THE COMING CAESARS

The English, after having cut off the head of one king, and expelled another from his throne, were still wont to address the successors of those princes only upon their knees. On the other hand, when a republic falls under the sway of one single man, the demeanor of the sovereign remains as simple and unpretending as if his authority was not yet paramount. When the emperors exercised an unlimited control over the fortunes and the lives of their fellow citizens, it was customary to call them Caesar in conversation; and they were in the habit of supping without formality at their friends' houses.

Alexis de Tocqueville,
Democracy in America

AMAURY de RIENCOURT

Also by Amaury de Riencourt
ROOF OF THE WORLD

The Coming
Caesars

Coward-McCann, Inc.
New York

interference, he is all at once Chief of State and head of government in control of all cabinet appointments as well as Commander in Chief of the most powerful armed forces in the world. He is the only statesman in the Western world who can make major decisions alone in an emergency. He is in control of a *de facto* empire into which the scattered fragments of the dissolving British Commonwealth are gradually being merged. Everywhere, on the European continent, in the Western Hemisphere, and in the Far East, he can make the weight of his incalculable power felt with immediate and crushing speed.

Yet, all this is nothing but the reflection of an underlying reality. The prime element in this situation is neither political nor strategic— it is essentially psychological. It is the growing "father complex" that is increasingly evident in America, the willingness to follow in any emergency, economic or military, the leadership of one man. It is the growing distrust of parliaments, congresses, and all other representative assemblies, the growing impatience of Western public opinion at their irresponsibility, lack of foresight, sluggishness, indecisiveness. This distrust and impatience is evident in America as in Europe. Further, it is the impulsive emotionalism of American public opinion, which swings wildly from apathetic isolationalism to dynamic internationalism, lacks continuity in its global views, stumbles from one emergency into another, and mistakes temporary lulls for the long-expected millennium. Such was Rome's public opinion in the first century B.C. Each new crisis calls for a strong man and there are always strong men present who are willing to shoulder responsibilities shirked by timid legislatures.

When, at the beginning of 1955, for instance, President Eisenhower went to Congress and requested emergency powers to deal with Formosa's offshore islands, how many Congressmen recoiled in fear and pointed out to him that he already had those powers, implying in effect that they wanted no part of this terrifying responsibility? Even with the utmost good will, a President who sincerely attempts to build up the sense of responsibility of the legislature cannot halt a secular trend. And this development suits public opinion perfectly well. The public wants to personalize issues and responsibilities and instinctively looks down upon the collective anonymity of assemblies. Those who doubt that today an American President might be elected for life should remember that no constitutional amendment, such as was voted after World War II, can stand in the way of public opinion if it truly wishes to elect a Caesar for life. In fact, the amendment limiting presidential terms of office is itself proof that many in America saw in Franklin Roosevelt the first pre-Caesarian who was, as it turned out, virtually elected for life.

The purpose of this book is to demonstrate that such concentration of power is no accident due to unexpected emergencies, but the natural outcome of an historical evolution. Those who believe that swift revolutions or accidents can alter the course of history should keep in mind the Roman saying *Historia non facit saltum,* history makes no leaps. What happens today germinated generations ago. Yesterday's seeds are today's blossoms. We must recognize exactly what kind of seeds we are sowing today if we want to know what tomorrow's blossoms are going to be.

In the following pages, we are going to attempt to discover the distant roots of our present situation and, starting as far back in history as may be necessary, retrace their growth and proliferation. Seen in this light, the approaching Caesars are no longer historical accidents, temporary tyrants, reactionary dictators who attempt to turn the clock back, all of whom are merely replicas of Classical Greece's tyrants. Those short-lived despots have nothing in common with the Caesars who eventually will organize the universal empire toward which their civilization has been tending. The coming Caesars are the lethal product of centuries of historical evolution, each succeeding generation having unconsciously added its stone to the towering pedestal on which they are going to stand.

Before we undertake our journey through history, we must do a certain amount of spadework. In the process, we shall for a time lose sight of our main objective: the coming Caesars. But we will explore the background without which this formidable possibility towering over us is meaningless. This background is nothing less than a complete interpretation of America's destiny in the light of world history. In the process, Europe and Asia are also considered, but the primary focus is on the New World and on its meaning for the entire human race. Our journey through the past, which will follow a chronological order for the sake of convenience and clarity, will not be a marshaling of mere facts but an interpretation of their symbolic significance. This whole undertaking, therefore, is based on the premise that history has a hidden logic and significance of its own that can give meaning and purpose to our lives.

What is the essence of history? Not so much the recorded facts as the thoughts, dreams, emotions, ideals, and aspirations of the human beings who have acted on its grand stage. History is life itself. Behind the disconnected facts, there is the continuous evolution of human societies; behind the outward forms, the living essence. Like everything else that is alive, history experiences ebbs and flows. It has a beating pulse which manifests itself in recurrences and cycles, moving from tension to relaxation and back again to renewed tension. We see it in a minor way in politics, in economics, in cultural development. Overwhelmed by the explosive changes of the past two centuries, we tend sometimes to overlook this sort of cosmic rhythm and look upon our own historical development as a one-way street leading ever upward, as if a strenuous effort of the human race could be kept up indefinitely without temporary relaxation. Nothing could be more misleading. It is not, for instance, the dramatic progress of technology that gives us the key to our future, but the aspirations that, many centuries ago, generated scientific thought and made today's scientific knowledge possible. The secret of our future is not located in the atom or in interstellar space but in our hearts and minds.

Man, like all living beings, individually or collectively, is geared to rhythm. It is this cyclical rhythm that exhausts a particular segment of humanity after a number of generations that compels it to lay down its tools and take a rest, as the Pharaonic Egyptians did three thousand years ago when the Greek star rose in the firmament of history and took over the leadership of the human race. The question is, then, how are we going to find out what these cycles are, and where we stand today in our own cycle?

If we are to solve this problem we must create a new system of references. And since all human activities are related to one another, this new system has to be all inclusive. As in physical science, the true test of a valid interpretation of history is whether it can explain the greatest number of phenomena with the smallest and simplest formula.

We must first of all define the social unit with which we are dealing, isolate it from other neighboring societies, and watch its historical development. A human society thus delineated is not merely an aggregate of separate human individuals; it is an entity in its own right, endowed with a life of its own, a collective life greater and far more lasting than the lives of the separate individuals who belong to it: it is a spiritual organism. Its reality is recognizable in that it has a definite spiritual source and that from this source flows a coherent stream of religious, philosophic, artistic, scientific, and political creations which are all interrelated, which have, all of them, a profound symbolic unity within the broad framework of a distinctive world-outlook belonging specifically to that particular society and to no other. And like all organisms that are alive, a particular society is compelled to follow certain biological laws throughout its historical development: it is born, grows, blooms, decays, and eventually dies.

We are now in a position to define the two key words in our present undertaking: *Culture* and *Civilization,* two expressions that have been used more or less indiscriminately and interchangeably in the past. The distinction between them, in this book, is going to be in the periodic sense of youth followed by maturity, that is, of organic *succession.* They do not coincide in time but follow each other during the life span of a particular human society: each Culture engenders its own Civilization.[1]

Their definition springs from their allotted task in history. Culture predominates in young societies awakening to life, grows like a young organism endowed with exuberant vitality, and represents a new world outlook. It implies original creation of new values, of new religious symbols and artistic styles, of new intellectual and spiritual structures, new sciences, new legislations, new moral codes. It emphasizes the individual rather than society, original creation rather than preservation and duplication, prototypes rather than mass production, an aesthetic outlook on life rather than an ethical one. Culture is essentially trail-blazing.

Civilization, on the other hand, represents the crystallization on a gigantic scale of the preceding Culture's deepest and greatest thoughts and styles, living on the petrified stock forms created by the parent Culture, basically uncreative, culturally sterile, but efficient in its mass organization, practical and ethical, spreading over large surfaces of the globe, finally ending in a universal state under the sway of a Caesarian ruler: India's Asoka, China's Shih Huang-ti, Egypt's Thutmose III, Babylon's Hammurabi, pre-Columbian Peru's Inca Roka, Mexico's Aztec emperor Itzcoatl, Islam's Turkish sultans, and Rome's Caesars who organized under their personal rules the universal societies toward which all the higher Cultures tend when they pass into

Civilizations. Our coming Caesars, therefore, have to be seen in the light of this profound and recurrent urge for a world-wide empire in which the compelling desire for unity, peace, and the preservation of traditional values plays a predominant part.

Civilization aims at the gradual standardization of increasingly large masses of men within a rigidly mechanical framework—masses of "common men" who think alike, feel alike, thrive on conformism, are willing to bow to vast bureaucratic structures, and in whom the social instinct predominates over that of the creative individual. It could be said metaphorically that Cultures are the systoles and Civilizations the diastoles of human evolution, relaying each other endlessly, the pulsating heartbeats of history.

This interpretation of history's inner development has a special meaning for us today because we are in the very process of switching from European Culture to American Civilization. In this sense, we are experiencing a momentous and baffling change of historical phase, one that no one can correctly understand who does not grasp the fact that we are reaching the culmination of a process that started a thousand years ago when the first Gothic spires began to dot the European landscape: it is the final winding up of European Culture. The twentieth century is the dramatic watershed separating the Culture behind us from the Civilization that lies ahead.

Our historical past, as distinct from that of Oriental civilizations, lies partly within the realm of Classical Greece and Rome. Our philosophies, languages, political institutions, legislations, sciences, are all more or less offshoots of that remote Mediterranean world. A careful study of comparative history can convince us that the evolutions of the Classical world and our own have largely been parallel and symmetrical to this day. Superimposing the thousand years of Greek Culture that started in Homeric days with the thousand years of European Culture that started at the dawn of the Gothic age, we can roughly estimate our present historical position.

The following chapters are going to follow step by step the development of Western society—in Europe and especially America—during the past four hundred years. Constantly hovering in the background, we shall have the ominous parallelism of Greece and Rome. What is being compared, let us remember, is not so much the facts of history as their symbolic meaning. It is this meaning which we need today in order to understand our predicament and overcome our difficulties. The growth and *civilized* greatness of Rome and America are no more accidental than the *cultural* endowments of Greeks and Europeans. In every developing Culture are the seeds of the oncoming Civilization that will eventually assume the burden of preserving the cultural heritage thus accumulated. Some chosen nations are the depositories of those seeds, and the world-wide responsibilities that fall upon their shoulders with startling suddenness have in fact been allocated to them centuries before by an inescapable destiny.

However, the way they handle these crushing responsibilities is *not* predetermined. So far, all Civilizations have chosen the easy solution of Caesarism. But Caesarism itself, if allowed to develop unchecked, implies organic death for the society that gives itself up to it out of fear of freedom. And whereas in the past a new Culture has always sprung from the ruins of an antecedent Civilization and blossomed forth, the wreck of our own Western Civilization might well mean absolute death for the entire human race. What was only an episodic drama in the past might be final tragedy tomorrow. Modern man's technological power will no longer allow him to make those grievous mistakes that past Civilizations were free to indulge in—nor can he ignore the lessons of a past that other Civilizations did not possess. Man's technical knowledge makes it possible for him to build heaven on earth or destroy his planet, and his historical knowledge makes it possible, for the first time, to avoid those deadly shoals on which every other Civilization has destroyed itself.*

* Roughly sketched in the Introduction, this interpretation of history is more fully developed in an Appendix which the reader will find at the end of the volume.

CONTENTS

13

PART I | *Europe: The New Greece*

CHAPTER I

Seedtime: Renaissance and Reformation

GREECE a thousand years before Christ and Western Europe a thousand years after—these were the birthplaces and birth times of two great human societies whose emotional roots dug deep into mythological eras filled with legendary figures, heroes and supermen, dreamlike eras depicted in the fantastic tales of Homer and Charlemagne's chroniclers. Both were emerging from chaotic Dark Ages replete with barbarian invasions—Boeotian and Dorian in Greece, Teutonic and Norman in Europe—receding nightmares of their collective childhoods.

Those who awoke to new life were entirely new breeds of men, dynamic offspring of the rape of old civilized populations by wild barbarians. Dorian Greeks and Gothic Europeans looked at the world with the puzzled, curious, and naïve eyes of newborn children. They looked at it as no one ever had before. They were moved to extreme tenderness or utter ruthlessness, excited to great joy or quick anger and often swept to sublime ecstasies by their vibrant faith. Compelled by a mysterious urge to materialize in stone, color, music, and verse their profound visions, they created new Cultures over the gaping ruins of dead Civilizations.

In Greece as in Europe, cultural creation was part of life itself, spontaneous, natural, and unreflective. The keynote of those "medieval" ages was synthesis, unity of meaning underlying variety of expression, an unfolding vision of the world in which religion, politics, economics, art, literature, philosophy, and science were all related.

17

All were looked upon as facets of a single spiritual truth. Religious celebrations, the Olympic games and Europe's chivalric tournaments, the tragedies of Sophocles and Dante's infernal visions, the Parthenon and the Gothic cathedrals, were all part of the same explosive impulses working out their new symbols, grouping them around the basic postulate of all Cultures in their springtime, which is that Beauty, Goodness, and Truth are equivalent reflections of the same underlying spiritual reality.

The prime concern of Culture in those days was the harmonious and simultaneous development of ideal man and ideal society. The goal was the development of life's highest creation, individual man—the development of excellence in body and soul, of human wholeness. But social concerns were never neglected. Society was conceived of as an organism analogous to the human body with its soul, mind, limbs, and organs, each of these having its appointed place, its tasks and duties, its privileges and rights. Society was a spiritual organism in which man, the living cell out of which the social body was made, was free to develop his individual potentialities to the full. The goal was a harmonious balance between individual and social requirements.

Unity was the fundamental idea in those days—same symbolism, same inspiration and style for art, literature, education, philosophy, political and scientific speculations, same economic theories, same social institutions, and same cultural language. Men could travel freely from one country to another. Pilgrims, students, scholars, merchants, professional soldiers, and knights could journey the length and breadth of their small worlds, facing untold hazards and hardships, yet always be at home in the Olympic and Christian commonwealths. Early Greece and Gothic Europe were like prisms, breaking up a single ray of spiritual light into a variety of scintillating colors. Contrasts were evident but religious feeling for the unseen held together all human beings, their institutions, their ideals and symbols. Contrasts were not viewed as irreconcilable antitheses but merely as stages of development within a broad unity which linked, through minute gradations, matter and spirit. The concrete and the abstract, the objective and the subjective were never sharply opposed but merged in a creative synthesis that was in a process of never-ending development. The connecting thread in this development was spiritual faith.

These cultural springtimes came to an end when the Ionic style appeared alongside the Doric, when Gothic metamorphosed itself into

Baroque. In Europe the grandiose unity was shattered by the Renaissance, which took the outward appearance of an anti-Gothic manifestation, a countermovement which, in fact, belonged to the same spiritual atmosphere. The Renaissance was no copy of the Classical spirit. That spirit was forever dead and gone. There was nothing in common between the smooth, static, poised statuary of Classical Greece and the forceful, dynamic sculpture of the European Renaissance, which had merely borrowed the old Classical forms and reshaped them to satisfy the intellectual and emotional requirements of a new Culture. The Renaissance was a prolongation of the Gothic upsurge in a different garb but its devotion to the same Christian spirit was just as intense. When the fiery Savonarola arose in Italy, the pseudo-Classical trappings disappeared, revealing the naked soul of Europe's vibrant Christian faith.

The Renaissance, however, was also a reaction against outmoded Gothic forms, as the Dionysiac movement had reacted against the Doric style and its Apollonian world-outlook.[1] They were both historical expressions of the yearning of their respective Cultures for ampler styles and more adequate forms. Their vitality and richness of soul were growing and could no longer be confined within the limits of their medieval ages. Both the Ionic and the Baroque continued and matured the deep trends that had shaped the Doric and Gothic styles, and both were destined to bring to full maturity—and therefore conclusion—the cultural growth of their respective worlds in the over-elaborate Corinthian and Rococo styles.

The Renaissance shattered the Gothic synthesis by putting the emphasis on the individual rather than society. Necessarily, the emphasis was also put on the increasing differentiation within the body of European Culture, on the separate components of European society rather than its over-all unity. Gradually, both the individuals and the diversified communities began to emerge from the collective unity of medieval Christendom, concentrating on their own distinctive developments. The strong links which had united them in their springtimes—the Olympic celebrations, the authority of the Christian Church—began to weaken steadily. Inner tensions developed to the point where they broke the medieval chains. But they were still essentially creative tensions.

In the Italian city-states, the teeming little worlds of the Medicis, the Sforzas, Borgias, and Malatestas, could be found the same vitality and exuberant artistic and literary output that characterized the bustling Hellenic world of the seventh and sixth centuries B.C. The ideal of Unity and harmonious synthesis had been abandoned in the Olympic and Christian *societies,* but only to be all the more emphasized in the creative *individual.* Glaucus of Chio and Leonardo da Vinci were universal geniuses who combined within themselves the talents of engineers, scientists, and artists. Everywhere, under the leadership of such universal men, there was a search for new forms, new symbols, new modes of expression, new outlets for the expansion of creative souls. Ionic and Eleatic philosophers paralleled the Humanists; Descartes and Anaximander, Leibnitz and Thales, all were searching for new formulations of eternal truths.

Men were becoming extreme individualists. They were men of giant stature, intellectual, artistic or scientific pioneers exploring a new universe which had been only dimly perceived by their medieval ancestors. They were towering personalities, endowed with profound originality, men impelled by some unknown inner compulsion to blaze new cultural trails, hammer out new symbols at a time when their contemporaries—Cortez, Vasco da Gama, Magellan—were discovering the globe. In fact, compared with all their predecessors, these Europeans were audacious supermen who had a new and more profound vision of the world, just as the Greeks had a far greater insight into the secret workings of the universe than their predecessors, the Egyptians and the Babylonians.

Simultaneously with this grand development in forms and styles, the Renaissance brought to a climax the tensions which Gothic Christianity had long kept in check, resulting in the atomization of Europe, the shattering of Christendom's political unity. The rise of internal tensions and discords was temporarily abated whenever the young societies were menaced by the assaults of barbarian hordes—when Greece repelled the vast Persian armies of Darius and Xerxes, when Europe faced the onslaughts of Moors, Mongols, and Turks. But as soon as the external threats disappeared, internal dissensions were renewed with greater bitterness than ever.

The outstanding characteristic of maturing Cultures is diversity and variety in the social and political body as well as among individual men. Between the numerous city-states of Italy—Florence under her tyrants, Venice under her commercial oligarchy, and the Papal States; the democratic cantons of Switzerland and the "bourgeois" Low Countries; the multitude of German kingdoms, principalities, bishoprics, and commercial cities; the elective kingdom of Poland and the more centralized monarchies of France and Spain —there were as many differences in political and social structure, in wealth and cultural activity, as there were among Athens, Sparta, Argos, Thebes, Syracuse, and Corinth. They were all moving away from the relative uniformity of medieval times and they matured in their own distinctive ways, leading to the cultural supremacy of Athens and France, the commercialism of Corinth and the Netherlands, the single-minded militarism of Sparta and Prussia.

. The inner structures of Greece and Europe were based on multiplicity and diversity, tensions and antagonisms, all of which generate a fabulous creativity in a Culture's summer and autumn—and self-destruction when the winter of cultural decline sets in.

Political and social evolutions followed parallel routes in Greece and Europe. Whereas feudal order and monarchy were the only social and political features of Homeric and early Gothic periods, the following eras saw the rise of new polities. Except for Sparta, the Greeks abolished royalty everywhere and all their city-states adopted some form of republican government. The traditional reverence toward kings disappeared and authority was transferred to oligarchic councils and assemblies. The new political *form* was now the rule of oligarchic nobilities, of the *few* instead of the *one,* the rule of feudal landowners. The same evolution in Europe is seen in Britain's Magna Charta in 1215, Aragon's General Privilege in 1283, France's establishment of the States General in 1302, the transformation of the German imperial crown into an elective office. These transformations indicated the gradual introduction of representative, almost republican features, which were more openly recognized in the Hanseatic, Swiss, and Italian republics.

But profound social transformations were also at work which counteracted this incipient republicanism. The oligarchies were soon superseded, in Greece as in Europe, by the "despots," the representatives of the rising middle classes competing with the traditional feudal nobility for political power—middle classes bred by expanding economic conditions, small landed proprietors, skilled artisans, traders, merchants, and bankers. For a time, the rule of the *few* was abandoned and a return to the rule of the *one* was carried out.

Despots rose to power on the strength of the growing dislike of those prosperous, vigorous, and self-assured middle classes for the decaying nobilities. The feudal order was gradually dissolving, new economic forces were coming into being, and yet no ruling class was qualified to replace it and take the lead. This interregnum could be filled only by tyrants, capable of easing the difficult transition from feudal order to the class-state ruled by the hereditary aristocracies, whose members, instead of ruling individually their separate fiefs, were to rule collectively the larger and more uniform states that were coming into being. The typical *condottieri* of the Renaissance—the Borgias, Wallensteins, Richelieus, and Cromwells—were the European replicas of Greece's early tyrants.

Despotism in Europe often fused with the monarchies when it could not destroy them, and such "absolute" monarchies became the acknowledged representatives of the middle classes—in France, especially—against the feudal aristocracies. Even in England the tyranny of the Tudors established its power over the ruins of the feudal nobility after the havoc wrought by the War of the Roses.

The destruction of the feudal order gave rise to the concept of "State." Men's allegiances were no longer given to an individual suzerain, who acted as intermediary between them and the kings, but directly to a more impersonal and abstract entity, the State. This new entity existed on the twin bases of internal tensions between social classes and external struggle, diplomatic and military, against similar States. And with its advent took place the first spectacular rise of the City, no longer a mere market place for a wholly agricultural society but an independent unit of its own, the embodiment of an emancipated Intellect antagonistic to the hitherto supreme countryside, stronghold of the instinctive forces of feudalism.

The Renaissance was only one phase of the reaction against the Gothic order. On the intellectual and religious level, a simultaneous reaction took place, a reaction against papal authority, against the Catholic Church's historic claims, and against medieval theology. The Renaissance had liberated southern Europe from the shackles of the Gothic and Teutonic spirit and had reclaimed its Mediterranean legacy. The Reformation liberated northern Europe from the Latin and Classical discipline of the Catholic Church. Although they did not operate on the same level, they both tore apart the organic unity of medieval Christendom and set its components traveling on their separate courses. Both movements joined hands, however, in exalting man's individualism and autonomy—the Renaissance in art and literature, the Reformation in religion, both in philosophy.

The Reformation itself broke up into two distinct movements. Luther's volcanic revolt vindicated man's right to free mystical experience, his right to seek for God's grace in his heart without priestly intervention, his right to salvation through *faith* alone. He brushed aside the theological legalism of the Vatican and completely divorced the secular from the religious, the material world from spiritual restraint. He was willing to transfer the external authority of the Church to the State and contributed to this deification of political authority which was to become the distinctive creed of modern Germany. Lutheranism was an impractical idealism which attempted to turn its back on a world of expanding economic development and preached a return to the primitive simplicity of rural life.

Calvinism was entirely different. Vigorous and life-affirming, this was a creed, not of faith alone, but of *works*. It did not merely attempt to save the individual but to rebuild Church and State. It was as much a political, social, and economic movement as a strictly religious one. It was as dynamic as Lutheranism was static, as reconciled to the new world that was coming into being as the Lutheran was indifferent to it. Furthermore, Luther's was still a rural outlook whereas Calvin's was essentially urban. The urban quality of Calvinism, appearing at a time when the city was just starting its fabulous development, guaranteed its eventual success. Calvinism became the creed of prosperous artisans, traders, merchants, and bankers. It was the spiritual counterpart of the despots, the religious faith of the rising middle classes.

Greece had experienced her own Reformation, her Orphism with its powerful reaction against the Homeric world-outlook.[2] When Xenophanes of Colophon inveighed against the "abominable" Olympus and its corrupt gods, he set in motion the Eleatic protest and his Reformation eventually culminated in Zeno's Stoicism. Sweeping away the Olympian pantheon was just as drastic as brushing aside the Catholic cult of the Virgin Mary and the saints. The practical results were the same in both cases: the rise of unmitigated nationalism through a transfer of religious sentiment to State and nation, the patriotic attachment to the Greek *polis* and to the European *State*.

In time, these reactions were bound to extend themselves. Having destroyed the feeling of reverence for the Olympic and Catholic poetic symbolism, they opened the way to critical inquiry untrammeled by theological safeguards, to an emancipated intellect left free to question, argue, and dissect. The tendency to explain the universe and man's destiny in naturalistic rather than in spiritual terms underlined the Renaissance and the Reformation. The dogmatic keystone which held together the Gothic hierarchy of values was removed, and the well-built structure that had embraced all human thoughts, aspirations, and activities disintegrated.

The disintegration, of course, was slow, but eventually religion was divorced from man's secular activities. Instead of having an organic connection establishing a hierarchy of values and linking lowly secular activities to man's higher spiritual purposes, we now have parallel and independent fields, regulated by different laws, amenable to different standards. It is this fatal dualism that gave rise to the accusation of "hypocrisy" that non-Westerners have long been hurling at Europe and America. The accusation is also made by Catholics against Anglo-Saxon Protestants, this dualism being essentially Protestant.

Calvin was the first to approve of the new world of economic development that was coming into being. He did not distrust capitalism or consider that economic and financial profit conflicted with true spiritual life, and approved of interest on invested capital provided the rate was reasonable. He pointed out, with an acute awareness of changing economic conditions, that financial interest was as legitimate as the payment of rent for land. Calvin blazed a new trail when he praised economic virtues and refused to consider poverty a benefit to spiritual progress. In all these respects, he turned his back on Luther as well as on Catholicism. Nevertheless, he always emphasized that luxury and ostentation were vicious. He reproved self-indulgence and was the spokesman of new generations who pursued wealth and attained it through sheer self-discipline and self-denial —generations of city-bred middle classes who were in search of a faith that justified spiritually the striving toward economic prosperity. Discipline, sobriety, and self-denial—these virtues were ruthlessly enforced by Calvin's totalitarian regime in Geneva. Later, they were to seem inborn in those followers of his whose souls were hammered into shape by his stern doctrine, followers who proved to be men of iron without any need of external compulsion. His emphasis on *works* rather than prayer, on *action* rather than thought, was mirrored in the mighty upheaval that was going to transform the economic structure of Europe and eventually the world.

Calvinistic predestination was a harsh and gloomy reality to his followers, one which necessarily excluded the greater part of mankind from any hope of salvation. But, if *works* were not a means to attain salvation, they were necessary to prove that salvation was within reach; and the energy with which Calvinists threw themselves into their work was considerably heightened by this conviction that they were a chosen group of men who could look down on the rest of a self-indulgent and weak humanity. Predestination guaranteed to its devotees that the forces of nature and history were on their sides. This liberation and moralization of rising economic energies was explosive.

Calvinism, like any other historical movement, is complex and displays apparent contradictions. Its success was due to the fact that it was able to combine in a workable synthesis the urge toward individualism that was then sweeping Europe and at the same time a strong social consciousness that could generate a genuine Christian socialism. These two contradictory features we shall find constantly displayed throughout the development of the English-speaking people. A strong sense of the community's paramount interest was inextricably mixed with the economic individualism of the rising middle class, to whom personal success and prosperity were a badge of spiritual salvation. But Calvin's doctrine as applied in Geneva was based on a spiritual legalism, mechanical, stern, without compassion and without appreciation for art, inhumanly practical, and in many respects iconoclastic. In Geneva were sown the spiritual seeds of what was to become the New Rome of the West.

Medieval England was a small marginal island on the fringe of the European continent, remote from the great centers of commerce, art, and literature in Germany and Italy, withdrawn from France since the fall of Calais, situated at the far end of the known world. A few centuries later, England stood as the earth's foremost commercial and industrial power, the main warehouse between Europe and the rest of the world, with an internal economic unity achieved several centuries before that of any Continental power.

England went through the complicated motions of a double reformation. The English Church rejected papal authority under Henry VIII but retained the entire Gothic symbolism and panoply complete with ecclesiastical hierarchy, the acceptance of apostolic succession, and retention of the view of society as being a spiritual organism in which every phase of human action and thought had its appointed station and purpose. In other words, nothing at all had been reformed. The Church of England had merely severed its connections with the Catholic-Mediterranean world and the papal authority had been transferred to the king.

But then, strident demands for a reformation which would reshape the entire political, social, and religious structure began to be heard with increasing frequency. This reshaping was to include philosophy, ethics, and economic doctrines. It was largely the expression of new social and economic forces which were attempting to overwhelm the dikes set up by Gothic medievalism, and which the Church of England insisted on retaining. The rule of the Tudors and Stuarts was frankly despotic and although this despotism represented the rising middle classes against the remnants of the feudal nobility, it retained the entire Gothic outlook on the organic structure of society. Religion was not merely personal salvation. It was the cement which held together the social structure, the ideas, the arts, and the economic functions. The only innovation was an insular nationalism which had made the State supreme over the Church.

Hooker and Laud, the two architects of this separate, autonomous English Catholicism, were profoundly imbued with the Gothic distrust of economic motives and financial profit, but they were no longer in step with the times.

During the hundred years from the middle of the sixteenth century to 1640, the clash between the rising forces of individualism and economic development, and an outdated medieval synthesis became increasingly bitter. Already, in Elizabethan times, a powerful capitalism had developed in mining and textiles. Cities had grown considerably, along with the urban middle classes. Trade and commerce increased with the gradual expansion of European enterprise all over the world. Pressure mounted steadily against the old medieval restraints on economic activities and the old opprobrium attached to financial profit. The old Gothic "Higher Law" was no longer a divine ordinance curbing material appetites but a "Natural Law" which upheld them. Hitherto, ethics was only a department of applied religion, and economic transactions a department of ethics. But the religious structure was collapsing. Ethics soon became divorced from religion, and economic activities from ethics. The ecclesiastical authorities resisted in vain; they could not stem the tide of public opinion. The Church no longer thought deeply about contemporary problems and refused to come to terms with the new economic and social forces. The emotional symbolism of the past was being routed by the dry intellect of the cities, overwhelmed by the rise of scientific thinking, political and economic mathematics, double-entry bookkeeping, joint-stock companies, banking, industry, and shipping. Gradually, the Church, its doctrine, and its ecclesiastical hierarchy began to seem odious to these rising and vigorous generations of men who looked forward to a bright future of unbelievable power and wealth. The desperate efforts of the Church to preserve the old structure and its over-all authority finally generated the storm that broke out in the Long Parliament and became the Puritan hurricane.

Early in the seventeenth century, the gap between the prevailing religious theories and the new realities of a fast-expanding economy had become unbridgeable. One or the other would have to give way, and the outcome could no longer be doubted. Calvinistic ideas had made tremendous inroads in England and Scotland, gathering strength among the middle classes and eventually instigating a religious, political, and social upheaval that was to shake England to its foundations. The ascending merchant and lawyer class, imbued with a new social and religious radicalism, wanted to erase the entire medieval structure, tearing out utterly and forever all traces of Catholic and aristocratic compromise. Thus arose the Puritan movement, the crystallization and fighting organ of the expanding energies of this new philosophy of life, which threw itself against an intimidated and confused Church and set in motion the Cromwellian revolution.

Puritanism was the real Reformation of England, the apex of the whole Protestant movement, the sharp edge of the righteous sword which cut the united Christendom of Gothic days to pieces. It was a fighting movement of soldier-saints inspired by Milton and Bunyan, fanatics who sought no consolation, absolution, or tenderness but virile exhortations, instructions, and military commands. The psalm-singing Puritans arose as the Pythagoreans did in the Hellenic world.

Cromwell's somber, fanatical Ironsides ravaged and put an end to Shakespeare's Merrie England as the followers of Pythagoras destroyed charming and glittering Sybaris with ruthless ferocity. The tragic beheading of King Charles I in a Europe still full of reverent respect for monarchical tradition was just as staggering as the annihilation of the gay metropolis of Magna Graecia by the Pythagorean Milo, the Cromwell of Classical Greece.

Strong, inhumanly self-reliant, endowed with an ecstatic dryness of temper which brushed aside the psychological complexities of mysticism, the Puritans were geared to a life of action. They shunned subjective contemplation and were determined to throw their fanatical energy into this struggle against nature—a struggle incipient in the Gothic spirit—remorselessly brushing aside all men who stood in their path. They fought their own selves with gloomy energy, repressing instincts and emotions, disciplining and rationalizing their entire lives.

A leading Puritan of the times claimed that "freeholders and tradesmen are the strength of religion and civility in the land, and gentlemen and beggars and servile tenants are the strength of iniquity," stamping the approaching revolution with a religious sanction.[3] Always uneasy under the Stuarts, who had a real inclination toward Catholicism, antagonized by James I's refusal to put an end to medieval rites, strengthened by a deep-rooted feeling of Calvinistic predestination, the Puritans engineered the historical earthquake which separated medieval from modern England.

Puritanism was not so much a religious doctrine as a way of life which animated to a greater or lesser extent Presbyterians, Congregationalists, and numerous other denominations. It was as contradictory as the original Calvinism had been, extremely individualistic and yet imbued with a strong social consciousness, devoted to capitalism and at the same time animated by strong socialistic instincts. But the remarkable feature was that its dominant theme was economics. Calvin had partly legitimized business, finance, and banking and had refused to condemn material wealth provided it was acquired through hard work and dedicated to the Lord. Calvin's was a practical concession to an existing situation. The Puritans went much further. To them business was a spiritual calling, economic prosperity was a sign of divine benediction, and earthly success the definite touchstone of a spiritual blessing that opened the gates of salvation. Merrie England,

the land of carefree aristocrats and boisterous laborers, was forever
swept away by the icy middle class fanaticism that despised all human
weakness. Self-reliance, thrift, and hard work became the guiding
principles of all those who parted company with bishops and clergy,
with medieval pageantry, and the refinement of a European Culture
in full development.

Pushing the Reformation to the extreme limit of its logical implications, the Puritans brushed aside the organic structure of society.
Social and ecclesiastical hierarchy, family ties, were swept away, leaving the self-reliant individual alone in front of his Maker, face to
face with a world that was no longer to be enjoyed but conquered
and subdued. Cambridge and Oxford were the main centers where
this intellectual revolution was worked out. The primary victim of
intellectual Puritanism was, of course, Aristotle and his comprehensive, all-inclusive philosophy which Thomas Aquinas had adapted to
Gothic Christianity. As befitted men who turned their backs on
Catholic spirituality and looked toward intellectual idealism, the Puritans substituted Plato for Aristotle. With a sure but totally unconscious instinct for historical parallelism, they rejected in Aristotle the
most *catholic* of all Greek philosophers, "the first of the Schoolmen,"
as Walter Pater called him,[4] the believer in practical wisdom and
the golden mean, the man who sought philosophical Beauty rather
than Goodness and who saw this Beauty in Unity, in the harmonious
cooperation between the parts and the whole—the philosopher who,
in his *Nicomachean Ethics,* sought not what makes men good, but
what makes them happy.

And when they adopted Plato, they chose the most *protestant* of
all Greek thinkers, the man who was deeply influenced by the re-
forming Pythagoreans and Orphists, who rebelled against Ionian
moral laxity as Puritans rebelled against the same laxity of the
Catholics, who distrusted human nature as evil and believed in original
sin, and yet who sought moral Goodness. As a true Puritan, Plato
saw Beauty as intellectual rather than physical; he shattered the
traditional Unity of body and soul, on which Greek aesthetics was
founded, by sharply divorcing the *evil* body from the *divine* soul.
Art was then thrown overboard, and true culture with it. "Why did
the Puritans object to the music and painting and gorgeous ritual
of the Catholic Church? You will find the answer in the tenth book of
the *Republic.*" [5]

It is easy to follow this remarkable duplication between the evolutions of Greek and European thought, two thousand years apart, and trace back to Plato many of the fundamental notions which underlie Europe's Puritan Reformation—the belief in the absolute metaphysical reality of abstract Ideas which views Matter as basically unreal, a mere principle of inertia which challenges God and man, and must be overcome by the human soul's strenuous exertions. There is, in Platonism, no pyramid of values connected organically and hierarchically as in Aristotle's philosophy, linking and coordinating everything from lowly matter to the most exalted spiritual reality. Instead, there is a sharp, absolute separation between the human will and the obstacles that are to be overcome. Plato is the father of utopias and would have recognized in the English Puritans and American Pilgrim Fathers his truest disciples.

Puritanism laid the foundations of a religion of the intellect, not of the heart. Like their intellectual master, Puritans believed in utopias, in the metaphysical reality of Ideas eternal and unchangeable, in the primacy of moral Goodness and its struggle against fundamental evil, and in the primacy, not of the creative individual, but of society. The Puritans were the human seed from which the New Rome of Western Civilization was to spring across the Atlantic Ocean.

The Puritan hurricane eventually blew away with the Restoration, leaving ruins in its wake. It had gone too far and the excessive radicalism of Levellers, Diggers, and suchlike had ended by antagonizing those very freeholders and merchants who had welcomed it at first. The revolutionary Cromwellian Puritans had emphasized their iron discipline and their collectivism, had frowned on a liberty which they equated with license, and yet had thrown overboard the compassionate fraternity of medieval days. With the Restoration, they forsook political and social agitation, shed their radicalism, and made their peace with the returned Cavaliers. The end result of the hurricane was a new spirit of tolerance and freedom which accepted the destruction of the old paternalistic medieval structure of the Stuarts while stamping out all traces of Puritan fanaticism.

What grew out of the scrambled ruins of medieval and Puritan England was a vast compromise that retained various features of contradictory political, social, and economic doctrines and blended them harmoniously, in fact if not in theory. The only element which disappeared almost entirely after the subsequent Glorious Revolution of 1688 was royal power. The Crown became a mere symbol, and political power fell into the hands of a new aristocracy that replaced the downfallen feudal nobility already largely destroyed by the Tudors and the Stuarts. This new aristocracy blended the traditional blood-nobility with the higher middle class. Alone of all the European ruling classes, it was able to mix successfully the virtues and political talents of an aristocracy with the keen business sense of the capitalist middle class. The Church of England made its peace with the Presbyterians and nonconformists and, securely ensconced in its official privileges, gave up all attempts at interfering in what had come to be none of its business—politics, social concerns, economics, and science. The resulting agreement between Cavalier and Puritan as to the new political, social, and economic philosophy of the Restoration gradually shaped the modern world as we know it.

This philosophy, like the social and political structure which it attempted to justify, rested on a compromise. It remained essentially aristocratic and reverted to Aristotle through the agency of Richard Hooker. The English Puritans gave up their search for a Platonic utopia as part of this bargain, leaving it to their American brethren to build it on the other side of the Atlantic. Society retained something of its organic and hierarchical nature, and was still conceived of as a living body whose various members and social classes had to play their appointed parts. The European emphasis on the protection of individual originality, the distinctive trait of all Cultures in full development, was fully retained.

But together with this pious reverence for a traditional outlook which the British insisted on preserving, they implicitly admitted that economic pursuits were man's prime function and that religious ethics should stop short of what was now deemed outside its province. Puritanism had shed its disciplined collectivism and brought forth the other side of its personality: a strong individualism that not only rejected the feeble interference of an impotent clergy, but the whole concept of the control of economic self-interest by religion. Spiritual significance was gradually drained out of business transactions and social relations. Society became a giant soulless mechanism regulated by economic appetites and requirements. Tolerance, political and religious, was emphasized, not so much out of idealistic motives but because it was good for business—the evidence of the wealth and prosperity of the extremely tolerant Netherlands was striking and was zealously studied by the British. Each department of what used to be a coherent and organic synthesis now went it own way. Theology was divorced from ethics, ethics from economics. Religion and science broke up their former partnership and philosophy was secularized.

The practical English were able to carry on with these conflicting philosophies for two centuries, right through the Age of Enlightenment, the Industrial Revolution, and the Victorian era. They were never logically reconciled but were somehow intuitively fused together into a successful way of life. It was left to the Puritans who crossed the Atlantic Ocean to attempt to create a new world in which there would be no need for compromise and where the development of their way of life could reach its ultimate limits.

CHAPTER II

Foundation of the New Rome

CLASSICAL Greece and Western Europe had too much surplus energy to remain physically contained within their geographical limits. Around both youthful societies, although twenty centuries apart, could be found the same barbarian darkness or, in other quarters, the crepuscular sadness of aging civilizations. The dynamic Greeks looked upon the Babylonians and Egyptians as the latter-day Europeans looked upon the Muslims, Indians and Chinese: decadent, overrefined, and enfeebled people, members of societies without creative powers. The barbarian Gauls and Iberians were to the Greeks what the Africans and American Indians were to the Europeans: savages without culture, begging to be civilized. Greek travelers could wonder at the splendors of Babylon's mysterious vastness and Herodotus could marvel at the awesome pyramids of Egypt as travelers from Europe were to gaze, later, at Constantinople, Delhi, and Peking. The fabulous power of Babylon's monarch Nebuchadnezzar or, two thousand years later, that of the Moghul emperor Akbar inspired the Greeks and Westerners with the same feeling of awe and yet contempt—contempt for the effeminate people who were unable to rule themselves through representative institutions and who crawled at the feet of despotic monarchs. And many Europeans in those later days echoed the remark of Euripides two thousand years before: "Asia serves as the slave of Europe." [1]

Heaving with expanding energies, the Greeks and Europeans began to overflow their small peninsulas and islands and spread themselves

33

all over their respective worlds—the Greeks throughout the Mediterranean, the Europeans throughout the entire globe. The Greeks founded so many colonies that the Mediterranean became a Grecian lake, just as the globe's five oceans later became so many European lakes. The vast and powerful Greek settlements in the new lands of Sicily and southern Italy were matched by the quick rise of Spanish America. The splendor and wealth of Peru and Mexico remind us of the glory of Syracuse, Rhegium, Agrigentum and Tarentum. Italy's Magna Graecia was in every respect a worthy predecessor of Latin America's New Spain. The agricultural wealth of the West Indies, the fabulous mines of Potosí, accelerated the economic development of Europe as did Greece's numerous offshoots. Agrigentum, called by Pindar "the fairest of mortal cities," enormous Syracuse with her five hundred thousand inhabitants—these and the other Greek settlements participated in the mother country's cultural life. The magnificent architecture of Posidonia was to the Classical world what the Baroque churches and palaces of Mexico and Lima were to the Western. The dynamism of youthful Cultures can never be confined to one domain and always overflows, exploring, digging, discovering, and exploiting in the spiritual as well as in the physical worlds, covering like tidal waves the known worlds of its respective ages. The wars waged by Spaniards, Portuguese, Dutch, French, and British all over the globe re-enacted the memorable colonial wars between Sybaris and Croton, Corinth and Corcyra. But the balance of power soon began to shift within the Classical and Western worlds. When Magna Graecia and Latin America began to decline under the weight of their own sloth and corruption, they gradually made way for new powers in being, new powers of an entirely different order: Rome and North America.

Early in the seventeenth century, a small group of dedicated men founded a modest colony which was to be the embryo of the world's most powerful nation. Man was making a new start. He was going to build a rational and supremely ethical society. He was going to attempt to emancipate himself from history and oppressive traditions, from the bondage of the past. He would trade space against time and attempt to use the time thus saved to shape a new human society according to his enlightened ideas.

Many speculative writers of the Renaissance such as Thomas More and Francis Bacon had conjured out of their daring imagination remarkable pictures of ideal Platonic republics and, late in the sixteenth century, many sober nonconformists of England had instinctively come to identify this mental ideal with the remote coast of North America—a savage, deserted coast, far removed from the brilliant and opulent world of the West Indies and Latin America with its glittering cities full of priceless Baroque churches and palaces, its mines and inexhaustible tropical resources. The wealth and splendor of Latin America must have seemed as distant to a lonely wayfarer on the Hudson River as the splendors of Greek Sicily did to a Roman farmer plowing along the Tiber. But this primeval wilderness, with its virgin land where life was still wholly prehistoric, was alluring to all those dissatisfied elements in English society who suffered from the political tyranny of the Stuarts and the Anglican reaction of Archbishop Laud.

So it was, translating long-meditated thoughts into action, that the stern Puritans founded on the coast of New England what they thought would be the land of Canaan, the new Jerusalem of their dreams, and what we can now label far more accurately the New Rome. In November, 1620, off Cape Cod, these Biblical-minded men concluded the Mayflower Compact, the original social contract that became the historic foundation of American political philosophy: government resting exclusively on the consent of the governed.

When they landed and began to penetrate the fringes of the immense forests, they took possession of an empty land—empty because, in those days, agricultural settlement, not nomadic hunting, constituted real possession. The roaming Indian tribes, in Puritan eyes, belonged to the animal rather than the human world and in spite of a few early attempts at missionary work among them—those of tender-hearted John Eliot and others like William Rogers—the early settlers developed a policy of pious but ruthless extermination. They were never deliberately cruel or bloodthirsty as the Spaniards had been further south. They were cold, implacable, and determined to clear the land of all obstacles—mosquitoes, Indians, and trees. They refused to be seduced or intimidated by what Cotton Mather called "pernicious creatures"—the redoutable Iroquois confederation of Mohawks, Oneidas, Senecas, Cayugas, and Onondagas. They had braved the fogs and storms of a vast ocean, the deep, awful silence of the immense forests, the howling winds and impetuous rivers, the terrifying solitude of an unexplored primeval world. They would brave anything else—but in so doing, they denied and cast out of their consciousness the undoubted seductions of the New World's savage life.

The sober fanaticism of the Puritans stood as an opaque screen between their sentiments and the overpowering nature all around them. They had left their sense of history behind them in Europe and had never possessed an intuitive feeling for the beauties of nature. They were iconoclasts who clung tenaciously to an abstract Idea— the idea of a perfect human society which would actualize on earth the Almighty's dream. All other settlers in America—Portuguese and Spaniards, the French in Louisiana and Canada—sooner or later succumbed to the overwhelming influence of American nature. They befriended the Indians and in their humane weakness reverted often to an entrancing form of primitive life to whose charms the English and the Dutch were immune. Archaic tendencies are always deeply embedded in every human being and the confused instincts of prehistoric life were often able to develop unchecked among the Latins who entered into full communion with the wild spirit of the American earth. Not so the iron-willed Puritans. They imposed their abstract plans and concepts on nature from the very start, making no concessions to the land, determined to dominate, not to bend and adapt.

Whereas the European Puritans soon had to compromise and amalgamate with the numerous other religious tendencies of the Old World and gradually disappeared as a separate entity, their migrating coreligionists took full physical possession of New England and later, through their moral influence, took mental possession of the whole continent. Thus they set the pattern of American life and thought from the very start: an absolute domination of rational man over a nature with which he refuses to enter into communion. America was destined to become the expression of Europe's dream, a dream which could never come true in the Old World because the cramping limitations imposed by tradition, and the pressure of relatively large populations impinging on one another in a limited space, stood in the way. In order to make an idealistic utopia come true in Europe, violent coercion was necessary because there was no virgin space where a new society might be built up without affecting unwilling neighbors. And Europe's past history with its accumulation of venerable traditions, deeply ingrained customs, its gradual elaboration of complex and conflicting philosophies and ideals, could not be dismissed simply as a troublesome nightmare. It was discovered, from the French Revolution onward, that no utopia could be attempted in Europe without violence and brutality, bloodshed and tears. It had to remain a dream.

The materialization of this dream was in American Puritan hands and in Puritanism was reborn the temper of the Biblical Jews, with their emphasis on strict morality, the terrible feeling of unbearable tension between God's will and man's hopeless inadequacy. To them, beauty was of no importance, sometimes even possessed of diabolic undertones. Purity, simplicity, were the bases of their life. This lack of aesthetic feeling, of taste for culture and for the resulting integration of man's manifold possibilities and aspirations into a harmonious whole, gave to the Pilgrim Fathers the characteristics of *civilized* rather than *cultured* men. Only a portion of man's countless potentialities was able to develop freely, but that to an unparalleled degree.

In the years following the Pilgrims' first landing, wave after wave of Puritan emigrants came ashore. One colony rose after another in quick succession: Salem, Boston, Charlestown, Dorchester, creeping up along the coast of Maine, founding little city-states that came to resemble closely their Classical counterparts. Communal freedom and decentralization were established from the very beginning, and all official positions were elective. But individual freedom was remarkably restricted. The franchise was tied to property qualifications and church membership. The local governments were empowered to regulate politics, religion, economics, and customs. The idea of mass democracy was repulsive to the Puritans, who were imbued with a Calvinistic faith in their predestined superiority. John Cotton, Winthrop, and other leaders believed firmly in class distinctions, so long as they themselves were the social and political elite, rid of a profligate aristocracy which had bothered them in England and contemptuous of the lazy lower classes. But theirs was no selfish desire to enjoy social superiority or political power for their own sake. They were God-fearing men, stern and self-reliant, who journeyed through life as through a probationary purgatory. "It is enough that we shall have heaven, though we should pass through hell to it," was Governor Winthrop's sober comment after the founding of Boston.[2]

Like the early Romans of the fifth and fourth centuries B.C., the

Puritans founded communities of self-disciplined men whose unremit-
ting toil was wholly dedicated to abstract entities—the abstract deities
of the Roman state, the Almighty of the New England "Saints." In
both cases, individual men were, in contradistinction to Greece and
Europe, ruled by the community and public opinion. Mutual vigi-
lance, methodical organization of communities, tyranny of the group,
devotion to duty and self-control, all these characteristics of the
coming American nation were born in these early days. Romans and
Puritans were dedicated to a severe, joyless life; determined men who
bowed to no other men, natural born republicans. Two thousand
years before, the Romans had come to loathe the very idea of monarchy to a degree never equaled by the Americans. After having
expelled the Tarquin dynasty in 508 B.C., Publius Valerius put through
a law according to which any man who attempted to make himself
king should be put to death without trial. The American Puritans
sympathized with their Cromwellian brethren when they beheaded
Charles I. Romans and Puritans were idealistic fanatics who had a
horror of useless luxury, vanity, self-indulgence. The loyal devotion
of both did not go to any human being but to the abstract, impersonal authority of Law. When they became a social elite later on they
felt strong and worthy enough to act sincerely and firmly as trustees
for those fast-increasing populations in their expanding realms who
were not yet deemed capable of sharing in the government. Discipline
was the motto of the Romans as well as "the very ark of the Puritan
covenant." [3]

Puritanism, under its moral aspect, eventually conquered the whole
of America as Stoicism was destined to conquer the entire Roman
world, this very Stoicism which John Buchan defined as "Puritanism
stripped of its element of rapture." [4] Both had in common the fact
that they were not so much elaborate philosophies as ways of life,
psychological attitudes, the ultimate ethical consequences of Protestant reformations. They made few demands on the mind but a great
many on the character and both stood opposed to the prevailing Epicureanism of Greek and European cultures. They espoused the *ethical*
point of view of Civilization rather than the *aesthetic* outlook of
Culture.

Roman religion was originally a cold, formal creed which did not
indulge in the warm mythology of Greece. Rome's ultimate acceptance of Stoicism could have been as easily forecast as the rise of the

European Reformation, which brushed aside the "mythology" of Catholicism. It was a question of psychological disposition, not of ultimate truths. Rome's austere gods were as impersonal, abstract, and formless as the Puritans' Almighty. They were embodiments of moral principles restraining passions, but were at an infinitely remote distance from the worshipers—such abstract deities hovering over Rome as Justitia, Fides, Veritas, who had little in common with the flamboyant and whimsical gods of the *catholic* Greek Olympus. Roman priests were "professors of spiritual jurisprudence" as Dean Inge expressed it. Greek priests served gods of pleasure, sensual or intellectual, gods capable of inspiring great cultural achievements, gods of art and literature, strong and weak gods, warm and humane. By contrast with Greeks and Europeans, neither the Romans nor the Anglo-Saxons were interested in metaphysics. Their emphasis was wholly on morality, on ethical standards.[5]

Theirs was therefore a psychological condition eminently favorable to the building of powerful, compact societies as efficiently and co-operatively organized as beehives. In New England, it was the regular practice of elective democracy in the townships that gave the coming democracy of America its character, a democracy which did not flow down gradually from the top of a society already organized along other lines but which grew up from townships to county to state, and eventually to nation. The townships were like so many little city-states, little republics whose allegiance to a distant monarch beyond the seas was largely nominal. They elected their magistrates, levied their own taxes, ran their own schools and their own police. Local government in parishes, boroughs, towns, and counties was more independent of the colony than the latter was of London. In each community, in the Roman and Latin communities as in the American, the prevailing ideology had two apparently contradictory goals in view: the preservation of human liberty and dignity and yet the curbing of men's selfishness whenever it came into conflict with public interest. How and why did the early Romans and Americans succeed where more creative societies failed? They had "character," they had the typical Roman virtues: *gravitas, pietas,* and *simplicitas.*[6] They were endowed with great will, courage, dignity, and a profound sense of duty, and they voluntarily surrendered a large part of their personal idiosyncrasies for the sake of collective freedom.

Since suffrage remained limited to church members and property-owners, the economic foundations of New England were laid in favor of the small ruling oligarchy. Thanks to their exclusive political power and keen sense of business, they were able to distribute among themselves extensive land grants which rose steadily in value as wave after wave of colonists swept in from the Old World. Inasmuch as economic prosperity was blessed by the Lord, members of the oligarchy felt that their establishments rested securely on spiritual foundations. What enabled them to maintain their supremacy against the mounting pressure of droves of newcomers was that they could always divert them to other virgin parts of the unlimited territory. Each colony was free to set up its own religious, social, and political structure without interference from its neighbors. Individual freedom and equality were just as restricted within these city-states as they were in their Classical counterparts, but they were complete realities as far as the relations between the self-enclosed communities were concerned.

Boston leaders, dedicated to their oligarchic and theocratic ideals, adopted Presbyterian principles but other Massachusetts churches were free to veer toward the more democratic Congregationalist organization. Democratic dissenters in a community usually had no other recourse but to emigrate to new lands and start new communities. Thus started America's traditional solution to most human conflicts—a solution made possible by the almost infinite extension of land in the interior—re-emigration of dissenters and foundation of new colonies away from the increasingly congested seaboard. Connecticut was founded by Puritans who were repelled by the undemocratic nature of the Boston settlement, whose Governor Winthrop asserted vigorously that democracy was "the meanest and worst of all forms of government." But the Connecticut leaders had scarcely founded Hartford and Wethersfield when they set up a new structure that was almost as undemocratic. Rhode Island was then founded by men who shunned not only oligarchy but theocracy as well, and this new colony became America's first liberal experiment.

And so it went for centuries, until the Latter-day Saints founded Salt Lake City's Mormon settlement in the wilderness of the western deserts. The American pattern was set. Mobility in space could dispose of most human conflicts by merely widening distances. The more adventurous among the new arrivals from the Old World refused to bow to the coastal oligarchies and pushed immediately inland, where virgin territory offered great opportunity to those who were bold and enterprising enough. Throughout her development, America was able to dispose of her democratic elements by distributing them along her mobile frontier, a fringe of pioneering men following the sun, generation after generation, across the length and breadth of a gigantic continent, endlessly re-enacting the bold landing at Plymouth Rock. In the same vein, Rome disposed of her adventurous elements —pioneers, democrats, and discharged legionaries—by sending them off to distant Italian colonies on the edge of her own expanding "frontier." It was thanks to this wise policy that Rome was able to ward off the terrible social conflicts which, starting in the fourth century B.C., eventually shook Greece to self-destruction.

In her early days, Rome was as much a modest democracy as New England's most democratic community. Her population was composed of self-reliant citizens whose distant roots were identical with those of their Greek cousins. They were the offshoots of the great Hellenic trunk—common linguistic roots, common type of building, same dress. Their social and political principles were almost identical but with a greater emphasis in Rome on the fundamental sovereignty of the people and in freedom of the individual from the whim of arbitrary tyrants. Any Roman citizen condemned by a magistrate to death or flogging had a right to appeal to the Assembly. Even under the tyranny of the Tarquins, legislative power was largely entrusted to the Assembly of citizens. The king proposed rather than commanded and the citizens replied as they saw fit. The resulting law was a contract proposed by him and endorsed or rejected by the people. Roman citizens had the rights and privileges of New England church members and like them, exercised those rights with a profound sense of responsibility to the community. The great historian Mommsen wrote that "in no other community [than Rome] could a citizen live so absolutely secure from encroachment, either on the part of his fellows or of the state itself"; and he added that it was always held "that the Council of Elders was the highest authority in the state." [7]

In other words, even under the despotism of Tarquins and Stuarts, Rome and the English-speaking world represented the two real centers of political liberty in their respective ages, lands where individual freedom was best preserved against the arbitrary whim of despots. And this, of course, became even more true after the fall of Tarquin and

Stuart dynasties. The expulsion of the Tarquins and the abolition of the Roman monarchy were essentially similar to the Glorious Revolution of 1688 in England, where monarchy was not altogether abolished but preserved as a symbolic but powerless link with the past. In 1689, the famous Declaration of Rights was proclaimed and William III became the willing tool of Parliament. Such protection for individual freedom was not afforded in Greece and continental Europe.

In Rome and Anglo-Saxondom, the protection of the individual was easily achieved because the citizens rarely abused liberty. Both had strongly rooted in their psychological temper a strong feeling for the community's interests, a social instinct which made them understand the advantages of social organization and self-imposed discipline, all this underlined by a basic altruism. Not only could it be said that their successful societies were able to promote individual freedom on the basis of a voluntary sacrifice of excessive individualism to society, but also that success was due to the fact that they could move with the times, remain socially fluid and adaptable—a feat of which Greeks and continental Europeans were incapable. Both the Romans and the English-speaking people showed their true political genius in solving their political and social problems with a minimum of bitterness and bloodshed, displaying a remarkable sense of legal continuity in their history. Whereas Greeks and Europeans lacked the spirit of compromise, Romans and Anglo-Saxons could solve the most intricate problems in the most pragmatic way.

Early Rome was not only the abode of real freedom, but also of a great deal of democratic equality. There were no class privileges and all Roman citizens wore the same simple woolen toga in public. "As the Latin immigrants had no conquered race to deal with, the nobility of Greece ... was unknown to them." [8] Rome gradually became the leading member of a Latin league of thirty autonomous townships, each of them equal in political rights, each with its own laws and constitution. To an extent, Rome was to the Latin federation what London was to the autonomous American colonies. Rome's growing supremacy, which ended in dwarfing and finally absorbing the other Latin communities, was due to her favorable geographic position and the expanding economic revolution which was linking the various parts of the Classical world together. "This commercial position stamped its peculiar mark on the Roman character, distinguishing them from the rest of the Latins and Italians as the citizen is distinguished from the rustic." ⁹ Thus, another aspect of the Roman-American convergence: the predominantly urban and commercial nature of their social structures. It was not peasants but largely urban middle-class men who settled New England, and even though farming remained for centuries the leading occupation, both in Rome and America, these men were citizen-farmers who looked toward the city, rather than peasants stubbornly tied to the earth (which the French promptly became in Canada). The city and not the countryside was the ruling element.

In an unconscious tribute to the immense formative power of the Puritan ideal, it is often overlooked that the early settlement of Virginia had taken place a number of years before any settler had set foot on New England soil. The New England settlers, however, were idealists, as the Virginians were not, and Puritan ideals were destined eventually to conquer the whole of America.

Actually, the early settlements in Virginia were run along more democratic lines than those in New England. But by the end of the century, a landowning aristocracy had formed itself and acquired complete predominance along the seaboard. The social transformation was quite remarkable. Until 1670, the General Assembly of Virginia was composed of a Council of State chosen by the governor from the leading families, and a House of Burgesses elected by all freemen. After 1670, however, democracy was on the defensive and only propertied voters could elect members to the House. The aristocratic character of the South gathered strength all through the second half of the century. With Lord Baltimore's foundation of Maryland, a new type of colony, the proprietary, came into being. English country squires crossed the Atlantic to establish in the South a type of aristocratic society closely patterned on that of England. Many wealthy immigrants laid the foundations of their baronial estates along the Potomac—men like William Fitzhugh who arrived as late as 1671 but was soon the proud owner of ninety-six thousand acres of timbered land between the Potomac and Rappahannock rivers. Huge plantations appeared in the wilderness, wrested from virgin forest and largely self-sufficient. Planters sent their staples to England and purchased directly in London what they needed in the way of manufactured goods. Scattered along the North American coast, the various highly differentiated colonies were widely separated from each other. Their common nexus was and remained for generations England.

The inexhaustible supply of virgin land was such that farming was wasteful and cultivators were always on the move, opening new tracts of land when they had exhausted the old ones. In a purely agricultural society which was not anchored to any one spot by fishing and trade, this semi-nomadism militated against the growth of large cities. By the end of the seventeenth century, Boston was already a leading metropolis when Virginia's more ancient Jamestown was still hardly more than an overgrown village.

Thus came into being the Cavalier type of American, the representative of an aristocratic society less rigid than England's squire-archy, but largely patterned after the mother country's traditional landowning nobility. The prevailing religious denomination was Anglican, which was only fitting for a society which did not sympathize with the middle-class Puritanism of New England. Negro slavery was not yet a major issue and was even discouraged. Many of the imported Negroes were simply indentured, like the white immigrant servants, and were usually released after their contract had been fulfilled. In 1700 there were eighty thousand whites in Virginia, but less than six thousand Negroes. It was only in the following century that the importation of Negro slaves gathered momentum. White indentured servants began to find the competition too severe and European immigration slowed down considerably. The trend away from social democracy to complete aristocratic ascendancy in the South was challenged at times, partly deflected, but never halted before the Revolution. Bacon's rebellion was the apex of the democratic protests and it established the pattern of all coming democratic and radical movements: the more democratic population of the frontier made common cause with the coastal yeomanry and indentured servants. And an addition to this recurring pattern made its appearance: the frontiersmen, always expansionist-minded, demanded a more ruthless policy toward the Indians.

A new characteristic of American politics thus came to light. The wealthy classes of the eastern seaboard were conservative and anti-imperialistic, the more democratic and equalitarian populations of the interior were radical and expansionist. This was the beginning of the natural alliance between social democracy and the expansionism which is also a constant factor in Roman history.

The defeat of Bacon's rebellion allowed the trend toward aristocracy to be resumed. Other colonies were founded in the South, colonies in which English aristocrats could hope to achieve a true manorial grandeur in the American wilderness that would have been impossible in overcrowded England. Carolina was founded by eight "proprietors." One of them, the Earl of Shaftesbury, put philosopher John Locke to work on an aristocratic constitution. Like all such theoretical plans designed to suit the convenience of small oligarchies, it met with the violent opposition of North Carolina's Quakers and small farmers.

Between North and South arose a variety of middle colonies— Pennsylvania, the "holy experiment," motivated by William Penn's remarkable idealism and his insistence on the rigid separation of church and state—and aristocratic New York, both of them great colonial melting pots for Dutch, Swedish, German, English, and Scotch immigrants, whereas the North and the South remained predominantly British. But whether New England Puritan, Pennsylvania Quaker or Virginian aristocrat, all the leading elements of early America were men outstanding in character, will power, self-reliance. All of them displayed to a greater or lesser extent some Puritanical traits. In their customs and mode of life, the Quakers were just as Puritanical as the most rigid New Englander. All favored stringent legislation against drinking, gambling, blasphemy. Their Protestant outlook suffered few exceptions and they retained a pronounced iconoclastic mentality that despised art's "sensuality" and "idolatry."

All those early immigrants set the American pattern and although they still occupied an insignificant fraction of the gigantic continent, they had already stamped it with their vigorous spirit. The millions of immigrants who would pour in during the following centuries would have to go through the filter thus set up along the eastern seaboard and slough off their European baggage. They would enter a New World whose soul was born in the seventeenth century and matured in the twentieth.

CHAPTER III

The Age of Enlightenment

THE eighteenth century saw the rise to global supremacy of the British Empire, the magnificent flowering of European Culture and the very beginning of the Industrial Revolution. It was to the West what the Age of Pericles was to the Classical world. These Ages of Enlightenment which seemed to so many in Greece and Europe as being the threshold of a wonderful new world, were in fact the supreme expressions of Cultures approaching their zenith, ages when everything was in style, when bad taste was still impossible, when no dissonance could yet mar the cultural harmony.

The Age of Enlightenment saw the decisive shaping of America, as it did of Rome. Both were still marginal societies, living in the shade of the glories of Greece and Europe. In them there was no real brilliance but subdued strength—strength of character, a sense of the practical and useful, self-discipline, lack of individualism and originality. America's early history had been one of great diversity among the scattered colonies, an overseas replica of Europe's own growing diversity. It became one of increasing uniformity in the eighteenth century, and this profound American tendency toward uniformity—political, social, and psychological—has been in evidence ever since.

Since both Rome and America were decisively shaped in those Ages of Enlightenment, it follows logically that they absorbed many of the principles, ideals, and characteristics of those Ages—and because of their basic conservatism and traditionalism, because of their geographic isolation from the history-making currents of their times, were able to live by them and preserve them long after catastrophic

46

wars and revolutions had annihilated them in Greece and Europe, their places of birth.

In the confusing ebb and flow of history, we often experience a certain difficulty in tracing the outlines of complex social and political movements. For instance, the convulsions of the Reformation and the revolutions of the seventeenth century had given the impression that democracy was on the march. But when the dust settled after England's Glorious Revolution it became clear that the Western world stood once again on the threshold of a new aristocratic age. The era of despots was closed and its main purpose had been fulfilled: the insurance of the rights of the new middle class, the merger of its upper layer with the remains of the former feudal nobility, the birth of a new aristocracy, and the decisive predominance of the city over the countryside.

With the resulting situation in continental Europe, we are not here concerned. Social integration proceeded easily in northern Europe, with far greater difficulty in central and southern Europe. But in England and America, the pattern was clearly set. In all English-speaking countries, as it had been in Rome, individual freedom was the basis of social and political life. At the same time, the aristocracy rose to supreme and undisputed pre-eminence, but it was no longer the same ruling class that had preceded the Tudors and Stuarts. It was a new one that had willingly incorporated the higher middle class and had become partly converted to its economic ideals. It was the first of the great *compromises* whereby the Anglo-Saxons were able to reduce political and social frictions to a bare minimum. Within the English aristocracy, the landed gentry (Tories) came to terms with the financial and business patricians (Whigs). It was a strange but workable alliance between the old feudal nobility based on landowning and blood ties and the new wealth of finance, commerce, and industry—between the old countryside and the new city. Both were willing to struggle for supremacy within the constitutional framework of a two-party system and thus virtually share the supreme power in the state. They had their club—the House of Commons—and all their trials of strength took the form of parliamentary debates.

Therefore, fluidity stamped their political and social structure, a fluidity that has endured until our times, that has made possible the plastic adaptation to changing conditions through peaceful evolution rather than violent revolution, that was able to launch the Industrial Revolution and absorb its terrific impact with a minimum of social trouble and none of the sanguinary upheavals that tore the rest of the world apart.

Rome followed the same enlightened road after the abolition of the Tarquin monarchy. Rome became wholly aristocratic. Because they were realistic, pragmatic, and remained sufficiently fluid to accept ceaselessly new recruits from the rising plebeians and middle classes, generation after generation, the Roman and Anglo-Saxon aristocracies enjoyed a "tradition of confidence" on the part of the people which was unknown to Greece and Europe. Both were societies expanding rapidly in wealth, territory, populations—and expansion meant that the ruling classes had to expand if they wanted to cover the same ground, retain their relative pre-eminence, and control the new sources of power that were coming into being. They had to have great powers of absorption and amalgamation. They were respected by the rising middle classes who sought admittance into their ranks because they represented an essential and vital link with the past, an all-important consideration among people who are both progressive and yet tradition-conscious.

The Romans' devotion to liberty was equaled by their genius for practical politics. After expelling the Tarquins, Rome widened her Assembly by granting suffrage to the Plebs. The aristocratic Senate saw its power increase tremendously, but it came to admit a growing number of wealthy plebeians. Acceptance among the ranks of the ruling class was neither quick nor easy but, given patience and determination, it could always be reached eventually. In the beginning, the newly accepted plebeians had neither magisterial prerogatives (*auctoritas*) nor the right to express their opinion and tender advice (*consilium*); they remained for a long time silent voters, *pedarii,* that is foot-members, men who voted with their feet. Thus humbled and trained for their new political responsibilities, the chosen plebeians came in time to absorb and revere the traditions that were still very much alive among the duty-conscious aristocracy.

As Rome grew through incorporation of neighboring city-states and came to occupy a preponderant position in Italy, so did its fluid aristocracy grow in numbers and wealth, always giving increasing leeway to the vocal plebeians. From the creation of the Tribunate in 495 B.C. to the democratic laws of Quintus Hortensius in 287 B.C., the decline of the old blood nobility proceeded steadily and peacefully, with the predominance shifting to the new aristocracy of money and commercial wealth. But there was no brutal break, no revolution, no rupture comparable to the frightful revolutions, civil wars and slaughters of contemporary Greece. Rome in ancient and the English-speaking nations in modern times were the only states to survive the great eras of revolutions and world wars with unimpaired constitutions. Aristocratic standards and traditions were regularly transmitted through osmosis, as it were.

The small elite that guided the destinies of a small Rome with its few thousand citizens metamorphosed itself gradually through the centuries into a much larger and complex ruling class which came to dominate the greater part of the Classical world. This progressive enlargement of the early nobility based on blood ties and tribal relationships to a far more numerous aristocracy based primarily on wealth and financial power was made possible by the gradual dilution of the traditional ruling class through the normal course of events —war, degeneration, and impoverishment.

The same phenomenon occurred in England, from the small feudal nobleman of pre-Tudor days to the nineteenth-century magnate who could just as well be First Lord of the Admiralty, Viceroy of India, a great steelmaker, or head of the Bank of England: the same preservation of form, the same transmission of traditional standards of aristocratic conduct, the same willingness to absorb and amalgamate with the rising elements from lower social strata. And the same phenomenon took place in America where the descendants of the early settlers found themselves gradually raised to the level of a small ruling class by the steady growth of a population swelled by a continuous stream of immigrants and jumping from thousands to millions. When social pressure became alarming, concessions were made. Rome was threatened with revolution when the fast-increasing plebeians became conscious of their strength and of their lack of political rights, but the democratic reforms of Servius Tullius came in time to stave off the impending conflict. When American frontiersmen became too numerous and powerful to be ignored, the seaboard gentry made the necessary concessions by granting them greater political rights. It nevertheless remains that eighteenth-century America had an aristocratic structure that did not exist in the preceding century and that even suffrage was far more limited, in relation to the total population, than it had been at the origin.

In early Rome, as in England and America, the land problem was paramount. Trade and industry were not yet powerful enough to overshadow agriculture. Under the Tarquins, as under the Tudors and Stuarts, the rulers had attempted to check the power of capital and increase the number of independent, prosperous farmers. But with the overthrow of despotic monarchs and the rise to power of wealthy aristocracies in Rome and the British Empire, the new ruling classes reversed the process and began to concentrate the land into fewer and fewer hands. The keen business sense and financial acumen of the Puritans had seeped down to the landowning gentry who now began to look upon land as a source of wealth on a par with mining and industry. Farming became more scientific and the good earth, from being the mother to whom the continental European peasant remained attached by sentimental bonds, became an impersonal source of wealth that could be properly fertilized and exploited on a large scale by businessmen-farmers. From being a calling, agriculture became a business, increasingly involved in the complicated financial network of credit transaction, money rates, growing capitalism, and the international level of food supplies. The destruction of the small independent farmer was the inevitable outcome of this social altera- tion, as the annihilation of the small artisan, later on, was to result from industrialism's mass production.

Rome had showed the way, two thousand years earlier. Under the aristocratic rule of the Roman Senate, Rome's large landowners began to claim the sole right to use the *ager publicus,* the public land, and soon incorporated into their private estates most of the communal lands, to the detriment of the powerless small farmers. On the large estates thus created they imported masses of slaves and concentrated on those staples that were exportable and profitable (vines and olives), now that every Mediterranean country was increasingly tied to an expanding Classical world economy. Scientific farming on a large scale was introduced and Classical agriculture was gradually caught in the vortex of an international balance of food supplies, commodity speculation, and massive imports of cheap foodstuffs from the East which threw the independent Roman farmers on their knees. Generation after generation, tradition-conscious Romans cried that the backbone of the nation was being hacked to pieces, that the sturdy independent yeomen were being priced out of the market and Italian agriculture crippled, but the trend seemed irresistible. The economic results of this agricultural concentration were far superior to those obtained by small-scale farming that did not have the necessary capital to invest in mass production. This soon became obvious in central Italy's *latifundia* near the Fucine Lake, in the districts of Ciris and Volturnus, then later in southern Italy where huge ranches appeared, stocked with herds of oxen and sheep.

And so it was in the eighteenth-century British Empire. The steady growth of the large English country estates through the "enclosure" system, the gradual seizure of the peasants' commons by the lords of the manor, drove small farmers to bankruptcy but raised the efficiency of scientific farming on a capitalistic scale. It was no different in America. The destruction of the small independent farmer became the main objective in Virginia and the Carolinas, where southern aristocrats were in full political control, and where they were able through their overwhelming predominance in the legislatures to appropriate to themselves huge tracts of virgin lands in the interior. Taxation worked in favor of the landowning ruling class, as it had in Rome, where the Senate discontinued levying taxes on the public lands cultivated by large landowners and consequently taxed the small farmers all the heavier. In both cases, the massive and growing importation of slaves priced free labor out of the market, ruining many Roman and American farmers, widening the gap between latifundia and plantations on the one hand, with their hundreds or thousands of slaves, and an increasing population of impoverished farmers on the other.

Even in the more democratic New England states the "manorial institution of the commons"—land shared communally and open to all for pasturage, fuel, and other purposes—was undermined by the tendency of aggressive patrician families to fence in sections of the commons and incorporate them into their own estates. Instead of keeping the old township method of granting land and a share in the commons to new settlers, the legislatures sold them directly to speculators who in turn helped to create a class of powerful absentee landlords who often dominated the town meetings and overawed the small farmers.

This aristocratic reaction and pre-eminence was accepted in the

British Empire for one simple reason. Alone among all the ruling classes in the world, this aristocracy was progressive, was "in form." It alone was living consciously in the new age of economic development that the continental Europeans did not understand. The exception was Holland. In many respects, Holland had shown the way to commercial success and against her England struggled "for the fairest mistress in the world—trade." [1] Alone of all the great world powers England fought only wars of economic supremacy. Wars of religion, dynastic conflicts, revolutions striving toward one or another utopia —all these outdated forms of conflict were left behind. With icy coldness and remarkable foresight, the British were going to fight strategic wars for raw materials, commercial connections and monopolies, mass markets for their industrial output—starting with the Dutch War of 1665-67, which was instigated by the Royal African Company for strictly commercial purposes. Rome's Punic Wars were the first great conflicts of the Classical world which were largely motivated by economic purposes (the commercial rivalry of Carthage), at a time when Greece and the East recklessly indulged in ideological or dynastic wars.

Economics and economic thinking began to dominate England and America. Having been made respectable by Calvin, having become a symbol of spiritual achievement through the agency of early Puritanism, the thirst for economic progress and profit gradually discarded its religious crutch as it had already relegated the Church of England to the position of a stately fossil. English society, fully emancipated after the Glorious Revolution, looked upon church and state interference in economic matters with great disfavor. Public policy's new role was to be the willing tool of economic interests and an old-fashioned morality was no longer to stand in the way.

The thirst for individual freedom linked up quite naturally with the obvious fact that freedom was good for business. In America, religious tolerance became inevitable in a land of militant dissenters, but economic compulsion always lay behind this tolerance as the only practical policy to promote quick settlement of new lands. This was the first outstanding example of the typical alliance of an idealistic reform with a hard-headed business sense and flair for economic profit that was to characterize modern American psychology. Although there were a few peevish protests from priests and ministers as well as laymen, nothing could be done to halt this evolution.

Economic science was developed in France in a purely speculative way by literary intellectuals, in Germany later on as a subordinate part of the state's administrative policy. In England, it was developed by businessmen and financiers who were more concerned with concrete achievements than theoretical speculations; and British philosophic thought merely rationalized this psychological disposition. John Locke and his followers of the Age of Enlightenment intellectualized the feelings of Protestants and Puritans by rejecting once and for all the Aristotelian and Thomist conception of society as an organic entity endowed with a life and meaning of its own, over and above that of the individual. Instead, society was now viewed as composed exclusively of free, equal, independent individuals moved by their own self-interest. Locke looked upon the revolution that overthrew the absolutist James II as fully justified by the twin theory of individual "natural rights" and the rational "natural law" to which all individuals could appeal against man-made laws. And although the British always retained a divided philosophic allegiance to both Hooker's Aristotelianism and Locke's extreme individualism, Americans followed Locke almost exclusively. It was Locke who provided the intellectual justification for the American Revolution—and from England's Glorious Revolution to the American one a century later, a clear legal thread springs from the very root of Anglo-Saxon psychology.

Locke interpreted in his philosophy the world outlook of Calvinistic Protestants and especially of latter-day Puritans. His theory, according to which persons are separate mental substances without other relations than those of human reason, hammered the last nail in the coffin of Gothic Thomism, Catholicism, and Anglicanism—or so his followers thought at the time. He visualized social problems as mechanical relations similar to those of Newton's planetary universe. Laws were no longer based on spiritual realities but became human transactions freely entered into by the participants. Therefore, the only justification for the existence of government was the protection of private property, which was itself only an extension of the individual's physical body. Although Locke professed to believe in God, the Almighty had become a superfluous relic of the past, as powerless in his philosophic system as the English monarch was in politics.

The direct connection between Puritanism and the prevailing rationalism of the Age of Enlightenment is unmistakable. From the lyricism

of Milton to the dry thinking of Hume, there is a logical and unbroken chain. Metaphysics was dismissed as mental fog and God
became an empty symbol. Belief in the supremacy of critical understanding ruled supreme—more pragmatic, sensual, and experimental
in England, more intellectual and theoretical in France.

The decline of religious faith stamps the so-called Age of Enlightenment and coincides with the zenith of cultural creation. The
Classical world's Age of Enlightenment—the Age of Pericles—saw
the greatest flowering of art and literature ever witnessed by man,
but also the beginning of the age of skepticism and irreligion. Thu-
cydides has left us a remarkable rendering of Pericles' funeral oration
in which patriotism sheds the religious clothing into which it had
grown and becomes nakedly secularized: Pericles loves Athens, not
because she is a favorite of the gods but because her democratic
institutions prescribe that all citizens be free and equal. Thus could
Voltaire visualize the future of France—both of them being unable
to foresee the full consequences of their irreverent agnosticism, the
approaching storms, revolutions, and wars of annihilation. The Ages
of Enlightenment, Periclean and Voltairian, prepare, through their
divorce between faith and reason, the inevitable chaos of the future.

With our historical perspective, we can see the line of Greek
evolution quite clearly. Aeschylus, Pindar, and Sophocles poured their
fervent faith in the Olympian deities into their great literary creations, as Phidias did in his statuary. But already Pythagoras, the
Eleatic philosophers, and the Orphic devotees had initiated the ideological reaction of the Classical world's Reformation, and their natural
successors were the skeptical Protagoras, the Sophists (who introduced the notion of relativity and denied the existence of any absolute), the materialistic Democritus, and the Voltairian Euripides.
Worship of speculative science appeared with Anaxagoras and Democritus, the counterpart of the French Encyclopedists of the eighteenth century. The same reaction against the Periclean and Voltairian
urban rationalism animated the romantic advocates of a "return to
nature": the Greek Cynics and France's Rousseau.

Greece and Europe, more intellectual and theoretical, went to the
logical end of their quest and ended in tragic confusion. They started
their secular progression toward self-destruction, revolutions, civil
and national wars. Their various components attempted time and
again to squeeze concrete reality into abstract schemes and theories

—and each time, destructive explosions occurred which weakened their cohesion and gradually destroyed their vitality. Nothing of the sort happened in the Roman and English-speaking commonwealths.

Neither England nor America immediately absorbed and lived by Locke's philosophy. Their aristocracies were at first closer to Hooker's vision of a hierarchical society than to Locke's atomistic democratization. But there was a slow rise in Locke's influence, leading to its eventual ascendancy in America. In any case, this extreme individualism was only workable because the Anglo-Americans retained their instinctive feeling for social cooperation—in fact, mainly because they never took any intellectual philosophy too literally.

The rise of economic supremacy in Anglo-Saxon thinking, of plain skepticism and belief in the supremacy of reason on the European continent, went hand in hand. In America, the old, stern, unbending Puritanism began to soften and dilute itself through its very expansion over all the colonies. In spreading, it shed its theocratic coloring but gave its business ethics to all other Protestants. There was a steady loosening of social taboos. The theocratic character of Massachusetts' government was being undermined by the example of more liberal constitutions such as Rhode Island's and strict Puritans of the old school could not prevent their followers from noticing that tolerance was more favorable to business. The predominant type in New England was no longer the stern, God-fearing Puritan of the old days but the sharp Yankee merchant. The triumph of the economic world outlook over the religious was symbolized by the gradual shift for franchise qualification from church membership to property ownership, to the "stake in society" that alone could qualify the ruling elite of landowners and businessmen.

With the disappearance of old-fashioned Puritanism, the Platonic idealism (the belief in the metaphysical reality of abstract ideas independent of experience) also vanished. Locke's materialism and empiricism replaced it. "No idea without an antecedent impression" expressed this new philosophy in brief.[2] The material environment was construed as being the main determinant of man's destiny on earth, a man who now was deemed emancipated from the shackles of original sin. The perfectibility of man became the creed of an optimistic and fluid American society which had more reason to be struck by man's unbounded power over virgin nature than were the older, crowded, and more skeptical societies of Europe. Locke's was the main credo of the rising generation, the generation of Benjamin Franklin, Thomas Paine, and Thomas Jefferson. The gloom of early Puritanism was progressively dispelled, spiritual awareness waned, and economic connections became paramount.

The transition from the deeply religious Puritan to the ruthless trader who never confuses business with ethics and sentiment was almost inevitable. Much later, in the following century, the southerners, stung by the hypocritical righteousness of the Yankees, reminded all and sundry that it was New Englanders who shipped the African slaves to America. Rhode Island, whose liberal constitution was in itself good business, sent slavers to West Africa year in and year out, all through the eighteenth century, and supplied the West Indies as well as the South at a great profit. But this apparent hypocrisy was only the end result of the destruction of the medieval synthesis. Old-fashioned Puritans who attempted to retain a feeble link between ethics and business were dismissed with a shrug. Was not the ruthless commercialism that was beginning to prevail the logical consequence of their views on man's self-reliant individuality? Theocratic Puritanism as conceived by New England Congregationalists implied a fundamental contradiction, an indigestible remnant of this very medieval authoritarianism against which the Reformation had rebelled. Puritans had to go to the end of the experiment and reach the logical fulfillment of the movement.

Americans followed their British cousins—and later overtook them —in slowly reducing man to an exclusively *homo economicus,* a producing and consuming machine who thought of little except economic laws and requirements, goods and production. Because their social instincts were, in fact, very strong, because their individualism was never as marked as that of Europeans, English economists such as Adam Smith and Jeremy Bentham could propound the most individualistic economic doctrines ever put forward by man without poisoning their society. Anglo-Saxons could absorb it, and live by it whereas the individualism of a Voltaire could only destroy the Latins.

Even the Anglo-Saxons, however, could not quite cope with the disastrous effects of the Industrial Revolution, which virtually enslaved millions of workers during the following century. But even so, this extreme individualism was tolerable because it was, in a sense, progressive; because it alone could foster the Industrial Revolution and promote private initiative. This spectacular taming of the unknown and unsuspected forces of nature overshadowed the social ills and enlisted the enthusiastic approval of the leading elements of society, along with the mute acquiescence of its victims.

Imprisoned in their narrow vista through which they saw economics as the beginning and end of man's serious purpose in life, the English-speaking people led the rest of the world economically and at the same time were spared the frightening convulsions that began to shake Europe from the French Revolution onward. The preservation of private property became their main goal. Inevitably, they soon came to embody the most conservative outlook in the West, a form of enlightened and progressive conservatism similar to that prevalent in Classical Rome, which frowned as much on the social revolutions of Greece as on the reactionary monarchies of the Hellenistic East.

The decline of religious faith, the rise of rationalism and materialism, were the outstanding characteristics of the eighteenth century. As always, compensatory movements checked the more extreme tendencies of this revolution in thought in the English-speaking world. While Europe, especially Catholic Europe, found itself in the throes of a withering skepticism, the basically religious Anglo-Saxons sought for compensation elsewhere. Since, intellectually, the philosophies of materialism seemed unchallengeable and since they had no taste for metaphysics, their religious instincts sought a purely emotional outlet. Somehow, here again, the increasing atomization which had started with the Reformation pursued its thoughtless course. Religion had been divorced from economics, economics from ethics, ethics from science, and politics from the whole lot. Now, religion was going to be separated from a secularized intellect that was wholly devoted to materialism and economic thought. Its only remaining crutch was emotionalism and sheer emotionalism sparked what was called the Great Awakening—the first of those revivalist movements which were going to sweep the English-speaking world from one end to another.

The Great Awakening was an irrational outburst attempting to slough off the bewildering intellectual confusion of a Culture that stood on the threshold of decline. An American phenomenon, the Great Awakening was the answer of the South and West's self-reliant, illiterate pioneers, whose practical wisdom refused to accept the skepticism of the more intellectual East. It shook off the increasing lethargy and indifference which, under the guise of tolerance, had slipped into the increasingly secularized Protestant denominations. As theocracy waned beyond recall, religion became increasingly personal. Independent sects multiplied. Men and women listened more and more to the "inner light." Faith externalized itself, no longer in theology or mystical meditation, but in good works, and the persistent humanitarian trend of the Protestant world became the indispensable counterpoise to the ruthless economic individualism of the Industrial Revolution.

German Pietists, English Methodists, Calvinist Presbyterians from Scotland and Northern Ireland, Baptists, all took part in the Great Awakening in an instinctive revolt against the unsatisfying ideals of the Enlightenment's dessicated rationalism. Persecuted in Europe, innumerable sects emigrated to America and made a telling contribution to this emotional explosion. Moravian Brethren, Mennonites, Dunkers flocked in from Germany. In England, John Wesley launched his twin attack on rationalism and the formal symbolism of the Church of England, adding his emphasis on good works rather than religious symbolism and intellectualism, a sentiment already lurking in the English-speaking masses. His Methodism grew up with the Industrial Revolution, feeding on the uprooted rural populations, on the droves of impoverished farmers who were being transformed into urban, slum-dwelling proletariats.

America, still untouched by the Industrial Revolution, had to cope with the problem of her rootless immigrants spread out in the vast wilderness west of the Allegheny Mountains. Scotch-Irish Presbyterians, Congregationalists, Welsh and German Baptists soon joined in an orgy of indiscriminate emotionalism, psalm-singing, mass hysteria, shrieking, and fainting. Crowds of convulsive men and women gathered in all parts of America but more especially along the frontier, creating tight emotional links between multitudes of isolated immigrants from different parts of Europe.

Revivalism confirmed the eclipse of Calvin's iron predestination, which had already been well under way for generations. In spite of many gruesome references to Hell's terrors, the former gloom faded in front of an optimistic faith in man's ability to win salvation for himself. Revivalism helped greatly in diluting the narrow-minded but stern and heroic greatness of the Pilgrims' creed into the vague, smiling humanitarianism that still prevails today. Thus did American

Christianity acquire the distinctive traits which put it in sharp opposition to its Old World counterpart: lack of intellectualism, reliance on emotional revivals, emphasis on good works rather than prayer and meditation, optimistic and positive approach to earthly problems.

During the great ages of Pericles and Enlightenment, Rome and America were living on the periphery of history, building up their physical power, concentrating on practical work. They produced nothing significant in the way of culture, being content to live on the fabulous output of their aging parents. In the glittering age of Voltaire, Rousseau, Mozart, and Bach, America produced Benjamin Franklin's *Poor Richard's Almanack,* a rather limited contribution. No brilliant or original creations in the world of architecture or painting, no sublime flight in the world of music, no profound philosophic insight, no scientific thought which was not motivated by strict utilitarian aims. The stern morality that enjoined thrift and frugality and useful work certainly made exemplary citizens of a free country but was hardly conducive to the great flights of creative originality of the world's greatest Culture epoch. In the age of Hogarth and Watteau, America produced painstakingly detailed pictures that never betrayed the slightest artistic inspiration. Georgian architectural styles were imported wholesale from the mother country.

With Benjamin Franklin as a living symbol, the true American soul began to emancipate itself from its European cocoon: pragmatic, compromising and conciliatory, profoundly devoted to freedom and fundamentally inclined toward equality, industrious and frugal, unrefined and comfortable. Here again there is a direct connection between the somber, iron-willed Pilgrim Fathers and the optimistic, skeptical Franklin in whom religious fanaticism metamorphosed itself into an idealist morality. This direct connection was a fundamental utilitarianism, a direct outgrowth of early Puritanism, which gradually ended by resorbing its parent into itself. Since material success is a sign of spiritual blessing, every production should be gauged by the test: "Does it work, is it useful?" Bach's fugues could not pass the test, but Franklin's lightning rod could. And so could his homely aphorisms, which were meant to be read near the family stove, another of his inventions. And so it was with the nameless but practical Romans who invented techniques and gadgets that were unknown to the more brilliant Greeks.

Since every coin has two sides, the necessary counterpart of an extreme utilitarianism bent on concrete achievements is an equally extreme idealism of a more abstract nature than any put forth in the Old World. And so, on one hand the American temper is remarkably tolerant, compromising, and realistic, and on the other it entertains a fanatical belief in vague abstractions, a fanaticism which conceives of no shades between black and white. The occasionally baffling nature of American thought and action—to foreigners—lies in this basic and unresolved contradiction within the American soul. Essentially uncompromising in its ideals, essentially devoted to pragmatism and compromise in practical life, this fundamental schism is another consequence of the atomistic outlook of the Reformation.

On the eve of the American Revolution, the basic difference between Americans and Europeans was already clear cut. It was the same fundamental opposition that set the Romans apart from the Greeks—the cult of Beauty and Theory in Greece and Europe, the cult of Morality and Pragmatism in Rome and America. Romans and Americans already displayed a genius for avoiding those social and political conflicts which tore apart Greeks and Europeans. They always worked at producing a uniform level of ability among all men rather than bringing into great prominence those individuals who were more highly gifted. The result was a far higher average than in Greece and Europe, and yet an almost complete absence of great creative personalities, a very high average of popular education but no outstanding originality, no real contribution to culture. In the Age of Pericles, there was no cultural output in Rome, nothing but the dogged, persistent extension of Roman power in central Italy, the gradual build-up of political institutions. While Socrates and Plato expounded their immortal philosophies, the Romans shunned intellectual speculation and concentrated on trade, scientific agriculture, irrigation, and road building. Roman frugality and simplicity of living in the third century B.C. were as legendary as the homely way of life of the Americans in the eighteenth century. Even when not enjoined by law, equality was a plain fact because the great majority enjoyed the basic comforts of a healthy although plain life without the refined luxury that was becoming the distinguishing feature of cultured living among upper-class Greeks and Europeans.

In the Greek and European worlds, we can watch the free expression of individual originality in thought and action, uninhibited by any conformism. The whole was resorbed into its parts and the emphasis was on the creative and original individual, not on society. Freedom was rarely guaranteed by law and was always insecure. But this old-fashioned despotic denial of freedom was too clumsy and inconsistent to be anything more than a stimulating opposition to be challenged. Protagoras could be forced out of Athens into exile because of his agnosticism and Voltaire might have to flee France. But in those days, thought could never be controlled and it burst forth with that much more explosive vigor. On the other hand, when the Olympic and Christian beliefs faded in front of free intellectual inquiry, when the Olympic deities and Catholic symbolism were dashed to the ground by an increasingly secular and critical philosophy, there was no intellectual or emotional thread connecting the various portions of the fragmented societies of Greece and Europe.

In Rome, and increasingly in America, it was the reverse: the individual was merged in the collectivity, psychological conformism was unconsciously enforced by the collectivity itself with great rigor, and there existed a developing sense of cooperative action in which the individual ultimately labored for the group. Even in the meaningless character of individual Roman names, contrasted with the originality and marked personalization of Greek names, one can sense the instinctive desire of the Romans to reduce all human beings to one uniform level, and raise that level as high as possible, instead of promoting the full development of individual idiosyncrasies as in Greece. The American saying "To be different is to be indecent" could just as well be applied to Roman society.

CHAPTER IV | *The Age of Revolution*

IN the eighteenth century, the narrow strip of inhabited land along the coast of North America was carved into thirteen small colonies—to an extent, thirteen highly decentralized, autonomous republics that thought of themselves as having made a voluntary contract with the ruler of the mother country: "The agreement with William and Mary, in which the colonists joined upon their accession following the Glorious Revolution." [1]

The end of the Seven Years' War in 1764 had given Great Britain complete supremacy in India and had transferred the huge French possessions in North America to the British Empire. England now learned at her expense that a great deal of the loyalty of the native Americans to their British connection was due to their fear of a redoubtable French imperialism. Having disposed of that threat, the British were no longer needed. In 1763, Britain had fulfilled part of her historic role in America. She had destroyed the one rival who could have divided the continent and who, by settling the immense territory stretching all the way from New Orleans to Montreal, could have founded an antagonistic and far more powerful Latin empire. The French threat had vanished and the Americans were now fully prepared to take their destiny into their own hands.

But the British now attempted to fasten upon America a tighter political and economic control than they had previously exercised. Until now, the North American settlements had been hardly more than convenient dependencies of the fabulously wealthy West Indies, secondary colonies that could hardly compete in prestige and influence. New England merchants and shipowners and Virginian landowners could not possibly cope in London with the powerful par-

62

liamentary lobby of the tropical planters. In past days, when the unfair Molasses Act of 1733 was imposed, for instance, they submitted for the sake of the protection afforded by the imperial forces. Now they no longer needed this protection. Furthermore, with the end of the Seven Years' War came the end of a century of unmitigated prosperity. A severe slump hit America. The ill-advised British chose this precise moment to assert their full authority. The Sugar Act of 1764 and the Stamp Act of 1765 were followed by a series of arbitrary measures promulgated in London without reference to American wishes. In addition, having destroyed the counterpoise of a menacing French empire on the North American continent, the British attempted to replace it with an Indian threat. A proclamation of 1763 forbade settlers to cross the Appalachians into Indian territory. In this clumsy way, Britain hoped to limit the alarming growth of the colonies and preserve a profitable fur trade with the large Indian nations that were under British influence. Nothing could have been better calculated to infuriate the expansionist frontiersmen.

By thus pyramiding the provocations, London made an American revolt inevitable. But, on what ideological grounds would this revolt take place? Benjamin Franklin provided a historical justification when, looking back at the past and tracing the origins of colonization in North America, he concluded: "That the colonies were originally constituted distinct states and intended to be continued such, is clear to me from a thorough consideration of their original charters, and the whole conduct of the Crown and nation towards them until the Restoration. Since that period, the Parliament here has usurped an authority of making laws for them which before it had not. We have, for some time, submitted to that usurpation." [2]

From this statement, it was easy to predict that the tenor of the coming American Revolution would be politically conservative, in the sense that it implied a return to past traditions. The innovation that had to be canceled was this new imperial authority that was asserting itself aggressively without any justification. But, on the deeper level of state of mind, the Americans had already become conscious of their un-European nature, conscious of the differences that separated them from their cousins beyond the ocean. To an often quoted remark of a British officer that "The people of America are at least a hundred years behind the old Countries in Refinement," an anonymous American replied in the *Connecticut Gazette:* "As to Humanity,

Temperance, Chastity, Justice, a Veneration for the Rights of Mankind, and every Moral Virtue, they [the Europeans] are a hundred years behind us." [3] As an American historian points out: "The appeal to ancient Rome for republican inspiration was especially favored . . . the way to exhort the Americans was to 'stir up all that's Roman in them'." [4]

Conscious of their moral superiority, the Americans were beginning to define their incipient nationhood in terms of ethics. Europe became to them the land of decadence, self-indulgence, and corruption which no amount of culture could justify, America the land of solid virtues—therefore the land of republics since, according to the French philosopher Montesquieu, republics thrive on virtue. This moralistic outlook prompted them to sharpen the contrast between the two continents, to insist that a republican form of government was "much more favorable to purity of morals," that "honesty, plain-dealing, and simple manners, were never made the patterns of courtly behavior. Artificial manners always prevail in kingly governments: and royal courts are reservoirs, from whence insincerity, hypocrisy, dissimulation, pride, luxury, and extravagance, deluge and overwhelm the body of the people. On the other hand, republics are favorable to truth, sincerity, frugality, industry and simplicity of manners." [5]

The issue was clear cut. The ways of life were different and not only separation but different political systems were needed to take into account these fundamental differences. Historically minded John Adams intuitively felt the true nature of his compatriots when he wrote that "with the high sentiments of the Romans, in the most prosperous and virtuous times of that commonwealth, they have the tender feelings of humanity and the noble benevolence of Christians." [6] This double nature of the Americans—Roman, yet Christian—characterized their revolution and struggle for independence. It would be a positive change for the better, a constructive emancipation, not a negative explosion of senseless hate.

Few Americans were prepared to sever all connections with the British Empire. The great Americans of those days—Jefferson, Franklin, John Adams—all thought in terms of a federal empire. But how was such an empire to be organized? No one had thought the problem through. In a sense, the constitutional problem that generated the American Revolution was similar, on a much broader scale, to that which faced the Greeks and the Romans. Classical man could think of no other political unit than the tight, limited *polis,* the city and its immediate neighborhood. Geographical extension of the *polis* was unthinkable in the Greek city-states. Classical man was psychologically limited to the "here and now." To him, extension could only be imperialistic and imply subordination, not association or amalgamation. But the gradual extension of Rome in Italy placed the problem squarely in front of the Roman statesmen: how to extend direct representative government beyond the visible, tangible boundaries of the limited *polis* and its center, the Forum? Elections to some sort of federal assembly was never thought of, because it was unthinkable in view of the psychological limitations of Classical man. Voters had to be physically present; otherwise, Roman citizens living in some far-off city had no influence on the course of events.

The constitutional problem facing Britain and America might easily have been solved by the establishment of a federal assembly in London, over and above the British parliament and the colonial legislatures. But it is enough to quote Samuel Adams' remarks in 1765 to grasp the psychological limitations of the times: "We are far from desiring any Representation there, because we think that the Colonies cannot be equally and fully represented, and if not equally then in Effect not at all. A Representative should be, and continue to be well acquainted with the internal circumstances of the People whom he represents . . . now the Colonies are at so great a Distance from the place where Parliament meets, from which they are separated by a wide Ocean." [7] It is obvious that, in spite of this argumentation, the outstanding differences between England and America were small enough to be easily straightened out by a federal legislature and that a full measure of decentralized autonomy would have taken care of the local problems of the colonies. But the vast stretches of the Atlantic Ocean stood far more as a psychological than as a physical barrier.

A political separation was therefore unavoidable. But even in American public opinion, the issue was not quite as clear cut as the most vocal advocates of revolution and independence implied. Although there was an incipient American patriotism—the beginning of a vague feeling of Americanism as opposed to Europeanism—local loyalties were still paramount. The colonists were New Englanders, New Yorkers, or Virginians first, and Americans second. Washington

himself complained bitterly about the divided loyalties of his compatriots, about the considerable help and sympathy enjoyed by the
British among large segments of the American people. John Adams
estimated that as much as one third of the Americans were loyalists.

The obstinate blindness of the British played into the hands of the
leaders of the independence movement. The passions aroused by the
war itself among the Americans made conciliation more difficult as
time went on. What started out as a struggle to retrieve the old rights
of the colonies ended up as a desperate war for full and unconditional
independence from the mother country. Lack of moderation and the
eclipse of the customary spirit of compromise created added antagonisms. The stress and bitterness of the hostilities sparked a miniature civil war among the Americans themselves, and the emigration
of some of the loyalists to Canada sealed the fate of a continent that
was to remain politically divided. Had there been more generous
understanding on both sides, one single nation might have occupied
all the land stretching from the Rio Grande to the North Pole.

A mild social revolution was wrapped up in the War of Independence. The war had started as a protest against adverse economic
conditions and unfair taxation, but it was difficult to whip up popular
enthusiasm for the cause of the unhappy New England merchants
and southern planters without considering the numerous grievances
of the less fortunate Americans against their own ruling classes. As
soon as the revolutionary issue became clear on the social side, the
upper classes became alarmed at the radicalism of the "mob." Their
fears lay behind many of their attempts to seek a compromise with
London. But the situation, of course, was beyond control. Having
transferred the motivating principle of the Revolution from the strictly
economic to the ideological battleground, the American elite was
gradually driven to curtail its own privileges in order to justify its
idealistic leadership.

Jefferson and his liberal friends remained in power during the
war and the first years of independence. Aligned against Jefferson
and his followers were most of the New England leaders like John
Adams and most southern aristocrats like George Washington,
whose strong convictions were made plain when he stated that
"mankind, when left to themselves, are unfit for their own government." [8] But democratization was now inevitable. In the very

process of defining the meaning of Americanism, the leaders were bound to discover, even if reluctantly, the profound currents of irresistible equalitarian feeling that were to become the psychological hallmark of America. The devotion to *equality* was a normal trend since it represented the ultimate goal of an essentially ethical idealism, but many upper-class Americans echoed Gouverneur Morris' nostalgic warning: "Farewell aristocracy. I see, and I see with fear and trembling that if disputes with Great Britain continue, we shall be under the domination of a riotous mob. It is to the interest of all men, therefore, to seek for reunion with the parent state." [9]

But reunion had become impossible and mob rule prevailed—an extremely mild and reasonable mob rule judged by the European standards soon to be set by the orgiastic French Revolution. The electoral franchise was considerably widened. From the limited number of Americans who signed the Declaration of Independence and constituted a small oligarchy, to those who voted for the adoption of the Constitution, there was a tremendous increase in number of popular voters. In most states, almost every taxpayer acquired the right to vote—still far from universal male franchise, but a considerable step in that direction. The equivalent democratization in Rome was the transfer of political rights and privileges from the limited Comitia Curiata to the much larger Comitia Centuriata, the assembled levy of those bound to military service—military service in Rome being a duty and source of political rights equivalent to taxpaying in the English-speaking world.

The aristocracy suffered further blows when Jefferson and the Virginia liberals destroyed its economic bulwarks—entail, primogeniture, and quitrents. Church and state were separated, a victory for religious indifferentism rather than tolerance, which at the time was largely absent from political and social conflicts. Even slavery came under attack. Since emancipation would have solved only part of the problem, many liberals thought of sending the colored freedmen to the still-virgin lands of the interior. Miscegenation was never seriously contemplated. Though the movement for emancipation came to a dead-end, the gradual democratization of American society proceeded on all other fronts. The colonial aristocracy could not raise the banner of an anti-British revolution in the name of the Rights of Man and, in the same breath, deny these rights to their own underprivileged compatriots.

In 1776, the Continental Congress instructed all the colonies to set up regular governments. Their formation during the war was in itself a remarkable achievement, calling for unusual self-discipline, restraint, and moderation. But, orderly though they were, the ruling majorities were frankly radical and their confused attitudes permitted sporadic social disorders in various parts of the country. Many wealthy merchants and landowners who had rebelled against British taxation and economic discrimination ended up fighting dangerously inflamed mobs to protect their property. Frontiersmen fought the coastal gentry. Westerners were still being as strongly discriminated against as the Latin allies and plebeians were by the Roman patricians. New lands were being settled but their political representation in the legislatures was totally inadequate, and the anger of the new settlers found ample opportunity of expression during the Revolution. Such explosions as the Regulator movement of North Carolina led to full-scale warfare. Everywhere, the political and economic privileges of the eastern oligarchies were being challenged, not only by the eastern "mobs" but but western social democracy.

This was no new problem. Rome had faced it time and again. It was the problem of geographic expansion and concomitant democratization. New Roman citizens were eventually granted full political rights, but were inscribed in a limited number of "tribes" regardless of their large numbers; they remained a minority in the Assembly. Underrepresentation always penalizes newcomers until they can revolt successfully, and this can only be achieved through a tight alliance between all the victims of an oligarchy—alliance between Roman plebeians and Latin allies, or, in America, between eastern lower classes and western frontiersmen. The problems of franchise, money rates, and debt in the settled areas and the fair representation of the American westerners were always linked. The Roman oligarchy always ended up giving way to the coalition of plebeians and Latin tributaries who resented their underrepresentation in the Assembly, whenever it felt that this coalition really meant business. It was no different in America where the eastern oligarchy faced the facts and accepted the inevitable change.

The rising American democrats displayed immediately a feature which recurs throughout history, and for which ideologists rarely credit them: their inherent imperialism. Their first decision was to cancel the restrictive proclamation of 1763 and the Quebec Act, and open the vast Indian territories beyond the Appalachians to white settlement. Imperial expansion and democracy—two features that are presumed to be contradictory and yet are often two sides of the same coin.

The independence of America meant that a large segment of the English-speaking world was splitting off from the main trunk, to seek its destiny alone and unhampered. There were few ill feelings left between the estranged daughter and mother—a few pin pricks throughout the nineteenth century, followed by an unwavering although often unofficial alliance in the twentieth, before a strange new world in full revolt against Western Civilization. There could be few ill feelings. Both countries had the same culture, language, laws, political and social principles, and to a large extent the same blood. America moved faster toward full democracy than Britain, but both were largely dedicated to the same economic pursuits to the exclusion of almost everything that moved most continental Europeans. They were natural allies even when they squabbled over details. The best proof is that throughout the nineteenth century, three times as many Englishmen emigrated to America as to all the British dominions and colonies put together, further tightening the instinctive bonds between them.

<table>
<tr><td>CHAPTER
V</td><td>*The Fateful*
Decisions</td></tr>
</table>

IN 1777 the Continental Congress approved the Articles of Confederation, and all the states ratified them by 1781. Jefferson and his democratic followers were in full control of the situation and had established what they thought would be the ideal structure, a league of virtually independent states: "Each state retains its sovereignty, freedom and independence, and every power, jurisdiction and right which is not by this confederation expressly delegated to the United States in Congress Assembled." [1] The sole agency of federal government was Congress and the delegates from the states acted chiefly as ambassadors. Congress had no direct authority over the states' citizens. There was no federal Executive.

The liberals who wrote the Articles were convinced that democracy was impossible under a central government holding sway over a large area, a conviction based on fear that such a government would evolve toward some form of hated monarchy. They thought that the smaller the political unit, the stronger the democracy. Moreover, most Americans in those days were farmers who looked forward to a simple, unsophisticated agrarian democracy; they viewed centralization as the rule of the wealthy, decentralization as the rule of the plain people.

Their aristocratic and middle-class opponents, on the defensive, saw clearly that the splitting up of the country into thirteen weak little republics was the sure road to political impotence and financial chaos. Further, the states would be at the mercy of any strong and determined European power. This conservative opposition was largely urban (and therefore northern) although it was bolstered by a growing number of southern planters. They were all frightened by the growing insolvency of the states and by the insecurity of property, a condition that had started during the Revolution when the estates of fleeing loyalists were confiscated and distributed to the patriots.

As usual, the main issue was not clearly seen. It takes a great effort of imagination to see beyond the contingencies of the moment and reckon the far-reaching consequences of today's decisions. The basic issue, temporarily obscured by critical emergencies, was: were the states to become exclusively devoted to the enjoyment of peace and democracy (and therefore follow the decentralizing lead of the Jeffersonians) or would they embark on the road to consolidation, centralization, and fusion, with all that it implied—territorial expansion, increasing national power, and eventual imperialism leading to a profound transformation of the political structure? Were the states to become a peaceful Switzerland and devote their talents to the building up of a small, contented, and loose confederation, or were they going to aim at extension and power?

It was George Washington who perceived the tight connection between centralization and territorial expansion, and saw the inevitability of the twin trend at the same time. His journeys in the West convinced him that the Mississippi Valley was destined to be rapidly colonized and that, under existing conditions, the new country would fall under Spanish domination since the mouth and the west bank of the great river belonged to Spanish Louisiana. Without trade outlet to the sea, the westerners would vote themselves into the Spanish Empire or, at any rate, secede from a loose confederation which could not protect them. The very safety of the original states would be endangered by the rise of another republic across the Appalachians. The safeguard of the United States therefore required the protection and incorporation of the West—and this could only be guaranteed by a strong central government.

Thus, even in those early days, the Americans were inevitably committed to expansion and centralization out of sheer self-protection; and thus started the fateful, unintentional, and unplanned expansionism which, in less than two centuries, was to establish the frontiers of American security well into the hearts of the European and Asiatic continents, all the way across the globe's two greatest oceans.

The expansion of Rome was no less motivated by a feeling of self-preservation and the Roman statesmen had to make the same fateful choice after having long refused to embark on a career of extension in Italy. They were forced into it by the need to protect themselves against the dreaded Etruscans who had once ruled over them. It was the requirements of national defense, not the spirit of aggression, that were the motivating forces behind Rome's involuntary imperialism; and in order to defeat the threatening Etruscans, Rome had to provide strong leadership to the hitherto loosely organized Latin League as set up by Spurius Cassius. This eventually led them to the dissolution of the Latin Confederation about 384 B.C. and the substitution of a new federal constitution, far more centralized than the old one, in which Rome assumed full executive power while the Roman franchise was gradually extended to the Latins. Thus the need to expand for the sake of self-preservation was tightly linked with the need to centralize, in Rome as in America. The transformation of a loose Latin confederation into a tightly-knit federation under Roman leadership was in all respects equivalent to the transition from America's Articles of Confederation to the far more centralized federal Constitution. The fact that Vermont was negotiating with London for a return to the British Empire proved that failure to adopt a centralized constitution would eventually have meant the breakup of the loose confederation itself.

By the middle of the decade following ratification of the Articles, the virtual bankruptcy of the whole structure was obvious. Everything was at a standstill, the credit of America abroad was nil, the political situation was chaotic, the economic and financial conditions of most states disastrous; and as James Bryce noted, it was in liberal states such as Rhode Island that the chaos was worst, this state that resembled a Classical republic more than any other: "The example of her disorders did much to bring the other states to adopt that Federal Constitution which she was herself the last to accept." [2]

The time for a conservative reaction was at hand and the gentry rallied around George Washington. A convention was summoned in Philadelphia in May, 1787, Washington presiding. The delegates were men of outstanding intellect, integrity, and political experience. Their instructions were merely to revise the Articles of Confederation, whose failures were glaring. But the hopelessness of attempting to patch up a machinery which had almost entirely broken down became obvious. With remarkable boldness and spirit of decision, they decided to disregard instructions and work on an entirely new scheme. This new Constitution was devised by basically conservative men who saw in the virtual independence of the states the sure road to catastrophe. They were security-holders, manufacturers, ship owners, planters— all those who had a "stake in society"—and they designed a strong central government powerful enough to check the demagogy of state legislatures dominated by insolvent debtors.

It had been Locke's conviction that a government's primary duty was the preservation of property and this view was followed by John Jay, Alexander Hamilton, and James Madison. These men were patricians who believed in the fundamental inequality of men. They upheld *liberty* with vibrant conviction and saw the greatest threat to it in *equality*. In view of the patent failure of Jeffersonian democracy, they had no inhibitions about making their views public. Many would have subscribed to John Adams' sharp remark that democracy was "the most ignoble, unjust and detestable form of government." Years later, in 1815, Adams warned his countrymen: "Democracy has never been and never can be so desirable as aristocracy or monarchy, but while it lasts, is more bloody than either. Remember, democracy never lasts long. It soon wastes, exhausts and murders itself. There never was a democracy that did not commit suicide." [3]

What was clear was that the antidemocratic feeling, blind as it might have been, was not the result of selfish motives, but of sincere and altruistic convictions. What was foremost in the minds of the Constitution drafters was freedom, and they were acutely conscious that the chaos engendered by demagogy was the major threat to that cherished freedom. Even in those days when the democratic reforms of the Revolution had been accepted and consolidated, property qualifications restricted suffrage to 15 per cent of the adult males. The adoption of the Constitution was therefore bound to be the work of a minority.

Since they saw themselves as trustees endowed with heavy responsibilities which they could not shirk, the members of the Philadelphia Convention decided to conduct their debates secretly. They knew, in their wisdom, that constructive decisions could not be reached in full view of emotional crowds. The intricate negotiations which were carried out proved more than once that the whole attempt was on the verge of breaking down, and certainly would have collapsed, had it not been for the secrecy which shrouded this masterpiece of diplomatic conciliation. The difficulties were such that even the agnostic Benjamin Franklin suggested opening the meetings with a prayer. Thus faced by

difficult realities, the fashionable skepticism of the Age of Enlightenment was quickly shed by men who were bent on positive achievements, men who had no intention of worshiping at the altar of
Robespierre's mythical goddess "Reason."

In the twentieth century, many wise Americans were to remember
the drafting of the Constitution and reflect that they themselves might
better resort to the traditional discretion in diplomacy rather than
confuse relations with foreign nations by appealing to public opinion's
mass emotionalism. They were also to recall that the Philadelphia
delegates were cultured men who had perused the whole gamut of
past experiences for the benefit of the present. Many of the Phila-
delphians drew on such age-old examples as the Achaean and Lycian
Leagues, searching for solutions to their contemporary problems.

The Constitution—one of the most remarkable documents of all
time—was a successful compromise, the first great compromise in
American politics, the forerunner of many more fruitful compromises
to come. J. R. Lowell could claim a century later that the members
of the Convention "had a profound disbelief in theory and knew better
than to commit the folly of breaking with the past. They were not
seduced by the French fallacy that a new system of government could
be ordered like a new suit of clothes. They would as soon have
thought of ordering a suit of flesh and skin. It is only on the roaring
loom of time that the stuff is woven for such a vesture of their thought
and experience as they were meditating." [4] And, going back two
thousand years, here is Cicero: "Cato used to say that our state excelled all others in its constitution; in them, for the most part, an
individual had established his own form of state by his laws and
institutions . . . our state, on the contrary, was the result, not of one
man's genius but of many men, not of one man's life but of several
centuries and periods . . . actual experience stretching over the ages
is needed." [5]

The spirit of compromise is always the fruit of intense realism and
of a healthy distrust for empty theories. But it is also the fruit of
teamwork, of a sense of social solidarity, of respect for differing
viewpoints. More than anything else, it can only work successfully
when differences of opinion take place on the level of contingent and
not fundamental things, when controversies center around the means,
not around the end itself. The men of the Convention were united
by their common faith in the future of their country as well as in their

inherent right, as representatives of a ruling and responsible elite, to shape that future.

For all of their reliance on Locke's philosophy of government, these Founding Fathers were still members of a gentry that felt closer to aristocratic Anglicanism and its organic view of society's natural hierarchy. These men—Washington, Madison, Monroe, Randolph, and especially Hamilton and Jay—were still steeped in an enlightened reverence for the past. They had all the strength of character and noble-mindedness of the old Pilgrim Fathers, but without the fanaticism of the original Puritans. Most of the leaders were Virginia aristocrats and it is quite likely that without their high-minded leadership, the newborn American nation would have floundered helplessly. They were men of transition, a last link with the past, conservative engineers of a healthy reaction that consolidated the young nation and, unknowingly, led it to the distant shores of full-fledged democracy.

The Convention decided to appeal for ratification, not to the states but to the people themselves. This was the first substantial indication that the United States had become a nation rather than a league of separate sovereign states. It must be kept in mind that in those days, although the Americans were united by a common religion, language, and legislation, they were widely scattered over a large area. Geography, as much as anything else, made the existence of separate states a concrete reality. It took as long to travel overland from Boston to Charleston as to cross the ocean from Boston to Europe. It was no mean feat, therefore, to create a strong federal government and obtain from all Americans its acceptance.

The cardinal feature of the new Constitution was the creation of an autonomous Executive, and the cardinal principle was the separation of powers. The fear of tyranny and the ardent desire to protect freedom were in the mind and heart of every Founding Father. The members of the Convention thought that they had found the answer in Montesquieu's system of "checks and balances" whereby the various powers would more or less cancel each other out and be prevented from usurping absolute control. It was similar in spirit to the system prevailing in the Roman republic. Authority had to be diluted and scattered. In their search for workable formulas, the Founding Fathers had of course borrowed a great deal from England. But they had borrowed even more from their own colonial experience and much of their political philosophy was native to the American soil.

Since the early days when the Council and Burgesses of Virginia had congregated in a little church in Jamestown, the struggle between elected legislatures and the colonial governors had been ceaseless—in Classical times, the struggle between the Roman Senate and the Tarquin monarchs. The Founding Fathers blended their colonial experience with the ideas of Locke about the separation of powers and ended in creating an entirely new form of government adapted to free institutions. The Presidential system, barely outlined in a Constitution that was necessarily vague since it had to be a satisfying compromise, was destined to grow organically over a period of generations through trial and error. In so doing, American institutions moved in a direction that was diametrically opposed to Britain's parliamentary system. Britain's Parliament was gradually joining together and gathering all powers into itself, giving a collective and yet united leadership to the nation. This system was workable because Britain's social structure preserved, well into the twentieth century, the organic, hierarchical, and aristocratic character which America was going to discard early in the nineteenth century.

America was enjoined to separate as rigidly as possible the executive, legislative and judiciary powers. The same fear of tyranny had induced Rome to choose a similar course. Referring to the Roman creation of the Tribunate, Mommsen wrote: "Thus in this remarkable institution absolute prohibition was in the most stern and abrupt fashion opposed to absolute command," [6] a fitting description of the American system as conceived by the Founding Fathers. In the long run, these visions of proper constitutions with mechanical articulations proved unworkable in both cases. Successful so long as there was the connecting tissue of a ruling elite dominating in fact and joining together the fragmented powers, it proved increasingly difficult to apply when the ruling classes collapsed and mass democracy became triumphant.

Edmund Randolph saw the danger and warned: "Our chief danger rises from the democratic parts of our constitution. It is a maxim which I hold incontrovertible that the powers of government exercised by the people swallow up the other branches." [7] Time and subsequent events were to give ample confirmation to this warning. Nothing would have surprised the conservative members of the Philadelphia Convention as much as the subsequent development of the Executive and its transformation into a *tribunician* power. But then, like the early Romans, they were defending liberty, not equality. Their sole aim was to prevent the turbulent mob from controlling the federal government, as they had controlled so many state legislatures. They conceived of the Presidency as the mild mouthpiece of the ruling gentry. There were plenty of forebodings, however. George Mason of Virginia claimed: "We are not indeed constituting a British government, but a more dangerous monarchy, an elective one." [8]

What had happened, of course, was that they had created an Executive whose powers were virtually unlimited, and since they did not foresee the triumphant rise of democracy and equality in the following century, they had no thought of limiting the powers of an office which would apparently be held and controlled forever by the ruling gentry. They did not foresee that, from being merely the first magistrate of a mildly aristocratic republic, the President would be metamorphosed, from Jackson onward, into a powerful tribune of the people. They never thought that their careful separation of powers could be thus bypassed because new circumstances would compel the slow transformation of their republican institutions.

The full irony of this lack of foresight is brought into bold relief when it is remembered that on Jefferson's return from France in 1789, he expressed his "wonder and mortification" at the atmosphere he found: "Politics were the chief topic and a preference of kingly over republican government was evidently the favorite sentiment." [9] The conservative reaction was then in full swing. But that was not the important point. Later on, starting with "King Andrew" Jackson, strong Presidents were repeatedly accused of royal ambitions, and the danger of strong presidential power was always assimilated to the absolutism of monarchy—until in the twentieth century, the cry that was raised was no longer "king" but "dictator." No one accused Franklin Roosevelt of wanting to be crowned king but he was frequently censured for his alleged dictatorial ambitions. In this apparently slight transformation lies the metamorphosis of aristocratic monarch into democratic Caesar, of Culture-symbol into Civilization-symbol.

The creations of the Tribunate in Rome and of the Presidency in America were remarkable examples of political flair. Such vaguely defined offices paved the way for legal evolution rather than violent revolution, through very gradual changes within their plastic structures. Tribunes and Presidents represented or came to represent the whole people as opposed to local and particular pressure groups and privileged minorities entrenched in legislatures, senates, and other assemblies. It was from the Tribunate that Caesarism sprung almost legally in Rome. The remarkable metamorphosis of the Presidency from Washington to Franklin Roosevelt was carried out peacefully and constitutionally. Everywhere else, in Greece and Europe, institutions were fast losing their holy character and were being violently destroyed. But Rome and America could adapt themselves, thanks to the acute realism and pragmatism of their citizens.

In Greece, Athens overthrew her aristocratic Areopagus and established an unmitigated tribunician rule. Sparta, on the other hand, reverted to an unmitigated oligarchy. Everywhere, there was an impractical, intolerant attempt to fit the perpetual flux of changing conditions within the rigid framework of frozen abstractions. Thus it was in Europe, from the French Revolution onward. It was either one "or" the other, never a workable blend of both. Political struggles could take place only *outside* and *over* constitutions, never *within*. Nowhere was there the almost perfect balance of Roman Tribune-and-Senate, or American President-and-Congress, that smoothed their internal evolution and allowed one or the other to predominate according to the requirements of the time. This was made possible by the major premise on which Roman and American politics were built. Both sought the rule of abstract principles—the rule of law—Rome's Twelve Tables, America's Constitution—on which everyone agreed. Therefore, political passions were concerned far more with men than with universally accepted institutions. Political conflicts took place within the framework of accepted institutions, not outside through civil wars and revolutions.

America almost went back to an elective monarchy when strong-minded Alexander Hamilton suggested appointing the head of the state for life, an idea which was not retained but "received the support of persons as democratically minded as Madison and Edmund Randolph." [10] Just as in Rome, after the abolition of the monarchy, the republican instincts were too strongly entrenched in public opinion and the four-year term was finally adopted—a great improvement over Rome's two-year consuls who, more than once, had to resort to legal but temporary dictatorship to tide them over various critical periods.

When George Washington became America's first President, neither he nor any other American would have been able to describe the duties and powers of his office. But his contemporaries had inherited the unparalleled political flair of the British, their empirical tact, their instinctive understanding that reality shapes theory. They knew that *time* and nothing else would build up their institutions, although many of them would have been surprised to learn that *time* itself would take these rudimentary institutions and, in the very process of developing them, would stand them on their head. The conservative Founding Fathers thought that they had decisively checked the progress of democracy and yet democracy triumphed through their own Constitution—a democracy of a type which no one could have visualized at so early a stage. They wanted to adapt the British constitution to their republic and ended by creating an entirely different and original type of government.

With their eyes on Classical history, these men thought in terms of a static America. They did not foresee (nor did their Jeffersonian opponents) the dramatic impact of the Industrial Revolution, the swift extension of the American empire, and the steady growth of the executive power. Even Hamilton could not imagine the fabulous riches that were to accrue to their descendants, the staggering economic development that eventually would produce the highest standard of living in the world. They saw only the contemporary tension between rich and poor in terms of static immutability. How blind they could be to the dynamic implications of the Industrial Revolution can be gauged by Madison's remarks at the Convention: "The Freeholders of the country would be the safest depositaries of republican liberty. In future times a great majority of the people will be not only without land, but any other sort of property." [11]

However, what was important was that most critics of democracy were not feudal-minded aristocrats but town-dwelling patricians and prosperous bourgeois who saw in democracy a threat to private property. It was this relationship between property and political power that haunted them, not the establishment of a strong ruler or ruling class. They had not shaken loose from British domination and its unjust taxation to see their estates lost through political chaos. They were determined to return political power to the hands of the property-owning minority, but were totally uninterested in preserving a British-type ruling class with its aristocratic traditions.

The emphasis, now, was squarely placed on economics and property, and this psychological change spelled the doom of aristocratic rule—as it had in Rome when the same gradual shift appeared, the same growth of economic thinking, the same emphasis on the sanctity of private property and the same decline of the old landowning, blood aristocracy. Rome's Servian constitution reshaped the political structure along democratic-capitalistic lines, separated the freeholders (*asidui*) from the propertyless (*proletarii*), and virtually eliminated the blood aristocracy, which had retained until then the aura of religious prestige and reverence. Economically minded, eighteenth-century Americans saw in the existence of private property the best guarantee of freedom, the main obstacle to tyranny.

They also saw a guarantee of freedom in the separation of powers. But the problem was complicated by the federal structure of the government and the existence of the individual states. In order to protect the states' autonomy, the Constitution makers ended by weakening the federal House of Representatives and, unwittingly, by increasing the relative power of the President. As understood by the Founding Fathers, and as argued subsequently by Hamilton, Congress could do nothing except what was specifically authorized in the eighteen paragraphs, whereas the President could do anything that was not specifically forbidden. In time, since the logic of growth and expansion fostered increasing centralization and concentration of power, an enormous amount of unforeseen authority came into the hands of the federal government—and the greater part of it went straight to the White House, since the door was open for it at that end and closed at the other. The immense neutral territory lying between the White House and Capitol Hill remained undefined and uncommitted, but belonged potentially to the Executive. Time and History took charge of filling it and the shadow of the White House grew to encompass most of it, leaving Congress stranded—fettered by the basic impotence of all deliberative assemblies in times of emergency as well as by the Founding Fathers' constitutional strings.

Washington's first administration faced the difficult task of applying an abstract and untried Constitution to concrete realities, and in fact shaping the unborn government in the very process of applying it.

With great wisdom and courage, he insisted on appointing to his cabinet the two great antagonists, Hamilton and Jefferson. They were fundamentally opposed in many ways: Hamilton, the spokesman of commerce, industry, and finance, of urban and capitalistic interests, of those realists who were acutely aware of the natural corruption of human nature, of those who believed in the fundamental inequality of men—Jefferson, representing the rural and agrarian majority, optimistic, idealistic and democratic, afraid of the corruption bred by power rather than the corruption inherent in man. Forced to work together, they were able up to a point to act in unison for the good of a country which needed both of them desperately.

From the start, Congress could have made the heads of the executive departments responsible to itself. The Senate was small in those days and the Founding Fathers had vaguely hoped that it would become a sort of advisory committee at the President's disposal, since the Constitution did not provide for an official cabinet. The Senate could have been a bridge between the executive and legislative branches, but Washington's attempt to collaborate with it backfired. The suspicious senators felt that pressure was being put on them and reacted frigidly. Profoundly mortified, Washington walked out of the Senate, never to return. From then on, the custom was established that there would be no direct collaboration between the two branches, and the Constitution makers understood belatedly that an elective body can hardly act as a cabinet or a council of ministers. Since the general assumption at that time was that the administration would consist of President and Senate acting in conjunction, some new feature had to be provided to fill the gap created by the breakdown. The Senate, therefore, was largely confined to legislative action and a separate cabinet entirely devoted to the Executive replaced it.

At this point, the separation between executive and legislative powers was wider even than the Founding Fathers had anticipated. It illustrated the profound distrust of most Americans at the time for concentrated political power. Yet, a second attempt to join them in fruitful collaboration was carried out by Hamilton when he made a bid to appear before the House of Representatives. He, too, was excluded and denied permission to defend his budget personally. Refusing to seek guidance and information from the executive departments, the House created its own standing committees alongside the departments, duplicating them and acting as watchdogs.

Thus it was that, offended in its dignity by the efforts of the executive branch to collaborate loyally, Congress rejected it and made it able to develop its immense potentialities unhindered—new situations, unexpected crises, and the extraordinary development of the country being the main reservoirs from which this power was to draw its increasing strength. But this is not what Congress thought at the time. Having defended itself against the imaginary attempts of the executive power to influence and dominate it, Congress took the offensive. For thirty years, the House was to attempt to usurp executive power and use its committees as so many executive departments, only to prove irrefutably that it was unable to formulate and carry out a consistent policy.

Washington's personality and the circumstances of the world had more influence in shaping the political structure of the United States than the Constitution itself. It was his immense dignity and prestige that enabled the American nation to get the best out of bitter antagonists such as Hamilton and Jefferson. Austere, aloof, an acute judge of human nature, thin-lipped Washington represented the typical Roman-like quality of the Founding Fathers. The contrast between these men and the flamboyant, dramatic and unstable personalities who dominated revolutionary Europe at the time could not have been more striking. Washington never courted popularity, never failed to impress his inflexible will on his compatriots when he had decided on a definite course of action. He had the high wisdom and great courage to stand up to the wave of Francophile feeling which swept America during the French Revolution. Undaunted by threats and insults, he refused to be dragged into a futile war against Britain in spite of petty grievances, and he expressed his farsighted judgment in advocating peace and neutrality: "Sure I am that if this country is preserved in tranquillity twenty years longer, it may bid defiance in a just cause to any power whatever; such in that time will be its population, wealth and resources." [12]

Washington was a gentleman living in an aristocratic age and he saw his office as a freedom-loving gentleman would. He certainly never foresaw the vast changes that would alter the role of the Presidency and certainly never dreamed of the almost unlimited powers that his remote successors would collect in their own hands. All he saw was that the United States needed time to consolidate itself, a generation of peace in order to mature their new institutions and grow to a stature that would guarantee their independence from foreign greed.

In his memorable Farewell Address, he pointed out the four major dangers which threatened the new nation: secession, weakening of the central government, political parties, foreign affairs. In regard to the fourth, he laid down what was to become the gospel of American isolationism. He warned his compatriots against emotional sympathy or antipathy toward other nations and pointed out: "The nation which indulges toward another an habitual hatred or an habitual fondness is in some degree a slave. It is a slave to its animosity or to its affection, each of which is sufficient to lead it astray from its duty and interest." The violent and conflicting outbursts of feeling for and against France and England at the time made this reminder as topical as those similar warnings addressed by wise and farsighted Roman statesmen at the time of Rome's gradual involvement in international politics during the Punic Wars. Washington then added: "It is our true policy to steer clear of permanent alliances with any portion of the foreign world . . ."

American isolationism, thus stated, found its counterpart in Rome at the end of the Second Punic War when the abysmal danger of increasing foreign commitments stared Rome in the face. A political party was formed by Publius Scipio, the great victor of Zama, to check the growing Roman tendency to become emotionally involved in foreign affairs—and also to curb the incipient imperialism which was beginning to raise its head. Similar imperialism was already finding growing acceptance in American public opinion—designs on Canada, on Spanish Florida, on Mexican territory. But these designs were confined to the Western Hemisphere. Time passed, the French Revolution became a memory, passions cooled (except during a brief war with the British), and America entered the nineteenth century with no desire to become involved in world politics. Washington's Farewell Address set the road on which generation after generation of Americans were going to march away from the Old World, determined to occupy and build up their own continent without outside interference. In a sense, they were withdrawing from historical Time and entering into almost unlimited Space.

PART II | *America: The New Rome*

CHAPTER VI

Hellenistic and Victorian Ages

✓ VERY much like the Victorian Europeans, the Greeks who lived in the Hellenistic Age following Alexander the Great felt that they were living in a new, modern era of prosperity, of economic expansion, of discovery of the world with its strange petrified civilizations—Egypt, Babylon, Persia, and India. They had no feeling of cultural decline, no inkling that the Age of Pericles was the summit of creative power and inspiration from which they were slowly descending. There was profound reverence for the cultural creations of the past on the one hand, and on the other, a definite preference for an age that promised greater comfort and a more staid happiness. It was the beginning of the cosmopolitan age in which the tight and narrow bounds of the Classical *polis* were broken as two thousand years later saw the age when Europe's multitude of independent city-states, dukedoms, and principalities could no longer survive in the midst of rising bureaucratic nations and empires. They were ages which saw the rise of Alexandria as a Greco-Egyptian and Calcutta as an Anglo-Indian metropolis, of Hellenistic Antioch and "modern" Shanghai, the beginning of bad taste and ostentation, of insincerity in art, of pomposity, of grandiose and ornate pseudostyles, of vulgarity, ages in which the grand stylistic developments of the past—Doric-Ionic-Corinthian, and Gothic-Baroque-Rococo—came to an end.

They were also the very beginning of the "utilitarian" ages, the eras of city planning, hygiene, and comfort; of modern pavements, improved sewers, aqueducts, impressive highways and harbors, fast-expanding networks of world-wide economic relations. They were eras of museums (the first one was founded by the Ptolemies in Alex-

87

andria), of pedantic scholars, critics, grammarians, commentators, editors, eras of growing cultural fragmentation and specialization. They were essentially ages of transition—from Greek and European Cultures to Roman and American Civilizations.

But they were still ages of powerful creations along certain lines. In the Classical world there were philosophers like Aristotle, scientists like the physician Galen, the physicist Archimedes, the astronomer Ptolemy, the mathematician Euclid. The emphasis was on facts rather than symbols, on science rather than art—on a science that was still disinterested, speculative, and theoretical, still inspired and dealing with fundamentals but soon to be overcome by the strictly utilitarian outlook of pure Civilization. It was an age of expanding business, of the slow and steady rise to supremacy of *bourgeois* middle classes, prosperous, devoted to comfort and security, but not wholly divorced from cultural aspirations as Rhodes and Pergamum testify. Such also was Victorian Europe—culture still growing vigorously along certain lines in the midst of bad taste and evident decadence of many other forms of art and literature.

Decline in creative power manifests itself in an attempted emancipation from proportion and harmony, a desperate attempt to get rid of devalued forms and threadbare symbols that have lost their potency, to replace lasting styles growing out of each other in organic sequence by quick superficial changes of fashion, a restless pursuit of new artistic canons, an exaggerated emphasis on the technical rather than the symbolic and intuitive side of art, a pathetic attempt to go back to primitive fundamentals through the medium of exotic and rudimentary barbarian styles. The atrocious taste of the Victorian Age reigns supreme, alongside the last flashes of a once vigorous Culture—Wagnerian music, Nietzschean philosophy, and impressionistic painting. The European world was no longer in living communion with its former symbols—religious and artistic—and was desperately seeking to re-establish the lost connection, to undo the terrifying nihilism which was creeping in before nihilism itself destroyed its weakening heart.

In the course of this decline the grand philosophies find their supreme formulations—Plato and Kant, Aristotle and Hegel—in huge systems of abstractions that crown the whole edifice of a Culture's profound thought, and are in fact the closing chapter of systematic philosophy. And soon, systematic philosophy, this last attempt to retrieve on the intellectual plane the creative synthesis of the Culture's springtime, dies out. Ethics replace metaphysics, sociology replaces logic and dialectics, analysis replaces synthesis. Stoics, Cyrenaics, Epicureans, and Cynics vie with one another as Positivists, Transcendentalists, Existentialists, Pragmatists, and Socialists in modern times. The attempt at a synthetic comprehension of the whole body of the Culture breaks up into so many careful analyses of its unrelated parts. The Hellenistic Age is increasingly blinded by the vast accumulation of knowledge which no single man can now encompass in his heart and mind. An ever-increasing collection of facts and figures fails to be digested by man's baffled brain. Inspiration wanes, the will to bring intellectual order into a disorganized world fades away.

Instead of the Athens of Pericles with its noble Acropolis delicately outlined against the background of an Olympian sky, we have the colossal buildings of Antioch, the gigantic harbor of Alexandria with its world-famous Pharos. The plumbing and fixtures in Hellenistic Antioch were undoubtedly as superior to those of Periclean Athens as were those of Victorian London to Voltaire's Paris. The huge Mausoleum of Halicarnassus and the Colossus of Rhodes were gigantic, mechanical, lifeless reproductions. It was then and still is today an age of "Eiffel Towers"—an age of vast bureaucratic states where symbols and knowledge worked out over the past centuries are accumulated, stored, sifted, classified, distributed by countless experts, rhetoricians, compilers, an age of academics and gigantic libraries, of anthologies, encyclopedias, the age of the supremacy of the Alexandrian scholar who works over the original creations of the giants of the past. Cultural *creation* slowly gives way to civilized *preservation*.

Polybius could express his admiration in 148 B.C. at "the present day when the progress of arts and sciences has been so rapid," [1] and look with wonderment at the great technological progress displayed throughout the Hellenistic world—as the Victorian European gazing out at a conquered and subdued world, just as unconscious of the seething volcano he was sitting on as Polybius and his contemporaries were two thousand years earlier. In the Alexandrian emporium of world trade, we no longer have true creative genius but a great deal of interpretative work. Art and literature become specialized professions classified as "business." Hordes of grammarians, lexicographers, and critics compile records of past creations and make a business of exploiting the disinterested geniuses whose ashes were burned long ago. They invent better grammar, better punctuation. Aristarchus and

Aristophanes of Byzantium, the latter chief librarian of the Ptolemies in Alexandria, were remarkably cultured men in their own right. They selected the best authors of the past with unerring judgment. But what paltry figures they were against such giants as Sophocles or Socrates! The dusk slowly falls on the Hellenistic world as it fell on Berlin, Paris, and London during the nineteenth and early twentieth centuries.

With the Hellenistic Age, Culture Man gradually gives way to Civilization Man. Because it is an age of transition both still live side by side, but to the farsighted, the future belongs inevitably to Civilization Man—the man who lives in the world of facts, not of symbols, this world in which Anglo-Saxon and Roman commercialism take the upper hand, the world in which individual creation is gradually overcome by organization and mass production. The true individualism of the Age of Pericles can no longer flourish. Old Greece and *ancien régime* Europe were a confusion of perpetually clashing personalities and warring states. Classical Greece had ended by virtually destroying herself in her succession of senseless Peloponnesian wars as France did during the Revolution and Napoleonic wars. But still, what a blossom of cultural masterpieces! There was little freedom in the political sense. Socrates was sentenced to drink his cup of hemlock by the Athenian court of justice. Aristotle was condemned to death. Antiphon, the founder of Athenian rhetoric, was executed for political reasons. Demosthenes was killed by Antipater's Macedonians. But at least there *were* Socrates and Aristotle! Physical oppression seemed to stimulate their creative powers and failed to dull their brains or destroy their hearts. In the same manner continental Europe persecuted some of her greatest geniuses and never pretended to establish political liberty (except in Switzerland and the Netherlands, whose shrewd citizens knew that tolerance and good business were inseparable). Men could live and create under external tyranny because they had inner freedom, and from Galileo to Voltaire, it was clear that antagonistic pressure was more a stimulating challenge to be overcome than a danger to be feared and avoided at all costs.

In the Hellenistic Age longing for security and stability, the rise of middle-class public opinion and shallow conformism destroy the originality and individualism of former days. The process is gradual but ideas soon begin to lose their vital importance. New mediums of mass communication arise and crystallize this growing mental conformism. Greece saw the rise of rhetoric as a specialized profession and whereas eloquence appealed to the free and discriminating mind, rhetoric gripped the sentiments and emotions of the Greek masses. Europe saw the rise of journalism, publicity, and advertising, as Athens saw the rise of Aeschines' and Demosthenes' Attic oratory— new means of shaping public opinion to suit the convenience of whoever handles it. Plato, who knew that rhetoric and diatribe would eventually be fatal to democracy and hated this art of deception, was powerless against the profound trend.

Economics became the dominant preoccupation of the dawning age of Civilization—the main background of the Punic and modern wars. Chaeronea and Valmy were still fought largely for ideals,[2] but ideals are soon overwhelmed by economic imperatives. Rome's vast slavery system, organized on an impersonal scale in contrast to the more personal and humane Greek slavery, had to be provided for, just as the rising industrialism of Europe and America had to secure its raw materials and its mass markets. The inclination to go to war for mere ideals survives alongside the economic motives but, after a disastrous flare-up at the close of the Hellenistic and Victorian Ages, will disappear in the furnace of the coming World Wars.

The Hellenistic Greeks became cynical and devitalized, and the Europeans followed the same course in the nineteenth and twentieth centuries. Some countries—Macedonia and Prussianized Germany— were able to develop their military power in the midst of disintegration through their single-minded ambition and ruthlessness, through their fanatical determination to impose their will and unify their anarchic sister states under their autocratic rule. These last outbursts of idealism and emotional patriotism created temporary miracles. Philopoemen, *strategus* of the Achaen League, could still rouse his sluggish compatriots against Sparta as Clemenceau roused the exhausted French in World War I. But it was too late. They had played their part in history and, overcome by epicureanism and cynicism, had to yield the stage to others who were younger, more dynamic, and who knew how to combine realism with idealism.

The establishment of a Hellenistic and Victorian world order follows the slow ripening and expansion of a Culture, and serves as a prelude to the sterilized comfort of unmitigated Civilization. But it does not burst upon the world with the startling suddenness of the French Revolution. Greek and European expansion had started long before this Hellenistic and Victorian flowering. Greeks had settled all over the known world, had penetrated inland as explorers, soldiers, traders, physicians, scholars, had occupied influential positions in Asia Minor, Syria, Egypt, and Persia, as Europeans had settled in Russia and Asia since the Renaissance. They had both prepared the ground for the fabulous expansion of Hellenistic and European power in the East that was to come. Alexander's meteoric conquest and Hellenization of the East could have been predicted long before it took place—as early indeed as the civil war between the Persian rulers Cyrus and Artaxerxes, in which the overwhelming superiority of Greek over Asian soldiers was strikingly displayed. Cyrus knew the worth of Greek troops and saw how they could strike terror in the hearts of the Persians; Alexander himself had to fight Darius' thirty thousand Greek mercenaries at Issus and his fifty thousand choice Hellenes at Arbela. Greeks in those days assumed the same superiority vis-à-vis the Orientals as the Europeans later on, preening themselves on their greater vitality, technical ability, will power, and determination.

The Hellenistic Age was a brilliant flowering but its roots lay deep in the past. It was ushered into Classical times by Alexander of Macedonia and in Europe by Napoleon. But whereas Alexander established the Hellenistic Age all over the Near and Middle East, Napoleon failed to establish it in Europe and in that part of the globe which had fallen under European influence. Alexander defeated the Persians and Hellenized them for a time. Napoleon failed to defeat the half-Westernized Russians, largely because Peter the Great had Europeanized them almost two centuries before. In spite of the disparity in their personal achievements, the short-term results were the same: a temporary acceleration of the Westernization of vast Eastern countries.

Napoleon went to Cairo, Madrid, and Moscow, planned a grand march through Turkey and Persia to India—and failed. Everywhere he found the same elusive enemy with which he could never come to grips: British sea power.

Having destroyed the modern Alexander, the British undertook the establishment of the Hellenistic order themselves. Their success was due to a simple reason: they alone among the European powers were in tune with the modern temper, they alone lived consciously in a world of economic expansion. They had engineered the Industrial Revolution, an upheaval of much greater consequences in the long run than the French Revolution. This, combined with their unchallengeable domination of the oceans after Trafalgar, enabled them to preside over the vast expansion of European influence throughout the world, just as the Macedonian war machine had considerably widened the Greek sphere of influence throughout the known world of Classical times. Britain became the clearinghouse of the globe. London banks and exchanges were the throbbing heart of world economy, the pound sterling was the blood of world trade, British corporations the global limbs embracing Egyptian and American cotton, Malayan tin and rubber, Arabian and Persian oil, Australian wool, Canadian and Scandinavian timber, Argentine cattle. Britain bought and sold everything, insured against all risks and hazards, provided capital for any commercial or industrial venture anywhere in the world.

But, of course, all this had been in preparation for centuries. Britain's leadership was no accident of history that could possibly have been prevented by defeats at Trafalgar and Waterloo. The reasons for Britain's triumph lay in her working out to their logical conclusion the new trends initiated by the Reformation and the Puritan upheaval —without ever breaking with the past. From the early Puritan outlook to Locke, then to the philosopher Hume and to his pupil, economist Adam Smith, the thread is visible and unbroken. It was the only major European nation where liberty was fruitful, constructive, and dynamic, because it was wholly applied to the development of economic power. Liberty had meant intellectual freedom, but with the steady rise of economic mindedness, it came to mean a profitable freedom of trade as well. There could be no drastic opposition between concrete facts and abstract theories such as tore apart almost every other European nation, because Englishmen lived and worked entirely in the world of business, trade, and finance.

English freedom was home grown, insular, exclusive, and not exportable. The British knew that their freedom was largely due to their insular position. They never blindly believed, as their American cousins did later on, that freedom could possibly mean the same thing on a continent stretching from Spain to China in which vast populations alien to each other were constantly shifting and clashing. When Edmund Burke replied to a French statesman that "we demand our liberties, not as rights of man, but as rights of Englishmen," he pointed out the essentially parochial and insular outlook of his countrymen. It was not very generous, but it was realistic; and at that very moment, across the Atlantic, the more idealistic Americans were basing their whole political philosophy on the "rights of man," all men. However unrealistic it may have been, and however often American actions have failed to live up to the proclaimed ideal, it did indicate that in the long run, a global "Roman" consciousness was America's rather than Britain's.

The remarkable trait of Britain's Hellenistic Age was a unique social plasticity that enabled democracy to grow up gradually within an enduring aristocratic social structure. Britain was the home of freedom and parliamentarism, but in 1793, at the height of the French Terror, there were 306 members of the House of Commons who were elected by 106 voters. It still was an unmitigated aristocracy—wise, far-sighted, capable of producing the iron-willed statesmanship of the Pitts. It was always willing and able to absorb the rising members of the middle class who were being propelled socially upward in increasing numbers. The Industrial Revolution was stimulating a profound social evolution. Britain's ruling class faced the fact and began to draw into itself the cream of the new industrial bourgeoisie after 1832. This aristocratic ruling class knew that politics, diplomacy, and statesmanship are matters of training, not of planning, that they are arts rather than sciences. They knew that they had to be played by heart with the unerring instinct of tactful men who have been brought up to look upon world politics as a keyboard. The Victorian rulers were able to prove that they could keep their fingers on the pulse of the world as no other ruling class since the downfall of the Roman aristocracy, with an unparalleled flair for the underlying realities of the times.

The contrast with continental Europe was glaring. French aristocrats and the European nobility generally were no more able to reconcile themselves to the changing social landscape than were the noble *eupatridae* of Athens. They could not accept the coming economic revolution, the rising dominance of money and business, and failed to absorb the rising middle classes against which they raised the flimsy barriers of a steadily weakening tradition. They despised and neglected trade, finance, and industry and insisted on clinging to unjustified privileges. Romans and Anglo-Americans never made that mistake and realistically faced the new economic forces, determined to control them and let the organic transformation of society take its course through the gradual adjustments of a peaceful evolution. Continental Europe, like Classical Greece, had no other choice but blind reaction or brutal revolution. The unique durability of the British and American institutions was due to the fact that they were organic growths, like those of Rome, and not intellectual schemes. Greek and European revolts turned out to be essentially negative movements— against aristocracy, against dynasties, against capitalism, business, socialism, or any other institutional form which did not fit into their prefabricated theories. The gradual collapse of Greek institutions started with the revolutionary upheavals and massacres of Corcyra and Argos (370 B.C.), and the breakdown of European institutions began in 1789 with the French Revolution.

The result of such political and social instability is that, if the victimized nations are to live at all, they must entrust a large share of their destiny to some nonpolitical organization; and thus it is that the contrast between Hellenistic and Roman, European and American administrative structures rested on the predominance of permanent bureaucracies in the Hellenistic and European states, as compared with the elective and nonbureaucratic institutions of Rome and America. The multiplicity and frequency of elections in America, which baffled so many European travelers in the nineteenth century, was duplicated in a Rome that refused to organize a permanent civil service. Hellenistic and European bureaucracies were almost autonomous bodies administrating countries whose politics were so unstable that living conditions would have become intolerable if statesmen and politicians had more than a fraction of the bureaucracies' influence. If France has survived six revolutions and countless minor upheavals and has been able to stand the most anarchic form of political life, it is entirely due to the bureaucratic structure set up by Napoleon and run by intellectual mandarins who steer clear of all political commitments.

By now, the historic role of England has become clear. In reference to the Classical world, England stands halfway between Greece and Rome—or, the other way around, Rome was both Britain and America. While Britain's aristocracy and Parliament represent to a large extent the self-reliant, wise Roman aristocracy and Senate, America's rising democracy and Presidential-tribunician power represent the rise of its Roman counterparts; and in the latter part of the Hellenistic Age, the slow decline of Britain in front of America's developing power, as well as the decline of her own ruling class within the British

nation, finds its counterpart in the decline of Rome's traditional aristocracy with the concomitant rise of democracy and capitalism. Therefore, it is possible to view the political split between America and
Britain as a superficial rather than a fundamental event, and their
subsequent history bears out the contention that they both remained
natural allies, tied together by innumerable invisible strings that no
outsider could possibly snap.

The true nature of America's historic destiny thus comes to light:
quite unconsciously, the British aristocracy made the world safe for
the development of the American democracy. The British fleet stood
as a shield behind which America could pursue her social experiment
in splendid isolation, protected by vast oceans in friendly hands, preceded and guided by England in an Industrial Revolution which she
was to exploit to the utmost, free to expand in a virgin continent with
next to no neighbors, free to preserve *freedom* and extend *equality*.
British power stood guard for more than a century while the fledgling
American democracy grew up, safe from the brutal aggressors who
tore Europe apart and raped a slumbering Orient.

Britain's other historic role was to keep Europe divided through
her favorite foreign policy, the balance of power. Napoleon's dream
of a united Europe under French hegemony was doomed by Waterloo
as Alexander's dream of a united Hellenistic empire was frustrated
by his untimely death. Time and again, as Athens, Sparta, and Thebes
had attempted to unify Greece and had failed, so did the German
Holy Empire, Spain, and France make the same attempt in Europe
and experience the same failure. Then, with the Hellenistic Age and
the aftermath of the French Revolution, unity almost came—but this
time under the military despotism of Macedonia and Prussia in the
century and a half following Alexander and Napoleon. But it was the
military despotism of outsiders, semibarbarians who were Hellenized
and Europeanized but who traced their ancestry to full-blooded barbarians: the Macedonians to the Illyrians, the Prussians to Slavic
tribes.

The Hellenistic and European worlds had no other choice but to
settle permanently in chaos—a limited chaos, kept in check for generations by subtle diplomacy and secret intrigues, but chaos nevertheless. After the fall of Napoleon, the Congress of Vienna patched up
the remains of Europe's *ancien régime* and this era of relative peace
and prosperity lasted, with minor changes, until World War I, a

peace enjoyed by the Hellenistic world amidst limited storms and stresses. The Congress of Vienna and the solemn meeting of Alexander's generals and viceroys at Triparadeisos in Syria are equivalent events, swan songs of the Greek and European orders outliving themselves for a few generations through a precarious balance of power. Ptolemaic Egypt lasted as long as the British Empire in India, the Seleucid and Austro-Hungarian empires disintegrated under the centrifugal pressures of their multitudes of component nationalities, and Prussianized Germany eventually shared the cataclysmic fate of Macedonia. All of them finally collapsed through their sheer inability to establish the peaceful world orders for which all civilized human beings were beginning to thirst.

Neither the Classical world, centered around the Mediterranean, nor the Western, centered around the Atlantic, was living in a vacuum. Both had been for centuries in contact with other civilizations in the East, old petrified civilizations upon which they looked with a mixture of contempt and admiration. But a new element had made its appearance on the margin of those disintegrating civilizations. In order to appreciate what this new element represents in history, we have to add another stage of development to those which make up our Culture-Civilization sequence. This is the pre-Cultural, the Dark Ages that precede the so-called Middle Ages. The pre-Cultural stage is that of a new human society not yet born to true historical life, leading a purely instinctive existence, groping in cultural darkness like the child in the womb. Such was the state of the Persians before the beginning of the Christian era, such has been the state of Russia until our days, and such was pre-Homeric Greece or Carlovingian Europe.

Accustomed to dealing with ancient Civilizations such as Pharaonic Egypt and the Babylonian world, the Greeks had failed to see in the oncoming Persians a new breed of men, culturally younger than themselves and infinitely younger than the old Civilizations with which they had come in contact. To the Greeks, the Persians, Babylonians, Syrians, Jews, and Egyptians were all the same, half-barbarian, half-decadent, overrefined Orientals who were bound to be drawn into the orbit of what was to them the only true Culture: the Greek. They failed to see that out of the grandiose ruins of these Eastern Civilizations, new and younger people were slowly awakening to life, formless and uncertain of themselves, fundamentally hostile to the dominant

Greek Culture, yet compelled by its overwhelming superiority to imitate it and adopt many of its shapes and styles. Pre-Alexandrian Persia, the so-called Achaemenian Empire, was essentially a pre-Cultural state which had slowly fallen under the spell of Greek Culture through its conquest of the Greek cities of Ionia—which cities played the same part that eastern Europe was to play two thousand years later vis-à-vis Russia.

The Greeks could not readily differentiate between old decadent Civilizations whose Babylonian petrifacts were strewn all over the East and young barbarian, pre-Cultural nations: they had no historical perspective. But we have, and it is all the more inexcusable for us to label Russia an "Oriental" or "Asian" nation. Russia is neither European nor Asian, but a separate entity in its own right, *sui generis*. If we focus our historical lenses, we will see quite clearly that the Persians of the past were the Russians of today. Both share the same organic youth, the same irrepressible vitality, the same rustic strength sucked from virgin soil stretching far beyond the geographical pale of former civilizations (the Iranian highlands, the Russian steppes), the same stubborn clinging to their inaccessible home lands. Everything about them is huge, on a scale which dwarfs the neighboring Cultures of the west. Juxtapose a map of Russia's nine thousand miles with tiny Europe dangling at its western extremity, and a map of Darius' empire stretching thousands miles to the Oxus with puny Greece hanging onto its western tip; the scale is different but the proportions are identical. Everything else about the two empires is big, as big as their vast home lands. The vast masses of Persian manpower astounded the Greeks; the armies of hundreds of thousand Russians struggling against the Mongols of the Golden Horde astounded the sixteenth-century Europeans. The inner structure of those barbaric empires was the same. The Persian "Great King-of-kings" and Russian "Tzar of all the Russias" were birds of a feather, absolute monarchs who ruled like Charlemagne over a huge people not even started on its social evolution, still in the semi-collectivist clan stage where there are no independent social classes that can curb the absolute power of their imperious monarchs—nothing but the opposition between conqueror and conquered, barbarian Persian clans and fellaheen relics of doomed civilizations, barbarian Russians and Muslim relics of the former glories of Central Asia. Socially, they are not yet integrated. It is not that they are either socialists or individualists;

they are still in the pre-individualistic stage where those terms are meaningless.

Persian *vithpaitis* and Russian *boyars* were not a genuine aristocracy, nor were they proud feudal lords in their own right with the sturdy autonomy and high-minded codes and traditions of a "medieval" chivalry; they were nothing but temporary lords, cowed and trembling under the knout of their autocratic masters, the imperious Xerxes and Ivan the Terrible. They were a pre-feudal social element like the Frankish "barons" under Charlemagne—half chiefs of tribe and half government officials. There was no genuine Persian aristocracy before the beginning of our era, just as there never was a genuine Russian aristocracy that was anything but a crude replica of the European nobility. What stood in their stead was an artificial conglomeration of Hellenized and Europeanized pseudo-aristocrats who were entirely dependent on the whims of Persian Emperors and Russian Tzars.

Nor was there any middle class, nor real towns, nor urban living. Towns were overgrown villages, rural market places; and capital cities were the creations of despotic rulers. Susa was an imperial creation of Darius and Moscow was a collection of hamlets surrounding the Tzar's fortified *Kreml'*—agglomerations of soldiers, government officials, traders, and merchants catering to their imperial courts. And later, when the pressure of the dominant Cultures in their full flowering became irresistible, Hellenistic Seleucids and Europeanized Romanovs built new capitals to ape those of Greeks and Europeans. In their cold and soulless Persepolis and St. Petersburg, the borrowings from alien styles were in evidence although the rulers sought by instinct to compensate for their cultural inferiority by building them on colossal scales. In their vast empires, there was none of that free enterprise and individual initiative which characterized Greece and Europe. Everything was owned, regulated, and commanded by the imperial monarchs; their primitive but gigantic economic systems were state planned and monopolistic. "The highest refinement of a planned economy known in the new world before the twentieth century," characterized the Seleucid Empire, according to some scholars.[3]

Born in faraway highlands and steppes beyond the compass of any of the old Civilizations or dominant Cultures, these new nations cast about eagerly, searching for forms, shapes, styles, philosophies they cannot create—and yet, hating them all along because they find them unsatisfying. The hybrid character of their pseudo-culture and art springs from the indiscriminate merging of borrowed elements—Babylonian and Greek, Byzantine and European Baroque—into incongruous creations. Achaemenian art was like Russian art—hardly a living art at all, although here and there a genuinely native inspiration twisted new shapes hesitantly into Persian fire altars and Russian onion-shaped cupolas. As times goes on, and the dominant Cultures gradually pass into Civilizations, the borrowing begins to shift from a medley of cultural elements to mere techniques—to build up a technical power with which to defend their unborn souls against the growing pressure of alien Civilizations.

Their profound patriotism has nothing to do with nationalism in the modern sense of the word. It is an instinctive feeling of belonging soul and body to a great organic whole. Herodotus remarked long ago that no Persian ever prayed to Ahuramazda, the Zoroastrian Almighty, for a personal benefit: "But he prays for the welfare of the king and of the whole Persian people, among whom he is of necessity included." [4] And such is Russian patriotism in our times—collectivist, static, resilient, big hearted, and indestructible because, regardless of temporary political or social conditions, it is based on the profound instinct of spiritual purpose. It did not matter that their Seleucid rulers compelled the higher strata of Persians to Hellenize themselves, nor that Peter the Great enforced his Europeanization with consummate brutality: they never reached what was most profound in the great masses under their rule.

That Alexander the Great succeeded where Napoleon failed may partly be due to a mere accident of military strategy—the fact that the "scorched earth" policy which was suggested to Darius by his commander in chief was not followed, leading inevitably to disaster at the Granicus, whereas the Russians followed it two thousand years later, burned Moscow, and destroyed Napoleon's Grand Army. Yet, the ultimate result was the same because, regardless of their political relationship with the Greek and European West, the cultural subordination of Persians and Russians was the important fact. And the important sequel was, in both cases, the gradual collapse of the West's cultural pre-eminence because it was at all times superficial. Below the thin sheet of Hellenization and Europeanization that covered Persians and Russians, there were simmering volcanos. We can sense in Russian history the Messianic spirit that moved the Zoroastrian Persians. Facing the Greek and European West, the thickly bearded

Magian priests of Persia and Orthodox patriarchs of Russia stood as clumsy but fanatical guardians of the unborn souls of their coming Cultures. And when in our twentieth century the revolutionary Father Gapon and the somber Rasputin decided to take a hand in the disintegrating political situation, they seemed to be reincarnations of the old Magian clergy, who cared nought for Western Culture, in any shape or form. Neither the old Persians nor the modern Russians could really be seduced; they rejected Western ethics, laws, and religions. The Messianic spirit of Zoroaster and of the monk Philoteus (as reinterpreted by Dostoevski and the Slavophils) seemed, through their prophetic visions, to open entirely new vistas on the possibilities of development of the human soul; this Messianic spirit stood as an opaque screen between them and the dominant Cultures against which they instinctively struggled with all their might.

CHAPTER VII

The Turning Point

↓ IN the days of Alexander the Great, Rome was busy extending her domination over central Italy by crushing the power of the Samnites in a generation-long war. In the days of the French Revolution and Napoleonic wars, the United States launched her policy of western expansion—swift occupation of the trans-Appalachian West and purchase of the immense territory of Louisiana. Both Rome and America forged their destinies irrevocably in those days. Quietly, away from the main streams of world history, they were busy extending their dominions, not out of conscious imperialism but largely out of self-protection. They could not entirely avoid being involved in the titanic struggles of the Old Worlds but they never lost sight of their own true interests: the building up of their own nations. Alexander the Molossian, uncle of his great namesake, attempted to help and defend the Greeks of southern Italy as Napoleon hoped to vindicate the right of Louisiana to defend its Latin heritage and offset the growing power of the United States. They both failed.

Thus, from now on, the center of attention must shift to Rome and America, new world powers in formation, expanding doggedly, building up their strength in comparative isolation. America's task was twofold: the shaping of her political institutions, the preservation of her geographical freedom. Both tasks were well under way during the two decades following Washington's retirement. The first President's successor was the politically inept but farsighted John Adams, a hard, stern Puritan who frowned on relaxation, art, and poetry, a typical Civilization Man of the Roman stamp who claimed that "my sons ought to study mathematics and philosophy, geography, natural history and naval architecture, in order to give their children a right to study painting, poetry, music, architecture, statuary, tapestry and porcelain" [1]—the stark expression of an instinctive preference for Civilization over Culture, the faith of men for whom Culture is mere decorative froth on the periphery of life's serious pursuits. Benjamin Franklin had already long ago sounded the keynote of this American temper when he had proudly claimed that in America "very few are rich enough ... to pay the high prices given in Europe for Paintings, Statues, Architecture, and other work of Art, that are more curious than useful." [2] America would build a Civilization rather than a Culture and would come into her own when the exhausted Western world would thirst for *civilized* order.

Yet, true American aristocrats such as Jefferson were able to appreciate the great loss entailed by such an outlook. Jefferson was as much dazzled by the last days of Europe's *ancien régime* as the Romans were by Periclean Athens. Writing from Paris to Charles Bellini, he stated: "You are, perhaps, curious to know how this new scene has struck a savage of the mountains of America." After expressing his repulsion at the low standard of living of the bulk of the French population, he went on: "Were I to tell you how much I enjoy their architecture, sculpture, painting, music, I should want words. It is in these arts they shine. The last of them, particularly, is an enjoyment the deprivation of which with us cannot be calculated. I am almost ready to say it is the only thing which from my heart I envy them, and which, in spite of all the authority of the Decalogue, I do covet." [3]

At the Philadelphia Convention, Hamilton had declared that "inequality would exist as long as liberty existed and that it would unavoidably result from that liberty itself." [4] Those were brave words in a country which was to dedicate itself increasingly to an equality of an extreme type. Hamilton foresaw with uncanny prescience that the Industrial Revolution was the most momentous event of the times and that, for better or for worse, it was bound to alter the world. Even before his Jeffersonian rivals were about to begin seizing the whole continent, Hamilton made it clear that he did not believe in an idyllic agrarian America. He wanted a dynamic industrialism and mechanical power. He was the ancestor of the non-idealistic Americans who are masters of fact and reality, cold, sober, practical, and forceful. In him, there was the clear-sighted Roman-like quality of men who consciously shape the destiny of coming empires, who refuse to become lost in abstract and impractical idealism. Hamilton was the ancestor of modern planning, protective tariffs, and government subsidies for weaker industries. He initiated the master-minding of gigantic economic resources that were scarcely tapped in those days, and stood for the sturdy New England capitalists, industrialists, merchants, and shipowners against the agrarian South and West. He stood for the future, for the erection of those "dark satanic mills" the Jeffersonians feared and hated. He also stood for a strong paternalistic federal government acting as trustee for the people.

In this sense, he was no Adam Smith liberal and turned his back on a *laissez faire* policy which was well suited to England's predominant position as the world's leading industrial nation, but totally inadequate for an agrarian America starting from scratch. His "Report on Manufacturers" outlined a systematic economic policy of tariff duties for growing industry, of roads and waterways to be built by the federal government, of official inspection of goods and of over-all government planning for the nation's economy. But though he was able to push through his plans on the reorganization of finance and commerce, the Jeffersonians had become strong enough in 1792 to defeat Hamilton's plans for industry. The Jeffersonians were not only the Union's liberals and the democrats; they were also the aristocratic planters of the South. Their ideology rested on the fear that instead of becoming an agrarian state, America would be transformed into a bad replica of the Old World with its growing industry, its social inequities, its slums and misery. Hamilton was after industrial power on the British model and a strong Executive that resembled suspiciously a powerful elective monarchy. Jefferson was in favor of the "pursuit of happiness," republicanism, decentralization, and agrarian democracy.

The result of this conflict was a partial blend while Washington could make both antagonists work in his cabinet, and open rupture afterward. This rupture initiated the birth of what the Founding Fathers had always wanted to avoid: political parties. They had elaborated a Constitution which seemed to preclude political parties. They had foreseen temporary pressure groups and momentary alliances between sectional interests. They never foresaw the birth of huge political machines. Neither had they foreseen the amazing growth of presidential power over the years. Yet it was this very power that made the existence of permanent parties indispensable if a consistent policy was to be carried out. The policy-makers had to control the Presidency, whose over-all importance had been considerably boosted by the failure of Congress to associate itself with it. Unsteady coalitions of shifting interests had to become permanent and find a common candidate for the highest office in the land—and all the opposition groups had to band together in order to wrest this power from those in office. Since opposition in practical-minded countries like Britain and America can only be constructive, the actual seizure of power was the primary consideration, overriding all doctrinal and theoretical differences between sections of the opposition. Thus came into being the two-party system on the British model, not as a copy of the mother country's but a genuine growth on native soil. The struggle was on between those who were in power and those who were out.

American parties, unlike their tight-knit and cohesive British counterparts, straddled an entire continent with its vast distances and scattered populations; they had to be coalitions and their programs therefore based on compromise. They had to be concrete, undogmatic, and flexible. The more necessary the compromises, the more conservative the platforms. They had to defer to innumerable regional interests. On the local level they could afford to be as extreme as they wanted, but on the federal they had to be moderate. The immense size of the country fostered a cautious conservatism, a pragmatic approach, and a mistrust of general ideas and abstract principles. When party coalitions and compromises were sacrificed to idealistic principles, the Union broke down and Civil War was the unavoidable outcome. This was to remain a bitter lesson to generations of post-Civil War Americans.

Time and again, the administration had to preserve a balance between the commercial and industrial interests in the North, the agricultural and expansionist interests of the West, and the one-crop plantations of the South. Each solution favoring one section was purchased at the price of bargains and concessions to others. When the problem of the annexation of Texas arose, the danger of upsetting the federal balance in favor of the slave-owning South prompted the northerners to seek a compensatory expansion in Oregon. It required a constant exercise of American political ingenuity to keep this precarious balance, an ingenuity that was matched in the Classical world

only by the spirit of constructive compromise of innumerable Roman
statesmen. The First Punic War was undertaken for the sake of
Rome's powerful commercial interests who feared and hated their
Carthaginian rivals. As a compensation, Roman democrats then
undertook to wrest the Po Valley (Cisalpine Gaul) from its Celtic
rulers in order to find room for their expansionist-minded farmers.
Cisalpine Gaul became Rome's "Middle West."

Such was the long-range pattern. But when America started shaping
her political institutions, there was no prearranged plan, no theoretical doctrine. It just happened. As sectional strife increased and
the Hamiltonian North became increasingly bitter against the Jeffersonian South, decision had to come about in the geographical center,
New York. There it was that the first bosses and party machines made
their appearance, and it was in New York that Jefferson founded
America's most enduring and incongruous coalition: that of the northern political machines and the aristocratic southern agrarians. New
York had no political principles and aligned itself with either con-
tender with equal facility, treating the whole matter as a straight
business proposition; and Jefferson's idealistic principles never stood
in the way of his respect for realities. His political genius prompted
him to launch the most improbable of all alliances, setting the tenor
of all American political transactions of the future, and defeating the
Hamiltonian New Englanders in the process.

Embryonic political parties appeared shortly after Washington's
first inauguration. The basic conflict, underlying all sectional differences, was the opposition of the aristocratic planters and slave-owners
of the South, in conjunction with the democratic western farmers and
pioneers, to the bankers, merchants, and industrialists of the North.
It was a struggle between the men who despised or feared money
and those who manipulated credit and high finance. Alongside this
basic opposition and yet inextricably mixed up with it was the nulli-
fication problem. Had the individual states the right to decide whether
an act of the federal government was constitutional or not? If the
answer was yes, the nation was back where it started with the Articles
of Confederation, in fact was faced with the threat of secession at
every step. The Federalists, Hamilton's followers, became the staunch
exponents of the centralizing theory which denied any such freedom
to the individual states. The Republican party, founded by Jefferson,
adopted the platform of decentralization and states' rights.

The birth of political parties unquestionably violated the spirit of a Constitution drawn by aristocrats and patricians to restrain democracy and preserve an unadulterated freedom—the freedom deserved by strong men who did not have to court public favors, who could ride through emotional storms without wavering, argue doggedly their points and come to rational conclusions. But from the very start, the members of the college which elected the President gave up their inherent right to vote as they pleased and fell under the sway of party discipline. In so doing, they altered the original conception of the Executive—from being the nominee of an oligarchy to becoming gradually a tribune of the whole people. It was only a first step in that direction but it was significant.

It was under John Adams' Presidency that the power of political machines was felt for the first time on the federal level. Although he was out of office, Hamilton kept running the administration over the head of a powerless President, a President who had the making of a farsighted statesman but not the shrewd politician he should have been. John Adams had a prophetic vision of America's future greatness, a profound understanding of the paramount role played by the Founding Fathers in casting the mold into which would be poured millions of immigrants who would build the future nation together with the native Americans. He knew that the fate of America would be decided by those iron men whose principles, manners and political institutions would shape the future of an entire continent. Although a bitter personal enemy of Hamilton, Adams shared his views on the need for strong government and a strong Executive. He shared Hamilton's pessimistic view of human nature although he realistically extended his distrust of his fellowmen to include rich as well as poor. He was fanatically devoted to the constitutional system of checks and balances to avoid exploitation of one class, whichever it was, by another.

Such a personality could not for long submit to having Hamilton run his administration. His strenuous effort to break Hamilton's power wrecked the Federalist party, and it virtually disappeared from the scene of history at the turn of the century. This was a first lesson in practical politics. From now on no politician could ignore that collaboration between party and President was vital. But for all their swift and decisive fall from power, the Federalists really founded America's machinery of state. Their strong Executive alarmed all those who had been brought up to fear tyranny, but when their Jeffersonian opponents rose to power, they in turn were compelled not only to use the great presidential power at their disposal but to extend it considerably. Instead of reverting to their favored formula—a weak President and a parliamentary system—they increased the speed of the flight away from parliamentary rule. The cabinet became the exclusive instrument of the President, a tool over which Congress had no constitutional authority whatsoever; and later, James Bryce was to write that "an American administration resembles not so much the Cabinets of England and France as the group of ministers who surround the Czar or the Sultan, or who executed the bidding of a Roman emperor." [5]

Jefferson's election at the turn of the century was the signal for a return of triumphant democracy—although he himself, like so many outstanding democrats in all ages, was essentially an aristocrat. All the way to Franklin Roosevelt, democrats and radicals have frequently been led to victory over conservatives and reactionaries by isolated aristocrats, who, like all converts, embraced their new politicals faith with the fervor of neophytes. Rome's outstanding democratic leaders, from the noble Gracchi brothers to Julius Caesar, whose ancestry was as old as the dawn of Rome herself, were all blue-blooded aristocrats who turned against their narrow-minded peers and led the aroused people against them.

Thus, what made the democratic evolution of America relatively peaceful was the self-immolation of the founding oligarchy. Thomas Jefferson and his aristocratic friends split it wide open and unconsciously built the necessary constitutional channel for a political and social evolution that was inevitable in any case. Alone, except for the British Empire and Commonwealth, America went through the entire period from the French Revolution to the twentieth century with an unimpaired Constitution which no one thought of overthrowing. Alone in the Classical world, Rome was able to perform a similar feat—from the creation of the Tribunate in 495, through the establishment of the Plebeian Assembly in 471, the legalization of marriage between plebeians and patricians through the Canuleian law of 445, the opening of the Quaestorship in 421 and of the Consulship in 367 to plebeians, to the last blow struck against patricians with the famous Lex Hortensia of 287, which placed the democratic Assembly on a par with the aristocratic Senate. Rome experienced no brutal revolution, no upheaval, nothing but a steady democratization working lawfully through constitutional channels. No more than in the English-speaking world did the Roman people drag the ruling class down to them, but on the contrary rose to ruling level in full parity with the former oligarchies.

However, behind the shield provided by Britain's aristocracy, American democracy came about with far greater speed than anywhere else in human experience. American political parties could afford to start from the grass roots, unlike their British counterparts, which started from the top. They were tending in Jefferson's days to become less cliques within an oligarchic ruling circle than coalitions of local and divergent interests—an easy matter in a country with next to no foreign policy or commitments. And so what in the Rome of the second century B.C. had to become a revolutionary social struggle of immense magnitude when the Gracchi found the constitutional channels closed to further democratization, remained in America a slow, peaceful evolution because American democracy and British aristocracy evolved peacefully side by side without intermingling, geographically separate, each serving the purpose of the other instead of being superimposed on one another as in Rome. Britain's ruling class with its uncanny political flair policed the world and unwittingly made it safe for American democracy; and meanwhile America remained open to all the dissatisfied Britons who freely immigrated to the vast New World of social equality and unlimited opportunities.

Jefferson was the link between the aristocratic America of the past and the democratic America of the future. His claim to historical fame rests chiefly on the fact that he smoothed the path for the inevitable and far-reaching change. Jefferson was an intuitive, pragmatic man and his unerring instinct made him the master politician of all times—and a great statesman as well when he shed his idealistic illusions. He was no thinker but a man of action who, faced with reality, lost no time in throwing out all the ideological abstractions with which he so generously cluttered his utterances when in opposition. He succinctly expressed his philosophy of life when he stated that "what is practical must often control what is pure theory." The triumvirate Jefferson-Madison-Gallatin sought power in order to put their isolationism into practice and to prove that a peaceful, idealistic nation could exist and prosper along liberal lines, that the new American nation could find in its foreign policy a substitute for force. The saving grace of such abstract idealism is that it vanishes with amazing speed in front of hard realities, that its former promoters become pragmatic realists in the world of power politics—the source of a long-standing accusation of hypocrisy on the part of other nations who take this impractical idealism without the Anglo-Saxon grain of salt.

A steely realist like Hamilton could not help being shrewd enough to predict that, once in office, Jefferson would be more autocratic than any of his Federalist opponents would ever dare to be. He also saw that the pressure of events would compel Jefferson to enlarge, even against his own will, the sphere of action of the Executive; and, indeed, that is exactly what happened. Jefferson had watched Washington behave in office as a reluctant constitutional monarch with Hamilton as prime minister. He had then watched Hamilton, now out of office, run Adams' administration through the party channels which he still controlled. Jefferson quickly came to understand that the President and the head of the party must be one and the same man. Jefferson was both, and so were all the successful Presidents after him. Thus it was that the rigid separation of powers as provided by the Constitution, widened by the break between Congress and the Executive under Washington's first Presidency, was gradually nullified by the growth of the party system—by those political parties that brought together and fused the powers the Founding Fathers had so carefully separated. Life always prevails over abstraction. Thus started the unofficial gathering of scattered powers within the *caucus,* where the President could confer with and influence Congressional leaders under the cloak of semisecrecy. This regrouping of sundered powers was carried out by the President and therefore brought an immense increment of power directly to the White House, not to Congress.

Jefferson's Presidency was fateful because European events were then world shaking. This was the Napoleonic era, an era of upheavals of unprecedented magnitude that, in one way or another, could not help involving the young Union. Shortly after the third President's inauguration, Napoleon obtained from a weakened Spain the retrocession of Louisiana and sent a powerful army to reoccupy San Domingo, the first step toward the establishment of a French empire in the American West. Henry Adams, looking at the heroic resistance of Toussaint L'Ouverture, wrote that "if he and his blacks should succumb easily to their fate, the wave of French empire would roll on to Louisiana and sweep far up the Mississippi; if San Domingo should resist, and succeed in resistance, the recoil would spend its force in Europe, while America would be left to pursue her democratic destiny in peace." [6] Jefferson rose immediately to the situation, threw overboard his isolationism and wrote to the American minister in Paris in 1802: "There is on the globe one single spot, the possessor of which is our natural and habitual enemy. It is New Orleans, through which the produce of three eighths of our territory must pass to market . . . the day that France takes possession of New Orleans . . . we must marry ourselves to the British fleet and nation" [7]—the most distasteful of all possible marriages for Anglophobe Jefferson.

At least, in a similar situation, the Romans had to come to grips with Pyrrhus and then Hannibal's Carthaginians on Italian soil. More fortunate, the Americans were spared the horrors and devastation of such a war against the redoubtable French veterans under some Napoleonic marshal. The war was fought for them by the wildly brave Negroes of Haiti. Entire French armies vanished in the tropical jungles, melting away like butter under the sun; fifty thousand crack troops belonging to the most powerful army in the world disappeared in "the fiery furnace of San Domingo." Appalled by the disaster, Napoleon gave up his American dream and decided to sell Louisiana, lock, stock, and barrel, to Jefferson.

The purchase was made in an atmosphere of urgency. Talleyrand's policy of peace in Europe and French expansion in America would have, if carried out, changed a great deal of the history of the world. With the considerable means at their disposal, by far the largest army, the greatest population of any European nation—outnumbering the Americans ten to one—the French might have speedily occupied and effectively settled the Mississippi and Missouri valleys and linked up with Canada, surrounding the territory of the United States and preventing any further expansion. Indirectly, this might have caused the breakup of the Union. The sense of urgency came from the fact that the modern Alexander had given up his grandiose schemes overnight, and might just as easily have retrieved them overnight again.[8] But Britain's tacit consent would have been indispensable for the success of Napoleon's plans, and it was not forthcoming. In those distant days, the mutual hatred of European nations was already one of the prime elements favoring the growth of a united America. With unmatched prophetic vision, Napoleon claimed: "I have just given to England a rival which will, sooner or later, break her pride." [9]

Dealing with a mercurial despot, Jefferson was driven to behave with dictatorial speed and to become, in fact, far more autocratic than his Federalist opponent Hamilton would ever have dreamed of becoming. It was thus demonstrated for the first time in America, but not the last, that we always drift into adopting our opponent's methods and styles if they prove to be more effective. The Romans, too, learned that lesson in their dealings with the East. There was no time to wait for a constitutional amendment or for haggling with Congress. Jefferson knew that his action was unconstitutional but he went through with it and was persuaded by Gallatin not even to ask for a constitutional amendment after the fact. Nor was that all. The following year he decided, in spite of the "inalienable rights" guarantee of 1776, to create a territorial government in Louisiana in which the local inhabitants had no share. He appointed personally the governor, the legislative council, and the judges. Henry Adams summed up the whole operation in the following terms: "Within three years of his inauguration Jefferson bought a foreign colony without its consent and against its will, annexed it to the United States by an act which he said made blank paper of the Constitution, and then he who had found his predecessors too monarchical and the Constitution too liberal in powers—he who nearly dissolved the bonds of society rather than allow his predecessors to order a dangerous alien out of the country in time of threatened war, made himself monarch of the new territory, and wielded over it, against its protests, the powers of its old kings." [10]

When the American flag went up over New Orleans, many of the twenty-six thousand Latin Catholic Louisianians wept at the prospect of the coming invasion of dynamic Anglo-Saxon Protestants. But they were isolated, as the Greeks of southern Italy in front of the Romans, without support from a weak Spanish empire or from a France that was busy elsewhere. The dictatorial regime set up by Jefferson eased the transition for them and elective democracy took root later on when Anglo-Saxon immigrants began to flood Louisiana.

The logic of imperial expansion is implacable and makes a mockery of abstract idealism. The new western states of those days—Tennessee, Kentucky, and Ohio—depended for their trade outlet on the mouth of the Mississippi and would certainly not have remained in the Union if Louisiana had not been secured. With their withdrawal the Union would have shrunk to half its size, would have been denied all possibility of further expansion, and would have been constantly threatened with further disruption. As it was, it doubled its territorial surface at one stroke. Then and there, America's destiny became set irrevocably in the twin trends of expansion and growing power of the Executive. Congress was in no way involved.

Just the same, Rome, in order to be safe, had to conquer Latium and to make Latium safe, was driven to the piecemeal conquest of Italy. Then, to protect the trade of Italy, Rome had to go to war against Carthage in Africa and in Spain. To eliminate pirates in the Adriatic, she had to conquer the Illyrian coast. From then on, reluctant bit by reluctant bit, Rome had to meddle in the infinitely complex politics of Greece and the Orient, and was thus driven by the inexorable logic of endless expansion. And yet, Rome was so determined to exclude imperialistic extension from her foreign policy that she had a special regulation, the law of the *fetiales,* which forbade all except defensive wars. The religious character of this legislation was so powerful that it was only with extreme reluctance that far-sighted Roman leaders embarked on distant military campaigns.

The power of the Executive grows alongside the expansion of the nation, an inevitable trend if the nation dedicates itself increasingly to democratic equality. The slow metamorphosis of the Presidency into a tribunate of the people was boldly accelerated by Jefferson's purchase of Louisiana. From now on, the federal power, and within the federal structure, the executive power, grew almost continuously along with the democratization of the nation. Momentarily checked from time to time, it has never really retreated in any significant way; and it was when Jefferson discovered that the Union could not be ruled effectively if he adhered strictly to the orthodox constitutional theories of a dying gentry that this development became inevitable.

It might have been thought that the Louisiana Purchase had satisfied Jefferson, since this demonstration of unchecked executive power appeared to do violence to his innermost feelings and convictions. But this was not the case. Jefferson had a remarkable ability for being cynical without being aware of it, of being ruthlessly realistic when he thought himself impelled by the loftiest idealism. By stealth, he attempted to acquire West Florida and failed. But in the process he gave a brilliant demonstration of his presidential power by smashing, without so much as the flicker of an eyelid, John Randolph, a true idealist, popular and powerful. Then, the Napoleonic wars having . made matters difficult in Europe, Jefferson went on grasping more power by obtaining from Congress in 1807 the authorization to clamp an absolute embargo on all American commerce. Foreign circumstances, driving the Jeffersonians further away from their own ideals, prompted them to sponsor the ill-fated but drastic Enforcement Act, to the amazement of the Federalists who had been accused of rank tyranny for much less.

With James Madison in the White House, presidential power and prestige experienced the first of a number of recurrent slumps. His administration failed to devise a consistent policy and Congress almost wrecked the Union in the process of substituting for a weak Executive. The result was the unnecessary War of 1812 with Britain. Madison was the first American of stature to believe that economic appetites and requirements are the mainspring of human action and this led him into miscalculating England's reactions to his policy of "peaceful coercion." This belief was a landmark in the development of the American temper, a psychological trait that was to lead to many disastrous consequences in the twentieth century.

The main result of the Nonintercourse Act and the inconclusive war was the increase of the administration's economic powers along Hamiltonian lines—a new grievous blow to the Jeffersonian theories, inflicted by the Jeffersonians themselves. The outcome was virtual ruin for the agrarian South and the promotion of northern industrialism. Virginians themselves engineered the economic alteration that was to make their South poorer, the North wealthier and more powerful. But then, did not Jefferson himself cast a melancholy look at his agrarian dream in shambles and admit in 1816 the inevitability of the Industrial Revolution?—"Experience has taught me that manufactures are now as necessary to our independence as to our comfort." [11]

The paradox was that New England was opposed to the war from the start and almost seceded from the Union after having fought for a strong federal government for more than two decades. The Federalist party, trapped in the same contradictions as its Republican rival, died of having sponsored this secessionist movement, and with it died the antidemocratic party of patricians who failed to cope with the rising strength of democracy. Disgusted by politics, these patricians were driven to concern themselves almost exclusively with trade, finance, and industry, leaving the field to professional political machines and expanding democracy.

Nobody won the unwanted war, which had occurred through misunderstanding. The jubilation with which the Peace of Ghent was received in America was not so much due to the end of hostilities with Britain, as to the end of a quarter of a century of European wars in which the United States could not help becoming entangled. From now on, America was on her own, free from all ties with a Europe on which she deliberately turned her back. America's basic isolationism was now triumphant and the country could concentrate on its task of conquering, settling, and building up the New Rome with a minimum of interference. Napoleon's empire was destroyed as Alexander's had been, and in the long run, the chief beneficiaries were America and Rome. America could now grow, safe behind the British navy, a human shield she often mistook for a decree of nature. The United States stood on the threshold of a vast continent as the dominating power in the Western Hemisphere. From now on, for a full century, her domestic politics were free from serious foreign problems.

CHAPTER VIII

The Rule of Law

AMERICAN institutions, like the Roman, were solidly based on the principle of the rule of law, not men. This is one of the sharpest differences between the political and legal traditions of Classical Greece and Europe on the one hand, and of Rome and America on the other.} Under such rule, law becomes automatically and inevitably involved in politics, whereas in Europe it does not. The rule of law sets up as supreme authority, not men, individually or collectively, but written documents, frozen abstractions such as Rome's Twelve Tables or America's Constitution—and a great deal of the political activities of the nation revolve around the interpretation of these documents. The Declaration of Independence, the Constitution, the Bill of Rights, the various amendments, and all the memorable speeches of great Presidents are studied and reinterpreted generation after generation with an almost religious passion. The sacred character of these documents gave to those who were entrusted with their interpretation—mostly lawyers—an inordinate importance in American history. Such simple words as *person* in the Fifth Amendment have been analyzed to a degree that seems senseless to a European. Momentous political consequences have resulted from such interpretations. This is a direct outcome of the fact that American justice is based on the Constitution rather than on laws, since the latter can be invalidated by branding them unconstitutional. This power to cancel legislation is an original feature of America's legal code and the major difference between the American and the European judiciaries.

The immense political power of the American judiciary is unique in Western Civilization. The American judge is not entitled to invalidate a law on the ground of some abstract principle but he can

116

invalidate it in a specific case. American justice can only break down the validity of a law by refusing to apply it to a concrete situation and providing that it is in conflict with the supreme document of the land. It is significant of American legal history that its every landmark is symbolized by a definite case. In this sense, it plays a far more positive and constructive role than its European counterparts. The political incidence of American justice on the legislative power is always indirect; it can never attack the legislation of Congress openly. It is only through the refusal to apply laws that violate the spirit of the Constitution—as it happens to be interpreted at the time —that the judiciary limits the power of the other branches.

Thus, law and politics are inextricably mixed and the legal privilege of interpreting the Constitution, the power of "judicial review," allows it to stand up against President and Congress, to act as a conservative brake on political and social evolution. Americans may not always be law-abiding but they are, like the old Romans, more law-minded than any other nation. Freedom of the individual from arbitrary tyranny and the paramountcy of law are inseparable.

Europeans were often struck by the superior power invested in the American magistrates through the right of *injunction*. European magistrates, servants of bureaucratic states, were and are also *servants* of precise codes of law, not *interpreters* of the constitutionality of those laws. But the American injunction is the natural replica of the Roman *edictum* by which Latin magistrates were empowered to compensate for the deficiencies in the law. American and Roman magistrates were not only servants of the written law but living guardians of the community's general welfare and free to use their own judgment in its application. This was the result of an elective as opposed to a bureaucratic system, which would be paralyzed if the elected magistrates did not have far greater power than their bureaucratic colleagues; and comparing *Ancient Rome and Modern America,* Guglielmo Ferrero foresaw that "in the new world also, we should expect to see a society regulated by elective and authoritative institutions become bureaucratic and at the same time fetter every branch of political and administrative powers with the tight bonds of rigid juridical principles." [1]

The roots of this conception of law are deep in the old Puritanism of the Pilgrim Fathers and in English common law, each of which has given its own particular flavor. Puritanism had from the start established the over-all supremacy of the undefinable Natural Law, a blend of the Roman Stoics' "natural law" and the Biblical Law of God— a law which was to overrule even the Constitution and to which the Secessionists appealed to justify their decisions. This equivalent of Rome's *ius naturale,* the law imposed by human reason, or rather common sense, became the distinguishing feature of American legal philosophy. ✓

The other root lies deep in centuries of English common law, imported by the Pilgrim Fathers, considerably altered and simplified by discarding "a great mass of antiquated and useless rubbish" as a New Hampshire judge put it.[2] ✓ The influence of the West and the frontier in amending it were tremendous. It is largely due to the democratic instincts of the westerners that the aristocratic English features of entail and primogeniture were eventually dropped. ✓

Early in the American colonies, lawyers had been discouraged by not being allowed to collect legal fees. In Massachusetts they were forbidden to practice. The Fundamental Constitution of Carolina declared that it was "a false and vile thing to plead for money or reward." [3] Thus it was in early Rome where all lawyers were well-to-do patricians who were not allowed to collect fees and pleaded as an unrewarded public service. The law of Cincius (204 B.C.) forbade fees for legal services. But sooner or later, as society expanded and legal matters became more complicated, the practice of law had to be entrusted to paid professionals. Common law in all its complexity could not be handled without them, and some accommodation had to be found. Simplification of the common law and growing tolerance of paid lawyers were the answers. This did not come about easily. Lawyers were always hated by debtors and the indentured class in Virginia. During the Puritan revolution the southern gentry was on the defensive and the popular elements were able to cut legal fees and often ban "mercenary lawyers" altogether. Then came the reaction with men like William Fitzhugh attempting to restore common law in its English purity. Finally, they compromised on a simplified common law and the lawyer began his social and political ascension.

This growing ascendancy, unknown on the European continent, was due to the influence of English legalistic thinking. Anglo-Saxon law is a law of *precedents,* entailing a pragmatic concern for time and tradition, for organic growth rather than timeless logic. A law of *precedents* is utterly opposed to a law of *reasons* and fosters an immense conservatism. This has been reflected time and again in American history. The result is that whereas any layman can understand a European code if he cares to read the logical and permanently fixed document, nothing is more obscure than British and American legislation in its illogical accumulation of precedents, tradition bound, tied to concrete and particular cases and not abstract generalities, and always in a state of change. Tocqueville expressed it this way: "The French lawyer is simply a man extensively acquainted with the statutes of his country; but the English or American lawyer resembles the hierophants of Egypt, for like them he is the sole interpreter of an occult science." [4]

The result has been to transform American lawyers into a class endowed with immense influence, an influence which increased steadily as democracy gained the upper hand and destroyed the privileges of the gentry. In time, the lawyers came to substitute for the departed gentry and their influence on American politics can never be overestimated. The absence of marked disorders and upheavals in America's growing democracy is wholly due to this prestige and power of the lawyer class. The historical result is today clear: twenty-four out of thirty-two Presidents have been either lawyers or connected with the legal profession; between half and two-thirds of the seats in Congress have usually been filled by lawyers. Whereas Britain's ruling aristocracy has always been able to absorb and control British lawyers, their American counterparts have remained unchallenged in a country where democratic equality had made them indispensable. They alone lived in *time* and shared an *organic* outlook in a country that was living almost exclusively in geographical *space* with a *mechanical* outlook on things. They became the trustees of America's historic destiny.

During the American Revolution, the colonists' best and most understanding English friend, Edmund Burke, pointed out that the "intractable spirit" of the Americans was due to the fact that "in no country perhaps in the world is the law so general a study." [5] The legalistic temper of America was clearly set even before the Revolution. It was largely responsible for the careful wording of the Constitution and for the establishment of the system of checks and balances that attempted to impose a rigid separation between the powers under the over-all supremacy of an abstract document.

This was also the beginning of America's distinctive and, in many ways, absolutely un-British political structure with its roots deep in America's legalistic conception. The British Parliament remained the sole depositary of legal power in a country that did not believe in the sharp separation of powers; it was a collective leadership, effective because based on an aristocratic social structure with its organic articulations. Britain's Parliament, like the Roman Senate, was the private club of a responsible ruling class, and an often quoted remark makes it clear that "it is a fundamental principle with the English lawyers, that Parliament can do everything except make a woman a man, or a man a woman." [6] The authority and power of Parliament are transcendent and absolute. In the words of Sir Edward Coke: "It hath sovereign and uncontrollable authority in the making, confirming, enlarging, restraining, abrogating, repealing, reviving, and expounding of laws, concerning matters of all possible denominations; ecclesiastical, or temporal; civil, military, maritime or criminal; this being the place where absolute despotic power which must, in all governments, reside somewhere, is entrusted by the Constitution of these kingdoms. . . . It can, in short, do everything that is not naturally impossible to be done; and, therefore, some have not scrupled to call its power, by a figure rather too bold, the omnipotence of Parliament." [7]

Nothing of the kind was set up in America, where an almost morbid fear of human thirst for power fostered the checks-and-balances system. Adams expressed a deep-rooted American feeling when he stated that from Plato to Montesquieu, men had sought for the best possible laws and constitutions and that "every project has been found to be no better than committing the lamb to the custody of the wolf, except that one which is called a 'balance of power.' " [8] The growing belief in the power of some external machinery to influence and shape the behavior of men has become an ineradicable part of the American psychology. [9]

So it was that after Washington, Hamilton and Jefferson, the greatest single influence in shaping the political structure of America was that of John Marshall, the fourth Chief Justice of a largely untried Supreme Court. Marshall was appointed by the last Federalist in power, John Adams, and was himself an arch-Federalist whose thirty-five years on the bench were fateful for America. Taking office simultaneously with Jefferson, he was instrumental in building up the powers, both of the Supreme Court and of the federal government, to a degree that might have stunned the Founding Fathers. It is doubtful whether they had consciously wanted to hand over the power of judicial review to the Court, but Marshall took it without the slightest hesitation.

It was during Jefferson's Presidency that the decisive battle was fought between the Republican idealists and the Supreme Court—and was speedily won by John Marshall. In the celebrated case of *Marbury* v. *Madison,* the theory was firmly established that the Supreme Court was the one and only interpreter of the Constitution. Time sanctioned this decision even though it first seemed a usurpation at the expense of the legislative branch. John Marshall remained firm— the Supreme Court had the right to declare that an act of Congress was null and void if unconstitutional, as interpreted by the Supreme Court. Simultaneously, he reasserted the Federalist doctrine that the Union was supreme over the individual states, a doctrine that was intensely distasteful to the Jeffersonians. Like all subsequent strong Presidents, Jefferson went to war against the Court but failed. In the Chase case, the Senate turned against him and refused to become a court of appeals in the manner of Britain's House of Lords. Jefferson's theories, already battered by the Louisiana purchase, were a shambles after John Marshall had done his work.

Undeterred by the hostility of Jeffersonians and states' rights advocates, the Supreme Court went on quietly, doggedly building up the power of the federal government. The states were gradually reduced to mere administrative subdivisions of an expanding empire. Commenting on the case *Fletcher* v. *Peck,* John Marshall wrote: "Georgia cannot be viewed as a single, unconnected, sovereign power, on whose legislature no other restrictions are imposed than may be found in its own constitution. She is part of a large empire; she is a member of the American union; and that union has a constitution, the supremacy of which all acknowledge, and which imposes limits to the legislatures of the several states." [10]

The legal basis of the coming empire was decisively set by many decisions of this kind. But it would always take executive approval and action to translate legal decisions into actual practice. It took the Civil War to vindicate Marshall's legal doctrine and defeat the "states' rightists" by force of arms. The need for executive backing could have been predicted long before, as early as Jackson's Presidency. In those days, Georgia tore up the federal treaties with several Indian nations and confiscated their land. The Supreme Court intervened on behalf of the Indians and ordered Georgia to desist. Georgia refused and President Jackson, the Indian-hater, made no move to coerce the rebellious state. "John Marshall has made his decision," he is alleged to have said, "now let him enforce it." [11] Yet if a decision pleased Jackson, he was quite willing and able to enforce it—as he did against the South Carolinians who were urged by Calhoun to disregard a federal tariff law. It became obvious that the sanction of a law depended on the Executive's good will. Aging John Marshall had to face that sad fact. Jackson impressed on all concerned that the President, as sole tribune of the people, was ultimately the last court of appeals because he alone had the power to enforce his decisions.

Thus, although they freely borrowed from Europe, the Americans ended up by formulating an entirely new Constitution, framing an entirely new system of government, and working out, generation after generation, an entirely new legislation. When the Romans went to Athens to look into Solon's remarkable code of laws, they returned, adapted Greek legislation to Roman circumstances, and ended up by producing in the Twelve Tables of the Decemvirs an original legislation. Augmented and perfected over the following centuries from Sulla to Justinian, it became the most perfect legislation yet known. The Roman and American pattern in law as in everything else was not invention but skillful adaptation, attention to reality rather than abstract theory, and ability to let institutions grow organically over long periods of time rather than attempt to plan them logically on the spur of the moment.

CHAPTER IX

Growth and Expansion

AS opposed to Greece and Europe, Rome and America discovered early in their history the key to organic growth. They found it through trial and error, instinctively, without seeking it consciously or laying down rational plans. Organic growth implies not the brutal overpowering and subjugation of neighboring people to an imperial rule such as Athens, Sparta, and Thebes attempted time and again, or the bureaucratic empires of Macedonia, the Seleucids in Syria, or the Ptolemies in Egypt, or the imperialistic policies of European powers in Asia, Africa, or even Europe itself. Organic growth implies gradual extension through incorporation of aliens, neighboring people, or immigrants, as new cells join older ones in the process of building up the physical body as an organic unit. It precludes a policy of exploitation or subordination and implies a willingness to share, after a probationary period, one's traditions, duties, riches, and privileges with the newcomers.

What is most important, perhaps, is the existence of an indestructible link between social and political stability and the expansion of the society, a stability which is progressive and constructive, not stagnating. Rome and America grew prodigiously because, alone in their respective worlds, their ruling classes were willing to raise the lower classes up to their level, to share their knowledge, skill, and privileges with them, and thus remain in a state of constant growth. They had fluid, "open" societies. Having established this supremely successful pattern, they could not help growing by drawing to themselves all those who were dissatisfied with worse conditions—with narrow-minded clinging to unjustified privileges or revolutionary instability as in Europe, with economic stagnation as in the Orient, with

123

political chaos as in Latin America. They had a unique pattern that, even if it entailed an unusual degree of psychological conformism and social discipline, was supremely tempting and rewarding to those aliens who were willing to make the necessary sacrifices in order to become part of it.

When the United States became independent, the thirteen original states found themselves owning large territories beyond the Appalachians. With unmatched public spirit, they handed over their claims to the confederal and then federal authority. They accepted the principle that their own geographical growth was terminated in order that the Union as a whole should grow; and when the oligarchies of the coastal states gave up their privileges and granted equal representation to their underrepresented western settlers, they took the first step toward sound organic expansion. American expansion would have been fraught with terrible dangers had the Union not found a formula that permitted admittance of the fast-developing western territories as new states with all the rights and privileges of the older states. This was an innovation of far-reaching importance, and one that few European nations would have contemplated in those days.

The Roman policy of expansion was on par with the American in its generous boldness. Rome could never have grown in Italy if she had followed the expansionist pattern of the Greeks, no more than America could have grown by duplicating the colonial policy of Europe. Furthering their expansion with deep political instinct, the Romans gradually extended to allied, dependent, or vanquished states the Roman and Latin franchise while granting them local municipal autonomy. It was due to the remarkable self-discipline of her upper classes that Rome was able to succeed where the Etruscans had failed, and rise slowly above all other states in Italy. In the fifth and fourth centuries, Rome led the Latin League in a number of wars against Etruscans, Volsci, and Aequi. The defeated nations were enrolled in four additional voting "tribes," and Latin colonists went out to settle hundreds of thousands of acres of confiscated land among their former enemies. Then came the wars against Sabines and Samnites in the third century, then against the Gauls on the Adriatic coast and the Greeks of southern Italy. Defeated nations were systematically granted the duties and privileges of *cives sine suffragio*, a probationary status entailing military service without voting rights. Then franchise was gradually extended to the nonvoting citizens: in 268 B.C. to the

Sabines of Norcia, Rieti, and Amiterno; about 241 B.C. to the citizens of Picenum and Velletri for instance; and thus, decade after decade, century after century, the Roman nation grew steadily, extending the unique pattern of Roman life—political stability, higher standard of living, puritanical way of life, self-discipline, individual freedom from the arbitrary tyranny of despots, psychological conformity, concentration on the practical details of economic prosperity rather than concern for art, literature, philosophy, or the refinements of cultured living. In Italy, no community of depressed Helots could come into being such as disgraced Sparta. There were no tributary states and the Romans were wise enough not to tax their Italian subjects without their consent. A feeling of nationhood was thus slowly built up in Italy, fanned by common dangers from alien Celts and Greeks, just as the feeling of American nationhood grew steadily as Americans came into closer contact with Spaniards, Mexicans, French, and Russians on their own continent. The very name "Italian" came into use in the third century B.C. as the name "American" appeared in the eighteenth.

Rome's farsighted policy was a great innovation. Hitherto, Classical expansion of the Greek and Hellenistic type had always ended in the juxtaposition of two political structures: the ruling city and the conquered territory—a scrap heap of protectorates, colonies, and dependencies exploited for the benefit of the ruling city. The *res publica,* the commonwealth, was strictly confined to the corporeal body of the city; and it was only after a great inner struggle that Rome developed the entirely new concept of an Italian *nation* that was no longer limited to Rome, of a continental rather than a city-wide *res publica* in which all citizens had equal rights. Roman Italy was the only nation in the full sense of the word in Classical times.

We can even compare, on Italian soil, the imperialistic extension of the tyrant Dionysius of Syracuse and his organization of terrified tributary states, which the Syracusans regarded as "booty," and the organic growth of Rome through steady absorption and amalgamation. Elsewhere we can also visualize the typical Hellenistic structure. Alexandria was Egypt and the rest of the Nile Valley with its millions of toiling fellahs participated in no way in the life of the Ptolemaic realm. Antioch absorbed into itself the whole life of the Seleucid empire, regardless of its immense territorial expansion. Every one of those Hellenistic empires was merely an overgrown *polis* that could not be metamorposed into a *nation*—a metamorphosis which, alone in the Classical world, the Romans were able to work out. Even for the Romans it was not easy. Many farsighted Romans, sensing the creeping sclerosis that was beginning to harden their institutions, advocated conferring Roman citizenship on all Italians before it was too late—Flaccus in 125 B.C., Drusus thirty odd years later. But many other Romans were stubbornly clinging to their privileges, not so much to their voting rights as to the civil rights involved in citizenship. The result was the Social War, which finally conferred the citizenship on all Italians and completed the Romanization of Italy. The Social War was waged against Rome by her Italian allies, not in order to shake off Roman domination, but on the contrary, to be allowed to become full-fledged Roman citizens; they sought full integration within the Roman Commonwealth on a basis of equality. They won it and even in the days of Sulla's reactionary restoration, there was no attempt to go back to the past. From now on, the Roman citizen body included all Italy south of the Rubicon—to which Julius Caesar added, later on, Cisalpine Gaul.

What was so arduous in the Roman world was no easier in the English-speaking world. The American Revolution was in part a replica of Italy's Social War; but two thousand years later geographical circumstances were different and compelled the Anglo-Saxons, scattered all over the globe, to search for equality on a federal basis. Yet, the philosophy behind those upheavals was identical. It was essentially constructive and sought to build, not to tear down. While the Americans solved their problem by gradually transforming the federal territories into autonomous states and by progressively extending the franchise to the adult male population in a few generations, the British solved theirs by working out the steady metamorphosis of their global empire into a commonwealth of scattered self-governing dominions. In either case, wisdom avoided the paralyzing mistakes of Greeks and Europeans, even though wisdom did not shine before some trial of strength—the Social War and the American Revolution —had made them see the light.

Thus it was that the English-speaking world grew from a few million in the eighteenth century to two hundred and fifty million in the twentieth, while France grew from twenty-five to only forty million. Between the first census of Servius Tullius and the beginning of the Social War (before citizenship was extended to the whole of

Italy), the number of Roman citizens increased from 83 to 463 thousand, while Athens in her most prosperous period saw the number of her citizens decline from 30 to 21 thousand.[1]

The process of expansion was linked in Rome and America with the process of organic growth; and growth is the result of a successful pattern of absorption and assimilation.\While Rome was sending colonists all over Italy, and then all over the Mediterranean, spreading in this manner Roman speech, customs, and traditions and thus Romanizing a large part of the Classical world, she began to receive the "immigrants" of the times: the slaves, who were imported wholesale from every quarter of the Mediterranean.

The word *slave* should not mislead us. Classical slavery had nothing in common with European and American slavery in modern times. It was based on the fortune of war and most slaves were unlucky captives who were freed after a few generations, to become in time full-fledged citizens. Many of those slaves were more highly cultured than the Romans themselves and rendered invaluable services to the Roman community; they provided most of the doctors, scientists, engineers, writers, teachers, and professors, men who were often the leading experts in their various fields. European and American slavery was based on racial distinctions totally unknown to the Classical world, the victims recruited from defenseless savages who had no culture of their own, whose ethnic "inferiority" was taken for granted and presumed to be everlasting, and who, if freed, could look forward only to the status of pariahs. Western slavery had far more in common with India's caste system than with Classical slavery.

The Roman slave trade, practiced on a gigantic scale unknown to the Hellenistic East, filled Rome and Italy with multitudes of involuntary immigrants as fast as Rome sent out colonists to the far corners of the world. The successful absorption of these immigrants—who in time came to constitute the bulk of Rome's population (it is estimated that between 81 B.C. and 49 B.C. half a million of slaves were freed in the city of Rome alone [2])—can be compared only to the remarkable record of America's "melting pot" policy in the twentieth century. Success came from the fact that both nations had learned early the secret of organic growth—the social secret first, through the generous self-immolation of their ruling classes, then the territorial secret through the success of their geographical expansion.

The subsequent success of their "melting pot" policies was only the extension of earlier achievements in the social and territorial fields.

Romanization and Americanization imply a definite pattern of amalgamation and expansionism. They imply the triumph of the social over the individual outlook. They succeed in merging into their expanding communities a large number of scattered and lonely individuals who are, often unconsciously, longing for this social integration; and they add their weight to the remarkable decline of true individualism which characterizes nations like Rome and America, and which eventually becomes one of the hallmarks of Civilization as opposed to Culture. The immigrant is quite willing to leave his full individuality behind and immerse himself in a new society that is remarkably cohesive precisely because it restricts the free play of individualism. His acceptance in this new society makes him more Roman or American than the natives ever were. As a convert, he contributes more than one would think to enhance and even exaggerate their characteristics.

The pattern of this emigration of Romans to new lands and Americans to the West included the compensatory immigration of Greeks and Europeans to the old homesteads in Rome and America's eastern seaboard. While Greeks poured into Rome and Latium, Romans and Latins expanded into northern Italy, southern Gaul, Spain, and Africa. While Americans were on the move westward, crossing the entire breadth of the continent, European newcomers, especially those belonging to the latest wave of immigration, often stayed in the East and absorbed the American characteristics of a land that was already becoming old. This made Americanization far easier than would have been the case if the Europeans had settled heavily in the virgin West while the native Americans remained in the East. This happened in a few isolated instances and the intractable nature of large groups of German immigrants in the Middle West made this danger quite plain. Some states might have become as distinctively German, Scandinavian, Italian, or Polish as Canada's Quebec has remained doggedly French to this day.

The policy of dynamic growth has another consequence in that it ensures social and political stability in those nations that are great enough to apply it, while it relieves the Old World of congestion. Emigration in the nineteenth century rescued Europe from undue social pressure and contributed immeasurably to the relative peace secured by the Congress of Vienna. But it did far more for the New World. Rome's and America's expanding frontiers and apparently unlimited opportunities for daring pioneers made it easy to eliminate social discontent in the old settled areas. It was only with the end of these frontiers and opportunities that real social problems arose. Until then, the process of expansion tended to raise the old native stock ever higher in wealth, social prestige, and political influence, and each new immigrant looked forward to the time when other immigrants would come in and raise him up in turn, almost automatically. The process was a continuous one and those who were involved in it were willing to put up with any amount of present hardship for the sake of a bright future. Thus did Rome's middle class rise in numbers, wealth, and influence, drowning peacefully the small upper classes of former days and gradually replacing them as the dominant social strata, not merely of Rome or Italy but eventually of the entire Classical world.

This peaceful growth explains a great deal of the relative social stability of Rome and America up to the end of their frontiers and the advent of first great social crises—the Gracchi era and the revolution of Marius in Rome, Bryan's Populists and the New Deal in America. By then, the situation had become radically different. New problems arose and new solutions had to be devised.

At the beginning of the nineteenth century, the pattern of America's development was clearly set. The United States could look across a virtually unoccupied continent and back at an Old World ever willing to send forth its increasing millions. The ideals and customs of a small number of men hugging the Atlantic coast of North America were, within a few generations, to become the common property of almost two hundred million men and a world-significant phenomenon.

Yet in the days of Jefferson, Americans thought that it would take a thousand years to settle and develop the West—not merely the old trans-Appalachian West, but the new one extending to the distant Pacific, most of which did not even belong to the Union. The full implications of the Industrial Revolution were not yet guessed at, and Americans, Jeffersonians especially, saw the gradual settlement of the West in strictly agricultural terms.

By the time of the War of 1812, a new generation had grown up in the United States that had no firsthand knowledge of large-scale fighting, not having been of age during the Revolution. Men took their republic and their freedom for granted and never thought for an instant that their expansionism was going to set America's destiny for centuries to come. These men were hungry for land. The westerners, especially, wanted to absorb Canada and Spanish Florida.

The dismantling of the two remaining great empires of the New World became the unconscious goal of American expansionism. But the destruction of British power in North America was never achieved. A durable coalition between the French Canadians and the Loyalists of Ontario gave birth to a new nation that refused to be drawn into the Union. On the other hand, Spanish Florida was grabbed by American military forces without much discussion. In 1819 the United States paid Spain an indemnity of five million dollars, setting a precedent for its coming policy of conquest and cash settlements. The payment of money somehow soothed the nation's puritanical conscience.

By the time of the Congress of Vienna, the Union had already more than doubled its size and Europe had to face an unpalatable fact: the Napoleonic wars had made this expansion possible by weakening all European powers in their dealings with the Western Hemisphere, by inducing Napoleon to sell Louisiana and stab the Spanish empire in its European heart.

The next territorial growth took place a generation later with the annexation of Texas and the Oregon settlement with the British. The vast Mexican territories north of the Rio Grande were largely empty, Spain and Mexico having been unable to fill the new lands with immigrants. When Texas seceded from Mexico in 1836 it had already a small population of Anglo-Saxon farmers who longed to join the Union. President Van Buren, however, was reluctant to upset the precarious balance between the slave-owning South and the North. The problem was debated in Washington until Texas was finally admitted in 1845—a memorable date comparable to Rome's semi-reluctant acceptance of the pleading Mamertine republic, threatened by the tyrant Hiero of Syracuse, into the Italian Confederacy in 265 B.C. Syracuse's and Mexico's obsolete tyrannies and unstable politics were no match for the progressive dynamism of Rome and America. The same thing happened again when the Campanians offered to join Rome in order to be protected from the depredations of the Samnite mountaineers. Strong political institutions based on sound economic development always have an irresistible appeal for those who are threatened by backward tyranny or ceaseless revolutions.

American appetites had been whetted by the annexation of Texas, and California lay as a tantalizing prize, along with the huge piece of territory in between. The ethical side of the problem tickled the conscience of many Americans. Calhoun dared to say that "Mexico is the forbidden fruit" and Emerson emphasized that "Mexico will poison us." [3] Wise Romans were equally alarmed by the rise of imperialism in Rome and the great Publius Scipio, after the decisive victory of Zama, attempted to stem the expansionist tide. His peace terms with Carthage were generous to the extreme but he could not restrain a historical evolution whose roots lay deep in the past.

Although in many respects a colorless President, James Polk was a staunch expansionist and he had long cast covetous eyes on California. This meant war, for Mexico was determined not to sell. A pretext for starting hostilities can always be found if the will to fight exists. Polk provoked the Mexicans repeatedly until they handed him the desired pretext. The war was short and completely successful: Mexico surrendered a huge territory, larger than France and Germany combined. Again, to ease her conscience, the United States paid cash, giving the Mexicans fifteen million dollars.

Rome triumphed over the degenerate Etruscans for the same reasons that allowed the Americans to dominate the anarchic Mexicans: general decay of moral fiber had sapped their strength. The abolition of the monarchy by the Etruscans was as empty a symbol of progressiveness as the revolt of Mexico against the Spanish crown. In both cases, the worst form of self-indulgent oligarchic rule prevailed over the less corruptible administration of despotic kings. The result was political chaos, increasing social revolts among the Etruscans and political pronunciamentos among the Mexicans, both weakening their resistance against the more cohesive and determined Romans and Americans.

In America, all the conquered territories experienced an immediate economic boom. Settlement and the exploitation of economic resources went hand in hand, progressing faster in a few years than they had in centuries of Spanish and Mexican rule. From five thousand white settlers in 1845, California's population jumped to almost four hundred thousand in 1860. The unfortunate Indians, deprived of the paternalistic protection of Mexico, sank to the level of Negroes.

The result of this staggering territorial expansion, from the Louisiana Purchase to the Mexican War, was that, at the outbreak of the Civil War, the population west of the Mississippi was greater than that of the entire Union when Washington became President: four and a half million, only one tenth of which was of foreign birth.

The Mexican War rounded off the immense American domain. It was also a turning point. For the first time, America had started a war of aggression and had become uncomfortably conscious of her latent expansionism. In 1845, a Democratic editor coined the apt expression "manifest destiny"—manifest destiny to increase American power and territory, bolstered by the firm conviction that American institutions and way of life were the best to be had in the world. This might involve going to war against anyone who did not agree, but in all fairness, it was also the same imperative need to fill a vacuum that drew Rome into the Classical world, rather than imperial conquest for its own sake.

But there is always a penalty to pay. Lewis Cass, the leading imperialist of the time, wanted to grab the whole of Oregon and almost all of Mexico, and advertised his greed with shrill insistence. The penalty for the exacerbation of patriotic extremism and the arousing of uncontrollable passions was the shattering of the great North-South compromise and the Civil War. Calhoun, the wise compromiser, sensed the danger and feared the Mexican War because of its effect on the cohesion of the Union. But there was no turning back. Compromise is a state of mind that is rarely compatible with conscious imperialism.

It was not likely that the great Hellenistic and European powers would look upon the rise of the young western giants without misgivings. Napoleon knew quite well what he was doing when he sold Louisiana to the United States out of anti-British spite. After Napoleon's defeat by the Holy Alliance, Europe began to look on America as an unsuspected genie out of an Arabian Nights bottle, a young colossus whose growth should be stopped. Throughout the nineteenth century, various European powers made repeated but vain attempts to do so.

In Classical times, the mainland Greeks attempted several times to interfere in Italy on behalf of their compatriots of Magna Graecia. During one of Rome's protracted wars, the Spartan ruler Cleonymies compelled Rome's Lucanian enemies to make peace with the Greek city of Tarentum and form an anti-Roman coalition. But he did not dare enter the war directly by allying himself with the Samnites and the coalition collapsed. Similarly, Britain was hopeful that the War of 1812 would break up the Union by encouraging the reluctant Federalists and seafaring New Englanders to secede and either join Canada or set up a separate union of their own. Britain's wish was of course not fulfilled, but she did not give up hope. Her hope revived when the United States manifested a certain reluctance to admit Texas into the Union.

Lord Aberdeen and the French premier Guizot attempted, through diplomatic recognition and loans, to sustain Texas' independence and re-establish a balance of power in the Western Hemisphere by preventing further American expansion in the Southwest. In 1844, Britain and France offered Mexico a plan for a joint guarantee of both Texas and Mexico against the United States. The Mexicans unwisely turned it down and paid for it with the subsequent loss to the United States of half their territory. Even when the alarmed Americans had finally made up their minds to annex Texas. Guizot hopefully stated: "France has a lasting interest in the maintenance of independent states in America, and in the balance of forces which exists in that part of the world." [4] The precarious balance was soon shattered. President James Polk promptly replied to Guizot in no uncertain tone: "Jealousy among the different sovereigns of Europe . . . has caused them anxiously to desire the establishment of what they term the 'balance of power.' It cannot be permitted to have any application on the North American continent, and especially to the United States." [5]

Hellenistic and European powers could play the balance-of-power game within their continents but Italy was Rome's as America was the United States' and compact unity was their motto. The Old World's only remaining hope lay in a possible dislocation of the growing giant and the American Civil War provided their last chance. Such a sympathetic observer as Anthony Trollope reflected Europe's expectations when he wrote during this hectic period: "This widespread nationality of the United States, with its enormous territorial possessions and increasing population, has fallen asunder, torn to pieces by the weight of its own discordant parts—as a congregation when its size has become unwieldy will separate and reform itself into two wholesome wholes." [6] But, given their chance, the Europeans misjudged the true character of America, and especially her determination to preserve unity at any cost.

It was this hope that induced Napoleon III to launch his ill-fated expedition to Mexico. Europe had long believed that if something was not done to restore order in Mexico, the United States would incorporate the entire country down to Central America and become an even more formidable power. The Civil War seemed a unique opportunity for action and in the fall of 1861, France, Britain, and Spain dispatched an international army—quickly reduced to a strictly French expedition when Britain and Spain became aware of Napoleon's unrealistic megalomania. As soon as the American Civil War was over, Ulysses Grant suggested sending an American army to drive the French out. The move turned out to be unnecessary since Mexican resistance compelled Napoleon to recall his troops. But by now an entirely new fact impressed Europe: America had been able to raise for the purposes of the Civil War the largest and most efficient armies ever seen. For the first time, it was not merely the British fleet but American manpower and technical proficiency that guaranteed the Union's pre-eminence in America.

Napoleon III's dream of a new Latin Catholic empire in the Western Hemisphere collapsed as completely as Alexander the Molossian's equally impossible scheme of building up a new Hellenic empire in southern Italy. The last Greek attempt to establish a balance of power in Italy occurred in 216 when Philip of Macedonia concluded an alliance with Hannibal providing for an expulsion of the Romans from the eastern coast of the Adriatic and a Macedonian invasion of Italy. But it was far too late for any attempt of this kind. Napoleon III was indirectly compelled by Grant's threat to withdraw his army from Mexico and Philip was thrown out of Illyria by Valerius Laevinus. Hellenistic and European powers could no longer challenge Roman and American power on their own continents. The Spanish historian Navarro y Rodrigo, throwing a melancholy look at what might have been, wrote: "A little audacity and France was assured of her possessions, England of Canada . . . ourselves of the treasure of our Antilles, and the future of the Spanish race. Mexico and the Southern States . . . were the two advanced redoubts which Europe in its own interest should have thrown up against the American colossus." [7] This was the wisdom of hindsight.

Long before the Civil War, President Monroe had announced in blunt terms the new American doctrine of "hands off" the Western Hemisphere. Monroe made it plain that the Holy Alliance's political and social principles were obnoxious to Americans, that their presence would therefore not be tolerated. The Monroe Doctrine, set forth when Latin America was separating from Spain and Portugal, was a high-sounding document but, in those days, it took a British fleet to enforce it, especially in distant South America. Unconscious of the inconsistency between principles and the power to enforce them, the Americans failed to see the reality behind the doctrine's doubtful validity. That reality was simply that Britain expected to develop new economic markets and sources of raw materials for her booming industries; it was this British power and self-interest, nothing else, that made the Monroe Doctrine workable.

The Monroe Doctrine implied a virtual American protectorate over the entire Western Hemisphere. The Latin Americans never appreciated this, knowing perfectly well that they owed their national freedom to the Polignac Agreement, imposed by Britain's naval power on reluctant French and Spanish monarchs. Britain alone ruled the waves and policed the modern "Hellenistic" world. It was only in the course of time that America's growth and economic power began to seem threatening to the Latin Americans and that the Monroe Doctrine acquired definite imperialistic undertones. Rome, too, intimated to the Greeks that their interference in Italy was unwelcome. Rome's Monroe Doctrine was her war against Pyrrhus. But where the Americans could, for a few generations, speak with the protection of Britain's navy behind them, Rome had to go to war to prove that she was in earnest.

CHAPTER X

The Rise of Democracy

WHATEVER Jefferson and his immediate successors at the Presidency might have thought, they were all members of an aristocratic gentry, steeped in the eighteenth century. America was still ruled by an oligarchy and the downfall of this ruling class was a slow process which reached its conclusion under Andrew Jackson. Until and including James Monroe's Presidency, all the Chief Executives belonged to the "Virginia dynasty," Virginian aristocrats who provided the bulk of America's political leadership from the Revolution onward.[1] New England provided the substance of the ideology but the South provided the outstanding men; and it was under their leadership that democracy rose steadily until it felt strong enough, with Andrew Jackson, to discard the aristocracy altogether.

The two major forces shaping America's destiny in those days were the Industrial Revolution and the rise of the West. The first sign of the Industrial Age to come was the invention and introduction of the cotton gin in the South. The social result of this shot-in-the-arm administered to a sick cotton economy was to reverse the trend toward a gradual abolition of slavery. The hope of liberal Jeffersonians that this institution could be done away with and the Negroes eventually shipped back to Africa was shattered by a powerful resurgence of pro-slavery feeling largely based on new economic prospects. Some time before, plantations had become a burden to their owners, ruined by land exhaustion, the Embargo Act of 1807, and protective tariffs favorable to northern industries but disastrous for the raw-material South. Now, however, the opening of new lands along the Gulf and the extension of cotton plantations provided an expanding market for slave-dealers. Virginia lost her primacy to the Deep South and Southwest. Not only did slavery revive but the peaceful Cherokee Indians who had settled down to an agricultural life were expelled. And so the first result of the Industrial Revolution was a social disaster in the South—as it was in the slum areas of the North and Europe.

The North was industrializing rapidly and was the main instigator of high tariffs. The South wanted low tariffs or, better, none at all, to sell its raw cotton unhampered in overseas markets. These conflicting economic interests were to plague the Union until the Civil War. Meanwhile, the Industrial Revolution helped to open up the West at an undreamed-of rate. Steamboats soon paddled the waters of the Mississippi. The Erie Canal, connecting the East with the Great Lakes, was completed in 1825. A fast-increasing network of roads began to link North, West, South, and Southwest. The momentum of the Industrial Revolution gathered speed when the first railroads began to spread their metallic sinews. The westward trickle of population became a flood and the formidable Appalachian barrier was virtually washed away. It became obvious that the occupation and settlement of the whole continent would be, at most, a matter of generations, not centuries.

The great issue in those days was the disposal of the vast "imperial" public domain, a problem that had plagued Rome's corresponding *ager publicus* in the great days of the republic. Hamilton and the conservatives had hoped to put a brake on western expansion and concentrate on building the industrial might of the East. But Jefferson and the democrats had the better of them. For their own political purposes, they wanted to open up the West in order to create a population of democratically-minded freeholding farmers. The two programs were actually carried out simultaneously, thanks to the massive European immigration that provided manpower for both. Various Land Acts fixed the minimum unit of land and the moderate price which encouraged western settlement.

America's rising democracy owed a great deal to the new type of American, the westerner—a staunch, rough democrat who was both an irrepressibly self-reliant individual and yet was permeated by the strong social spirit which was becoming the distinctive trait of American civilization. Voluntary cooperation and logrolling cemented the solidarity of widely scattered communities in the immense forests of the west. Frontier stores at boat landings and crossroads were, with churches, the meeting place of scattered pioneers, social centers where public opinion could take shape and make its impact felt on the more civilized and sedate East. These meeting places were also the main centers of New England influence throughout the immense continent, the bases from which the Yankee peddlers imposed their Biblical narrow-mindedness and moralism on the more generous, easygoing westerners and southerners.

Alexis de Tocqueville has left us a memorable picture of the pioneer in his log cabin: "Nothing can offer a more miserable aspect than these isolated dwellings. The traveler who approaches one of them towards nightfall sees the flicker of the hearth flame through the chinks in the walls; and at night, if the wind rises, he hears the roof of boughs shake to and fro in the midst of the great forest trees. Who could not suppose that this poor hut is the asylum of rudeness and ignorance? Yet no sort of comparison can be drawn between the pioneer and the dwelling that shelters him. Everything about him is primitive and wild, but he is himself the result of the labor and experience of eighteen centuries. He wears the dress and speaks the language of cities; he is acquainted with the past, curious about the future, and ready for argument about the present; he is in short a highly civilized being, who consents for a time to inhabit the backwoods, and who penetrates into the wilds of the New World with the Bible, an axe and some newspapers." [2]

From this description, it is clear that Civilization was going to rise in the West without going through the intermediate stage of Culture.

This is how, in time, the West became the mainstay of American power and vigor, the home of an Americanism that looked down on the slightly decadent easterners who stayed behind, as the sturdy Romans of Cisalpine Gaul looked down upon the more effete Romans dwelling south of the Rubicon. Those Cisalpine Romans were as much a new breed as the American westerners, although they had recently emigrated from central Italy as America's westerners came from New England or Pennsylvania. Pushing always further, they Americanized the whole continent as the Romans pushed further in theirs to Latinized Transalpine Gaul. The American frontier saw a seemingly endless re-enactment of the first landing of the Pilgrim Fathers by men who were often their direct descendants.

And thus the rising democracy was expansionist—as it had been in Rome. From the early days, when the great censor Appius Claudius acted, like Jefferson, as a reluctant empire builder and completed in 313 B.C. the great military road from Rome to Capua across the Pontine marshes, Rome's rising democracy had never failed to be expansionist and even imperialistic. It was the same in America. At first, expansion had to halt on the edge of the Great Plains, where the lack of trees and water seemed to preclude colonization. The emigrants had to jump all the way to the Pacific Coast to find once again the watered, forested lands to which they had been accustomed east of the Mississippi. Thus came into being the Oregon Trail, whose Roman parallel was the famed Via Flaminia, the Great North Road which connected Rome with the Po Valley and along which traveled countless Roman emigrants in search of the free land of Italy's northern "West." Gaius Flaminius, its sponsor, was Rome's most outstanding democrat of those days, the leader who undertook the great Gallic War in order to make room for Roman settlers in northern Italy.

Roman aristocrats, like wealthy eastern Americans, were rarely expansionist-minded, comfortably ensconced as they were in their old lands. But the pioneers and the rising power of democracy in Rome and America imposed this expansion from sheer biological vitality—ruthless expansion whenever ruthlessness became unavoidable. Rome's drastic policy toward Senones, Picini, Celts, and countless other semi-barbarians was matched by the terrible punishment inflicted by Americans on the Indians, overcoming the scruples and reluctance of Roman and American conservatives. As Tocqueville expressed it when this policy was in full swing: "The Spaniards were unable to exterminate the Indian race by those unparalleled atrocities which brand them with indelible shame, nor did they succeed in wholly depriving it of its right; but the Americans of the United States accomplished this twofold purpose with a singular felicity, tranquilly, legally, philanthropically, without shedding blood and without violating a single great principle of morality in the eyes of the world. It is impossible to destroy men with more respect for the laws of humanity." [3]

The excuse that nomadic Indians had no right to occupy extensive tracts of land was no longer as valid as it used to be. The Cherokees had settled peacefully on the land granted them after Jackson's Indian war in 1814. A few years later, tearing up the federal treaties, the state of Georgia expropriated their lands and threw them out along with the Creeks. The state of Alabama followed suit and confiscated the land of the Chickasaws and Choctaws. The natural and often implacable expansionism of vigorous democracy has often been blurred by ideological misconceptions; but it is a stark reality. It was the Democrat Polk who thirsted for war and expansion at the expense of Mexico, and it was the conservative, pro-British Whigs who were dead set against imperialism. It was a Democrat, Lewis Cass, who was the leading imperialist in those days. And many easterners had understood early that the imperialism of expanding democracy leads, sooner or later, to Caesarism. In the old days of Jackson's successful wars against Seminoles and Spaniards, "Jackson returned, to be acclaimed once more a hero by the West; but Easterners thought of Roman history and trembled. 'It was in the provinces that were laid the seeds of the ambitious projects that overturned the liberties of Rome,' said Clay. In Monroe's cabinet, Adams alone took the high ground that Jackson's every act was justified by the incompetence of Spanish authority to police its own territory." [4] How many times did Roman democrats use a similar excuse to extend their domination against the wishes of Roman conservatives!

Religion brought its own specific contribution to the rise of democracy. Revivalist movements kept rolling along the expanding frontier, gathering force and eventually snowballing into the Second Awakening. Feeding on the naked religious emotionalism of rootless populations, revivalism offered a psychological compensation for the desiccated rationalism that was born in the euphoria of the Age of Enlightenment and was being tremendously encouraged by the materialism of the dawning Industrial Age. Like the Neo-Pythagoreans, who at times shook Roman Italy in their attempts to fight the irresistible flood of skepticism that swept Rome after the Punic Wars, revivalism was partly a throwback to the past. Older sects in the East remained more conservative, staying aloof and imitating Varro's attempt in Rome to salvage the most venerable and endearing symbols and customs of the past—and like him, these sects became in fact the embalmers of petrified cults. The emotional West would have none of it; by banishing the rational intellect from the field of religion, revivalism democratized it by making it acceptable and understandable to all, regardless not only of social background but of mental stature.

Thousands upon thousands of westerners gathered around camp-fires, singing hymns, communicating their religious flame to all who thirsted for brotherhood and a feeling of belonging in the vast empti-ness of the American West. The pattern had been set at the turn of the century in Logan County, Kentucky, and from there it swept the larger part of the West like a prairie fire. "Old time" religion with its Biblical atmosphere was well-suited to the new type of nomadic people who found no roots in the new West and who were forever on the march, looking for the blessed land of Canaan. There were no peasants in America, no men rooted in the soil, belonging body and soul to the good earth. There were only nomadic farmers with-out emotional attachment to their dwelling place, who exhausted the soil in a few years of careless tilling and then moved on. Their entire emotionalism was spent in religious revivals, their ecstatic behavior being a necessary counterpoise to their acute realism and dry prac-ticality.

The democratization of religion helped the liberals in their vic-torious struggle to disestablish all official churches which had become too closely associated with the ruling gentry. From New Hampshire's disestablishment of the Congregational Church after the War of 1812, to Massachusetts' in 1833, a steady reform separated church and state, a movement made far easier by the disruptive influence of evangelical religion and its multiplication of sects and denominations. But the most important feature of this reform is that it indicated the coming of age of a distinctive American Christianity that differed from its European counterparts as Roman religious feeling differed from the Greek. Since American life tended to emphasize the ex-ploitation of nature to an extent that seemed almost inhuman to Europeans, American religiosity was bound to emphasize the polar opposite by way of compensation. From the early Puritans who believed that God's will was written in the language of earthly success to the twentieth-century churches run like business corporations, the emphasis on material rewards tended to find a compensation in an exaggerated emphasis of strictly abstract principles, as seen in Chris-tian Science's concentration on Mind as opposed to Matter, or the revival of Platonic idealism by men like William Ellery Channing.

American was distinguished from European Christianity in other ways. Primitive influences filtered in, usually unnoticed, from American Indian shamanism, African witch-doctoring, and other sources. Christian Science was a rebirth of primitive magic on a higher and more technical level, an exorcistic form of mental healing that dismissed the demons of illness. The Rollers and similar sects reproduced old tribal ceremonies with their paraphernalia of incantations and hypnotic spells. And in the Classical world, it was not in Athens, Sparta, Thebes, or Corinth that one found the most incredible excesses of religiosity but in hardheaded Rome. Her hospitality to the most absurd forms of religious fantasy became proverbial—a reputation matched in our century by California's similar cordiality to a jungle of pseudo-Oriental creeds and cults.

Nevertheless, to this day and in spite of seeming evidence to the contrary, religious feeling is more intense in America than it is in Europe—as it was in Rome as against Greece. It is easy to discover the reason. In the Roman and American religiosity, one can find an extreme tension between a ruthless materialism and an ethereal idealism. The psychological pendulum swings wildly from one extreme to another. In Greece and Europe, on the other hand, one finds an intermediary stage between materialism and spiritualism, suffused with mild skepticism. The opposition is fundamental. This Greek and European skepticism had a compensation that was largely denied to Rome and America and could substitute up to a point for religion. It had a Culture in which true religious feeling could find an outlet—in poetry, art, even scientific speculation. In Rome and America, lands of developing Civilization without profound cultural life, there was no such outlet and religious feeling had to express itself through purely religious channels.

Democracy was becoming the basis of America's faith in her destiny. Yet the rise of democracy in America was as conservative as it was in Rome, a conservatism that always baffled the impatient Europeans who, in their smaller and more homogeneous states, were able to carry out revolutionary policies in a short space of time. Nothing of the kind was possible in America because of her gigantic size, the unquestionable necessity of working out compromises; and with the steady decline of the ruling gentry, went the rise of the equally conservative lawyer class. From now on, for all her democratic realities and ideals, America was to become the reluctant champion of true social conservatism, of slow, methodical, "Roman" evolution which refuses to break sharply with the past. This occurred while Europe's old societies were gradually getting up steam for formidable wars and revolutions.

The turning point was James Monroe's Presidency and the end of the "Virginia Dynasty." Monroe was a figure of transition, an aristocrat, but also the first professional politician. The national consolidation following the Revolution had been due to a remarkable combination of New England idealism, practical training in self-government, and Virginian aristocratic leadership. Members of the Virginia Dynasty which ruled until 1824 (Jefferson, Madison, and Monroe were granted two terms each) were nominated with the approval of the oligarchic Congressional caucus. All this was now coming to an end.

Except in foreign affairs, James Monroe was not a strong President, and Congress, quite naturally, made a new bid for political leadership. Jefferson's magic ability had devised the caucus to extend Executive power down to Congress. But now, the legislative branch was going to attempt to reverse the process and use the caucus in order to overpower the Executive. Since the Federalist party had collapsed, there was no organized opposition, no restraining discipline, no constructive criticism. There was nothing but personal ambition, envy, greed, and irresponsibility. Individual craftiness, corruption, and intrigue flooded Washington. There was no party structure to unite the opposition, canalize the claims, soothe the discontented, put down extremism, bring perfectionists to a sense of proportion, work out suitable compromises, and devise a consistent policy. There was nothing but paralyzing chaos. The need for a rebirth of the two-party system became glaring. It was obvious that the freedom from party spirit which the Founding Fathers had advocated was lethal, but it took some time to make this truth plain.

The steady increase in governmental impotence made the need for a disciplined and organized opposition more urgent. Realists are always willing to combine with others and compromise for the sake of obtaining power. This automatically puts the extremists out of the federal picture, relegating them down to state or county level where they are relatively harmless. The higher the politician rises on the political ladder, the greater the need for diplomatic tact, for a plastic mind, for an ability to compromise skillfully. Political parties established the needed hierarchy through which alone the countless, conflicting, parochial extremisms could be filtered, rid of their destructive implications, gradually worked into a constructive pattern on the national scale and cemented into a consistent, practical policy. Henry Clay, an outstanding speaker of the House, explained later: "All legislation, all government, all society is founded upon the principle of mutual concession, politeness, comity, courtesy; upon these, everything is based. . . . Let him who elevates himself above humanity, above its weaknesses, its infirmities, its wants, its necessities, say, if he pleases, I will never compromise; but let no one who is not above the frailties of our common nature disdain compromise." [5]

One of the noteworthy ironies of American history is that constitutional collapse was averted at the end of Monroe's eight years in office by the rebirth of an organized opposition party under the leadership of Andrew Jackson, the very same man who had previously asked Monroe "to exterminate the monster called party spirit." [6] Those who organized the party were no idealists. They had no plan, no doctrine, and no policy. They felt by instinct that union is strength and they banded together to put themselves into office. They saw what political organization could do on the local level and they also saw that the days of oligarchic rule by the gentry were over. The ruling class was losing touch with a vastly expanding electorate and had no control over the rising democratic West.

A last attempt to rule without political parties was carried out by John Quincy Adams and it led to a frustrating deadlock. The great bitterness provoked by his unsavory election, the flaring up of personal hatreds which were to poison American politics for a generation, all prompted the defeated Andrew Jackson to build a political machine in the spring of 1825. The electorate had tremendously increased since Jefferson's days. The fast-rising population and the gradual extension of electoral franchise by wiping out property qualifications had multiplied it to a staggering extent. Maryland, Connecticut, New York, and Massachusetts had joined the new western states in coming close to white adult male suffrage. Popular elections without voting qualifications had been adopted far more readily in states such as Wisconsin, Mississippi, and Illinois than in the East, still influenced by its ruling gentry.

Democracy was on the march and Jackson's new political machine began to organize this immense human raw material. With the defeat of Adams in 1828, one era of American history came to an end—the era of oligarchic rule.

| CHAPTER XI | *Jackson and the New Presidency* |

THE election of Andrew Jackson had a profound significance. For some time already, the state legislatures had been gradually forgoing their privilege of appointing the presidential electors themselves and had handed them to the popular vote. By 1832, all states save one had adopted this new method. This, plus the vastly expanding electorate, was swiftly changing the whole scope of the Presidency and transforming it into a new institution. The President was becoming a tribune of the people and as such, his already great constitutional powers and privileges were going to be considerably augmented and completely metamorphized. This evolution had been gradual, but it found its dramatic expression in the Jacksonian revolution. A rising democracy was to demand a strong Executive as the living expression of the popular will against the vested and sectional interests represented in the legislatures and Congress. The new Democratic political machine crystallized this rising feeling, injected party discipline and mass propaganda into the electoral campaigns, and at the same time brought to a pitch of perfection the spoils system— federal and state patronage being the bounties that were to reward party discipline and obedience.

A new look at Roman history will help us understand the full meaning of the Jacksonian revolution and the introduction of the new Presidency. From the creation of the Tribunate to the fateful Hortensian Law of 287 B.C., democracy had progressed with the growth and expansion of Rome. But with the Hortensian Law, this constitutional process came to an end and the plebs in Rome disappeared as a separate entity [1]—which meant that the old traditional aristocracy lost the last shreds of its legal powers and privileges, as it did in America in the days of Andrew Jackson. And it is with the Hortensian Law that the Roman Tribune lost his wholly negative role as mere protector of the people and acquired an entirely new, positive character. He became the most powerful figure, the dynamic representative of the people against vested interests, powerful enough to arrest censors and consuls in the second century B.C., the real depositary of popular sovereignty, the concrete embodiment of the will of the people.

Since the Tribunate had become the most powerful office in Rome as in America, the struggle was on to capture it—a struggle between the democrats and the new oligarchy of wealth that was substituting for the vanishing gentry. It could be captured by the business and financial oligarchy, as it was in Rome after the Second Punic War, or in America after the Civil War, or recaptured by the Democrats as it was under the Gracchi in Rome and under Wilson and Franklin Roosevelt in America. It had become the supreme political prize. It was as inviolable Tribunes that the Gracchi started their social revolution. The sacred character of Tribune was a greater asset to Julius Caesar even than his legions and it was on the Tribunician office that Augustus eventually established the imperial dignity.[2] Tacitus saw long ago that the source of the Roman emperors' power lay in the tribunician office, which entailed inviolability, the right of summoning the Senate and directing its debates, nominating candidates, vetoing the acts of all magistrates and, indirectly, controlling the judiciary. The seeds of Caesarism lay buried for a long time in the tribunician office before they burst forth in the open.

Thus the rise of democracy in Rome and America produced simultaneously the rise of strong executive power—far stronger in America because the one single office which was raised above all others became merged in this modern form of one-man tribunate. With it begins the tension between democratic political parties in place of the former social tension between gentry and people. It was in those days that parties really started on a massive scale with all their trappings —machines, bosses, Rome's *hetaeriae* (political clubs), the spoils system, and patronage. From then on, revolutionary class struggle in the old Culture-sense, such as still went on in Greece and Europe, disappears. In the new lands dedicated unconsciously to the building of a Civilization, the old constitutional struggle between patricians and plebeians, gentry and people, comes to an end whereas it rages on more fiercely than ever in Greece and Europe, the old homesteads of Culture. The struggle is transferred to mass political parties and it becomes increasingly the struggle of people against *Big Money,* liberals against conservatives. In America it was Democrats against National Whigs (later Republicans); in Rome it was Populares versus Optimates. Public offices no longer belong to traditional ruling classes but to contending parties who use them as spoils of victory at the polls.

Even in strongly aristocratic Britain, the same evolution took place around 1830. The ruling cliques' Whigs and Tories became Liberals and Conservatives. Elections became a business like any other business.

The declining aristocracy was gradually replaced or absorbed by a new upper class based exclusively on wealth and which no longer aspired to be a ruling class. The enduring traditions of England's aristocracy in its full splendor were able to mask this transformation in Britain. But in America, the contrast was stark. Against the elusive and tentacular power of money, no longer controlled by traditional ethics, the powerless people appeal to their elected tribunes and the road to Caesarism is open. The stage was especially well prepared in America because the President attracted from the days of Jackson onward a personal following which often cut across party lines—American parties being vast and often discordant agglomerations of private and regional interests. The evolution toward Caesarism—from "ideas" and programs to "men"—from Populares and Optimates to Caesarians and Pompeians—was remarkably smoothed by America's political institutions and the practical, untheoretical temper of the American people. The soulless party machinery tends to become the tool of the powerful tribune rather than an autonomous organism in its own right. Rome saw also the same birth of caucuses, Tammany Halls, election committees ruling wards and precincts, buying and controlling masses of votes, manipulating elections, and so on. The belief in programs slowly disappeared until the electoral masses put all their trust and confidence in specific men rather than abstract theories and plans.

Thus, as President, Andrew Jackson was the first popular hero in American history who was truly loved and who had the ability to stir up deep emotions in the people. The great men of the Revolution were admired and revered as iron-willed Roman Senators used to be, who placed duty and patriotism and public service above all personal considerations. Washington inspired awe, Hamilton admiration, and Jefferson both. But with Jackson, mass emotionalism began to play a preponderant part in American politics. As a contemporary Senator put it: "The people believed in general Jackson as the Turks in their prophet." [3] With Jackson, democracy put an end to the oligarchic rule of a respected gentry and in the process revolutionized the Presidency itself.

Andrew Jackson—"King Andrew" to his enemies—knew exactly where he stood. He told the Senate that the President alone is "the direct representative of the people, and responsible to them," the Senate itself being "a body not directly amenable to the people." [4] Until then, in forty years of American political life, only nine bills had been vetoed by the Executive. Jackson alone vetoed twelve—and thus started the steady rise of executive pressure on the legislative branch, the transformation of the negative veto into a positive force at the Executive's disposal, until the days when Franklin Roosevelt would veto 631 acts of Congress. The Senate protested vehemently and Henry Clay could rightly point out: "Really and in practice, the veto power drew after it the power of initiating laws, and in its effects must ultimately amount to conferring on the executive the entire legislative power of the government. With the power to initiate and the power to consummate legislation, to give vitality and vigor to every law, or to strike it dead at his pleasure, the President must ultimately become the ruler of the nation." And he added: "The government will have been transformed into an elective monarchy." [5] The Senate mourned its diminished stature but the House lost even more power and prestige. The democratic revolution had considerably damaged the practice of representative government, but it was the inevitable counterpart of the changing social and psychological landscape.

In addition, it was obvious that the obligation for Congressmen to be residents of their states and even districts destroyed all possibility for Congress to represent collectively the American nation. It became an assembly of local delegates, local ambassadors who come to terms with one another and with the nation as a whole, but whose primary duty is the defense of their particular constituents, not of the national interest. Only the President is elected by the entire nation and he alone speaks with the voice of the entire people.

"King Andrew," the tribune of the people, was often accused of being a tyrant by his rivals and opponents? The cult of Napoleon was widespread in America and the American thirst for hero worship was already marked in those days. Napoleonism somehow affected American public opinion to such an extent that an early portrait of Jackson, the victorious liberator of New Orleans, pictured him crowned with Napoleon's spit curls rather than his own bushy hair. There is no doubt that Napoleonism had a real influence in determining the political posture of strong popular leaders in America as in Europe, as Alexander the Great's impact affected not only Hellenistic statesmen but even distant Roman leaders, all the way from the censor Appius Claudius to the democratic leader and conquering general Gaius Flaminius—and the whole political history of the transition from Culture's twilight to Civilization's dawn lies in the transition from romantic Napoleonism to realistic Caesarism.

But Alexis de Tocqueville, who was a contemporary observer, and probably the most penetrating of all, remarked: "It has been imagined that General Jackson is bent on establishing a dictatorship in America, introducing a military spirit, and giving a degree of influence to the central authority that cannot but be dangerous to provincial liberty." Then he added those ominous words: "But in America the time for similar undertakings and the age for men of this kind, has not yet come." [6]

Under Washington's Presidency, there were four million people in the United States, immigration was a trickle, the Industrial Revolution had barely started, and the West was almost empty. When Jackson became President, there were twelve million people, immigration was becoming a flood, the Industrial Revolution was beginning to upset the social structure of the East, and western emigration was already leaping beyond the Mississippi. Quite naturally, the Presidency's stature rose with that of the nation. The Industrial Revolution, after having revived a dying slavery in the South, was creating the first miserable proletariat in America, with its slums, long working hours, and grinding poverty. Radicalism among the depressed classes of the East linked up automatically with democratic radicalism in the agrarian West.

Brought up as a poor man, Jackson became one of the wealthy landowners of Tennessee, the not-so-squeamish owner of hordes of slaves. But he retained, not so much democratic opinions and ideals, as democratic prejudices, directing his hatred toward Indians, Englishmen, and upper classes in general, so that it was not so much his engaging personality as his political skill that carried him to power. It was his shrewd alliance with Martin Van Buren, the first successful political boss on the national scale, that made his election a certainty. It was Van Buren who worked out all the compromises that welded the democratic West, the New York machine, the Virginia Jeffersonians, and the aristocratic planters of the Deep South into a working, disciplined political force. By building a gigantic political party, Van Buren put an end to twenty years of governmental impotence and reunited the powers that the Founding Fathers had purposely scattered. Popular interest in the presidential campaign, hitherto conducted by oligarchic gatherings, trebled the number of voters between 1824 and 1828; and from Jackson's election in 1828 onward, the presidential election came to overshadow in importance all the legislative elections put together. It did not matter that the people did not know what Jackson stood for, any more than it did at the time of Franklin Roosevelt's first election, a hundred years later. They knew or sensed that he was "the people's friend." The remnants of the hitherto ruling gentry could shiver at the prospects ahead, but there was no turning back.

The rise of the spoils system went hand in hand with the triumph of democracy. Jefferson himself had favored a limited system of that kind in order to prevent the rise of the most dangerous monster in the eyes of American liberals: a powerful bureaucracy. In spite of the Senators' cries of proscription, Van Buren's machine went into action stealthily and effectively. All decisions were made in secret; no explanations, or justifications were given for removals or appointments. Insisting on iron party discipline, he conveyed with unmistakable power that the administration could reward or punish at its own discretion.

A ticklish problem had to be solved. Since it became imperative that each party concentrate on one single candidate, how was this candidate to be chosen? The former nomination by Congressional caucuses was as discredited as the Congressional attempts to overpower the Executive. The solution was found in the Nominating Convention in 1832. Here was the supreme test and triumph of party discipline over personal jealousies and bitterness. Apparently created for the sake of free discussion, it became in reality a dramatized platform on which stood the party bosses and the supreme boss of all: the President, who could have himself renominated or virtually designate his successor. Then and there, its real purpose was to make sure that Jackson was unquestioningly obeyed by his disciplined followers; and Jackson's blunt, autocratic nature fitted this new Presidency like a custom-made glove.

The dictatorial power of a manipulated majority was nevertheless kept in check for a full century by the "two-thirds" rule, which gave a virtual veto power to the minority—only to be brushed aside at Franklin Roosevelt's request in 1936 when the potential Caesarism of the presidential office took a bold leap toward actuality. But from now on, in any case, President and party together could always dominate Congress, and never failed to do so when the President's stature was adequate. No constitutional means had been provided for the enforcement of the presidential will on a reluctant legislative branch, but the party machinery filled the gap so carefully laid out by the Founding Fathers. This gap, narrowed and covered up by the rule of an oligarchic gentry until then, had become glaringly wide after the gentry's downfall and begged to be filled. This extraconstitutional device filled it and became a sort of connective tissue that grew organically out of sheer necessity and imposed itself when it became obvious that there was no other solution. Through this connective tissue, the presidential will could flow down into Congress and manipulate it— if the will was strong enough.

How was it in Rome? A quick glance at the past shows us that the rise of political parties was as inevitable in Rome as it was in America, that it took place simultaneously with the rise of Roman democracy (second and first centuries B.C.)—but with the major difference that no single office as powerful as the American Presidency had been devised and that Roman politics were in consequence more disorderly. Optimates and Populares fought each other as America's Republicans and Democrats and Rome had her political machines, her Tammany bosses—men like Publius Cethegus who knew how to manipulate elections and made full use of caucuses, patronage, and the spoils system.[7]

The decline of the traditional ruling classes and the rise of democracy always lead to the same results. From being an art and a vocation, politics becomes a business and falls into the hands of professionals. With the rise in the standard of living, the wealthy, financial, and commercial classes look upon politics with contempt as being a "dirty" business that has to be manipulated in the interest of "clean" business. Rome in the second century B.C. and America in the nineteenth experienced this profound change in their political thinking and practice. The major difference was, of course, that Rome already had vast overseas commitments and America did not. America's relations with the world were indirectly handled by Britain, while Rome had to handle simultaneously Italy and an increasingly complex foreign policy. Britain's ruling class still performed for America the task which Rome's declining Senatorial aristocracy performed in the Classical world. It was only in the twentieth century that America's true position in the world burst out in the open after having remained concealed under the shadow of Britain's global empire.

Simultaneously, public opinion arose with the awakened interest and participation of the people in politics. It was no longer the sober, informed opinion of a small public-minded ruling elite debating wisely and acting cautiously, but a massive public opinion which swayed violently from indifference or downright apathy to extreme emotionalism, stirred by wild enthusiasm or wild fears. Public opinion made Jackson the popular hero of the day and from then onward, America experienced the recurrent phenomena of mass emotionalism raising leaders onto the presidential platform and entrusting them with such extensive powers as to make the most autocratic monarch in Europe green with envy.

By 1850, Whigs and Democrats had built up the modern party structures that still endure today, quite outside constitutional legality, with their hierarchy of conventions and parallel committees—ward, precinct, county, and state—pyramiding into national conventions whose duties are to choose leaders and platforms. Each party was not a monolithic structure, but a discordant clutter of local parochialisms and interests, conflicting and compromising for the sake of efficiency and power.

Radicalism often flourished on the local level, shedding its virulence as it went up from precinct to county to state, to become almost conservative on the federal level. Compromise is by essence conservative and compromise was the stuff of American politics. The party machines had to be repeatedly greased and oiled and repaired if they were to function efficiently and establish the indispensable liaison between President and Congress.

The contrast between the rigid discipline enforced by a party machine on the local level and its weakness on the federal was remarkable. True democracy was often flouted by the local machines run by dictatorial bosses but remained a reality on the federal level because the living politics of an isolated America without foreign commitments was local, not national. The real test was to come in the twentieth century when America emerged as the world's leading power and the need for national discipline and leadership became vital.

The main characteristic of the political machine was its nonpolitical character—nonpolitical in the sense of being primarily aimed at, not the triumph of a political doctrine or principle, but seizing power, controlling nominations and elections, distributing spoils. It is basically indifferent to politics and exists merely to gratify the feeling of power of its leaders and their taste for plunder. Until large-scale immigration came to an end in the 1920's, machines performed a useful role, alongside their discreditable activities. They gave cohesion and a semblance of organization to a fluctuating society, acted as charitable institutions, provided help and insurance as well as "Roman" circuses and festivities. They manipulated the votes of millions of ignorant immigrants as their Roman counterparts manipulated those of the vast crowds of freedmen and foreigners to whom citizenship had been granted in a hurry. In America, their power came from a certain allegiance of the bulk of the people in whom fear and gratitude were inextricably mixed. The extreme longevity of an institution such as Tammany Hall is proof that the machines fill a necessary purpose in a fluid, nomadic, and increasingly egalitarian society.

Americans, even in the days of Jackson, were eager for leadership, willing to let professionals handle their political responsibilities. The downfall of the gentry and the absence of a leisured ruling class made the rise of such professional machines inevitable.

The tragic predicament of the old-fashioned Jeffersonian liberals who still upheld states' rights was dramatically illustrated by Calhoun's vain efforts to revive a political philosophy condemned by the changing economic pattern. Jackson's Democratic party had politically centralized the administration to an unprecedented degree, without much regard for the autonomy of the states. His Whig opponents represented the growing power of an industrial capitalism uninterested in states' rights. Its growing corporations, industries, and railroads were already beginning to straddle dozens of individual states and were economically unifying the country. They thrived on harnessing the mysterious forces of nature and in the process overlapped the artificial and out-of-date boundaries of states. Wherever Calhoun and the southern ruling class looked, they could only see growing centralization and unification—political, social, and economic. The root of the problem was that, behind the defense of states' rights, lay concealed the last-ditch defense of the southern aristocracy and way of life. The increasing divorce between an industrializing North falling into the hands of Big Business and a patriarchal, agricultural South with its old-fashioned code of ethics, was threatening to tear the nation apart.

Thus it was that, whereas in the old days the conservative gentry wanted a strong central government, the aristocratic South now wanted to preserve states' rights. In the days of the Revolution, radicals and liberals fought for those states' rights because they believed that democracy was more effective on the local than on the national scale. They wanted a decentralized agrarian democracy, and therefore a weak central government. The overwhelming majority of the population was made up of farmers who believed that they could control the states but not a distant federal government. On the other hand, centralization was favored by the gentry and the wealthy because a strong central government would stabilize currency, pay its debts, and stiffen American credit abroad.

So long as the weak Confederation survived, debtors were in control of most of the state legislatures and paid back their creditors with worthless paper money. Wherever the commercial patricians remained in control—in Massachusetts, for instance—the desperately indebted farmers faced the alternative of bankruptcy or rebellion. The new Constitution and the conservative reaction that went with it put an end to the financial chaos of the Confederation. Hamilton insisted on transferring the war debts to the federal government and on the creation of a Bank of America on the model of the Bank of England. He insisted on refunding the federal debt at par and on the imposition of import duties to provide federal revenues. In two years, America's credit was restored and was as good as gold, even though the agrarian South was victimized in the process; and the wealthy upper classes knew that their personal interests were firmly welded to the strong central government that was then in their power.

A new Bank of America was chartered in 1816 after the first one had expired and its policy of easy credit had helped the great economic development of the country. It preserved a stable currency and was, naturally enough, hated by all those debtors who suffered from the depression of 1820's. The Bank worked efficiently but was not controlled by the government. It was in the hands of the wealthy patricians who were relaxing their grip on politics. Jackson hated this independent power, but could not be blind to the other evil which it counteracted—the irresponsibility and downright dishonesty of many state banks whose notes, often worthless, were used to pay the wages of the working class.

But, by now, the political problem was reversed. The Democrats wanted a strong central government, since they had come to control it through the metamorphosis of the Presidency into a tribunate. They wanted this central government to look after the people's financial security and the independent Bank of America was blamed for the misdeeds of the local banks. Jackson went to war against the Bank of America—the first clash between the tribune and Big Money. Claiming that the Bank was unconstitutional, he vetoed a bill providing for an immediate recharter. The veto was upheld in Congress and, indirectly, by Jackson's triumphant success at the polls. Without waiting for the expiration of the old charter, Jackson took the government business away from the Bank, which retaliated by tightening credit and starting an economic depression, clumsily and unwittingly proving that its enemies were correct in trying to destroy its independent power. Jackson was not to be intimidated. Fearless and ruthless, he forced the Bank to give up the struggle. In the meantime the state banks had run riot and uncontrollable inflation swept the country, a situation not improved by the destruction of the Bank of America and by Jackson's decision to distribute its deposits to the irresponsible state banks.

Eventually, over the loud protests of the conservatives, Van Buren promoted the creation of an independent Treasury without any ties with the banks, an autonomous organism in which the federal government would store its deposits and against which it would issue its own currency. Americans found it difficult to combine private and public interest as the British did so skillfully with the Bank of England. Their rising democracy demanded a government-controlled financial apparatus without capitalist participation. But, the fight having been won, the victorious Jackson became a convert to a hard-money policy and in so doing found that his main support switched to the commercial and industrial North and East, and that he lost the expanding West where inflation was popular, as it always is with debtors.

Thus Jackson undermined his own Jacksonian democracy. Subsequent events transformed this undermining into a complete collapse. A momentous alteration in the internal balance of power began to take place, culminating in the fifties. The problem of the disposal of the public domain in the West was the spark. The South, long an advocate of free land for the pioneering settlers, now turned against this policy because it favored the small independent farmer at the expense of the large landowning planter—and the South was now politically dominated by the aristocratic ruling class. The old Jacksonian alliance between South and West, already battered by his hard-money policy, broke up completely. Jackson's successors could not make up for it in the business-minded North. The slavery issue was coming to the fore and tempers flared. Gradually, a new coalition was formed when the North shrewdly altered its own attitude and adopted the free-land policy in exchange for western support for its main concern: high tariffs.

The South was now isolated. Another profound alteration was taking place which cemented this new North-West alliance: the growth of railroads cutting across the normal North-South lines of communication. In the 1850's, federal land grants and the flood of immigrant labor helped the fantastic boom in railroad construction. However, most lines went east-west, not north-south. The channels of trade and communications followed the parallels, no longer the meridians. The main fault lay in the South's failure to industrialize and throw its own railroads up north fast enough to retain its grasp on the slipping West; and this lack of economic progress was primarily due to the lethal influence of slavery. As it was, by the time the Civil War broke out, the North and West were firmly welded, with good communications and a rising industrial power amounting to 92 per cent of the national capacity, leaving the South way behind in its feudal agrarianism.

The Jacksonian revolution consolidated the simultaneous rise of democracy and tribunician-presidential power. Its democratic element was partly abortive, in the sense that it was merely a prelude to the rule of Big Business. It had destroyed the rule of the old gentry, only to let it fall later into the hands of a new and exclusively financial plutocracy. Several generations would have to go by before there was democratic progress in the field of economics. But Andrew Jackson left a legacy: the notion of a democratic, popular, and powerful Executive who could, if he wanted to, dominate Big Business and overpower economic oligarchy and financial privilege. In his days, the issue was not yet clear cut. The gentry was not wholly done with, Business was still a fledgling and the South was still dominated by its aristocracy. Those obstacles had to be swept away by the Civil War before the naked power of Big Business came into its own—as it did in Rome after the democratic Hortensian Law and the Second Punic War. But from now on, popular attention focused on the new Presidency as the champion of democracy and social equality.

The
Civil War

FROM 1840 onward, the vast increase in presidential power and prestige was curbed by the only device left at the disposal of oligarchies and vested interests: the election of obscure men who could be manipulated by the political machines. It took wars and economic depressions to break down the systematic endeavor of the politicians to put the lid on the tribune of the people. In normal circumstances, there was no great need for Executive initiative and the isolated United States could afford a minimum of centralization. But in times of crisis, with the election of military heroes or great personalities, there were next to no limits to the overriding power of the Executive. As Lincoln's Secretary of State said to a British correspondent: "We elect a king for four years, and give him absolute powers within certain limits, which after all he can interpret for himself." [1]

A short-lived attempt by Webster and Clay to restore to Congress the power and authority which had been absorbed by the Jacksonian Presidency failed through the untimely death of President Harrison. His successor's inaugural address comforted them for a while: "In view of the fact, well attested by history, that the tendency of all human institutions is to concentrate power in the hands of a single man, and that their ultimate downfall has proceeded from this cause, I deem it of the most essential importance that a complete separation should take place between the sword and the purse." [2] But Tyler's subsequent actions did not quite follow his speech. Tyler was a southern gentleman who believed in weakening the federal government in favor of the states, not the executive power in favor of the legislative. He refused to follow Clay and wrecked the newborn Whig party by seeking support among the old Jacksonians; and Clay's furor found no echo in a country that obviously enjoyed being firmly ruled and had other causes of anxiety.

Those causes lay in the gradual disruption of the political organization that alone could close the widening gap between the South and the North-West coalition. Jacksonian democracy died in 1844. The huge party machinery and its farmer-laborer following were captured by the southern slave-owning planters and made to serve the last aristocratic attempt to seize power in Washington. Almost simultaneously, the Whig banking and business party was made a shambles by Tyler.[3] The Whig planters of the South returned to a Democratic party that was purged of its western Jacksonian radicals. Calhoun was able to convince the southern aristocracy that it had to capture the Democratic party in order to defend itself on the federal and national level against its most insidious enemy: northern industrial business. The South had become more united and determined than it ever was in the past, more wealthy and powerful with the development of the Southwest, more aristocratic with the growth of the planter ruling class and the rising value of slaves. Slavery was in fact becoming the paramount issue, even for the majority of the southerners who owned no slaves but feared the economic competition of black labor if slavery were to be abolished.

The real social problems resulting from the expanding industrialization of the North made northerners more anxious to find an outlet for their pent-up tensions at the expense of southern slavery. Life was wretched for the northern industrial worker, especially in times of depression. The injection of moral principles into the already serious economic problem of slavery aroused tempers and passions that should have been left dormant, and overshadowed for a time America's great political asset: the spirit of compromise. Sooner or later, politics would have to give way to arms. Between two societies drifting apart, between northern industrial democracy and southern slave-owning aristocracy, war became inevitable.

√ The Civil War decided once and for all that America was not a federation of sovereign states but a united nation\ Except in the South, national feeling had been growing everywhere at the expense of state loyalty. There were many reasons for this alteration in public feeling. Progress in transportation and industrialization was unifying the country at a fast, almost dismaying pace, uprooting populations, increasing their already well-developed nomadic instincts. Millions of immigrants were pouring into the eastern harbors, bent on becoming Americans as opposed to Europeans, not on becoming New Yorkers or Pennsylvanians. The feeling that the national will should prevail against states' rights was growing apace. The concept of the autonomy of the individual states was weakened for the majority of the American people long before the Civil War shattered it.

ᴵThe outbreak of the war was preceded by a collapse of the party system in the 1850'sᴵ The slavery issue could not have disrupted the Union if it had not smashed the unifying Democratic party beforehand. It was in party conventions and nowhere else that the basic issue, war or compromise, was settled. As a Mississippi delegate said: "We are for principles, damn the party," which meant virtually "damn the Union." [4] Whenever one or the other of America's two major parties decided to adhere to hard and fast principles, the breakup of the vast Union was predictable; and this collapse was accelerated by the succession of weak and ineffective Presidents—Pierce, Buchanan —who no longer knew how to instill the feeling of party loyalty and impose discipline on their followers.

The result of the Democratic party's collapse and of the Whig's breakdown was the rise of the new Republican party, a crystallization of industrial capitalist philosophy and Puritan moralism which grew up in those days of executive weakness. The new party combined railroad potentates, northern protectionists, western homesteaders, and abolitionists. Furthermore, America was beginning to experience a substantial amount of literary production. The popular writers of the time seized the slavery issue with considerable eagerness and put it in a moral, idealistic context. The ill-fated John Brown was praised as a "saint" by Emerson, and as an "angel of light" by Thoreau.[5] This intervention of idealistic, uncompromising intellectuals inflamed a public opinion already sufficiently aroused and stiffened southern opposition to any concession of the issue of states' rights.

This intellectual movement sprang up in the New England of the 1820's and found its ideological roots in a rebirth of Puritan moralism. Puritanism had been partly overshadowed by strict Calvinism early in the eighteenth century, then by the optimism of the Age of Enlightenment. Its rebirth with Channing and Webster produced in Emerson a strange blend called Transcendentalism, a romantic adaptation and popularization of Kant's philosophy combined with a semi-mystical introspection, a reaction against American Protestantism's vigorous emphasis on action and good works. Emerson was conscious of America's cultural poverty and her exaggerated reliance on imitations of European models, and attempted to counteract this imitative dependence. Cato deplored Rome's dependence on Greek culture in almost the same terms.

Emerson's appeal for cultural independence had hardly any more success than Cato's in Rome, and this for profound historical reasons. New England did have what Santayana called an "Indian summer of the mind" but it came to an end fairly soon; it was a "moonlight" reflection of Europe's last brilliant upsurge of literary and philosophic culture. New England's narrow, bloodless intellectualism was quickly smothered in the prevailing Puritan atmosphere: ". . . it was all a harvest of leaves; these worthies had an expurgated and barren conception of life; theirs was the purity of sweet old age." [6] Emerson's own philosophy of contrast attempted in vain to escape from these limitations by proclaiming that man's value lies in his nonconformity—at a time when psychological conformity was slowly becoming the typical trait of America's expanding democracy.

A share of the blame for this failure to develop an autonomous culture must be attributed to an old and enduring trait of American psychology: its fundamental anti-intellectualism, its profound distrust of needless abstractions, philosophies, and doctrines in which the more unstable Europeans had been indulging but without which there can be no true culture. In the old Revolutionary days, John Adams had already been the articulate spokesman for this distrust when he claimed: "We have too many French philosophers already, and I really begin to think, or rather to suspect, that learned academies . . . have disorganized the world, and are incompatible with social order." [7] True Civilization Men are bound to be distrustful of all intellectual work which is not clearly aimed at the social good; and just as the example of the disorders which were tearing the Greek world apart filled the Romans with apprehensive distrust of intellectuals, the wars and revolutions of Europe seemed to the Americans to be the direct outcome of too much speculative thought.

If there could have been a genuinely original culture in North America, it was in the South and especially in Virginia, not in New England, that it could have developed—in the Cavalier atmosphere where business and money were relegated to the background, where the emphasis was placed on man's original individuality rather than his social function, where the atmosphere was still aristocratic and freed from the thwarting conformism that democracy's social equality was spreading all over the rest of the Union. As it was, nothing developed in a South whose atmosphere was poisoned by the slavery problem and by tortured intellectual justifications for the existence of an outdated institution.

If anything, Abraham Lincoln's imperishable greatness came from the fact that he was never carried away by the abolitionist fever, that his cool judgment clung steadfastly to the cardinal virtue of American political life: moderation and conciliation. His nomination was not in itself the signal for the war he had worked hard to avoid. The die was cast by then, and only strength could decide the issue although even Lincoln did not fully realize this on the eve of his election.

On the political level, the Civil War was largely the outcome of executive weakness and, as was only natural, the Executive came out of the ordeal more powerful than ever. Wise and cautious, yet able to shoulder crushing responsibilities without flinching, Lincoln built up from the very first, through his patronage policy, the federal structure of his party at the expense of local and state organizations. The new party structure set the pattern for the new Union of the future. The Civil War produced a new nation over the ruins of the old federation, a far more centralized Union—and most of the increase in central power devolved upon the Presidency. Lincoln brought to full maturity the immense potentialities built up by his predecessors in the White House and added more of his own. Yet, Lincoln himself was tormented by this inevitable growth of his own power and said mournfully: "Must a government, of necessity, be too strong for the liberties of its own people, or too weak to maintain its own existence?" [8]

Lincoln was no vague idealist but a stern and often humorous realist who had an acute perception of the relative strength and weaknesses of the conflicting parties. He was no abolitionist although he hated slavery. He knew that century-old customs and traditions could not be brushed aside, that profound changes take time and have to be carefully nursed along. He never embarked on a course of action without having weighed all possible consequences and always took a long-range view of things. He was tolerant, yet inflexible when he had decided on a definite policy. He had no personal vanity and the hard life of his pioneering youth would have dispelled any illusions he might have entertained. His sunken eyes were sad with his profound knowledge of human folly. Skeptical as to human strength and virtue, he had a complete, almost fatalistic faith in the Almighty. It was this profound faith that saw him through the ordeal.

Once the war started, Lincoln was inflexibly determined to win it by any and every means available, even though he intended to be generous and forgiving after the war was over. Unsure of his Union party's standing with northern voters, he even went so far as to condone fraudulent elections in 1864 in order to insure his retention of power. He condoned unconstitutional pressure on the wavering border states. He shouldered immense responsibilities alone during the hostilities, made all the basic military decisions as Commander in Chief. He suspended the writ of habeas corpus over the protests of the Chief Justice, asked for troops without legal authority, started the war before calling Congress in 1861, built a national army instead of relying on local militias, issued his Emancipation Proclamations in 1862 and 1863 without previous legislative sanction, indeed without even consulting his cabinet.[9] Never in American history had so much power been concentrated in the hands of one man. In stark contrast, power was so diffused in the aristocratic South that southern political leadership was almost unconsciously guiding its followers toward a parliamentary regime.

When Lincoln condoned frauds and illegal pressures, he went far beyond any powers which accrued to him in an emergency and created a highly dangerous precedent—dangerous because of the extreme greatness of his personality and the reverence with which posterity will always look upon him. "The Union with him, in sentiment, rose to the sublimity of religious mysticism," said his enemy Alexander Stephens.[10] And so it did. His virtual dictatorship was based on a sober but ruthless idealism which, once in action, stops at nothing. But in the precedent he established, many strong men of the future can find almost any justification for assuming unlimited power and adopting unscrupulous means to reach an idealistic end.

The Civil War destroyed the last remnants of aristocratic rule and way of life in America—and was instinctively understood in this sense by the entire English-speaking world. Britain, the greatest world power in those days, viewed the whole struggle with mixed feelings. The rising strength of Britain's incipient democracy, her working classes and intellectual socialists, gave a ringing endorsement to the North even though they were the main victims of the hardships provoked by the blockade of southern cotton. The workingmen of Manchester asked Lincoln "for your honor and welfare, not to faint in your providential mission. While your enthusiasm is aflame, and the tide of events runs high, let the work be finished effectually. . . . We are truly one people, though locally separate." [11] The American Civil War was the tail end of the two-century-old struggle between Puritan Roundheads and aristocratic Cavaliers—who had successfully merged in Britain, but had remained geographically separate in America.

One half of the British soul perceived that its own social struggle was being enacted on American soil and that America's internal evolution would have repercussions in Britain for generations to come. The southern gentleman was a cousin of the British landowning aristocrat who could feel that his own predominant position in England was threatened by his cousin's downfall. The other half of the British soul mirrored, as we know, the wishful thinking of a Europe that had become alarmed at the rapid growth of the American giant and was hoping that the break-up of the Union would become permanent.

The South that went down in the Civil War had many faults—the greatest and most unforgivable of which was that it was simply no longer in tune with the times. It was anachronistic. But the South also had a good many virtues that might have been preserved if the North had proved more generous and understanding. The southern gentleman, stubborn on the slavery issue, was remarkably more tolerant and liberal than the narrow-minded Yankee business leaders. Southerners were, for instance, far more hospitable to Jews and the only Jewish members of the United States Senate came from the South— Judas P. Benjamin of Louisiana, and David Levy Yulee of Florida. Many Jews fought valiantly in the Confederate army. This liberalism was largely the attitude of self-confident aristocrats who did not have to bow to the pressure of democratic public opinion with its erratic fanaticism, conformity, taboos, and prejudices. Only one southerner in ten owned slaves and most of the slaves were held by a small group of a few thousand wealthy planters who perpetuated the manners and traditions of the Virginian Founding Fathers, the aristocratic gentlemen whose remarkable qualities had made America's independence possible.

It was a feudal way of life that was destroyed by the Civil War, with its good and its bad side, its lords living in their "Plantation Greek" mansions, in their rice, sugar, and cotton palaces overlooking the Mississippi. It is quite certain that it was not an economically sound structure and that it was financially inefficient. It was a way of life, not a road to wealth. The South was static and did not believe in democracy. General education was poor but the universities for the social elite were splendid. Potentially, the South was "cultured" rather than "civilized."

American slavery had to give way as it had everywhere else in the world—to give way socially to a temporary caste system, economically to the great new forces of nature which the Industrial Revolution had conjured up and mastered. Man-fuel had to be replaced by coal and oil-fuel, human muscles by mechanical gadgets. Since slaves were not "persons" but "things," according to southern legal thinking, this substitution was merely an economic improvement that Classical Civilization had never been able to work out because it could never devise the technical means to do so.

When John Wilkes Booth murdered Lincoln he was merely re-enacting once again, but in real life this time, the theatrical role of Brutus. Like the Roman aristocrat, he wanted to kill the democratic Caesar who had destroyed the chivalrous South. Caesar's death plunged the Roman world in chaos for another decade, leading to the slaughters of the Proscriptions and the liquidation of the Roman aristocracy at Philippi, while Lincoln's death was a disaster for the South. Lincoln knew well and feared his own radicals, feared the demagogic passions of legislative assemblies unrestrained by a strong Executive. At his last cabinet meeting Lincoln said that he "thought it providential that this great rebellion was crushed just as Congress had adjourned and there were none of the disturbing elements of that body to hinder and embarrass us. If we were wise and discreet, we should reanimate the states and get their governments in successful operation, with order prevailing and the union reestablished before

Congress came together in December." [12] Lincoln was prepared to use his dictatorial powers to put an end to bitterness and crush the spirit of vengeance before more harm was done. By his death the South lost its best friend and paved the way for the rise to power of the northern radicals.

CHAPTER XIII

The New Union

THE South came out of the war largely ruined, a quarter of its productive white men killed or out of action, its small industrial establishment a shambles, its territory devastated. The world had to wait until the following century to see any greater destruction and demoralization. The North, on the contrary, came out more prosperous and powerful than ever, its economy greatly stimulated by war contracts, its losses in men well compensated by an immigration that was never interrupted. Industry and agriculture prospered to an unprecedented degree. But labor benefited little because of inflation and war taxes. Contract labor was declared legal and businessmen were entitled to hire cheap labor in Europe, thus underselling the higher priced American workers. Yet those very same capitalists insisted on being protected from foreign competition by high tariffs. Free enterprise, as understood by the businessmen of those days, was a one-way process.

The southern aristocracy had gone the way of the rest of America's old gentry. The rule of Money was now firmly established in conjunction with a victorious democracy, and Big Business rose to social and financial supremacy. Social unrest could always be avoided, thanks to the expanding West and the unlimited opportunities for all the enterprising laborers who were willing to face the hardships and risks of the frontier. Those who did not have the courage and energy to do so were not likely to muster those qualities to start social unrest in the East. There was and could be no opposition to the protean capitalist power, anonymous, fluid, penetrating, totally amoral, and always expanding. This power seized Washington, dominated it, and eliminated all rivals, letting politicians do as they pleased so long as they did not thwart Business—and while it dominated Washington, it also set up its own financial capital in Wall Street. The relative financial autonomy of the states was ended by the Currency Acts of 1863 and 1864, centralizing financial power in New York.

❧It is only after the Civil War that the full effect of the Industrial Revolution was felt in America.❡Delayed until then by lack of capital and the controversies that led to Civil War, it seized a united, powerful America that was fast catching up with Britain, covered her with steel, extracted her minerals, bathed her in oil. America had vast spaces, immense natural resources, fast-increasing manpower.❡ She seemed to have been selected by nature herself to become the most successful exponent of the dawning Industrial Age. ❧

A great deal of America's swift adaptation to the new age was due to various traits of her psychology—the inherited Puritan emphasis on will power and the application of that will to the process of transforming human beings through a voluntary surrender of excessive individualism. Technological progress was considerably helped by the American tendency to look upon human beings as machines; in fact, the assimilation of human traits to the workings of machinery indicates a tendency toward psychological mechanization, and this is reflected in the political, social, and economic life of America. This in turn tended to stifle the full development of the human personality and thwart true creativity. But original ideas could always be imported from Europe along with the immigrants and investment capital. Skillful adaptation and efficient mass production could multiply their effectiveness millions of times.

As industrialization developed, man soon became a mere adjunct to the machine, a part of the whole mechanism, indispensable to the extent that no piece of machinery could as yet replace him. In a sense, the remarkable technological power of America was created at the expense of the mechanized human being who remained psychologically undeveloped, robot-like. Having atomized man's productive capacity, analyzed in great detail his minutest reflexes and gestures, and having found gadgets to duplicate them, Americans then proceeded to treat intellectual knowledge in the same way, breaking it up into separate, disconnected fragments. Americans were taught increasingly to live in a world of encapsulated facts, rather than ideas. And this, in turn, was nothing more than the extreme development of the atomistic explosion which had started with the Reformation itself.

American efficiency was already famous before the Civil War and more than one European traveler expressed his admiration at the way in which large armies were trained and equipped in a minimum amount of time and maintained in the field for relatively long periods. Such efficiency borrowed a great deal from this fragmentation of knowledge and its resulting specialization, and was able to organize the entire American economy into an effective machinery of gigantic dimensions demanding a minimum of effort on the part of the individual.

The overpowering character of America's economic development after the Civil War was bound to enhance all those psychological traits which fit into an industrial society. Americans were thus tempted to reduce all psychological, economic, social, and political problems to the level of strictly mechanical questions. Europeans, with their mental background of historical Time, think largely in biological terms of *organic* development. Americans, with their background of apparently limitless Space which was being effectively tamed, began to think increasingly in *mechanical* terms. The salutary compensation was that in their actual historical development—in law, politics, and social relations—the Americans remained pragmatic, "time" conscious, careful to help the organic growth of their institutions instead of rebelling against the "time" element as did the European radicals or reactionaries who attempted to uproot historical growth.

It became obvious after the Civil War that the old America with her small-scale manufacturers and majority of small farmers was gone forever. A giant made of steel, steam, and oil was rising instead, drawing into its expanding cities millions of immigrants and native farmers, uprooting entire rural populations, and spreading tentacles over the entire continent. The typical American tendency toward rootless nomadism was enhanced, but at the same time gave to the rising industry an extremely adaptable supply of skilled labor; and the huge continental market accelerated the increasing specialization that was soon to overtake and surpass Europe's. The American farmer and log-cabin pioneer had never been a peasant, anyway. He was a transient, a would-be city dweller whose opportunity came with the Industrial Revolution and the fabulous mushrooming of cities all over the continent.

To a political centralization which resulted from the war itself, the rising industrial empire was adding its own centralized structure with its gigantic corporations and railroads straddling dozens of states, controlling many of them as so many departments of their business undertakings.

This Industrial Revolution is outwardly one of the basic differences between our modern world and its Classical counterpart. But it is largely a difference in size and scope. All the profoundly significant parallels that can be drawn between their cultural, social, and political evolutions are still valid. Rome, too, experienced a rudimentary Industrial Revolution in the second century B.C. In ancient Italy, between the seventh and third centuries B.C., the peasant and town-dweller were economically self-sufficient. However, industrialization and the rise of a Classical world economy gradually broke down this family autarchy through the agency of what could be called at least an economic revolution. Industrialization and mass production started in the new lands of the north. From Vercelli to Milan, Rimini, and Modena highly skilled artisans specialized in lamps and pottery; in Verona and Padua rugs and carpets were mass produced; the increasing proletariat of Parma and Modena found employment in textile plants; the shrewd industrialists of Genoa worked timber and hides. Gradually, technical progress sprouted industries all over Italy. Mines began to be efficiently exploited. The iron of Elba generated a hardware industry (swords, helmets, nails, screws). Specialization increased apace, feeding on an expanding market that linked the minerals of Spain to the cereals of Egypt. Every trade subdivided itself into highly skilled departments to satisfy the rising standard of living of a large segment of the population. First-century Italy was certainly as different from pre-Hannibalic Italy as twentieth-century America was different from the eighteenth-century colonies.

The Classical world experienced only an embryonic industrial revolution but underwent a complete economic revolution that created a classical world-wide economic market from the second century B.C. onward. Its impact on the political and social problems of the Classical world were not too different from the impact which our own Industrial Revolution has had and is still having on the modern world.

After four years of virtual executive dictatorship, Congress was burning with an impotent feeling of revenge. Kept in total subjection during the hostilities, unable to make policy, the legislature was determined to cancel all those changes and recapture part of its former influence. An incompetent President was all that was needed and in Andrew Johnson, Congress found its victim. Johnson was as unintelligent and tactless as he was stubborn, and from the very first, antagonized Congress by declaring emphatically: "Your President is now the Tribune of the people, and thank God I am, and intend to assert the power which the people have placed in me." [1] The clash was inevitable and the outcome predictable.

While Big Business dominated and manipulated Washington for its own specific purposes, it abandoned politics and the fate of the prostrate South to the professional politicians. Through Johnson's ineptitude, the leadership in Congress was promptly captured by the radicals, the bigoted anti-southerners who intended to keep the South as a conquered colonial area as long as they could.

The destruction of slavery had solved nothing. A great Negro leader stated after the war that the freedman was "free from the individual master but a slave of society. He had neither money, property nor friends. He was free from the old plantation, but he had nothing but the dusty road under his feet." [2] A generation later, the pattern of change became clear. Slavery had been replaced by a new caste system, the first of its type to rise on such a scale since India's, three thousand years before. Centuries before the birth of Christ, Indian Civilization had astonished the Greek ambassador Megasthenes because it knew no slavery—but the penalty was caste. So far, conflict between the widely different human races has produced either slavery, caste, or miscegenation. Having destroyed the first and refused the third, America, North as well as South, soon set up the barriers of the second solution.

Northern radicals were much too busy destroying the southern aristocracy and way of life to work effectively at rehabilitating the Negro by giving him education and financial security instead of meaningless political rights. Triumphant capitalism could persuade the federal government to grant forty million acres to one gigantic railroad but was unwilling to have it grant ten million acres to the landless freedmen of the South. Overshadowing an incompetent although well-meaning President, the radical leader Thaddeus Stevens dominated Congress with his diabolic fanaticism for the next two years. Johnson's vetoes were consistently overruled. A South that was well on the way to pacification and reconstruction was reoccupied by federal armies and its governments declared illegal when Congress reconvened in December, 1865. A new social revolution was carried out by the radicals, leaving a legacy of bitterness that was to last for generations. The carpetbaggers devastated what remained of the South and northerners took an almost sadistic pleasure in humiliating the southern "gentleman," in ridiculing his code of honor and way of life in the name of democracy.

| Then Congress turned against President Johnson, unconstitutionally deprived him of his control of the army, denied him the right to control his administration without consent of the Senate, and finally, drunk with power, voted to impeach him when he attempted to get out of this straitjacket. But this was going too far. Alarmed at last, Big Business stepped in and compelled the Senate to vote down the impeachment. The presidential form of government was saved *in extremis,* not only by this Senatorial decision but also by the appalling record of Congressional government after the Civil War. |

It was the growing power of northern money that was now dictating the economic and financial terms of southern reconstruction— a power that generations of southerners had feared. The South did not understand the intricacies of high finance and had no influence in Washington. Now the South was being enslaved—and so was the West. Short of capital, the West was becoming less an ally of the North than an economic satellite. The ruling Republican party, mouthpiece of Big Business, maintained high tariffs, subsidized the private railroads at the expense of the nation, curbed American labor by encouraging massive immigration, centralized money power in Wall Street and maintained a hard-money policy disastrous to the debt-ridden South and West. The "political" growth of the new Union was still a remarkable display of statesmanship and democratic sagacity—except in the South. The "economic" growth, however, displayed all the features of the most ruthless colonialism exercised by the North over the West and South. The rural populations as well as the urban proletariat were enslaved by money.

The splendor of Rome was erected on the backs of subjugated people. As long as there remained spoils to be had in the Classical world, Roman business leaders grabbed them—through the ruthless destruction of such commercial rivals as Carthage and Corinth, outrageous taxation and confiscation in the provinces and protectorates. Money and business dominated Rome, demoralized the remains of the aristocracy, corrupted the masses, and virtually destroyed the freeholding farmers. The same unchallenged domination of money and business was exercised in America between the Civil War and the New Deal. New York's Wall Street erected its gigantic buildings on the backs of southern and western farming populations as well as on those of immigrants and industrial workers. All this started while the South remained a conquered province at the mercy of Washington and the West was still an expanding territory ruled directly or strongly influenced by the federal government. Big Business could do as it pleased. It was the real winner of the Civil War.

General Grant's election to the White House proved an important point: professional soldiers are not the stuff that Caesars are made of. There were no professional generals in the Classical world. Caesar himself was a remarkably astute politician and statesman, a businessman and a leader of the democratic party, rather than a conquering general. Neither Washington nor Jackson had been professional soldiers in the full sense of the term. The first was a remarkable statesman, the second an unparalleled leader of men. Both had political flair. Grant had nothing of the kind. Tactless, blunt, autocratic when he had no cause to be, without psychological insight, Grant was easily maneuvered by the triumphant legislative branch. Unable to rule, Grant virtually handed his presidential prerogatives to a Congress that had become the chaotic battleground of pressure groups and special interests. Big Business pushed through the increased Tariff Act of 1870 with the assistance of its hired Senators. The true interests of the nation were ignored because the tribune of the people remained silent. Washington was slowly sinking into a swamp of corruption unmatched in earlier American history. The "Black Friday" panic of 1869 was the outstanding example of an irresponsible capitalism, risen to supreme power, pursuing its own interests at the expense of the national welfare. In the face of this degradation of the new democracy, public indifference and even cynicism stifled the voices of alarmed idealists.

Grant's attempt to secure a third term was defeated at the Republican Convention because of the widespread antagonism to this unprecedented step—not so much from fear of the establishment of an elective monarchy as from the desire of other politicians to step into the White House themselves. But while the President's power and influence were thus curbed by Congressional rule and the customary limitations imposed on his tenure of office, he could retain a far more subtle influence through his selection of the members of the Supreme Court. Chief Justice Marshall had spent his thirty-five years on the bench consolidating the Hamiltonian type of centralized government. Through his selection, John Adams had been able to outwit the Jeffersonians, extend his influence far into the future, and shape decisively the course of American history long after he had been voted out of office. The next Chief Justices, Taney and Chase, were less colorful and less determined in their political views. Lincoln's constitutional revolution was vindicated by the judiciary because five vacancies occurred during his four years in office, giving him the possibility of filling the Court with men of his own persuasion. Grant's selection of Morrison Waite as fourth Chief Justice proved that he could not even use this subtle influence and became the occasion for the first assault of Congress on the judiciary in 1869. An Amendment was almost passed which, in effect, would have pensioned off those Justices who stood in the way of Congressional will. The attempt failed but the Supreme Court shivered and took heed. Congress, dominated by the radicals, had effectively prevented the judiciary from interfering with the disastrous turn of Reconstruction in the South.

Driven to despair, meanwhile, the southern whites had turned to illegal action and open violence and nothing short of a new military regime could have curbed this revolt. Tired and disgusted with the radicals, the North eventually gave up the struggle. The retreat started in 1876 and was terminated in 1894. The embittered southern whites led by the realistic, conservative, and flamboyant "Bourbons," regained their former supremacy and substituted a full-fledged caste system for the paternalistic slavery of earlier days. Realistically taking into account northern lassitude and the need to use military strength to enforce radical laws, the Supreme Court eventually sanctioned the retreat and virtually handed back to the southern states their autonomy in all matters affecting race relations. The South, of course, was no longer what it was before the War and Reconstruction. The aristocracy had been destroyed as a ruling class and its Bourbon successors were overthrown in the 1890's. A new breed of Negro-hating demagogues rose to power on the ruins of the old social system like poisonous mushrooms, as virulent in their own way as the northern radicals had been before them. Violent radicalism always breeds as violent a counterradicalism. The main victim of all this was the Negro himself. Freed but disillusioned, many Negroes began to emigrate from the South, fostering the development of racial prejudice in the very same North and West that had clipped his chains. A similar although less stringent caste system began to develop above the Mason-Dixon line.

The disaster of Reconstruction was plainly the result of Congressional supremacy. The Executive had abdictated and, once more, Congress irrefutably proved that it was totally unable to frame an intelligent policy and carry it out consistently. Nowhere in the world was emancipation from slavery followed by such misery for the former slaves and such hatred on the part of the former owners. Slavery had been gradually abolished in the West Indies and elsewhere in a just, orderly manner, in striking contrast to the wreckage of the American South at a time of fabulous prosperity and dynamic economic development all over the world.

It was during the Civil War that the federal government exerted its influence over the economic life of the nation for the first time on such a broad scale. Wartime legislation had given direct control over the volume of currency to Washington. Private industry had been subsidized by the government through tariffs, land grants to railroads and corporations. Big Business, having captured the government and used it as a tool for its own purposes, was bound to see this build-up of governmental power strike back. When the last prewar depression came in 1857, no one expected the administration to do much about it. But the public temper had changed with the times. The capitalists manipulated Washington and when the great collapse of 1873 occurred, the public clamored for federal action. Pressure was put directly on Congress, whereas it was formerly put on the state legislatures—pressure for a cheap-money policy which would lighten the burden on debtors, pressure for public works to take care of unemployment, pressure for a moratorium. Popular anger turned against Big Business, the real master of government. The first great strikes took place between 1873 and 1877, and out of them emerged the effective but still limited and highly exclusive American Federation of Labor. The concentration and organization of labor power had been made inevitable by the rise of giant corporations and trusts.

But public outcries did not alleviate the burden put upon the working class. Labor conditions became appalling between 1870 and 1900. Social legislation that had formerly protected children was now disregarded. Most of the working families, especially those of immigrants, were housed in miserable tenements. In many respects, European social legislation was far ahead of America's, where a combination of factors—the still mobile frontier, the "rugged individualism" ideology, the absence of a permanent bureaucracy, massive immigration, and still unlimited opportunities—discouraged any such governmental action. While labor and capital were girding their loins for the great struggles to come, the debt-ridden agrarian West was vainly attempting to foster inflation. Capital was firmly in the saddle in Washington: credit remained restricted and money remained hard.

The elections of 1876 were a new turning point. Now returned to full power in the South but within the one-party framework that was to prevail for generations, the Democratic white southerners struck a bargain with the anti-Grant liberal Republicans who were sick and tired of the appalling corruption in Washington. Rutherford Hayes was elected President. According to the terms of the bargain, the southern Democrats were promised withdrawal of all northern troops and full acknowledgment of states' rights. Congressional government came to an end and the Presidency rose once more to a new crest of power. The attempt to establish a parliamentary form of government and transform the Executive into a powerless figurehead had failed. A last attempt of the Senate to brush off Hayes' cabinet appointments provoked such a fierce explosion of popular anger that the intimidated Senators yielded immediately. The people had come to the rescue of their new tribune who dared stand up against the powerful vested interests—the silver, tobacco, or railroad Senators.

Hayes had intended to reform the civil service, the first of any such attempts. But his promise to make appointments solely on the basis of ability could not be kept. The urgent requirements of politics, the paying off of electoral debts, the struggle against local bosses and machines, the obligation to strengthen the President's authority through patronage, all these factors made the continuation of the spoils system imperative. All Hayes could achieve was to recapture for the White House the vast patronage which Executive weakness had let fall in the lap of Congress. After a last skirmish against Hayes' successor, Congress surrendered.

Garfield completed Hayes' victorious struggle against the legislative branch and set up the Presidency on the high pedestal to which Lincoln had previously raised it. During the course of the conflict over presidential appointments, Garfield had to restate once more that the President alone is the tribune of the people. The Presidency "represents a whole independent function of government. The other is 1/76 of ½ of another independent branch of the government with which compound vulgar fractions the President is asked to compromise." [3]

It was under the Presidency of Chester Arthur that the first massive attack against the spoils system was launched. The rise of Washington's bureaucratic power was such that, sooner or later, new methods of recruitment would become imperative. The Pendleton Act of 1883 provided for a Civil Service Commission that was to preside over a permanent bureaucracy selected through the open competitive examinations of the merit system. Only 13 per cent of the federal offices were affected at the time, but the growth of the "classified" service—its regulation being entirely at the discretion of the President—was steadily encouraged by all the strong Presidents—Cleveland, Theodore Roosevelt, Wilson, and Franklin Roosevelt—to reach 92 per cent by the middle of the twentieth century. From 1883 onward, the spoils system on the federal level declined steadily without ever being completely abolished. The fast-expanding federal bureaucracy—rising from 3,000 in 1800 to 126,000 in the 1880's, and to more than two million in 1948—has been increasingly withdrawn from sheer politics to become the huge impersonal machinery through which executive policy is carried out and over which Congress can exercise virtually no influence.

A similar reform had been carried out quietly in Britain. The Indian Civil Service, the most remarkable institution of its kind in the world, had inspired Charles Trevelyan and William Gladstone to extend the system to the home country, recruitment being provided by similar competitive examinations. The steady rise of a "mandarin" system was unavoidable all over the Western world and it coincided with the equally steady decline of the aristocratic ruling classes. The British system came into being almost simultaneously with the great extension of the franchise in 1867, the first major breach in England's aristocratic rulership. It confirmed the gradual decline of the British ruling class's political power and at the time avoided the massive appearance of the political machines and spoils system that had replaced the American gentry. The main differences between the two countries were due to the fact that the equalitarian tendencies of America could not tolerate the appearance of a proud aristocracy of talent such as the one that was slowly growing into the frayed clothes of Britain's hereditary aristocracy. The old Jacksonian distrust for entrenched privilege and inequalities was still very much alive. American officials belonging to the "classified service" never enjoyed the prestige that surrounds their European counterparts.

The new Union reached the zenith of its Victorian splendor under President Cleveland. These were the days of unadulterated capitalistic rule at its best and worst, when the government was used to resist inflation and break strikes, but not to help farmers in their tragic plight or enforce social legislation for the protection of workers. Energetic, bold, and ruthless, this Victorian capitalism knew how to develop the country economically and efficiently But it was merciless in an age when social Darwinism ruled supreme, when Herbert Spencer's amalgamation of the old Puritan creed with a pseudoscientific biological outlook was almost unchallenged. The iron-willed Puritans saw the seal of Divine approval stamped on economic prosperity and their less religious descendants felt the need to bolster their secularized beliefs with the help of some philosophic or scientific argument less sordid than naked self-interest. With Roman-like ruthlessness, these Spencerian apostles confused mechanical expansion with historical progress and the very success of industrialization contributed to ensnare them in their own intellectual traps. Rockefeller could justify his industrial monopoly: "The growth of a large business is merely a survival of the fittest," and Andrew Carnegie could write about his own conversion to Spencer and Darwinism: "Light came as in a flood and all was clear. Not only had I got rid of theology and the supernatural, but I had found the truth of evolution." [4] The final, logical, inescapable conclusion was drawn from the stern faith of the early Pilgrims when the religious trappings were dropped and the secular ruthlessness of the hard core was left naked for all to see.

This philosophy of life was the world outlook of America's new upper classes, the "silk-stocking" aristocracy of respectable, urbane Victorian gentlemen, the financial and industrial leaders to whom business was everything and politics merely a tool of vested interests. Nor were they brilliant upstarts, as the famous legend of rags-to-riches has led so many Europeans and Americans to believe. Business was largely controlled by the older patrician families of the East, many of whom had turned to economic activities when politics had forsaken them. At the turn of the century, three out of four came from old colonial families, four out of five belonged to business and professional families and only 2 per cent came all the way up from the working class. Many of those who ended up as captains of industry had begun during the Civil War as commission merchants, as did their Roman counterparts, the *publicani,* during the Punic Wars.

This new upper class had nothing in common with the strong public-minded gentry of the past—the plantation aristocrats like Washington and Jefferson, the New England patricians like the Cabots and the Adamses. It was largely an unprincipled, amoral ruling class of fabulous wealth and power, of feudal barons who sliced out the new world of productive wealth disclosed by the Industrial Revolution. They no longer ruled territories and vassals but natural resources and means of communications. They were raw material kings, steel kings, coal kings, oil kings, industrial magnates who ruled over entirely new realms—razor blades, plumbing and fixtures, newspaper chains. There were banking empires and railroad empires whose clerks were often respectable Senators.

Many of these industrial corporations and trusts had become more powerful than the individual states in which they were located, dwarfing local governments, manipulating political machines, accentuating the centralizing trend that placed every major economic problem on the national scale where major politics had already preceded it. The result of this colossal concentration of wealth in a few hands was the cultural monstrosity known as the Gilded Age, in which a luxurious style of living was marked by the worst taste ever displayed, a lack of true distinction and refinement which had not been seen since the last century of republican Rome.

The rise to social supremacy of the American businessman was never duplicated in Europe. There business remained at all times the servant and not the master of politics, and the most powerful and wealthiest businessmen still sought admittance into the ranks of traditional upper classes and absorbed many of their aristocratic traits. Nowhere in Europe could the highest legislatures fit the description James Bryce gave of the American Senate of those days: "The Senate now contains many men of great wealth. Some, an increasing number, are Senators because they are rich; a few are rich because they are Senators; while in the remaining cases the same talents which have won success in law or commerce have brought their possessors to the top in politics also." [5]

The great business leaders of those days were ruthless men whose lack of ethics did not spring from evil or selfish motives but from sheer lack of interest in moral principles. They were highly intuitive, imaginative, bold, and enterprising, unconscious of either right or wrong. Success to them was still a symbol of some spiritual grace they had no time to investigate, and money was an instrument of power, nothing more. Once power had been obtained and their Napoleonic instincts had been gratified, these business leaders were often not interested in enjoying it or handing it down to their descendants. Thus it was that the bulk of their fortunes was given to charitable or educational institutions. Andrew Carnegie gave away nine-tenths of his gigantic fortune in his lifetime to various philanthropic foundations. Most of these men, ruthless individualists when building their fortunes, became social-minded and altruistic when disposing of them.

The history of America between the Civil War and World War I is largely the history of her economic development. Politics was only a reflection of the major business of taming raw nature. Presidential power remained largely in abeyance. Cleveland was strong but he still belonged to an age that conceived of government largely in negative terms. Essentially an honest obstructionist, he was dedicated to preventing the bad from happening, not to promoting the good.

In contrast to the situation in Europe, the American individual's private life prevailed absolutely over the authority of the national government. Jeremy Bentham had expressed this outlook by pointing out that "the interest of the community is . . . the sum of the interests of the several members who compose it." [6] Becoming part of the psychology of the equalitarian American society, this view showed the contrast between a mechanical and an organic vision of human society. It rests on the instinctive opposition between truthful, virtuous *nature* and artificial, evil *culture,* in the voluntary emancipation from social courtesy, and government in general. The recurrence in the American vocabulary of adjectives such as *rugged, raw,* and *tough,* symbolizes this refusal to countenance culture and breeding.

In this sense, America became a land of supreme individualism based on the priority of the individual's private interests rather than on his own inner freedom—a freedom which was anyway meaningless, since he was entirely geared to a life of action and had reduced his inner life to a bare minimum. In Europe, man was always part of a social, political, economic, and religious hierarchy but the full development of his individuality and therefore of his inner freedom was always stimulated by the variety of his social and national expressions and functions. In America, man wanted to live out his private interests, a thing he never could do in stratified and congested Europe. American freedom did not imply a strong development of originality and personality but freedom *from* social hierarchy, government, military draft, polite manners, and every other sort of compulsion.

In a sense this was a new freedom, one that did not belong to the original Puritan and Cavalier traditions but was evolved by the millions of immigrants who had left Europe and European culture as well. A century earlier, Americans had fought for independence from "arbitrary" government. Now, the new American longed to be free from everything else besides; thus, the predominance of private business and private interests to a degree that baffled most foreigners. All the violent protests against the rising power of the federal administration and bureaucracy in the twentieth century sprang from this fundamental outlook that always viewed the state as a *private trust* like any other, not as a religious symbol like the British crown or an emotional focal point like most European states.

Romans shared to a large extent the same views, especially after the Punic Wars. The devout respect for state and religion that had prevailed earlier largely disappeared. The prevalence of the private-trust outlook in Rome, as in America, coincided with the rise to almost undisputed power of finance and business, and inevitably entailed an alarming weakness of the state. But this weakness was always compensated by the citizens' unfailing self-discipline and public-mindedness. Fifteen years after the start of the First Punic War, when the Roman state was weaker than America ever was in its worst period of Congressional rule, the Romans had lost four fleets and the state was utterly powerless. By private subscription, a number of Roman citizens raised the money for two hundred superbly outfitted warships and presented them to the state together with sixty thousand sailors whose salaries were paid by these private citizens—and their reward was the decisive victory of Aegusa.

Just the same, American millionaires matched Roman millionaires in contributing to the welfare of their respective communities, supplying abundant funds for roads, bridges, churches, civic centers, temples and theaters. The generous grants of Roman millionaires were duly recorded in the monumental *Corpus Inscriptionum Latinarum.*[7] Such psychological attitude springs from a strong feeling of social duty, not imposed by the state but springing from the heart of the free individual. Every Roman city had its donations from its Fords, Morgans, and Rockefellers, and for every American Carnegie Hall there was an equivalent Agrippa's Pantheon.

The weakness of the absolute predominance of the private-trust outlook lies in its incompatibility with the increasingly world-wide responsibilities of such powerful communities as Rome and America. Because of the limited number of magistrates at its disposal, the Roman state had to entrust the building of roads, bridges, fleets, the supplying of armies, and the collection of taxes to private contractors. The rise of middlemen contractors during the Punic Wars, of companies of *publicani* who exploited the state-owned forests, agricultural or pastoral lands and mines under lease from the government, was the equivalent of the rise of American business contractors during the Civil War. In both cases, the absolute domination of pliable administrations by Big Business was the inevitable outcome. In Rome as in America, the peculiar outlook of business leaders did not prepare them for the world-wide responsibilities that were soon going to be theirs.

CHAPTER XIV

From One Century to Another

IN 1880, there were fifty million Americans, forty million of them living in rural areas. The next fifty years witnessed the dramatic metamorphosis of a predominantly rural America into an overwhelmingly urban society. The flight from the land was partly masked by the steady increase in immigration from the Old World, but the flight had nonetheless become alarming in the eastern United States. Like Roman Italy, America was becoming a land of city-dwellers, of rootless populations divorced from the soil, conglomerating into gregarious and increasingly impersonal crowds. By 1880, half of the eastern population had become urban and the waning of eastern agriculture was proceeding at a fast rate. The steady progress of urbanization can be gauged from the fact that in 1790 city dwellers totaled less than 4 per cent of the population whereas in 1860 they totaled already 16 per cent.

The growing cities were absorbing and concentrating an increasing portion of the national wealth while the farmers were losing their political importance. Farms were heavily mortgaged, and farmers were becoming the rebellious and unwilling tools of city merchants and bankers. The new American West, now developing in the Great Plains beyond the Mississippi, linked up politically with the agrarian South and attempted to fight the urban industrialist-capitalist octopus that was slowly devouring the traditional rural America. This defensive movement eventually became, in the 1890's, the Bryan-Populist revolt.

√The frontier was coming to an end. The Great Plains were filling up, the last Indians were confined in their reservations, and the colorful epic of the Far West was drawing to a close.⌋Cosmopolitan life with its increasing mechanization was slowly extending over the entire continent, as it was all over the world. Soon, there would be no wild refuge for those who wanted to escape from the class distinctions that seem to permeate every civilization, for those whose self-reliance and boldness found no outlet in the tameness of more settled areas. America was now changing much faster than Europe, becoming more unified and more mobile. Instead of the thousand years predicted by the post-Revolutionary generation, American settlements had reached the Mississippi in twenty-five years and another quarter of a century had seen them on the Pacific.⌋By 1900, the continent was virtually settled from coast to coast.⌋

The economic depression of 1873 had started the long tale of agricultural woes. Farmers were in the same desperate straits as their Roman counterparts when large-scale slave farming had made the lot of the old-fashioned Roman homesteader intolerable. ⌊A similar revolution, on a much higher technical level, was taking place in American agriculture. The huge treeless prairies—what used to be called the "great American desert"—were brought under cultivation thanks to products of the Industrial Revolution: the dense network of railroads, barbed wire fencing, the tractor, and the automatic binder. The older, smaller farms of the East and the wooded West were ruined by the large-scale farming of the plains. New England's barren fields could no longer support its traditional sheep-raising and sent thousands of impoverished farmers to city slums and industrial work, where they had to compete with Irish immigrants at depressed wages. Mechanical devices were doing to old-fashioned agriculture what the imported slaves did to Roman farmers. They lowered production costs and priced nonmechanized individual farming out of the market. The days of the farm as a self-sufficient economic unit providing its owner with food, clothing, and building material were gone forever. Agriculture was drawn into the vortex of an industrial society, tightly linked to capital, a mere cog in the spreading machinery of railroads, industrial plants, and fluctuating international markets. Vastly increased transportation facilities could dump cheap Argentine wheat on the

American market and depress American agriculture as Egyptian cereals had ruined Rome's individual farming.

Italy's old peasant population, the free yeomen who had been the mainstay of Roman power as America's farmers had been the backbone of the United States, disintegrated. The formation in Italy of vast latifundia manned by thousands of slaves, the technical improvements of Roman agriculture and cattle breeding (introduced from the Hellenistic East), concentration on the cultivation of vines and olives while the production of cereals collapsed—all these changes contributed to the disappearance of the traditional Roman peasant. A new type of farmer was to appear in the first century B.C. alongside the big landlord, a middle-class farmer equipped with a "modern" outlook and far greater technical knowledge as well as some capital and a few slaves, corresponding to the new midwestern American farmer with his highly mechanized methods of cultivation. Together with the vast cattle ranches of wealthy men like Domitius Ahenobarbus, which find their counterpart in Texas and other cattle raising areas, Rome's northern "Midwest," the Po Valley, was soon covered by medium-sized properties where scientific and specialized farming gave greater yields than had been possible in the days of the one-man farms. Such properties could compete more advantageously in the Mediterranean world market then coming into existence.

Neither Rome nor America took those sweeping changes unconcerned. Wise statesmen knew that what might be a sound economic transformation might also be a social disaster. Rome attempted time and again to recreate a class of small independent farmers through grants of land and settlement of retired legionaires on new land, only to find that Roman capitalists and bankers ruined them by cornering grain markets. In America, the Homestead Act of 1862 solved the problem of the resettlement of the Civil War veterans by granting them free land. Hundreds of thousands of veterans settled beyond the Mississippi on their 160 acres. Two hundred and twenty-six million acres thus passed into private ownership. (For purposes of comparison, the total area of Great Britain and Northern Ireland is only 62 million acres.) But most of this land eventually fell into the hands of the large corporations, while another 158 million acres was given directly to the railroads.[1] Nebraska, for example, was largely settled by homesteading veterans. Less than a generation afterward virtually the entire state was owned by railroad corporations and insurance companies. The Union Pacific Railroad alone had been given almost five million acres of the best land, and under its leadership eastern capitalists came to control the state government, giving them dictatorial authority over all phases of Nebraska's life.

The land gifts to veterans had seemed at the time a generous bounty, but they were nothing of the kind. Without capital, the new farmers had to mortgage their land and borrow money that rose in value while agricultural prices fell steadily. It required three times as much wheat to pay off a mortgage in 1885 as was required in 1865. Southern farmers were tied to falling world prices by their disastrous one-crop system, and western farmers were tied to eastern capital by their rising debts and a hard-money policy.

The rise of unbridled capitalism was perhaps the most demoralizing social factor in America in the period 1880-1890, especially now that the counterbalancing influence of a service-minded aristocracy of the British type no longer existed. Roman capitalism, master in Rome in the second century B.C. as American capitalism was master in Washington after the Civil War, profited from official favors, in the same way. The fabulous gold mines of Macedonia, together with the crown lands of the fallen dynasty, were leased under very advantageous terms to a corporation of Roman capitalists. Carthage and Corinth were destroyed to please Roman merchants and bankers who wanted to eliminate commercial competitors. In 143, Appius Claudius invaded the Piedmont in order to confiscate the gold mines of the Salassi, following which the Roman authorities leased them to a Roman corporation for whose benefit the enslaved Salassi were forced to work their own mines. In Rome as in America Big Business enjoyed an unadulterated triumph.

Since the grip of capitalism could not be loosened by economic means, it had to be done politically. The rise of western radicalism was inevitable. Bryan's Populist party arose in the downcast South and swept the vigorous West where contempt for the easterners was rife. The sturdy Romans of the new Cisalpine Gaul looked down upon the decadent Italians further south with as much contempt and as much determination to escape from the control of Roman capitalism. Bryan's proposals to alleviate the plight of countless debtors, his inflationary program of cheaper money, matched similar radical programs put forth in Rome. Revolutionary proposals, all the way from the Gracchi's to Catiline's program of moratorium on all debts, played on the radical sentiments of masses of discontented Romans. From then on, politics was going to attempt to stand up to naked financial power. The struggle was on, and in America, half a century after Bryan, Franklin Roosevelt was to stand on the Populist platform as Rome's Marius was to stand on the Gracchan program.

The first ominous signs of the coming evolution of public sentiment, the bartering away of freedom against security, were sounded when Bryan declared: "I come to speak to you in defense of a cause as holy as the cause of liberty—the cause of humanity." [2] The platform of the Populist party in 1892 started off: "We meet in the midst of a nation brought to the verge of moral, political and material ruin. Corruption dominates the ballot-box, the legislatures, the Congress and touches the ermine of the bench . . . the newspapers are largely subsidized or muzzled, public opinion silenced . . . homes covered with mortgages, labor impoverished, and the land concentrated in the hands of capitalists. . . . From the same prolific womb of governmental injustice we breed two great classes—tramps and millionaires." [3]

The Populist was the most, indeed almost the only, influential third party in the history of America and its success was made possible by the fact that both major parties had been largely captured by Big Business. A popular revolt that could no longer express itself through regular party channels had to create a new outlet. Most of its actual program—a flexible currency controlled by the government and not by private banks, a progressive income tax, restriction of immigration in order to protect American labor, the direct election of Senators instead of their election by state legislatures, the eight-hour day—were later incorporated in the programs of either the Republican or the Democratic parties as soon as they were able to develop their progressive wings.

The problem of immigration was tackled piecemeal but it was the first to be tackled at all. In 1860, the total population of the United States was thirty million. In the following seventy years, another thirty million European immigrants came to America. The absorption of this staggering influx was in itself a tremendous problem, but it was made more difficult by the change in the sources of immigration. The ethnic homogeneity of the American people began to be affected as the similar immigration of slaves and freemen from all over the Mediterranean world had affected Rome. American industrial leaders began drawing on eastern and southern rather than northern Europe for new sources of cheap manpower. The troublesome Irish were no longer welcome in the coal mines and Germany's quick industrialization kept her citizens at home. Nordic immigration dried up and was replaced by a steadily mounting flood from Italy, Greece, Poland, Hungary, and other parts of eastern Europe. Northern Europeans had been inclined to settle on the land but the latter immigrants conglomerated in the cities and stayed there. Viewing the cosmopolitan masses of Mediterranean and eastern European immigrants streaming into the United States and congesting most of the large cities, native Americans could echo Juvenal's alarmed cry in Rome: "The Orontes is flowing into the Tiber," and recall that in the days of Julius Caesar almost 90 per cent of the population of Rome was of foreign extraction.

The result was a succession of stringent immigration laws, leading from the first, promulgated against Chinese and Japanese immigration to the West Coast in the 1880's, to the act of 1924 that reduced European immigration to a trickle. The great human current that had flowed steadily across the Atlantic for centuries came to an end. At the time, no one could assess the final results of this great migration. It certainly deprived Europe of countless citizens who were more democratically minded than those who stayed behind, and weakened the democratic movements of their homelands by their departure. On the other hand, they fitted into the democratic structure of their adopted country like hand in glove. They had fled from Europe, at first, for the same idealistic reasons—religious or political—that had motivated the earlier settlements of the Pilgrims: the desire to materialize their ideas in a new world. But as the nineteenth century drew to a close, escape from economic adversity became the prime motive and the quality of the immigrants declined, making legal limitations unavoidable. The "melting pot" was no longer equal to the task.

None of the other problems set forth in the Populist platform was tackled that soon. Depression struck time and again, and the administrations seemed unwilling to act. The steady decline of agricultural income eventually recoiled on the Eastern capitalists themselves. Railroads went bankrupt, banks closed their doors, and by the middle of the 1890's the whole of America was wrapped in gloom. The Pullman strike was put down with bloody violence while crowds of hungry men wandered about the country, begging or looting, marching on Washington to compel the administration to do something about their plight.

The greatest obstacle to governmental action, actually, was not so much the reluctance of an awakening administration as the paralyzing influence of the judiciary. The legal mind is conservative; it moves slowly and is not always adaptable to fast-changing conditions. It frowns on political and social revolutions, but it was totally unprepared for the Industrial Revolution. The Supreme Court's main duty was to protect the property and privileges of the citizens against state and federal encroachments, but it was psychologically unable to protect them against giant capitalist corporations, trusts, cartels, and monopolies because they were phenomena without precedents. Unwittingly, the Supreme Court fostered the rise of those Cyclopean concerns, blind to the fact that they were not merely aggregates of individual properties but giant organisms in their own right, whose powers were often greater than those of the government, monsters conjured up unpredictably by the rise of industrialism—that they should therefore be amenable to an entirely new legal code which would have to be devised for them.

The legal mind persisted in viewing corporations as ordinary "persons," and therefore fully entitled to protection against the encroachments of legislators. These mammoth structures were given the full protection of the Fifth and Fourteenth Amendments, putting them on a par with powerless individuals. It was not surprising, therefore, to see administrations push through antitrust acts only to have them nullified time and again by the Supreme Court. Only against labor unions were the acts upheld. The Whisky Trust and the Sugar Trust went unscathed but the full weight of judicial action fell on the American Railway Union.

In 1895, the Supreme Court decided that the income tax was unconstitutional. Western agrarians and the eastern poor joined in denouncing a decision which favored capital. Yet, the court was in good faith and branded the income tax as "class legislation." To this Justice Field added: "Whenever a distinction is made in the burdens a law imposes or in the benefits it confers on any citizen by reasons of their birth, or wealth or religion, it is class legislation and leads inevitably to oppression and abuses . . . the present assault upon capital is but the beginning. It will be but a stepping stone to others, larger and more sweeping, till our political contests will become a war of the poor against the rich; a war constantly growing in intensity and bitterness." [4]

Capitalism was still firmly in the saddle but the premonitory mutterings of the New Deal could be heard as early as the turn of the century.

The election of 1896 consecrated the inevitable defeat of agrarian America that went down before the rising industrial power. The capitalist-controlled cities and industries now carried too much weight, and timorous labor in the cities, barely organized, was not strong enough to conclude an alliance with the agrarians. So it was that McKinley was overwhelmingly elected by the East and the Northwest, defeating Bryan, who had carried the West and the South. The way was clear for a capitalism that would now have to be curbed from inside the cities and their industrial strongholds. Rural America was no longer a basic but a marginal factor. The New Rome's political strength shifted from the farmers to the the great city masses, as it had in the Old Rome.

From Grant to McKinley, Republican Presidents had given little political leadership. America had to wait until Theodore Roosevelt for a new offensive of executive leadership—due rather to the great personality and Gargantuan energy of the man than to compelling circumstances. His vitality and will stamped him as the typical man of action, while his remarkable sense of publicity and his profound intuition made him a first-rate politician. Roosevelt had no definite philosophy. He was a force of nature who represented the mood of the times, the last outburst of unthinking youth and yet the first qualms of an awakening social conscience. His election made Big Business uneasy for it sensed in him some democratic instincts combined with a definite yearning for the power of a popular tribune. He was the first of the "progressives," a man of transition—the epoch-making transition from the horse-and-buggy era to that of the automobile and the airplane, the optimistic opening of the new world of supermechanization.

With Theodore Roosevelt, Congress was once more overpowered by an exuberant Executive. When Congress expressed its surprise at the brutal seizure of Panama, Roosevelt steam-rollered it: "I took the

Canal Zone and let Congress debate, and while the debate goes on, the Canal does also." [5] Browbeating Congress was no new thing. What was new was Roosevelt's intention to bring the independent power of Money and Business under the supervision of the administration and reverse the trend that had lasted since the Civil War. Political democracy was not enough. Economic democracy became the new goal. Roosevelt set in motion a complex political machinery to overpower Big Business: an Interstate Commerce Commission to curb the railroad empires, agencies to preserve the nation's natural resources from plunder by thoughtless farmers and lumber kings, a Department of Commerce and Labor to bring industrial kingdoms under federal control, antitrust legislation to break up a threatening industrial feudalism.

As time went on, Theodore Roosevelt became more conscious of the potential power of the presidential office. Writing to the historian George Trevelyan, he said: "I have a definite philosophy about the Presidency. I think it should be a very powerful office and I think the President should be a very strong man who uses without hesitation every power that the position yields." And he added in his autobiography: "I did not usurp power but I did greatly broaden the use of executive power." [6] Here was a clear indication that each new power created by political and economic expansion ended up in the White House. Congress might still have the same power as in 1800 but the Executive was immensely more influential since new powers in an expanding age accrued steadily to the presidential office.

Theodore Roosevelt was the first President to base his tribunician appeal on the new means of communication that linked the White House directly to public opinion over the heads of Congress and the Supreme Court. He was the first, since Andrew Jackson, to play on the undiscriminating emotions of the masses. If the Executive failed to arouse an apathetic public opinion, Congress once again revolted, as it did under his stodgy successor, Taft. Roosevelt exerted considerable influence on the Supreme Court, for which he had little respect, and indirectly prevailed upon it to reverse itself on more than one occasion. At the same time he went further than any of his predecessors in demonstrating that presidential appointments to the Court are essentially political. But his outstanding trait was his distaste for ruthless capitalism as exemplified by J. P. Morgan, a distaste he pungently expressed in his autobiography: "Of all forms of tyranny the least attractive and the most vulgar is the tyranny of mere wealth, the tyranny of a plutocracy." [7]

√ It was during this era that America, having largely terminated her internal expansion, began to look beyond her geographical borders and take an active interest in world affairs. Richard Olney, President Cleveland's Secretary of State, claimed in 1894 that "today the United States is practically sovereign on this continent and its fiat is law . . ." [8] Canadians and Latin Americans did not appreciate such a statement, but they could not dispute its truth. The New Rome was speedily becoming a world power and the other world powers were invited to take notice—especially Britain with whom the United States was at odds again. The wrangle over Venezuela and British Guiana was the last serious quarrel to mar Anglo-American relations. The internal difficulties of an economic depression had encouraged the United States to "let slip the dogs of war." Public opinion was roused to a pitch of excitement and it was only Britain's polite restraint that prevented an actual military collision. Quickly sobered, America began to realize that her power, indeed her very existence, depended more than ever on the British fleet. Then and there, the decision was made to rehabilitate the United States Navy.

There were ominous signs that Britain's mastery of the seas was being challenged by Germany and Japan—a challenge indirectly directed at America herself. Now it was that America became vaguely conscious of an alarming fact: that, sooner or later, the burden of policing the high seas would be hers to assume—an irretrievable step toward a new "Roman" stewardship in the twilight of Europe's "Hellenistic" Age. Alexander had not had time to conquer the Roman West and Napoleon's desire to conquer the civilized world had been held in check by the British fleet. How long could Britain's trusteeship last?

From now on, Britain and America moved closer together in an implicit alliance which the coming storms of the twentieth century were going to strengthen. Britain was about to become America's main bastion across the ocean, and western Europe her new overseas frontier. As Henry Adams expressed it in 1905: "We have got to support France against Germany, and fortify an Atlantic system beyond attack; for if Germany breaks down England or France, she will become the center of a military world and we are lost." [9]

America as a whole was rather more jingoistic than alarmed at this stage. The public excitement over the Venezuela affair had not died down and was directing its fire toward any potential victim in sight. The end of the frontier had left the nation without material outlet for its expansive energy. These were the days when Senator Cullom of Illinois howled: "It is time someone woke up and realized the necessity of annexing some property. We want all this northern hemisphere." Senators and journalists joined the outcry. Even Theodore Roosevelt claimed at the time of the Venezuela explosion: "The clamor of the peace faction had convinced me that this country needs a war." [10]

Expansionism was welling up in the New Rome and a suitable victim was found: Spain, against whom Cuba was in full revolt. Spain's colonial domination was tyrannical and inefficient although her temper was not warlike. But America was flexing her young muscles and McKinley gave in to a public clamor stimulated by such newspaper magnates as Hearst and Pulitzer. No great prophetic insight was required to foresee that Spain would go down as she actually did, losing Cuba and the Philippines. But in the process, America acquired an embarrassing colonial empire. At one stroke, the American frontier crossed the entire breadth of the Pacific to the Far East; and although Cuba was granted conditional independence two years later, the island became part of another American empire— the invisible but powerful empire of the Dollar. Belonging largely to New York banks that had invested one and a half billion dollars in her rich crops, Cuba joined the select group of "banana republics" that were virtual satellites of Wall Street.

From this time on, the United States established her supremacy over the Western Hemisphere. Her only serious rival, Britain, gave in completely and withdrew from that part of the world in order to cement the new Anglo-American alliance. British withdrawal from Panama and surrender of Canadian claims in Alaska, military withdrawal from the Caribbean and Canada, all pointed to the rise of undisputed American supremacy in the Western Hemisphere, prelude to a greater supremacy to come across the oceans. And while America criticized all European spheres of influence in the rest of the world as immoral, she established her firm grip on Latin America without sensing any paradox. Colombia—"The contemptible little creatures in Bogota" as Theodore Roosevelt put it—raised some objections about the projected canal across the isthmus of Panama. A convenient revolution—"a most just and proper revolution," [11] he added—detached Panama from Colombia while American warships were on hand in case of misfire. A new republic of Panama, recognized by the United States less than two hours after its Caesarian birth, handed over the future Canal Zone to America. This was outright imperialism at the expense of what Roosevelt called "inefficient bandits," a jingoistic imperialism that was only a passing phase. But it indicated unmistakably that the United States intended to have her way on the American continent, an intention that led to outright interventions in Cuba, Mexico, the Dominican Republic, or more subtle but equally effective pressure on other Latin American republics.

The first conscious formulation of America's global imperialism began to arise at the end of the nineteenth century. Idealism and religious proselytism often assumed an expansionist tinge, as expressed by the famous missionary Josiah Strong of Ohio, for instance: "It is manifest that the Anglo-Saxon holds in his hands the destinies of mankind, and it is evident that the United States is to become the home of this race, the principle seat of its power, the great center of its influence." [12] The Romans hardly dared think this bluntly in the twilight of the Hellenistic Age. Other Americans, more secularminded, expressed their faith in their racial superiority—a notion that was basically alien to the Classical world and is a distinctive characteristic of the northern Europeans and North Americans. John Fiske expressed his Darwinian racialism in his celebrated article "Manifest Destiny" and joined many others in expressing their belief in the racial superiority of northern people, a conviction that led a generation later to closing the gates of immigration not only to Asians but to southern and eastern Europeans. Senator Beveridge of Indiana linked racialism and expansionism in an 1898 speech eulogizing Ulysses Grant: "He never forgot that we are a conquering race and that we must obey our blood and occupy new markets and, if necessary, new lands. He had the prophet's seerlike sight which beheld, as part of the Almighty's plan, the disappearance of debased civilizations and decaying races before the higher civilization of the nobler and more virile types of men." [13]

It was Admiral Alfred Thayer Mahan who expressed most clearly America's geopolitical imperialism, who was conscious of the overwhelming importance of sea power for the Anglo-American world and who advocated global supremacy for America's fleets. True Roman realism suffuses his thesis that "self-interest is not only a legitimate but a fundamental cause for national policy, one which needs no cloak of hypocrisy. . . . Governments are corporations, and as corporations they have no souls." [14] Big Business would soon fall under the heel of Big Government but not without making an attempt at transferring to it its soulless philosophy of might without morality.

Mahan inspired America to seize Hawaii, to extend its influence in Central America and the Caribbean, explaining to his compatriots what was already becoming evident: America was a continental island endowed with a higher civilization than the rest of the world, in urgent need of a powerful navy that would one day displace Britain's Royal Navy as the supreme ruler of oceans. We can now look back at Tocqueville's prophetic words: "When I contemplate the ardor with which the Anglo-Americans prosecute commerce, the advantages which aid them, and the success of their undertakings, I cannot help believing that they will one day become the foremost maritime power of the globe. They are born to rule the seas, as the Romans were to conquer the world." [15]

Beveridge, Mahan, and Roosevelt found additional support for their imperialism in an argument of the Supreme Court on the case *Downes* v. *Bidwell* dealing with the status of Puerto Rico: "A false step at this time might be fatal to what Chief Justice Marshall called the American Empire. Choice in some cases, the natural gravitation of small bodies towards large ones in others, the result of a successful war in still others, may bring about conditions which would render the annexation of distant possessions desirable." [16]

What really limited America's latent colonialism was not so much a generous idealism as the realization that the old formula of statehood no longer worked where large alien populations were concerned. Racialism stood in the way; and what is more, open colonialism implied great responsibilities as well as privileges which discreet economic imperialism did not entail. Puerto Rico or the Philippines could never be admitted as states within the relatively homogeneous, white, and overwhelmingly Protestant Union without disrupting the whole structure. America began to face her limitations as Rome had in the past. Italy could be Romanized, and so could Spain and Gaul to a certain extent; but there were stringent limitations to the Romanization of Africa, Egypt, or Syria. America's remarkable ability to absorb and digest millions of European immigrants began to fail when it came to overseas territories populated by entirely alien stocks.

Two leading imperialists fought it out in those days. Whitelaw Reid refused to admit that overseas possessions could ever be admitted to statehood and Andrew Carnegie replied that they would have to be admitted as such, whether Reid liked it or not. Time was to prove that they were both wrong. What no one could foresee then, in Europe as well as in America, was the revolt of the Orient, the downfall of Europe's colonial empires, and America's voluntary surrender of this old-fashioned imperialism that she had developed in those immature days when she attempted to emulate the great powers of the Old World. It did not matter much whether the Philippines were eventually given up because powerful private interests in America wanted to end their economic competition, rather than out of sheer idealism. No one could foresee at the turn of the century that European colonialism was an antiquated formula that would have to be replaced by a new type of imperialism—more responsible, more universal in scope, more subtle, and in the end more generous and more effective than any devised so far. America was no more to copy European colonialism than Rome was to copy Greek imperialism. Real American imperialism could spring only from the heart of her generous but uncomprehending anti-imperialists, as an idealistic expansion bolstered by irrepressible economic forces.

What became evident during this phase of premature expansion overseas was that a great deal of what passes for a true characteristic of America—buoyancy, capacity for enthusiasm and idealism, exuberant youthfulness and naïveté—is nothing more than a psychological compensation for the indestructible bedrock of the American temper: fundamental seriousness, shrewd calculating power, and implacable determination to overcome obstacles. What may seem amateurish or childish in American life is nothing but an escape on the plane of imagination. The core is still the rock-hard realism of men who have a profound distrust for all abstract generalities and indulge in them only as a hobby.

Theodore Roosevelt closed the optimistic, dynamic era of American growth with a great flourish. The power of the Executive had increased immeasurably and all eras of transition had been managed by strong Presidents—Jackson's establishment of the rising democracy, his institution of tribunician power in the White House and decent burial of the former ruling gentry; Lincoln's preservation and consolidation of the Union; Theodore Roosevelt's partial establishment of administrative ascendancy over Big Business. Weak Presidents had permitted the disastrous drift toward the Civil War. Lincoln's towering strength through the war years was followed by renewed presidential weakness and the tragedy of Reconstruction. Historical evidence now pointed to the inevitable trend toward presidential Caesarism as being the natural counterpart of the trend toward democratic equality. Writing at the turn of the century, James Bryce remarked: "The tendency everywhere in America to concentrate power and responsibility in one man is unmistakable." [17] And this in a time of peace and world prosperity. Nothing more would be needed than the great era of wars and revolutions and national emergencies of the twentieth century to bring this long-term trend to its natural conclusion. Rome was saved time and again by her temporary constitutional dictators as America had been by her strong Presidents—until Caesars came along to establish their personal rule on a permanent footing.

Meanwhile, no one expressed better the economic implications of the new social conscience that was emerging than Theodore Roosevelt. He advocated a new centralization that was to have far-reaching consequences—a new vision into the future structure of the world's mightiest economic empire. "They [the advocates of the Sherman Act] tried to bolster up an individualism already proved to be both futile and mischievous; to remedy by more individualism the concentration that was the inevitable result of the already existing individualism. They saw the evil done by the big combinations, and sought to remedy it by destroying them and restoring the country to the economic conditions of the middle of the nineteenth century. This was a hopeless effort, and those who went into it ... really represented a form of sincere rural toryism. ... On the other hand a few men recognized that corporations and combinations had become indispensable in the business world, that it was futile to try to prohibit them, but that it was also folly to leave them without thoroughgoing control. ... Government must now interfere to protect labor, to subordinate the big corporations to the public welfare, and to shackle cunning and fraud." [18]

The end of the old rural era with its Jeffersonian ideology could not have been more cogently expressed, along with the need for some form of state control over the independent power of money and business. But against Theodore Roosevelt's prophetic vision of the social and economic world to come, arose Woodrow Wilson's middle-class attempt, with agrarian and labor support, to backtrack, to destroy the big corporations altogether by enforcing the rules of competition. Both agreed that government should step massively into the economic sphere, and this was already a revolution by nineteenth-century standards. But while Roosevelt saw clearly that the government would find it more convenient to use and control the colossal corporations, Wilson attempted to break them up and inject more competition into the industrial structure.

Woodrow Wilson himself was a strong President. A staunch Democrat, his rise to power was made possible by the split in the Republican ranks between Roosevelt's Progressives and the die-hard reactionaries—who eventually captured control of the party and expelled their liberal opponents. Wilson did not hesitate to attack Big Business. The Underwood Tariff, reducing the average duties by almost 27 per cent, the Federal Reserve Act, which brought money management further under government control, and a long series of acts bringing further sections of economic activity under the supervision of the administration were all wrung from a reluctant Congress by a willful Executive.

Democracy was also making further progress. The most important change took place in the recruitment of the Senate, hitherto an assembly of ambassadors chosen by state legislatures, with the faintly aristocratic flavor attached to such indirect elections. In 1913, the adoption of the Seventeenth Amendment provided for the direct election of Senators by the people. This put an end to the Senatorial "millionaires' club"; however, it did not end the Senate's most characteristic feature: that of overrepresenting the slowly dwindling rural population. But a cardinal factor of American politics is the almost holy reverence for the waning rural life—a nostalgic feeling for America's "log-cabin" roots, a psychological compensation for the extraordinary industrialization and urbanization of the new century. As already noted, America never had a real peasantry. Such organizations as the Grange attempted to compensate for this by developing in their dwindling numbers some feeling of emotional attachment to the land, along with programs of economic welfare.

And so, with the passing of the "horse-and-buggy" era, America and the world entered a new age. The first World War was about to sweep away forever the old world with its unique charms and evils. The Hellenistic Age of Europe was ending in a blood-bath; and the burden of world-wide responsibilities was going to fall on America's shoulders with a swift brutality unmatched in history.

PART III | *The Decline of Europe*

CHAPTER XV

Twilight of Europe's Hellenistic Age

NOTHING could have been more brilliant than European life in the Victorian and Edwardian periods. It was an age of great wealth accumulated during a century of peace and fabulous economic development, the age of Viennese waltzes and dazzling court life, of relative social stability, of courtesy and culture, aristocratic leadership and middle-class prosperity. Europe dominated the world, her pre-eminence unchallenged, powerful in the physical might of her huge armies and colossal industrial structure, powerful as the acknowledged fountainhead of ideas, art, literature, and philosophy. Few could hear the premonitory rumblings of the earthquake that was to destroy it all.

The last blaze of cultural creation had centered largely in music, the most truly representative art-medium of European Culture, which found in its Wagnerian Twilight of the Gods the conclusion that Greek art found in Pergamene sculpture. But cultural exhaustion was becoming evident. Sculpture, painting, and architecture were losing their inspiration, either living on old stock-forms or strongly affected by technological revolution. There were vain attempts to formulate new styles and new symbols, ending in a confusion of scrambled styles and meaningless, empty symbols. Artists were giving way to engineers, technological inventions took the place of profound artistic insight. Great art is always spontaneous and self-evident, and nothing denotes senile decadence as much as the growing divorce between content and form. A pathetic attempt to emancipate art and culture from form and proportion, a morbid taste for neobarbarism, for the gigantic and colossal, for Eiffel Towers and sky-scraping buildings that ridiculed the dwarfed Gothic spires of the surviving churches— everything pointed to a Culture fading away in the night of historical death.

The organic growth of European Culture was coming to an end as Greek Culture once had in Athens, Pergamum, and Rhodes. In the restless search for new mediums and new techniques, in the naïve return to Pre-Raphaelites or the pathetic plunge into African or Polynesian barbarism, we can feel the desperation of Western man as he instinctively senses the increasing crystallization of a very old organism.

Cultural decline can and often does coincide with a staggering increase in power and prestige of the dominant Culture throughout the known world. The Russians struggling fiercely to Europeanize themselves, the formerly dreaded Turks becoming the enfeebled "sick man" of a condescending European diplomacy, Westernized Japan becoming the industrial giant of the Far East—all those manifestations pointed to this ascending prestige just as decadence was beginning to hollow out the soul of Europe. In fact, Western ideals, forms, and customs were penetrating everywhere from China to Africa. Only a few centuries before, a small and weak Europe still trembled and fought off the assaults of Turks and Moors, as the mainland Greeks had fought off the Persians at Salamis and the Sicilian Greeks had simultaneously repulsed the Carthaginians. Yet a few hundred years later the Persians and the Carthaginians were as Hellenized as the Russians, Turks, and many other Asians were Europeanized in our modern age.

Long before the World War broke out physically, it had broken out in Europe's mental life. No conflagration of such magnitude can take place if the mental balance of the Culture has not been disrupted beforehand, if its soul is not profoundly seared by some secret disease. Lack of tacit agreement on basic issues does not denote vitality, as Europeans thought at the time. It denotes the breakdown of a realistic spirit of synthesis or compromise, the loss of the awareness of a fundamental unity underlying the apparent diversity of expression, a unity which should have been too sacred ever to be put in question. The dislocation of Europe's unity had started centuries before, at the onset of the Renaissance and the Reformation. But powerful exponents of cultural union lived in Europe throughout the nineteenth century. Goethe, Beethoven, Saint-Saëns, Chopin, were not specifically German, French, or Polish. They were Europeans, just as Socrates, Plato, and Aristotle were Hellenes rather than citizens of specific Greek states. They thought, felt, and created within the framework of the same Culture, shared its world outlook, and felt like distant cousins, like offspring of a common ancestor.

But the steady rise of virulent nationalism—implicit in the Protestant Reformation, becoming explicit with the French Revolution —was inescapable. It began to affect Europe's waning Culture, its philosophies and literatures, and even invaded the arts. Profound discordances were welling up from the depths of the European soul and were soon to break out in the open, shattering the whole structure. The destructive triumph of nationalism could take place only after the last flicker of cultural vitality had exhausted the common European source of inspiration. There was no place in Bismarck's Germany for great philosophy or great art but only for the furnaces of the Ruhr. Clemenceau's France was no longer congenial to great literature nor was Victorian England to great music or great painting. Economic development and politics were absorbing what was left of European vitality. It did not matter whether their political structures were liberal or authoritarian, whether their social structures were aristocratic or democratic. The spirit of Culture was dying out, leaving nothing in its wake but discordant nationalisms—and after the Age of Pericles, there was nothing but senseless Peloponnesian and Hellenistic wars and revolutions.

Europe reached the peak of exasperated nationalism early in the twentieth century. No feeling of European brotherhood could restrain the clashing secular creeds that conferred upon state and nation the supreme religious aura of deification.[1] Christian internationalism had been breaking down steadily since the Reformation, communicating its own dislocation to one sphere of human activity after another. The Socialist International was now about to be betrayed by its adherents, overcome by patriotic passions. The excited French jingoism, the superb pride of the insular British, and the arrogant complex of superiority of the Germans were no longer curbed by a common feeling of cultural solidarity. Stimulating rivalry and creative competition had given way to bitter hatred and destructive antagonism. It was truly the end of a great historical epoch. And when the first World War broke out, Britain's Foreign Secretary, Sir Edward Grey, said prophetically: "The lamps are going out all over Europe; we shall not see them lit again in our own life-time." [2]

"Spartan" Prussia had gradually swallowed up the chaotic world of German principalities, free cities, dukedoms, and kingdoms, and made of the Second Reich the Macedonia of modern Europe. Strutting Kaiser Wilhelm was an insufferable reincarnation of the arrogant King Philip. When the Americans were constrained to enter the field in 1917, they felt and behaved very much like the Romans who went into Greece to put an end to Macedonian oppression, with all the generous impulses of a great overseas republic liberating the threatened cradle of the common Culture.

To the modern world, the German surrender in 1918 was as significant as the Macedonian defeat at Cynoscephalae. It was not merely the downfall of Macedonia and Germany but also the prelude to the twilight of the Hellenistic and European world orders. Germany had been no more able to establish a European unity based on national equality and an all-European patriotism than Macedonia had been able to unite Greece against the growing power of Rome. They both remained inveterate oppressors imbued with the superiority complex of younger nations, glorying in their greater vitality, discipline, organization, and martial pride, but without generosity, without power of absorption, and therefore without capacity for organic growth. Macedonia and Prussia were both close to their barbarian origins, while France and Britain were old, enfeebled, tired nations like Athens and the Aetolian League, who spent their remaining strength resisting the onslaughts of their younger and more barbaric neighbors.

Rome and Macedonia, America and Germany: these were the real antagonists struggling for world domination, and in both cases it was just as much geography as national character that determined the outcome. A much greater geographical base, wealth and population on the part of the great overseas republics as opposed to the autocratic monarchies, and also a certain psychological greatness adapted to their broader physical environment and their essentially "ethical" and legalistic outlook—these advantages, on which, alone, a world Civilization can be securely based, paved the way for victory. Rome and America were fluid, pragmatic, adaptable, and endowed with a capacity for organic growth and absorption. Macedonia and Germany were essentially rigid military structures, unadaptable, and incapable of organic growth. The world power they sought ended by devolving upon the great republics that did not want it. Macedonia was just as bent on outright world domination as Germany and their ruthless behavior initiated the terrible "total" wars of their respective ages. Neither Rome nor America could let them pursue their aggressive careers; both intervened in order to save their natural allies.

Neither of the great republics aspired to world domination. They were given it in spite of themselves and both behaved, for a time, with the same naïve idealism. A certain feeling of emotional reverence gripped both the Romans and the Americans at the sight of the seats of the great Cultures from which they sprang—Athens and Paris, Corinth and London. The delirious Greeks and western Europeans acclaimed Romans and Americans as liberators from the tyrants who had arisen on their own continents. Rome forced Macedonia to give up all her possessions in Asia Minor, Thrace, Greece, and the Aegean Islands; Europe's Central Powers were broken up and forced to liberate a dozen captive nations, two thousand years later. The defeated Macedonian army was limited to five thousand men; Germany's Reichswehr to a hundred thousand. The overseas republics then felt that their mission was accomplished: the "war to end all wars" had been fought and national freedom, brotherhood, and peace would be the outcome.

Rome had learned to dislike overseas possessions through her bitter experiences in Spain, as America had in the Philippines. These were old-fashioned colonial possessions on the pattern of the Greek and European colonial empires, and were repulsive to Romans and Americans, who, in their idealism, felt that the age of such outright colonialism was passing. Both, therefore, proclaimed liberty to be the cornerstore of their foreign policy, and Rome immediately restored full freedom to the Greek nations. Rome's reputation as the champion of national freedom lasted for generations after the fateful battle of Zama. For more than a century, Rome hardly increased her empire at all, and when forced to do so because the alternative was chaos, only with the greatest reluctance.

The position and failure of Woodrow Wilson can be better appreciated when the example of the great Roman democrat and victorious general Titus Quinctius Flamininus is set before our eyes. Rome had just smashed Macedonia's military machine as the Allies smashed Germany's in World War I. Flamininus was a generous democrat and an idealistic believer in freedom who proclaimed with ringing sincerity the complete restoration of freedom to Greece at the celebrated Isthmian Games—and Plutarch reports that the cheers of the assembled Greeks were so thunderous that crows flying overhead fell dead. The Roman herald announced: "The Senate of Rome, and Titus Quinctius the proconsul, having overcome King Philip and the Macedonians, leave the following people free, without garrisons, subject to no tribute, and governed by their own laws: the Corinthians, Phocians, Locrians, Euboeans, Phthiotic Achaeans, Magnesians, Thessalians . . ." and so on—a long list of Greek nations that read like the nations of modern Europe.[3]

Woodrow Wilson never stirred greater hopes and never earned such gratitude in Europe. And yet, behind these scenes of unmitigated enthusiasm, mutual suspicion was rife. All the old store of anti-Roman and anti-American feelings, of contemptuous condescension of the highly cultured Greeks and Europeans, was transmuted into an entirely new feeling of jealous inferiority. The former masters of the world had knocked each other senseless in their old age and were being set back on their feet by their well-meaning offsprings—an intolerable affront to their dignity. Tired and cynical Greeks could still attempt to look down upon the Romans and express their contempt for their bad manners and blunt ways in terms that are familiar to Europeans and Americans. But the days when Romans went on pilgrimages to Athens to copy Solon's laws and when Jefferson could be dazzled by Europe's Culture were gone forever. Times had changed, condescension gradually became a hateful feeling of impotence, and Greeks and Europeans clung that much more desperately to a cultural superiority that was becoming purely mythical.

Under such inauspicious circumstances, peace could only be precarious; and a student can well be amazed to learn that Greeks and Europeans, far from being chastened by their bitter experience and by the closeness of Macedonian and German servitude, felt more imperialistic than ever—as if they could compensate for their dreadful weakening by grasping some ghostly shadow. Against Roman wishes, many Greek states attempted immediately to extend their domination over other nations. Athens took Paros, Scyros, and Imbros; the gluttonous Aetolians took Phocis and Locris but were eventually denied Acarnania and Thessaly—and outraged, appealed to the tyrannical monarch Antiochus III against Rome's generosity at "their expense." It was no different in postwar Europe, absurdly partitioned by the Treaty of Versailles. European nations often incorporated alien territories against the wishes of the populations, while France and Britain carved up the defenseless Middle East into new colonial satellites.

Unstable peace prevailed, the peace that can only be a prelude to new storms. Flamininus acted with great fairness, generosity, and patience, attempting to inject some tolerance into the Greek souls, tolerance that he himself put into practice when dealing with the troublesome Boeotians who persisted in their peevish anti-Romanism. But disillusionment soon set in. The Romans withdrew in disgust from Greece in 194 B.C., leaving the quarrelsome Greeks to solve their own problems as best they could—as the Americans withdrew after the disastrous Treaty of Versailles. Greeks and Europeans gave full vent to their feelings of frustration against their overseas allies and yet were at each other's throats as soon as they felt free to indulge in their quarrels again. The Aetolian Greeks were soon asking Philip of Macedonia to join the tyrant of Sparta and the Asiatic potentate Antiochus in a war against Rome. Thus did Europe's Fascists join Nazi Germany in a new war against the West and, in their hatred, extend the hand of friendship to their worst enemy: Soviet Russia.

The pattern is clear, the logic of the whole historic development beyond argument. The compact western republics, unified, disciplined, efficient, cannot help being drawn against their will into the conflicts of the Old Worlds. The unrealistic idealism of Rome and America blinded them both to the fact that they were deeply involved in a process of disintegration and war which could only end in some form of world leadership for them—or in the collapse of their respective Civilizations altogether. Rome had forced the Macedonians to evacuate Asia Minor and now Antiochus proceeded to invade the liberated but undefended territory. Cries for help soon reached Rome: Pergamum, Smyrna, and many others appealed for protection against a new tyrant. But the Romans were as weary of war as the Americans after 1918, and like them, clung to a disastrous pacifism that could only postpone the day of reckoning. Flamininus did not want to abandon his role as generous liberator in spite of Antiochus' repeated provocations; and Mommsen could aptly remark: "History has a Nemesis for every sin—for an impotent craving for freedom, as well as for an injudicious generosity." [4] The Nemesis in the Classical world was the rise of Parthia and the coming war of Rome against Mithridates—in the context of our own century, the rise of Soviet Communism and World War II.

The Hellenization of the Orient, which had reached its zenith under Alexander, had continued for generations under the rule of the Hellenistic dynasty of Seleucus. But about the time when Flamininus was liberating the Greeks from Macedonian tyranny, a strong Asiatic reaction against Hellenism was beginning to sweep an awakening Orient. As in our own days, the reaction was sparked by an excess of European influence which jarred upon Asian nerves and the devastating counterattack of the East was triggered by Antiochus Epiphanes' reckless attempt to Hellenize his subjects. The result was, after a slow build-up, the dramatic rise of the Iranian Parthians to the imperial domination of Media, Persia, Turkestan, and Mesopotamia in the second half of the second century B.C. and the total collapse of the Hellenistic structure between the Indus and the Euphrates. Greek Culture, forcibly imposed on reluctant Asians for centuries, was thrown out and the Orientals gradually reverted to their own cultural traditions, considerably altered and "modernized" under the western impact: revival of the Iranian language, rebirth of the reformed Zoroastrian worship of the sun-god Mithra—the "Invincible Sun" of the East—and the religious supremacy of the Magi.

Thus, while Roman power was growing to such an extent as to impose its unofficial and still irresponsible influence over all the Hellenistic Mediterranean, the Hellenistic East was fast losing most of that Asiatic empire which had belonged to it for centuries. Roman blindness and unrealistic idealism were largely responsible for this disaster. Rome had enjoyed the fruits of power without responsibility, as well as the psychological gratification of an ephemeral popularity which apparently—to them—entailed no duty. Romans attempted to instill law and order in the Hellenistic world with gratifying speeches and platitudinous discourses without wanting to understand that they had to establish a much tighter control—that they had to assume the burdens of responsible rule. In the end, far from remedying anything, the spasmodic interference of Rome only increased the appalling chaos.

The Parthians of the modern world were the Soviet Russians. Rising to power at the end of World War I, they proceeded to undo the glittering and superficial Westernization that Peter the Great had undertaken, and they dragged Russia back to her Mongolian-Byzantine roots—in spite of the fact that they did it with all the technical trappings of the Industrial Age. The transfer of the capital from westernized St. Petersburg to the more oriental Moscow was symbolic of this rejection of all European values—save the strictly technological. Rome had contributed to the downfall of the Seleucid Empire, bulwark of Greek influence in the East, but having provided no substitute, reaped the Parthian threat that was to last for centuries. On the ruins of the Tzarist and Central European empires, of which America so righteously disapproved, arose the threatening power of a Soviet Russia backed by an Asia in full revolt against the West; and Mommsen's comment about Rome could apply dramatically to our modern world: "The Roman Senate sacrificed the first essential result of the policy of Alexander, and thereby paved the way for that retrograde movement whose last offshoots ended in the Alhambra of Granada and in the great mosque of Constantinople." [5]

All this might seem to be pure coincidence, mere accidents of history that might have been averted if Rome and America had pursued wiser policies, had been more aware of the long-term threats to the Civilizations for which they stood. But this would mean taking a superficial view of things. Without denying the fact that wiser policies might have blunted the long-term threat, neither Rome nor America were fundamentally responsible for its existence. The real villains were the declining Greek and European Cultures; it was primarily a failure of these disintegrating Cultures to influence the East "in depth" that broke the spell they had cast for centuries over their respective Orients. Cyrus the Great could fall under the spell of a Pericles as Catherine the Great under that of a Voltaire; but a century later, the developments of Greek and European Cultures were coming to an end and the magic charm was exorcized. The Russian Marxists in our century merely consolidated a feeling of hatred and disgust which the nineteenth-century Slavophils had directed at Europe—hatred of the narrowing of horizons that takes place when

Civilization overtakes Culture, of the gradual loss of imaginative vision and creative power, of the increasing selfishness of the dominant Civilization, of the shallow pragmatism that overcomes artistic inspiration, of the "bourgeois" pursuit of mere economic welfare that replaces the selfless impulses of the former days of cultural greatness.

Western thinkers have been inclined to concentrate on the social aspect of Russian Marxism, but this is only a small part of the whole problem, which is the profound antagonism of the Russian people—as distinct from the Soviet Communists—toward Western Civilization. The Marxist hatred of the "bourgeois" middle class conceals in Russia a primitive, instinctive hatred of Western-type city life as it had developed in the past century, and therefore of all the elements which go into making a Civilization. Furthermore, even the social aspect of the problem was as much in evidence in Classical times. In the Orient, the Greeks and the Hellenized Asians were the hated "bourgeois" of the day, the town-dwelling middle class upon which the native rural populations looked as alien and oppressive: "For them the real oppressors were not so much the officials of the royal administration as the Hellenized 'bourgeoisie'. . . . The eternal antagonism between labor and 'bourgeoisie' was aggravated by the national and religious contrasts. The city was born and with it reappeared the old incompatibility between town and country—an incompatibility aggravated for Iran at this period by the opposition that existed between the Greeks on the one hand and the far more numerous Iranians on the other." [6] Just the same, what was there in common between the sophisticated town-dweller of St. Petersburg who aped the civilized life of Paris and Vienna and the masses of Russian mujiks? And between the Chinese peasants and the westernized Chinese of Shanghai?

This deep-rooted antagonism that springs *outside* the area of a given Civilization always coincides with a social disintegration *inside* it—with a period of revolutions and social upheavals that always accompanies the collapse of a Culture and symbolizes the loss of that precious self-confidence of former times. The declining Cultures themselves provide plenty of fuel for this antibourgeois feeling by bringing out in bold relief the selfish, cynical, and irreligious character of the Greek and European middle classes. Balzac (who was immensely popular in Russia during his lifetime and who remains one of the most prized foreign authors in Soviet Russia) ripped the typical

French bourgeois apart, just as Aristophanes and Menander satirized his Athenian counterpart. What prestige could the Greek and European middle classes retain in the eyes of Asians and Russians when their own compatriots lampooned them so mercilessly?

History makes it quite plain that as the dominant West becomes more unsure of itself, the Orient slowly regains a new self-assurance. Yet, in those portions of the West that are most remote from the stages on which their drama is played—in Rome and America—such events take place almost unnoticed. The Greeks were aware of the collapse of their Hellenistic world, and the Europeans were not blind to the immense threat implied by a Soviet victory in Russia. They even made some half-hearted attempt to influence the course of Russia's civil war by sending token expeditionary forces. But the will to retrieve immense Russia was no longer there. Exhausted by World War I, corroded by internal social conflicts that at times even paralyzed their military forces through mutinies, they gave up the struggle. And when they gave up the struggle in Russia, they unwittingly made sure that, sooner or later, they would lose all their colonial empires, and, ultimately, their own political independence.

Once again, we must turn to the past and realize that Parthian victories alone did no more to destroy Greek power in the Orient than the Soviet victories in Russia destroyed Europe's global power. They were only the beginning of the whole process of disintegration, the spectacular inception of the widening rebellion of the entire Eastern world. The Iranian Parthians had plenty of allies in Mesopotamia, Syria, Arabia, Egypt, and Africa, among the remnants of deceased Civilizations as well as among new invaders from remote steppes and deserts, all men who refused to be drawn into the orbit of Classical Civilization and who had a feeling of oriental kinship with the Iranians—the Nabateans of Damascus, the Armenians, the Maccabean Jews in Palestine, the Arabs seeping in from the Arabian peninsula, the Palmyreans.

The feeling of tight kinship between Jews and Iranians was especially significant. Five hundred years before, the followers of Moses had hailed Cyrus, the Iranian monarch to whom they owed their deliverance from captivity in Babylon. The similarities between the Jewish and Zoroastrian faiths were remarkable, and the subsequent intermingling was an event of considerable importance. But the influence was largely one-sided. To a very great extent, the Jews borrowed heavily from the Iranians—for instance, their belief in immortality, as well as the notion of a duel between Satan and God that set the Sons of Darkness against the Sons of Light.[7] As the Christian Era began, Jewish sects borrowed increasingly from Zoroastrian offshoots—for instance, the Jewish Essenes, as described by Josephus, borrowed their sun-worshiping from the Iranian Mithraic faith. Most of these loans subsequently became part and parcel of the Christian faith itself. It is noteworthy that the metamorphosis of the Jewish concept of the Messiah as "Messenger" of God into the Christian concept of the Messiah as "Son" of God can be traced directly to the same pre-existing belief in Mithraism.[8] In fact, the influence of the Iranian creeds upon Judaism and Christianity, and then Islam, was so considerable that the whole religious awakening of the East between the Mediterranean and the Indus should be viewed as one single cultural movement, however numerous the superficial variations—a movement that was fundamentally opposed to Classical Culture.

Translated into the language of politics, the result of this cultural evolution was that the anti-Greek and then anti-Roman rebellions of the Jews and western Semites coincided more than once with Parthian offensives against Greeks and Romans. In fact, they were all allies in a long struggle against a Classical world whose Civilization they rejected, united in their common effort to build a new world based on the apocalyptic visions of their great prophets—Zoroaster, Moses, Isaiah, Mithra, Mani, and others. The stage was being slowly set for an awakening of the Orient that was eventually to smash Classical Civilization itself by destroying its cultural foundations.

Of all this, the Romans were not aware—no more than America understood the profound meaning of all the cataclysmic events that have taken place in the first half of our century. Neither Rome nor America understood that sooner or later they would be compelled to stand up against the East on behalf of the Greeks and Europeans who left them this dangerous legacy. As far as Rome was concerned, the eventual pay-off was the disaster at Carrhae where the proconsul Crassus lost three-quarters of his army, destroyed by the heavy cavalry of the Parthian *cataphracti*. By then, it was too late to roll back

the frontiers of an awakening Orient. "Rome realized that its statesmen and military leaders had, through their ignorance of the country,
made a grave mistake in despising Iran . . . Iran had forcibly thrown
back from its frontiers the Hellenism to which the Romans claimed
to be heirs." [9]

Ignorance and lack of understanding blended with indifference—
these were the factors that undermined from the very start Rome's
foreign policy. Rome had her anti-imperialists and her isolationists,
some form of isolationism being a long-standing Roman tradition—
unrealistic men like Cato who thought that the Roman state should
not extend beyond Italy, that overseas there should be mere zones of
influence, or better, no involvement at all. But it was far too late
in the century for such backward views. When Rome destroyed
Carthage and Macedonia, and when America entered World War I,
there was no turning back for either. The miscalculation of the Roman
Senate, unable to rise to the occasion and face entirely new problems,
was matched by the blindness of the American Senate when it turned
against Woodrow Wilson. American isolationists were to learn, as
did their Roman predecessors, that there is no power without responsibility. The mere existence of such entities as Rome and America
upsets the balance of power, attracts and antagonizes simultaneously
their weaker neighbors and associates. They can no more exist without upsetting the gravitational structure of the world than a new
star can fail to upset the astronomical structure of the universe. In
the long run, both are driven for the protection of their own safety
and ideals to step in forcibly and rule with an iron hand.

Mental blindness prompted Wilson and other idealists of the same
stamp to vindicate the rights and independence of small nations, as
if in an age of expanding economic development and interdepend-
ence, a small nation could ever be anything more than the satellite
of a big industrial power. The world was thirsting for high-minded
and generous leadership and got nothing but platitudinous speeches.
The problem, which no one could as yet formulate, was that the Western world was longing to get beyond both an outdated nationalism
and a vague internationalism that solved nothing, longing for a new
political conception of organic cooperation that would preserve what
was best in local patriotism but transcend it at the same time. It was
in fact and without knowing it, longing for a new Roman Age. It took

a second World War to bring this yearning into clearer, if still blurred, focus.

The first World War signified the destruction of the old aristocratic structure that had been patched up by the Congress of Vienna and still prevailed almost everywhere. The collapse of the Austro-Hungarian and German empires led to the downfall of former ruling classes although, here and there, some hereditary aristocracies still held their own, clinging desperately to power and tradition. The most powerful and clannish, the Prussian Junkers, still controlled Germany's armed forces. But Britain's ruling class accelerated its decline after the war. For the first time, Britain had fought as a "nation," no longer as a remote home base for "colonial" wars with limited expeditionary forces—whether in Europe, Asia, or Africa. Her ruling class had failed to foresee that, mobilized for war as a nation, the British people would remain politically mobilized in peacetime and would attempt to take matters in their own hands. Everywhere, the old social order was collapsing along with the antiquated political structures—which seemed to Americans to be all to the good.

But a new crop of tyrants was bound to arise. The collapse of the old social order did not give away to democracy on the Anglo-Saxon pattern nor to liberal parliamentarism, but to an entirely new type of despotic leaders who were misnamed "dictators." Crowns fell everywhere, but only to be replaced by far more autocratic rulers who styled themselves Duce, Führer, Caudillo, the fanatical "Leaders" of nations that had lost their souls and did not know where to turn. These tyrants were often the representatives of middle classes ruined by wars, revolutions, and inflations. European "dictators," in fact, were the modern replicas of the last crop of Greek tyrants and Hellenistic potentates, erratic, Machiavellian or fanatical, drunk with power, bombastic and theatrical. They were obvious symbols of a profound malaise that no one could diagnose accurately. It seemed no more possible to establish democratic freedom in postwar Europe than it had been in Greece during the twilight of the Hellenistic Age. Equality was progressing rapidly, but at the expense of the real measure of liberty that had formerly existed even in such autocratic empires as Germany and Austro-Hungary.

Postwar Europe turned out to be very far from the ideal that American democrats had visualized. The very rapacity of the Versailles Treaty was a sign of mortal weakness. That France's outburst of patriotic energy during the war was pregnant with the probability of future collapse was not foreseen. Italy's Fascist imperialism was a theatrical carnival, and Britain's attempt at playing the old game of balance of power in a shrinking continent was hopelessly outdated. No one could then tell what would come out of a Balkanized Europe with its civil wars and revolutions, its discordant claims and counter-claims, its flood of problems without solutions. Baffled and disgusted, America withdrew into isolationism.

CHAPTER XVI

The Lost Generation

AMERICA became fully conscious of her individuality during World War I. Until then, her history had merely been a chapter in the history of European expansion throughout the world. It took the momentous shock of a global war to start an entirely new phase of America's evolution, to emancipate her from European tutelage and to make her conscious of being something different and apart from the rest of the Western world—no longer a marginal society but a dominant factor in world politics and economics. Then, she truly became the New Rome as opposed to "Hellenistic" Europe. This metamorphosis was intimately involved with the end of the frontier, of large-scale immigration, and of the self-reliant individualism that had been a marked feature of her personality in the nineteenth century. It was a change of historical phase, the beginning of an autonomous Civilization in its own right, of a society that was becoming increasingly cohesive, whose standard of living was fast increasing while Europe's was stagnating or declining. It was the new age of mass production in which America excelled above all others, the age of what the admiring Germans called *Fordismus*.

Woodrow Wilson was at the helm when America entered the stormy waters of the World War. He had already proved to be a strong President so that there was no vacillation in executive authority, no Congressional government. America remained neutral for a time but many of her outstanding leaders saw clearly what was at stake—a struggle to the finish between the Germanic Central Powers and the English-speaking nations for leadership of the Western world. Many farsighted Americans felt that a German victory would deal a fatal blow to democracy as they conceived of it, besides forcing America

218

to build a large military machine against her own profound inclinations. The safety of the Atlantic Ocean required that America help preserve the independence of the old European nations on the opposite seaboard, a necessity that had been foreseen as early as the 1890's by men like Henry Adams and John Jay. Geopolitical facts were compelling. America could never remain neutral in a contest in which she was as basically involved as France and Britain.

The tragedy was that Wilson's leadership proved inadequate throughout the entire conflict. Instead of dominating the field and laying down a long-range policy, he let himself be swayed by the strong isolationist sentiments that prevailed in the Middle West, asking in his Proclamation of August 1914 for complete neutrality in thought as well as in deed. Later on, when compelled to switch to a war policy, he had to reverse himself completely—not only in action but, what was far more calamitous, on the ideological plane as well, and present the inevitable participation of America in the conflict in such emotionally charged terms that he became the prisoner of irrational forces which he no longer controlled.

Worse still, Wilson failed to rise to the required status of a national leader, failed to emancipate himself from party politics, and remained confined within the narrow bounds of his Democratic party. Failure to draw to himself the best among the Republicans and develop a bipartisan leadership paid sour dividends after the war. Unwittingly, he himself injected party politics into the peace talks and dragged global policy down to the level of American internal political squabbles. He had failed to become the true tribune of the whole nation that circumstances required.

Public opinion had completely rallied behind him during the hostilities and he had received bipartisan support. Yet he rejected the Republican overtures and appealed to the voters in 1918 to return a Democratic majority, the greatest blunder he could have made. The American people, emotionally shaken by the war, wanted a national leader, not a party chieftain who would make Democratic capital out of a national victory. Wilson behaved like a party politician and yet talked to the world like an inspired prophet. His Messianic speeches antagonized most Congressional leaders and tragically misled the Europeans who expected to see his policy backed by Congress, as it was in fact by American public opinion. He was a prophet but not a statesman and his unrealistic idealism made him an inept politician.

This catastrophic failure did not prevent him from behaving all through the war like a Roman constitutional dictator, taking the full "war powers" as they had already been developed by Abraham Lincoln, in addition to which he seized control of the nation's economic sinews—so vastly increased since the Civil War—with full Congressional approval. He had in fact become "a combination of King, Prime Minister in control of legislation, Commander-in-Chief, party leader, economic dictator and Secretary of State for foreign affairs." [1]

Vague attempts of Congress to recreate the "Congressional Committee on the conduct of the war" that had plagued Lincoln were firmly put down. Wilson even persuaded Congress to hand over to him all the powers that the lawmakers wanted to grant to an autonomous War Cabinet. Never had America seen such concentration of power in the hands of one single man. Wilson's failure after the war was all the more shattering, and Europeans never quite understood this brutal and complete collapse.

In order to destroy Wilson, American political leaders had to adopt a paradoxical attitude—as the Romans did after Cynoscephalae. The old nineteenth-century isolationism had, in fact, been dealt a death blow by the Americans themselves since the imperialistic development of the 1890's. But it was artificially revived by all those who rebelled against Wilson and were frightened by any form of involvement in the European nightmare from which they had been warned by the Founding Fathers. They had to justify their illogical attitude by attempting a radical withdrawal from all the foreign commitments in which they were already deeply engaged.

Isolationism was strongly bolstered by an emotional wave that swept a baffled and angry America. Hurt by European suspicions and ingratitude, Americans attempted to cut off all but economic relations with Europe, as if economics and politics could ever be divorced. Since Americans have a tendency to view situations separately rather than as part of an organic whole, they refused to see how hopelessly and inextricably world politics were mixed up with world economics. The idealistic "Wilsonism" that came under the heading of lovable public relations was quickly replaced by the "hard-headed" approach of the Yankee businessman, increasing European distrust and closing the vicious circle, since Europeans cannot look upon behavior as being motivated solely by the immediate circumstances of the present.

This swift metamorphosis of the idealistic Goddess of Liberty into a rugged Uncle Sam stunned them.

Conforming to the well-established pattern, a new period of Congressional rule followed on the heels of a bankrupt Executive. A small group of Republican Senators propelled the weak, ignorant, and unintelligent Harding into the White House. From then on, until the Great Depression, the Republican party was going to attempt to turn the clock back and cut the formidable Presidency down to size— not out of any idealistic motivation but rather for private reasons of business interest. The tribune had to be shackled and silenced by a coalition of vested interests. President Coolidge was hardly an improvement on Harding, and Herbert Hoover, although far more capable and intelligent than either, joined this select group of men who believed that the President should abdicate the immense powers that more than a century of American history had accumulated in the White House.

The reaction was bound to come, and with a vengeance. Not only was the long-term trend blindly resisted. The vast economic changes that had taken place in the past half-century had seen colossal financial and industrial corporations spread all over the continent, huge labor unions link in one organization the Atlantic and Pacific seaboards. The days of Hoover's "rugged individualism" were as over and done for as the horse-and-buggy era, but he did not see it. In addition, the World War itself had accelerated the trend toward increased state power, as all wars do. The draft and economic controls had brought the federal government—that is the executive power —to every doorstep in America. There was no turning back. When Depression struck in 1929, America was back in a national emergency greater than the World War and the people looked up to the government for even greater leadership than it had displayed in 1917.

In those postwar days of mixed euphoria and bafflement, the outstanding fact was that America was experiencing a change of historical phase. The end of the frontier and of immigration signified the end of the dynamic settlement of the country. America was cutting off the flow of European immigrants that had linked the Old and New Worlds for centuries. Now followed the drowsy lull of digestion, of prosperous contentment in the 1920's, of acute indigestion and despair in the 1930's. From the 1940's onward, the lull was at an end and

World War II started a reverse process: American expansion throughout the world.

In 1920, the Census Office recorded for the first time that America's town-dwellers had outstripped the rural population, itself becoming increasingly mechanized and urbanized. Like Roman Italy, America was an increasingly compact and mobile nation of highly civilized town-dwellers, towering above the smaller rustic states around her, unwilling to assume world-wide responsibilities which accrued to her, yet far too powerful to be ignored.

Growing urbanism and increasing nomadism made easier by the fabulous development of transportation, the tearing up of the flimsy rural roots planted only a few generations before—everything conspired to increase the gregariousness of the population, develop the herd instinct and mass suggestibility. True individualism and originality, already weak in Tocqueville's America, was sinking under the weight of a psychological socialization exceeding anything known in the past. Industrial standardization had fostered its psychological counterpart and every social phenomenon of the 1920's, from Prohibition to the moral breakdown and the speculation hysteria, assumed gigantic proportions. Everything became massive—bootlegging, gangsterism, vice, corruption, industrial corporations, buildings, financial speculation.

But, by way of psychological compensation for the frenzy and license of the "Jazz Age," this was also the era of the melancholy "Lost Generation," the age of the morbid revolt of American youth against the outdated ideals of their elders—ideals rooted in the eighteenth century's Age of Enlightenment, which had become incompatible with a new and baffling world. The vigorous dynamism of the turn of the century was gone, as was the reformist zeal of Populists, Progressives, and the apostles of the New Freedom. Prosperity dulled the social conscience, as it had in Rome after the Punic wars and the sudden increment of riches in Italy.

While the novelists of the twenties gave poignant descriptions of the Lost Generation's shriveled souls, Mencken's humorous cynicism, a reincarnation of Petronius' and Juvenal's turned its back on the cult of the "common man" and on democracy in general, proving in the process that the most sacred American beliefs and taboos can be challenged with impunity, so long as the challenge is based on disrespect and humor. It became fashionable to ridicule the great traditions of America's past, to cut down the revered leaders of bygone ages to contemporary size.

For the first time the seeds of moral decay became clearly visible in America's leading social stratas. Prohibition was as symptomatic of this decay as Rome's amazing Sumptuary Laws, the result of the same moralizing psychology and same belief in external compulsion as a substitute for inner strength and conviction. Both had to come to the same sad end. Both implied a nostalgia for the good old days of simple, healthy living when Rome and America were relatively poor, when luxury and self-indulgence were unknown.

The tension of early Puritanism, in Rome as in America, was bearable for austere men of great faith and iron will power. Such psychological tension and sternness had not existed in Greece and Europe, where a certain easygoing, harmonious balance was as much in evidence in the morals of the individuals as it was absent in the exasperated politics of Greek and European societies; whereas the moral breakdown of latter-day republican Rome and America gave rise to the most extreme rejection of all moral restraints. Pent-up frustrations and inhibitions, held in check by centuries of stringent moral taboos, were finally exploding in an orgy of self-indulgence on a fantastic scale. The era of Prohibition witnessed the same unloosening of moral fetters as in first-century Rome. Its repeal was an implicit admission of the failure of external compulsion to retrieve the lost virtues of the past and Pompey's building of the first gigantic circus for the pleasure-loving Romans compares symbolically with the Repeal as sounding the death knell of compulsory Puritanism.

But America could no more turn her back on moralism than Rome could. Roman and American Civilizations stand on *ethical* bedrocks from which they could never be removed without collapsing altogether. Rome's Sumptuary Laws are a remarkable example of legislation applied to the minutest details of private life and no more felt to threaten personal liberty than America's lingering puritanical laws. They regulated with minute precision the permissible private expenditures on housing, banquets, funerals, women's clothing, and a multitude of other details. Such puritanical stringency made the better-balanced and more individualistic Greeks shudder. There is no such thing as crass immorality for easygoing Epicureans, no great inner tension, and therefore no spectacular breakdown of morals such as affects Puritans and Stoics.

In the "business civilization" of the 1920's—"America's business is business" was the optimistic slogan of those thoughtless days, a fundamental expression of an outlook which is so alien to Europe —the insidious belief that an end had been put to economic cycles made great headway. The belief that the "war to end all wars" had disposed of all major problems, that it had, in fact, put an end to history altogether, convinced many men otherwise intelligent, that the world had entered an age of unlimited progress, the age known to the 1920's as the "New Era." The belief that cycles in human affairs eventually come to an end is as old as Methuselah—and about as outdated. Cycles, in economic as in historical development in general, are unavoidable. Efficient management of powerful public agencies—provided these agencies are as widely based as the economic structures with which they deal—can minimize the amplitude of these cycles, or break them up into minor cycles. But it can never abolish them, any more than it could abolish the blood pulse of human organisms or the cyclical recurrence of the seasons.

The American administration of the 1920's was pitifully weak and ineffective in the United States, let alone the virtual nonexistence of world organization. There was a world economy with a tight web of international connections and protean ramifications in every part of the globe, but no world management. The pygmy international agencies that attempted to nibble at the major economic problems were totally inadequate, dwarfed by the size of a world economy in full development.

So it was that, against this dark and cloudy background, Big Business experienced the Indian summer of its absolute predominance during the decade preceding the great collapse of 1929. This predominance was not merely economic and financial; it was also psychological. The whole of America came to believe that businessmen were the salt of the earth, that economic profit was or should be the main object of man's endeavor. Great business leaders became the heroes of the day. They were shrouded in an atmosphere of reverent respect as statesmen or generals or artists were in bygone ages. Never had the great captains of industry enjoyed such prestige, never had their shallow ideals been so enthusiastically adopted by millions of men and women thirsting for riches.

The postwar economic panorama was dazzling; endless, almost uninterrupted, growth seemed to be in sight. But the first outstanding economic and financial revolution in the international field had come about largely unnoticed in its profound implications: from being an international debtor, America had become the greatest creditor nation in the world. Her industries vastly expanded by the tremendous European demand for supplies and armaments, America entered the postwar era without noticing the grave symptoms of economic disequilibrium introduced by the world conflagration. For America was now both a creditor and a predominantly exporting nation. Europe was considerably impoverished and could no longer buy American goods with the returns on investments that had been liquidated to pay for the war. In order to re-establish the balance, European exports to the New World should have been substantially larger than the imports, but America's high tariffs stood in the way; and nothing could induce the Americans to lower those tariffs. Big Business was in control and blindly resisted the normal trend.

Inevitably, European gold began to flow in steady streams to America in exchange for her exports, compensating for Europe's liquidated prewar investments in the New World. On the other hand, massive American loans went to Europe—largely to Germany where they were eventually used to build up the Nazi war machine. The glaring incompatibility between an interlocking world economy and America's political isolationism should have seemed ludicrous, but it did not. Americans did not, and indeed had not wanted to understand the profound causes of the war. They could no more understand the basic problems of the postwar world. Economic and political leadership on a global scale was required and was not forthcoming, in spite of the fact that by 1927 American private enterprise had invested more than thirteen billion dollars abroad.

Yet, American business leaders could not close their eyes to some international problems that impinged directly on their interests. In 1925, unwilling to face the facts of inevitable historical decline, Britain took the catastrophic step of reverting to the gold standard. National pride, which should never have been left free to disturb international economic relations, led to this over-evaluation of the pound sterling. Britain was drained of her gold and slumped into a grave social crisis highlighted by the general strike of 1926. Alarmed, British and other European financial leaders went on a pilgrimage to Washington and persuaded the Americans to adopt an easy-money policy in 1927 in order to discourage the flow of European capital to the New World. Interest rates were thoughtlessly lowered in America with the unexpected but unavoidable result that a vast influx of loose money began to flood Wall Street—disrupting America's internal structure without appreciably improving Europe's financial situation.

Instead of realistically facing the international problem, America concentrated on herself and plunged into an orgy of speculation such as the world had never yet seen. Financial omnipotence and super-human wisdom were credited to the Big Business leaders of the day and both political parties became entangled in the fast-expanding network of promoted speculation. One of the outstanding speculators of the day, John J. Raskob, a director of General Motors, became Chairman of the Democratic National Committee. Politics and world problems were soon forgotten. The hysterical mood of the day can be gauged from the following comments of an influential economist: "Led by these mighty knights of the automobile industry, the steel industry, the radio industry . . . and finally joined in despair by many professional traders who . . . had caught the vision of progress, the Coolidge market had gone forward like the phalanxes of Cyrus. . ." [2]

Not only Wall Street but Washington was largely under the control of Big Business and the administration kept hands off. The Federal Reserve Board was made up of cowards or incompetents who dared not or could not stand up against the hysterical optimism that was sweeping the country. Worthy men like Benjamin Strong of the New York Federal Reserve Bank were scolded for their vague internationalism and Strong himself was labeled "a mental annex of Europe" by Herbert Hoover [3]—with the unmistakably contemptuous undertone of un-Americanism. The slogan of this era was "less government in business, more business in government," which would have been better rephrased "no government at all." The real heroes of the day were orgiastic speculators like Charles E. Mitchell of the National City Bank, who became a director of the Federal Reserve Bank of New York, men like William Crapo Durant, organizer of General Motors, Harrison Williams, one of the prophets of the volatile high-leverage investment trusts, Richard Whitney, vice-president and then president of the New York Stock Exchange. In the background stood awesome, almost legendary figures—J. P. Morgan, Henry Ford, John D. Rockefeller, and other empire builders of the same stamp.

In America's increasing financial frenzy, there was no more room for concern about the rest of the world than there was for America's own specific problems. Farmers had been in a permanent slump since the depression of 1920-21, the South was still underprivileged and streaked with slums. Concentration in industry had progressed to such an extent that in 1929 half the corporate wealth of the nation had fallen into the hands of two hundred giant corporations—many of them as powerful as dozens of foreign governments combined. It should have been apparent by then that there were grave weaknesses in the economic structure of America and that a cyclical downturn in business was already overdue. The basic weakness was an uneven distribution of the national wealth, most of the benefits of rising pro-ductivity going to a small minority of the people. Labor unions were too weak to force business leaders to share their benefits with the bulk of the working population and thus build up the general public's purchasing power. This lopsidedness only increased as the frantic speculation went on. John J. Raskob, having become Chairman of the Democratic National Committee, told the American public that "Everybody ought to be rich" in a celebrated article bearing the same title. The golden road to riches was paved with speculative investment trusts rather than with the sweat of hard work. Belief in incantations about the prospect of unlimited prosperity ahead was almost universal.

Never had politics disappeared so completely into the furnace of economics, high finance and eventually sky-rocketing speculation resting on doubtful manipulations, pools, and artificial promotions. What little interest there had been in art, literature, and culture in general, had entirely disappeared in the hectic summer of 1929 when Wall Street reached the boiling point. The stock market dominated the news and the thoughts of all, from financiers to cab drivers, even though the actual participants in Wall Street's volcanic activities were only a minority. By the autumn of 1929 an economic depression was under way but for a while this alarming trend put no damper on the speculative fireworks. Money from all over the world poured into the golden Mecca which, with its economic support slipping away, was by now floating on mythical clouds.

When the speculative bubble was pricked at last and the stock market began to collapse on "Black Thursday," an era came to an end—not merely the end of the speculative fury, but the end of seventy years of Big Business prestige and authority. It was a dramatic ending. The demoralization produced by the great crash in America amazed the rest of the world. But in a society that stakes most of its thoughts, actions, and pride on economic progress, such a collapse was shattering. To many in those awful days, it looked like the end of America itself. There was no recovery, only breathless pauses between sinking spells that engulfed fortunes as well as the small savings of millions of individuals. Money that had poured into Wall Street from the far corners of the world now reversed its flow and streamed out of the punctured heart of world finance like water out of a sieve, deepening the slump, draining the life blood out of America's financial structure, and drying up all possible sources of recovery.

The greatest event of those tragic weeks and months was not so much economic or financial but psychological. It was the irretrievable destruction of a traditional prestige, the downfall of a great money-power that had been almost unchallenged since the Civil War. It was the catastrophic loss of authority of Big Business. The people no longer believed in their former gods. The bankers and businessmen themselves lost all faith in their financial acumen and with it, lost all faith in their destiny. They looked foolish and behaved ineffectively. The old incantations no longer worked. Fords, Du Ponts, Morgans, and Rockefellers could claim to have retained their faith in the soundness of the economic structure but the magic spell was broken.

Loss of prestige soon gave way to contempt when a pyramid of frauds and embezzlements was disclosed by the fast-receding tide of money. The rank dishonesty of Albert H. Wiggin and Charles E. Mitchell, respectively heads of the Chase and National City banks, besmirched the entire financial community. During the following years, financiers became a fair target of politicians, the press, radio, and Congressional investigating committees. The climax of this precipitous decline was reached in 1938 when Richard Whitney, the respected head of the New York Stock Exchange, was convicted of grand larceny and sent to prison. It was truly the end of an era.[4]

President Hoover still had three grueling years to serve, years of deepening depression that were grinding to bits the economic fabric of America. Yet by the spring of 1931 there were signs that the worst might be over and that the economy was beginning to pick up. But by now, isolationist feelings had spread to economics, fanned by the psychological urge to discover some scapegoat. Turning their backs on the rest of the world, America's frantic business leaders compelled Congress to vote the disastrous Hawley-Smoot tariff of 1930. President Hoover did not dare impose his veto and the world was informed that the outflow of American loans and the inflow of American imports were being drastically curtailed, affecting the entire world economy and dragging it down into the abysmal slump. Europe's weak structure could not stand up to this last blow. The huge Kredit Anstalt of Austria collapsed in May, 1931. In September Britain was forced off the gold standard—and the growing depression of Europe rebounded on America, smashed the light upturn of the spring, and dragged the New World down again to lower depths of demoralization. In October, 1931, Franklin Roosevelt's "nameless, terrifying fear" gripped America again. There seemed to be no end to this recurring, deepening nightmare.

The fundamental element of the crisis being moral and emotional rather than economic, the people wanted moral comfort and reassurance as much as wise decisions. They received neither. Herbert Hoover was a typical self-made man of the old stamp, a self-reliant man of the dynamic West who believed in the old virtues that had made America great but were no longer applicable to a gigantic industrial machine of great complexity in which everything seemed to have gone wrong. Hoover's was still the America of unlimited opportunity for the individual, the America where failure was not society's fault or responsibility, but the individual's alone. It was the America of independent men of bold temperament, men who did not indulge in self-pity and who despised weakness. Those were democratic men who did not believe in class distinctions and therefore could not have any strong emotional feeling for the underprivileged. This lack of feeling paralyzed them when the time came to deal with the political implications of mass emotionalism. An engineer and not a lawyer, Hoover belonged to an age of empire builders who did not know that the era of unlimited opportunities was past, that vitality had declined under the impact of a rising standard of living. A lawyer, familiar with history and human psychology, might have understood, if only by instinct. But an engineer like Hoover, who was described by the

Philadelphia *Record* as "easily the most commanding figure in the modern science of 'engineering statesmanship,' " [5] was lost in his mechanics. Hoover and his Republican associates had mentally accepted the predominance of economics over politics and when economics failed, the Republican party lost an emancipated political power for a full generation. They did not believe in strong executive power and Hoover himself failed to give firm leadership to his own Republican party. Through their failure to grasp the situation as it really was, these men ushered into the White House the first of the outstanding pre-Caesarians.

CHAPTER
XVII

The New Deal

THE Great Depression shook America as no war ever had and shook the entire world in the process, a world dwarfed by the great economic power of the United States whose productivity was roughly equal to that of all the other nations combined. With the Depression, came the historical downfall of an irresponsible Big Business, metaphorically summed up in Franklin Roosevelt's Inaugural Address: "The money-changers have fled from their high seats in the temple of our civilization. We may now restore that temple to the ancient truths. . . ." [1] In its long struggle with money, political power was going to emerge victorious, but the cost was staggering. By 1932, the national income had fallen below that of 1912 when the population was smaller by thirty million people. From 1929 to 1933, the total production of the economy had fallen off by as much as one third. The Depression's devastation to America's highly complex structure exceeded anything experienced in the Old World. Farm income, estimated at almost eight billion dollars in 1929, fell to less than three billion in 1932. Hunger, breadlines, Hoovervilles, the tramping of the unemployed from one end of the land to another —all this was a shattering blow to the leadership of the economic and financial czars. During the terrible 1933-34 winter, twenty million people depended directly on federal relief for the basic elements of survival. From then on until 1941, except briefly in 1937, the number of unemployed remained over eight million, and as late as 1938, one person out of five was out of work. It was a prolonged disaster with no end in sight.

When the Depression began to have repercussions abroad, President Hoover attempted to shift the blame onto foreign nations. The economic leaders of America had been unable or unwilling to see that a world economy without some sort of world supervision was folly. As the crisis grew more acute in 1931 and the denizens of the international economic jungle began to devour each other, Hoover said: "As we look beyond the horizons of our own troubles and consider the events in other lands, we know that the main causes of the extreme violence and the long continuance of this depression came not from within but from without the United States." [2] And he added that "political instability had affected three-fourths of the population of the world." [3]

The emotional impulse to shirk responsibilities and blame the unsettled world for the disaster could be psychologically soothing but it solved nothing. Panic-stricken, the American people clamored for governmental action. Radicalism flared up again and minor Caesarian figures like Huey Long could and did become dictators in their states on the strength of their extreme demagogy. Not content to rule Louisiana with an iron hand, able and bold, Huey Long aspired to a dictatorial leadership on the national scale with his "Share-the-Wealth" platform. He was taken seriously enough to be considered a real threat—one made possible by President Hoover's complete lack of authority and imagination. Hoover's views on the limited role of the Presidency were outdated, not merely in terms of the early 1930's but in terms of the office as Theodore Roosevelt had reshaped it; and in view of the rising temper of the American people, such presidential leadership could not long be delayed.

The election of Franklin Roosevelt in 1932 was a major turning point in the history of America, and indirectly of the world. America elected a new tribune of the people, a tribune who was no longer the captive of business and vested interests but one who felt responsible to the entire nation. He was a Democrat but also the champion of a revolt that had started forty years before under the Populists' leadership and had often cut across party lines. Conscious of this national rather than merely partisan backing, Franklin Roosevelt was determined to establish a semidictatorial rule, a personal rule such as none of his strong predecessors would have dared contemplate in their wildest dreams. He had no wish to carry out a revolution and explained quite clearly that no such revolution was necessary: "Our Constitution is so simple and practical that it is possible always to meet extraordinary needs by changes in emphasis and arrangement without loss of essential form. . . ." [4]

During the four months between Roosevelt's election and his inauguration, Hoover's policy-making was utterly paralyzed and the Depression deepened to the extent of becoming a calamity. Respect for constitutional forms resulted in a grinding economic breakdown and illustrated the weakness of an outgoing President who could not come to terms with his successor. Years before, writing in a more peaceful age, James Bryce reminded his readers of a Classical parallel. Choosing one example among many, he explained that in an emergency the Greeks were quite willing to disregard constitutional forms. And he concluded: "This effort . . . to escape from the consequence of the system could not have occurred in governments like those of Rome, England or the United States, where the 'reign of law' is far stricter than it was in the Greek Republics" [5]—or for that matter than it was in any European country.

Respect for law and Constitution deepened the economic disaster in which America was plunged during the winter of 1932-33. The people wanted an immediate change of rulers but constitutional law stood in the way and it was respected. The tragedy was that there could be no meeting ground between the President and the President-elect, no agreement of any sort. They did not speak the same language and the President-elect would not assume the responsibility of underwriting his predecessor's fumbling decisions.

Victorious democrats often seem to find their greatest leaders among the remnants of former aristocracies in whom lurks the intense if unconscious dislike for money-making and sheer plutocracy. This pattern was quite in evidence in Rome among the intensely aristocratic leaders of Roman democracy: the Gracchi, Drusus, and Caesar. It was just as evident in the selection of Franklin Delano Roosevelt. It is these aristocratic leaders who, having been raised in an atmosphere of social privilege, apart from the people, can be moved by popular misfortune because they are not part of it but look at it from the outside. Belonging to a respectable squirearchy settled along the Hudson River, possessing wealth that made it easy for him to despise something he had never lacked, Franklin Roosevelt could let his generous impulses guide him uncritically. He despised money because he did not understand it. Although this attitude gave him the immense appeal of a true tribune, it colored his economic views with a dangerous amateurishness. Under his leadership, the New Deal was to engineer a great social revolution but would not solve the basic problem of a depression which threatened to become chronic. World War II finally put an end to it by mobilizing all the immense resources of a nation that seemed to have too much for full use in peacetime.

Leadership was asserted immediately after Roosevelt's inauguration with the proclamation of a "bank holiday" under a War Enabling Act dating back to Wilson's days—and Congress fell in line immediately, intimidated, cowed into complete submission by the catastrophic nature of the financial crisis. The people responded with an absolute faith in a man whose theoretical views were largely unknown but who was able to act boldly and decisively. The most popular and articulate spokesman of public opinion's feelings, Will Rogers, said in those days: "I don't know what additional authority Roosevelt may ask, but give it to him, even it's to drown all the boy babies. . . . It just shows you what a country can do when you take their affairs out of the hands of Congress." [6] No European dictator ever commanded such popular backing—backing voluntarily offered, not wrung out of the people by compulsion or terror.

The New Deal was launched in the first three months of the new Administration as an amalgamation of Theodore Roosevelt's Square Deal (partnership between business and government) and Wilson's New Freedom (control and limitation of business concentration), wrapped up in the emotionalism of Bryan's old Populist movement. It was essentially a practical attempt to deal with a grave emergency without any theoretical or doctrinal base, and it found deep roots in the widespread sentiments of the past half-century against the irresponsible power of Big Business. The heaviest blow against the financial magnates was a financial revolution that had been advocated by Bryan's Populists; it gave the Administration full power to manipulate the currency and foster inflation or deflation, as the need might be. The entire financial edifice was reconstructed, the independent power of the bankers smashed—but reform always stopped short of the radical measures advocated by the doctrinaire Socialists who pay more attention to form than to essence.

Throughout the first year of his rule, Roosevelt concentrated an increasing amount of power in his hands, overriding the reluctance of a disgruntled Congress. Administrative agencies assumed a degree of power and independence that left the legislative branch with very little influence on the dizzy course of events. Final decisions rested with a President who handled his huge power with increasing assurance as time went on. Roosevelt was not carrying out a constitutional revolution, as his enemies asserted, but was merely leading America back to the one and only path along which her history had been proceeding: the path toward growing executive power. It was not a fresh start but the fulfillment of a profound trend whose origin lay deep in the past. All those who deplored the trend, who lamented the waning of the former "rugged individualism," were belated romanticists who refused to move with the times. The spirit of the Roman *panem et circenses* was slowly pervading the atmosphere, without destroying the willingness to work but weakening the former self-reliance of pioneering days. The mainstay of American freedom— freedom *from* authority—began to give way now that a large majority of the people were willing to barter freedom for security.

The psychological change was profound and it made the emergence of an all-powerful, paternalistic state inevitable. It was not this Welfare State that weakened the individual's self-reliance, as its critics contend. The Welfare State merely sanctioned what had become a fact, a psychological change of profound scope, to which it adapted new social and economic institutions. The emergence of the Welfare State as a controlling apparatus, operating both on a gigantic scale and in a minutely differentiated field, was as much a result as a contributing cause of the gradual decline in the average individual's self-reliance and initiative. Individual man was increasingly trapped in the complex network of a colossal machinery of which he saw and understood only a very small part. This psychological evolution indicated a change of historical phase in the individual's outlook, from the dynamic to the static. Dwarfed by the size and complexity of modern society, he became willing to surrender a large part of his stimulating but dangerous freedom for the sake of economic security.

It was all in the cards that Franklin Roosevelt did not make but which he dealt with consummate skill. His leadership was not collective but intensely personal. He consulted many men but always made his own decisions alone. Nothing could have been further removed from a parliamentary type of government. The New Deal "brain trusts" were unique in their conception, a typical American creation attempting to mechanize and mass-produce ideas by pooling human minds. But they had nothing in common with parliamentary debates. They operated like general staffs under military discipline. Only the Commander in Chief was entitled to make decisions and he did not have to give any explanations. He was like another typical American creation, the master-mind sports coach who bosses his team, devises its tactics and strategy, switches players and substitutes at will. However, endowed with true political genius like all Caesarian figures, Roosevelt always knew how to give to the American people the feeling that his power and his decisions were theirs.

Much has been and will be written about Franklin Roosevelt's exceedingly complex character, his courage and yet his evasiveness, his idealism and his acute realism. Mommsen's succinct summing up of Julius Caesar's character—"the most supple master of intrigue" [7] —is perhaps the most fitting description of Roosevelt. What Roosevelt had to a supreme degree was a charismatic charm that poured out naturally, the irresistible charm of a born leader of men. As soon as he was in office he communicated with the American people through his "fireside chats," a remarkable exercise in mass hypnotism. The fact that he came, in time, to have the major part of the press against him did not make a dent in his popular appeal. A new device, the radio, had prevailed over the older printed word; and when his magnetic voice purred its way into the ears of millions of his compatriots, he managed to cast an unbreakable spell on America. Logical argumentation could no longer prevail, as it had in the days of the Founding Fathers. Political speeches had already long ago become what rhetoric and diatribe had become in the Classical world when they displaced eloquence: they were used for effect, not for content. They conjured emotions but did not appeal to the intellect; and at this game, Franklin Roosevelt was unrivaled.

The greatest reward of this projection of one man's warm personality on the national consciousness was a remarkable recrudescence of confidence which economic circumstances did not really warrant —and many political opponents were quick to point out the numerous flaws in the Administration's policy. But against Roosevelt's personality, conservatives were as powerless as radical demagogues like Huey Long. The Caesarian flavor of this highly personal rule was partly masked from his contemporaries by the easygoing familiarity of the man. As a New Dealer remarked: "The New Deal is a laughing revolution. It is purging our institutions in the fires of mockery, and it is led by a group of men who possess two supreme qualifications for the task: common sense and a sense of humor." [8] Certainly this leadership was closer to that of popular pre-Caesarian Rome than it was to the Wagnerian tyranny of Germany's Nazism with its terrifying *Götterdämmerung* atmosphere. But its humane and humorous aspect was only a mask, a psychological compensation for the almost absolute power behind it. It was not issued of a brutal revolution as was the fashion in the unstable worlds of the Hellenes and the Europeans; it was the actualization of an old trend and those who lived through it and trembled for the safety of their republican institutions could always attempt to comfort themselves by pointing out its familiar, even traditional features. But the lengthening shadow of growing Caesarism was unmistakably there.

Another source of Roosevelt's power was in his knowledge of how to handle the political world, Congress especially. He was a consummate politician whose leadership within his party could no longer be challenged, who used patronage with considerable effectiveness. Skill in handling Congress and full use of his veto power gave him, in fact, almost unlimited influence on lawmaking, thanks to the fact that he always had the initiative. It was all strictly constitutional and yet the separation of powers so fondly cherished by the Founding Fathers was no more than a ghost by then.

The New Deal implied simultaneous relief and recovery, and then profound reform of the economic and social structure. The speed with which the new Administration went to work on relief reduced Congress to the position of a rubber-stamping body. Individual Senators could hurl the epithet "dictator" at the President but the country at large trusted its tribune and repeatedly voted him back in office. Time and again, Congress was asked to vote huge sums of money without being given even a minimum of information as to how and by what organization the spending was to be carried out. Roosevelt's control over the fast-expanding network of agencies and committees was masterful and often left his closest advisers as much in the dark as regards his grand strategy as the Congressmen themselves.

Sixty different agencies were involved in relief undertakings and only the President knew all the twists, detours, and corners of his administrative labyrinth. The best example of his shrewd handling of men was his creation of two opposed and yet complementary agencies with confusing initials: Hopkins' W.P.A. and Ickes' P.W.A. —always quarreling, yet always forced into close collaboration by the White House's imperious arbitration.

Washington gradually became the seat of the world's greatest business enterprise: the Administration of the United States. A strange new world came into being, dwarfing and shattering the prestige of the old business world of bankers and industrial magnates. It was a world of pure politics and bureaucracy emancipated from business control, a world in which men competed for power and prestige, not for financial profits, a world of mandarins and brain-trust intellectuals. For the first time in the history of the United States, the despised intellectual reached a position of substantial power and even respectability. The American intellectual, the psychological "freedman" of the modern world, began his real emancipation under Franklin Roosevelt as Rome's equally despised intellectual freedmen (mostly of Greek extraction) reached power when Julius Caesar established his permanent bureaucracy after the downfall of Roman Big Business.

All this bewildered the former rulers of the country whose only world outlook was financial profit, who looked down upon politics as the handmaid of private business, and who bitterly resented their new master. And from the opposite direction left-wing radicals struck out at Roosevelt for not doing away with capitalism altogether. But he stood his ground, acting as a surgeon, not as an executioner.

Congress had been more or less disposed of, but across Roosevelt's path stood an old-fashioned, defiant judiciary that carried over into the new age the old limited views, the lack of comprehension that had made it for so long an unthinking ally of Big Business. A strong President always ends by clashing with the Supreme Court, but Roosevelt's clash was momentous. In 1935 the Supreme Court found that the National Industrial Recovery Act was unconstitutional because it granted too many legislative powers to the President; other acts were soon invalidated by the same judicial procedure. Emboldened by his tremendous success at the polls in 1936, Roosevelt overreached himself with his Supreme Court "packing" scheme—Congress refused to sanction it. But the Justices had been impressed by the demonstration of electoral will as well as alarmed by this undisguised threat to their autonomy. The Court virtually capitulated and approved the National Industrial Recovery Act—and with this the executive branch moved boldly into the legislative arena and carved out for itself an absolute predominance over the "fourth branch" that was coming into being: the autonomous agencies and commissions such as the Tennessee Valley Authority in which executive, legislative, and judiciary powers were inextricably intertwined. Henceforth the political parties were no longer the sole connective tissue joining together the separate powers of government. A new autonomous bureaucracy under executive control towered over them.

Like all the great reformers in Rome, Franklin Roosevelt had incurred at first the almost unanimous hostility of lawyers and jurists, always the first to react to arbitrary modes of procedure; and if he could always overpower Congress, he had to tread gingerly when it came to dealing with the conservative-minded judicial element. But he finally reached his goal by dint of skill and patience. He was eventually able, because of vacancies, to appoint seven out of nine members of the Supreme Court and reshape it decisively. The legal profession finally made its peace with the New Deal and provided many of its administrative brains, emphasizing the pragmatic nature of the great experiment with its reliance on American "legal realism," case law rather than logical legal philosophy, applied law rather than theoretical.

But, in this conflict, the President had unquestionably weakened the prestige of the Court among the people. In this sense, it is doubtful whether it could or would dare resist a new presidential assault which might be launched during some future emergency; and this psychological evolution further weakened the vanishing separation of powers.

The New Deal was in line with American tradition. It was essentially concrete-minded and pragmatic. It concentrated on practical issues, not on theoretical formulations; but although it alleviated the worst features of the Great Depression, it proved unable to cure the more fundamental national ills. Roosevelt's violent campaign speeches in 1936 frightened and antagonized the business community needlessly, and made a lasting reconciliation with the business managers impossible.

Roosevelt's lack of financial acumen was shared by most economists in those days and his stubborn insistence on a balanced budget eventually sparked the new collapse of 1937. In a few months, half of the progress made since 1932 was lost, industrial production declined 30 per cent and the number of unemployed reached more than ten million. Instead of being wildly inflationist, as many of his critics thought, Roosevelt was basically frightened of inflation and his uncertain fiscal policy reduced the Administration's contribution to the general purchasing power by several billion dollars. A new depression struck and, this time, the President lost his usual self-confidence. For the first time, he could not make up his mind as to what policy to pursue. The normal course of all depressions is to come to an end, but this one might have lasted indefinitely if it had not been for new inflationary appropriations wrung from Congress to the tune of three billion dollars for relief and public works. Even so, it was World War II and nothing else that put an end to massive unemployment and set the gigantic machinery of America humming again.

Hesitation in economic matters was not reflected in politics. Roosevelt now determined to tighten his iron grip on the Democratic party by purging it of all rebellious elements and accentuating the predominance of its liberal wing. In so doing, he completely altered both political parties by standing up before the electorate as a national leader rather than a party nominee. He was a tribune of the people, the "indispensable man" without whom his own party could not hope to win, whose lengthening shadow encompassed all other personalities and who, in fact, needed no party for support. In him, we can now see the true pre-Caesarian figure whose rule is no longer partisan but personal.

The rise of democratic political power in Rome took place, as it did in America, through the big political machines. The corrupt rule of ring-and-bossdom in an elective democracy is almost inevitable. Franklin Roosevelt's strength lay in his shrewd manipulation of the big city Democratic machines, not in the national Democratic party as such. National parties, agglomerations of discordant local interests without specific doctrine and philosophy, were and are increasingly dominated by the "indispensable man." Vitality resides in the local organizations, not in their federal structure. Roosevelt could fight relentlessly against Huey Long's machine in Louisiana and James Curley's machine in Massachusetts. But he could only do so successfully by depending on a majority of the other machines. His alliance with Edward Flynn, boss of the Bronx, was comparable to Caesar's reliance on Clodius' machine against Milo's "Tammany Hall." Clodius' machine was primarily a vote-buying organization that distributed free wheat to its clientele, standing on a platform advocating the emancipation of slaves and freedom for Roman labor to organize itself.

But centralization is greater in America than it was in Rome, in a sense at least. Political power is more concentrated in the one elected tribune instead of being parceled out among many officials of equal rank as was the case in Rome. So it was that Roosevelt was able to dominate most local machines by making the W.P.A. itself into a gigantic, nation-wide supermachine with extensive political ramifications. The vote-buying that characterizes local machines was applied on a federal scale and paid rich dividends to the Roosevelt Administration. From now on, this federal dwarfing of such petty machines as Tammany Hall became a prime factor in American politics. A great deal of the political credit still granted to local organizations depends on their ability to obtain funds from the federal treasury rather than on their own local resources.

Like the Americans, the Romans were an essentially practical people. They believed in pragmatism rather than logic, trial and error rather than theoretical schemes. They wanted no revolution but constructive evolution and they were hardly swayed at all by the revolutionary waves that swept the Greek and Hellenistic world. Polybius, who was born a Greek, saw with the keen eye of the outsider that the Roman constitution was not so much thought out and laid out in a rigid pattern as evolved gradually through a process of perpetual transformation and adaptation—which is just the way Americans looked upon their Constitution. Someone remarked with justice upon "Franklin Roosevelt's conscientious, deliberated effort to continue the Constitution as a truth and a hope, not as a mere collection of obsolete phrases." [9]

So it was that alone in the classical world, Rome experienced a succession of New Deals, pragmatic attempts to solve concrete problems without any theoretical doctrine. In Rome as in America, popular indignation did not strike down existing institutions but individual men —specific politicians, bankers and businessmen.[10] Capitalists who were swindlers were exposed, as Catulus was exposed by Julius Caesar for embezzling the funds provided for the rebuilding of the Capitoline temple. But capitalism as such was never seriously attacked, except by a handful of demagogues and radical intellectuals.

New Deals take place when dynamic expansion is over, when the frontier comes to an end, when expansive sources of new wealth are exhausted, when the problem becomes one of distribution and organization rather than bold creation. The New Deal started in Rome when Caius Gracchus pushed through his *Lex Frumentaria,* providing for distribution of corn to the poor at half its market price. Accusations of undermining the old Roman way of life were at once hurled at him. But the undermining had been proceeding for generations, ever since the successful conclusion of the Punic Wars, with the increase in wealth and leisure, the loosening of the old moral fiber, the increasing demoralization entailed by great riches, the virtual disappearance of the self-sufficient farmer. The apparition of the Gracchan New Deal was not the cause but the result of this psychological trend. It was a fateful step, nevertheless, one upon which there was no turning back, the beginning of the concept of "Welfare State," the end of a rugged individualism that had no place in a far more complex world. In Rome as in America, psychological conformity had in any case sharply limited individualism in all except economic matters. But when the latter were taken in hand by the state, an outcry went up whose intensity cannot be understood by nations that do not concentrate so exclusively on economic factors.

Henry Ford was a "rugged individualist" but unwittingly he did more to cripple individualism among his own workers caught in the grip of mechanized mass production than any other man. The step from individual Fordism to social New Deal and Welfare State is as unavoidable as the step from Big Business to Big Government. And in Rome, the Gracchi's partial failure lay in their inability to recreate the class of small individualistic farmers, not in their welfare-state measures that no one dared repeal after them—any more than the essence of Roosevelt's New Deal can ever be abolished.

Like the American New Deal's early measures, the Gracchi's reform appealed to farmers, the urban masses, and the small businessmen. Relief was provided partly by the *Lex Frumentaria,* partly by public works that lessened unemployment. The American Resettlement Administration was paralleled by the distribution of land in Italy and the foundation of new Roman colonies in other parts of the commonwealth. In Rome itself, hundreds of thousands of men were on grain relief for generations afterward in spite of efforts on the part of some bold politicians to repeal the law. Sometimes, half-priced wheat was not thought sufficient as a concession to the democrats, and shrewd demagogues like Clodius ran on a free-wheat platform. It was only under Julius Caesar that a means test was decreed, cutting relief rolls down to 150,000. But the towering personality of the Gracchi remained long after their death to haunt Roman statesmen and the substance of their New Deal remained unimpaired. Drusus, Marius, and then Caesar, leaders of the democratic party, were to take their stand on the Gracchan platform as Roosevelt's New Deal incorporated many features of Bryan's Populism.

The long series of reforms in Rome was continued by Drusus, whose father had helped overthrow his Gracchan predecessors. A proud aristocrat but nevertheless a convinced democrat, he was elected Tribune in 91 B.C. and "staked his strength and his life in the attempt to overthrow the domination of the merchants . . . he himself saw the merchants ruling more absolutely than ever, found all his ideas of reform frustrated." [11] Then came the democrat Marius and the conservative reaction of Sulla, who proved that even conservatives had to stand up against bankers and businessmen. Sulla hated mercantile wealth and after defeating Mithridates in the East, refused to let Roman capitalists revert to their former exploitation —in fact consolidated a part of Mithridates' social revolution and stamped out the extortions of Roman tax-farming. The anticapitalist trend was general. Proconsuls such as Piso lowered the outrageous interests owed by many Macedonian towns to Roman joint-stock companies, Gabinius in Syria struggled constantly against Roman capitalists and bankers. The conservative Lucullus lowered the interest rate to 1 per cent per month in Asia Minor, with its corollary that interests claimed could never be greater than the capital.

Generation after generation, the fight went on. The democratic party in Rome had always claimed the illegality of all interest, a viewpoint that had been codified as early as 342 B.C. in the *Lex Genucia,* but had been disregarded when business and capitalism rose to power after the Punic Wars—as the similar Catholic ban was disregarded in Europe after the Reformation. But now, in the dawn of Civilization, the Roman New Deal was slowly returning to the past and rekindling a social conscience that had been dormant for generations. Julius Caesar himself helped the debtors in 49 B.C. by canceling the interests in arrears, and creditors had to accept payment of property as it was valued before the inflation. "Caesar did what he could to repress permanently the fearful omnipotence of capital," explained

Mommsen.[12] Until then insolvent debtors became the slaves of their creditors. Caesar destroyed this cruel bondage and gave them the possibility of preserving their freedom. He then adopted Lucullus' laws as applied in Asia Minor and extended them by decree to the entire Classical world in 50 B.C.

As in America, each new economic depression and financial breakdown in Rome fostered inevitably the growth of state control—all the way from the collapse of Asiatic stocks in 86 B.C. with the freezing of credit, devaluation, and partial moratorium, to the panic of 63 B.C. with its speculation, flight of gold, and eventual embargo on all gold exports, as well as inflation and cheap credit, to the next panic of 49 B.C. Economic emergencies called for practical and concrete measures, not theoretical plans and ambitious schemes such as appealed to the more intellectual Greeks.

Roman Big Business was curbed under the impact of widening New and Fair Deals as American Big Business was curbed by Franklin Roosevelt and succeeding Democratic administrations. But in neither case were they destroyed as by a revolution. They fell under the domination of Big Government but in the end always managed to come to terms with it. In both cases, it was evolution rather than revolution. Roman Big Business still retained its over-all supremacy in the Classical world, with its vast financial resources and know-how, its remarkable organization, the destruction of its last Carthaginian and Corinthian rivals, and the tacit alliance of all the foreign business communities left in the Mediterranean world. The north side of Rome's Forum had become the Classical world's "Wall Street," with its tremendous accumulation of banks, stock exchanges, brokerage houses, and innumerable offices of financial corporations and joint-stock companies. Rome had become, like London and New York, the clearinghouse and banking center of the civilized world. No Roman New Deal could or wished to alter that fact; and it would be inconceivable that any future administration in Washington would want to cripple America's preponderant position in the world of business and finance.

Under Franklin Roosevelt's New Deal, America took a decisive step toward Caesarism. The remarkable feature of this subtle evolution was that it could take place constitutionally, without any illegal move, simply by stretching the extremely pliable fabric of America's political institutions. Romans had a far greater distrust of concentrated power than the Americans and they had so fragmented political authority that any man who aspired to full executive power had to hold, simultaneously and unconstitutionally, the official positions of Consul, Proconsul, Tribune, Quaestor, Censor, and Pontifex Maximus —never forgetting that each one of those offices, save the last, was split between several incumbents. In America, the existence of the Presidency makes the transition far easier and wholly constitutional. Where constitutional obstacles appear insurmountable—the hostility of the Supreme Court, mostly—intimidation can usually be just as effective if it is backed by public opinion. Roosevelt was quick to point this out when he insisted in the autumn of 1937 that the Supreme Court had been "forced" into line after his threatening message in February of the same year.

It is essential to keep in mind that all this is the result of profound historical trends, not of any one man's dictatorial ambitions. Circumstances, not conscious desires, create Caesarism. In the case of America, it is clear that psychological reasons favor this historical evolution. Americans are hero worshipers to a far greater extent than any European people. Concrete-minded and repelled by the abstract, they always tend to personalize issues, and in every walk of life they look up to the "boss." They are led by insensible degrees to foster a Caesarism that historical evolution favors anyway. A friend of Roosevelt's could write with great perception: "For one who knows the President it is impossible to believe that he is aiming at a future dictatorship; but it is also impossible not to recognize the packing of the Supreme Court as exactly what a dictator would adopt as his first step. The President may not know where he is going, but he is on his way." [13]

European-type dictatorship, like Greek tyranny, is usually the result of brutal revolutions, Caesarism the result of a long secular trend. One is temporary and often short lived, the other as lasting as the secular trend that fosters it. Caesarism is the natural counterpart of the leveling process of democratic equality. We can well trust Franklin Roosevelt's absolute sincerity when he disclaimed any intention of setting up a dictatorship in the United States. The great Roman Tribunes who hacked out the path toward Caesarism had no greater desire to imitate the tyrants of Greek city-states or the Hellenistic autocrats, all of whom had been destroyed or overpowered by the Roman Republic. It was historical destiny that made them the unconscious precursors of the coming Caesars—internal circumstances, to a certain extent, but even more the compelling nature of foreign involvements.

CHAPTER XVIII | *The Second World War*

AMERICAN public opinion was overwhelmingly isolationist between the two World Wars, as Roman opinion had been after the exhausting Punic and Macedonian wars. Americans felt somehow that their previous involvements in overseas conflicts had been great mistakes, that far from being popular in Europe, they had become intensely disliked, as the Romans had been in the Greek world.

What should have struck all those who pondered over the growing disagreements between Europe and America is the difference in psychological background. Europe's background, as we have already seen, is one of Time, America's one of Space. The major psychological disability of America in the twentieth century was the failure to understand historical connections and the teachings of the past—not that Europeans were so much wiser, but at least they could see quite clearly in their sober moments that their insane passions had upset their mental balance, that blind and unrestrained emotions had overcome reason, and that it was their own undigested past, their historical knowledge distorted by fierce nationalism, ancestral hatreds, jealousies, and lethal memories that had led to the disastrous conflicts. European faults were those of weakness unable to control passion, American faults were those of willful incomprehension.

America simply wanted to *ignore* the past history of the outside world as if it had never existed. Ethically minded, Americans thought in terms of an absolute and timeless justice that excluded all historical relativity. The clearest statement of this psychological blindness was Woodrow Wilson's in 1916 on the raging war, with whose causes, he said, "we are not concerned. The obscure foundations from which its

stupendous flood has burst forth we are not interested to search for
or explore." [1] This was the antihistorical statement of American foreign policy clearly set forth—the mental blindness of sleepwalkers.[2]

The postwar estrangement was unavoidable and the consequent
isolationism was largely grounded in this determined refusal to understand that historical connections were vital. America was psychologically a victim of her own unimpeded development on a virgin continent where most of the problems were those of taming of nature's
forces and extracting her resources, not those of dealing with masses
of alien men whose customs, traditions, and mental processes were
entirely different and had to be taken into vital consideration.

Isolationism was a political feeling that did not extend into economics in the 1920's. America was the essential thread in the world's
economic fabric and never contemplated retiring into an autarchic
ivory tower by cutting off external trade. But it was economics that
dragged the entire world down in the Great Depression and, far
from scrapping their former isolationism as dangerously outdated,
America's business leaders now extended it to the field of economics
with the Hawley-Smoot tariff. Uncompromising, all-inclusive isolationism became a matter of faith for a large part of the American
population. When Franklin Roosevelt came to power, the economic
emergency was such that he had to adopt some attitude in foreign
policy. World trade was paralyzed by high tariffs and monetary chaos,
and the urgency of some international understanding was obvious.

An International Economic Conference was held in London in
1933 in which the participation of America was obviously to be the
most important feature. Roosevelt had been an outspoken internationalist ever since he entered politics. But now, sensing both the
profound isolationism of the American people and the psychological
impossibility of linking the recovery of America with that of the world,
he ended by scuttling the Conference in his July 3d message known
as the "Bombshell." The response in the United States proved that
he had correctly sensed the mood of the people. The greater part
of the American press hailed this "second Declaration of Independence" with undisguised enthusiasm. International cooperation was
shattered because that was what American public opinion demanded
at the time. From now on, domestic problems remained alone on the
stage and the rest of the world was left to disentangle itself as well as

it could without American cooperation. As Cordell Hull remarked later on, this gave a blank check to the antidemocratic nations, allowing Germany and Japan to arm to the teeth and build up their economic self-sufficiency. America was becoming as passive in front of stepped-up aggression as Rome had been in the early days of Mithridates' insolent provocations. Unable to agree among themselves and formulate a coherent policy, the disunited democracies on both sides of the Atlantic made World War II inevitable.

Roosevelt's responsibility was great in this disastrous isolationism but it was the responsibility of a tribune who on the whole played the game of international relations as the American people wanted it played. It was only years later, when he awoke to the increasing threats of Germany and Japan, that he developed the statesmanship that enabled him to see far ahead of American public opinion and initiate long-range planning. In the meantime, having virtually refused to cooperate with Britain and France, Roosevelt proceeded to recognize Soviet Russia, whose Marxist prophecies had been so tragically confirmed by the Great Depression. With this exception, he made no particular move in foreign policy and concentrated almost exclusively on domestic problems. A proposal to join the World Court in 1935 faced such fierce opposition that he made no effort to push it through. The Nye Committee's investigations had sounded the keynote of isolationism by claiming that American involvements in foreign affairs in the early part of the century had been highly detrimental to the country—with the added charge (a kind often made in Rome) that selfish private interests, bankers, and war industries had been responsible for the involvement in World War I. Thus pacifism, conservative isolationism, and New Deal liberalism seemed to coalesce into a well-knit, united, and powerful movement, implacably opposed to any form of active foreign policy.

Under such psychological conditions, Roosevelt's hands were tied so long as he considered himself a tribune of the people rather than a forward-looking statesman; and with the passage in August, 1935, of Congress' Joint Resolution, American neutrality was proclaimed to the entire world, a dramatic declaration of indifference soon bolstered by the Neutrality Act of May, 1937.

But it was far too late to become a Western Hemisphere Switzerland. War was already raging in Africa, Spain, and the Far East. Britain's inability to police the world was glaring. The first indication that Roosevelt was rising above the isolationist feelings of the majority of his countrymen was the famous Quarantine Speech of October, 1937, with which he virtually made his comeback on the scene of international politics. By then he had become conscious of a definite resurgence of internationalist feeling in America. Without in any way indicating an American participation in foreign conflicts, he began by strengthening the sorely depleted American defenses. At the same time, the weakening isolationism became more vociferous. Spearheaded by Senator William E. Borah, this sentiment put stringent restrictions on the five-billion-dollar Work Relief Bill: "No part of the appropriations . . . shall be used for munitions, warships or military or naval matériel." [3] But the Democratic Administration effectively disregarded the restrictions.

It is in the nature of a dynamic democracy to be unconsciously expansionist and the worsening crisis in Europe and the Far East was going to bring this characteristic out in the open. A great deal of the W.P.A.'s construction work was of deliberate strategic importance and was carried out with the help of the Army Corps of Engineers, giving the latter training and experience which was to be useful in World War II. Appropriations for the armed forces were ridiculously small. In many ways the W.P.A. saved a great part of the American military establishment from disastrous obsolescence.

Whether Roosevelt did or did not say in a secret conference with Congressional leaders "The American frontier is on the Rhine" is of no great importance. What is quite certain is that all thoughtful Americans by then had come to realize this basic truth. When the war finally broke out in September, 1939, the painful uncertainty and suspense of the late 1930's came to an end. International conferences, pacifism, expressions of good will and peacefulness—everything had proved useless. When Congress failed to repeal the Neutrality Act, a new blank check was given to Germany and World War II was the outcome. Nothing but determined strength could oppose brute force.

Roosevelt's new strategy was then to convince the American people that the only way to avoid participation in the hostilities was to extend aid to the Atlantic democracies on the opposite seaboard. More farsighted than his predecessor Wilson, he was able to prepare public opinion gradually, urging his compatriots to remain neutral in action but not in thought, urging them in fact to search their conscience and align themselves emotionally with Britain and France.

From then on, the baffling and apparently unexpected course of the war made American involvement increasingly inevitable. The collapse of France in 1940 left Britain as the sole bastion defending the security of the Atlantic, a bastion as vital to the security of America as Long Island. When he prodded Congress to ratify the destroyer deal with Britain, Roosevelt pointed out: "This is the most important action in the reinforcement of our national defense that has been taken since the Louisiana Purchase. Then, as now, considerations of safety from overseas attack were fundamental." [4] The long historical trend was evident. When Secretary of State Hull said that "an Allied victory was essential to the security of the United States," [5] it implied not merely aid to beleaguered allies but growing control over those allies who would never have found themselves in such straits if they had not been fundamentally weak to start with. Thus were formerly strong world powers to become weak dependencies of America.

Increasing involvement in the global conflict brought with it an increase in the stature of the Presidency. The President gradually became a Commander in Chief who was to be obeyed unquestioningly, and the White House became world-wide headquarters. The same logic that had impelled Roosevelt to concentrate power in his hands during the Depression now compelled him to concentrate even more. A whole new set of war agencies came into being, responsible to Roosevelt alone, and not to cabinet members. This innovation was partly to offset enduring Congressional antipathy toward the steady increase in permanent federal departments, which antipathy reflected the long-standing distrust of the growing power of a permanent bureaucracy largely beyond legislative control. But Roosevelt, too, wanted to by-pass the slow, cumbersome bureaucracy by creating a new one directly controlled by the White House and better geared to deal with wartime emergencies. He had long ago manifested his distrust of such agencies as the State Department by dealing with heads of foreign governments outside the regular diplomatic channels.

No one in Washington saw the magnitude of the problem as Roosevelt did and there was plenty of evidence later on that only he had been able to foresee the full dimensions of America's inevitable participation in the war. This participation was largely his own personal doing—a Congress that had already been overwhelmed by the Depression could hardly challenge the Commander in Chief in this military emergency. He thus added to his immense powers that needed no Congressional approval a great many older powers that had never been rescinded—some dating back to World War I—which enabled him to set up agencies for price control, war production, transportation, food production. Some of these powers dated back to the Civil War (the National Defense Research Council). Furthermore, on September 8, 1939, Roosevelt issued his Limited National Emergency proclamation and simultaneously an Executive Order to which few people paid much attention in the excitement of the outbreak of the war in Europe. This order reorganized the Executive Office. In the process it transferred the Bureau of the Budget from the Treasury Department to the Executive Office, enabling Roosevelt to lay his hand directly on an agency that became responsible solely to himself and was entitled to send agents into every department of the administration. The Bureau of the Budget became, in fact, the President's private intelligence service.

Historical evidence thus shows that each new war adds to the already tremendous powers of a President, who is simultaneously Chief of State, Prime Minister in charge of all the Executive departments, and Commander in Chief of the armed forces. When Franklin Roosevelt talked about "his" ambassador, referring to an American envoy abroad, he was only stating, over the loud protests of his advisers as well as his Republican opponents, what was a plain fact: one man was already largely in control of the world's greatest power.

The basic American issue in 1940 was the coming presidential election and the third term dilemma. Roosevelt's decision to run a third time was a shattering blow to a revered tradition, although absolutely constitutional. In a country where precedents are all important, this fateful decision must be seen as marking a turning point in constitutional history. The war emergency, of course, justified the decision. But then, there were also eight years of Roosevelt's overpowering leadership, the total disorganization of the Republicans, and the purging of the Democratic party. The party, in fact, had become inconceivable without Franklin Roosevelt. As an American historian put it: "The national Democratic party, as such, had disappeared, although the forms and names remained." [6] Roosevelt had become the *indispensable man* without whom victory at the polls was more uncertain than with his tradition-shattering third term nomination;

and his control of the party was such that there was no Democratic leader of sufficient stature to challenge him. He imposed Henry Wallace as Vice-Presidential candidate in spite of the opposition of the overwhelming majority of his party. His will could not be resisted.

At the same time, he emphasized his personal rather than partisan Democratic leadership by avoiding Wilson's mistakes and creating a bipartisan policy, keeping constantly in touch with Republican leaders in Congress, appointing such outstanding Republicans to his cabinet as Henry Stimson and Frank Knox. He had so completely reshaped all the basic issues that, inevitably, the Republicans campaigned under Wendell Willkie almost in his own terms, on his own platform.

What was ominous in this situation was not so much Roosevelt's full use of powers that were of truly Caesarian magnitude. It was the American people's full acceptance of this concentration of immense powers in the hands of one man and their firm belief that it should remain there in spite of traditions against third, fourth, or more terms. An incident of the 1940 campaign epitomized this popular feeling: "In the Cleveland speech, he made his first and last reference to the third term issue. It was a glancing reference and produced a surprising reaction from the crowd. Roosevelt said that, when the next four years are over 'there will be another President'—at which point the crowd started to shout 'No! No!' Thinking remarkably quickly, Roosevelt thrust his mouth close to the microphone and went on talking so that the shouts which suggested that he might be elected permanently should not be heard over the radio." [7] The first ghostly contours of Caesarism were appearing and, as always, welling up from the people themselves.

⌐The war itself shifted more and more power to the White House.⌐ Congress was induced to approve the Lend-Lease Bill, including the controversial provision stipulating that Lend-Lease could be extended to "any country whose defenses the President deems vital to the defense of the United States," thus effectively transferring to the hands of the President a power that could well alter the entire complexion of the war and allow him to influence directly the internal politics of scores of foreign nations. From then on, Roosevelt could in fact commit the United States to long-range policies, could plan secretly without Congressional knowledge, and conclude binding agreements about which the great majority of Americans knew nothing. He could and did send American troops to Greenland, Iceland, Trinidad, and British Guiana, extend maritime patrol in the Atlantic Ocean, proclaim an unlimited emergency on May 27, 1941, place the Philippines' armed forces under American command and extend as much help to Britain as was needed.

Charles A. Beard, an alarmed American historian, passed judgment on those proceedings later on: "If these precedents are to stand unimpeached and to provide sanctions for the continued conduct of American foreign affairs, the Constitution may be nullified by the President, officials and officers who have taken the oath, and are under moral obligations to uphold it." [8] Of course, there are as many different interpretations of the Constitution as there are historians. The fact is that its very plasticity makes it so remarkably adaptable and durable; and mere nostalgic yearning for a very different past can never hope to check a profound historical trend.

The year 1940 was possibly the darkest period the Western world had known since it came into existence a thousand years ago. "Never before since Jamestown and Plymouth Rock has our American civilization been in such danger as now . . ." said Franklin Roosevelt, [9] with his more exclusively American perspective. The German alliance with Soviet Russia was remarkably similar to an alliance between Mithridates Eupator, King of Pontus, and the Parthians in the east— this very Mithridates whose policy was a strange blend of political reaction and social revolution that could be aptly termed the "National Socialism" of the Classical world. After the fall of France, the last bastion standing between the German-Russian threat and the Western Hemisphere was Britain, and in order to help the old mother country, America was prepared to go to any length. This implied that sooner or later America was to inherit the burden of policing the world. Having done this all through the "Hellenistic Age" of the West, Britain had slowly dwindled in stature, to become the forward island fortress of the Western Hemisphere, a mere outpost on the periphery of the New Rome's empire.

Gradually, America began to recover the Messianic spirit that would justify such global commitment—it had been temporarily overcast by distrust of Europe and by the Depression. The Four Freedoms and the Atlantic Charter were so many idealistic pronouncements to counteract the feeling of mortal peril. "If Great Britain goes down, the Axis powers will control the continents of Europe, Asia, Africa, Australasia, and the high seas—and they will be in a position to bring enormous military and naval resources against this hemisphere," said Roosevelt.[10]

Without being conscious of it, America was now going to rise to a new and unpredictable stature—that of a world power whose role is not merely to preserve the independence of democratic allies but actually to set up Western Civilization on a durable basis. World War II was the ultimate phase in the collapse of Europe's "Hellenistic" order. What was required now was a true "Roman" order—no longer a precarious balance of power between Western nations but a compact unity of the entire Western community against a new challenge aiming at the total destruction of its Civilization.

The German assault on Russia gave the West a first glimmer of hope that Nazism might be defeated after all, that there was no longer one invincible revolutionary Eurasian bloc extending from France to Japan. But it also provoked strategic and political errors of judgment which were to prove catastrophic. The principal error was naïvely expressed by Roosevelt himself: "Now comes this Russian diversion. If it is more than just that, it will mean the liberation of Europe from Nazi domination—and at the same time I do not think we need worry about any possibility of Russian domination." [11] The Romans had not foreseen, either, that the destruction of the hostile Seleucid Empire would be followed by the fabulous growth of the threatening Parthians and not by peace. It was not merely Roosevelt's mistake, but that of many Americans, Republicans as well as Democrats, who saw in Russia an anti-imperialistic counterpoise to the old-fashioned imperialism of European nations. Roosevelt's Republican opponent, Wendell Willkie, was not the least of these misguided idealists.

America was finally propelled into the war by the attack on Pearl Harbor. For all those who search for an understanding of the broad issue of the war, the controversy over the responsibilities for this disaster is unimportant. No one knows exactly what was in Roosevelt's mind, no one knows to what extent he could foresee what was going to happen. What is certain is that he knew by then that American participation in the war had become inevitable—and that, whether he did use it as such or not, he *had* the power to precipitate America into the war by using the fleet in Hawaii as a decoy. The mere fact that he *could* do it, that he alone could modify American policy in the Far East so as to stand across the path of Japanese imperialism and coordinate all the secret information indicating the imminence of an attack, is enough to prove that he had the power to shape decisively the future of America, and of the world in the process. How he actually used this tremendous power in those obscure days is an academic matter for historians to debate.

At any rate, America was now totally involved in the war, in Europe as in Asia. This time there could be no retreat such as had followed World War I. America was tied to allies, east and west, who were compelled by historical and geographical reasons to become satellites rather than partners of equal stature. A decisive turn in the course of world history had been taken; and it was Roosevelt's personal leadership that was to shape a great deal of the evolution of the war itself. It was under his leadership that, on New Year's Day, 1942, America signed the Declaration of the United Nations with twenty-five other countries. And it was not long before the Chinese foreign minister granted him the unofficial title of "Commander-in-Chief of the United Nations," an ominous label suggesting the possibility of sliding by insensible gradations from United States to world-wide United Nations.

The psychological temper in America was not what it had been in 1917. It was not the emotional and lighthearted elation for an entirely idealistic cause but rather a more realistic, grim determination to see the war through with all that it might imply in blood, tears, toil, and stress. There was still plenty of naïveté, incomprehension, and ignorance, most of which benefited world communism, but the more realistic undertone was unmistakable—as in Rome, the generous mood of Flamininus' idealism was gradually replaced by the grim exasperation of Lucius Mummius at Leucopatra, where the Greeks suffered a crushing and final defeat at the hands of the Romans—the prelude to the transformation of Greece into a Roman province. America had begun to look upon herself as a superpower, standing over and above all European nations, the main bastion of a Civilization in danger of being wiped out in the rest of the world. It was no longer Wilson's idealistic view of the United States as a mere nation among others, participating in a loose League of Nations on terms of democratic equality, but that of a superstate entitled to assume forceful leadership of the United Nations at war. It was Rome against

Mithridates, guiding and dominating the dwarfed Greek states to save them from a reactionary-revolutionary tyranny.

Within this pattern of rising American leadership the American President did not merely *represent* as Prime Minister Churchill did, but actually *was,* with all his powers of office. He had full authority over each individual member of his cabinet. Churchill had no such authority; the British Cabinet as a whole is responsible to Parliament and each minister individually to the Crown. At one point, for instance, Churchill wanted Foreign Minister Anthony Eden to go to Moscow. The Pearl Harbor attack having just taken place, Eden felt reluctant to leave England and would have been entitled to refuse. It was Churchill's persuasive arguments, not his constitutional authority, that finally induced Eden to leave for Russia at so critical a time.

The increasing stature of President Roosevelt as a world leader dimmed the authority of Congress. The recurrent pattern of the President-Congress relationship is suggested by the following incident, as described by Robert E. Sherwood. In 1942, the "President had the power to stabilize prices and wages by Executive order without reference to Congress and some of us believed that he should do just that immediately and not run the risk of hostile action or no action at all on Capitol Hill. There were unquestionably many Congressmen who fervently hoped that he would do it this way and thereby absolve them from all responsibility for decision on such a controversial issue (it was an ironic fact that many of the Congressmen who were loudest in accusing Roosevelt of dictatorial ambitions were the most anxious to have him act like a dictator on all measures which might be unpopular with the people but obviously valuable for the winning of the war)." [12] This fear of responsibility is perennial in all democratic assemblies, and nothing contributes more to the rise of Caesarism than this factual abdication masked by verbal denunciations. It was quite clear that Congress was almost voluntarily relegating itself to an entirely subordinate position since it could not control policy-making and could only envision the fluid situation as it would congeal years later.

With absolute power at home, the President could speak with full authority to other statesmen and extend his leadership to the entire world controlled by the United Nations. The fact that the British bulwark had been able to stand against the Nazi onslaught masked a fact of primary importance. This was the virtual dissolution of the British Empire into its component parts. One section (the Asian possessions) was soon to become independent, and the other (the scattered English-speaking dominions) were beginning to revolve around Washington and no longer around London. Had Britain fallen, of course, a great impetus would have been given this gradual redistribution of power. Canada had long been intimately connected with the United States for obvious geographical reasons and was not even part of the Sterling Area. But with the war against Japan, Australia and New Zealand began to depend increasingly on America's armed support, now that the hard-pressed British could no longer extend their imperial protection to the South Pacific. At the outbreak of the Far Eastern war, the alarmed Australians decided to recall their armed forces from the Middle East and Churchill's anxious pleas were curtly turned down. Churchill then induced Roosevelt to intervene and the President was able to convert the Australians to his point of view by promising to dispatch considerable American forces "down under." Further disputes between Britain and the Dominion induced Roosevelt to write bluntly to Churchill: "I sense in this country a growing feeling of impatience at what publicly appears to be a rather strained relationship at this critical time between the United Kingdom and Australia. . . . I say this to you because I myself feel greatly responsible for the turn of events." [13]

All through the war, this gradual transfer of global power and responsibilities from London to Washington went on ceaselessly, discreetly but irreversibly. It was not always welcome in Washington but Roosevelt's views and will always prevailed. It was even less welcome in London where Churchill was unwilling to accept the dramatic metamorphosis of Britain into a second-rate power, virtually shorn of her world-wide empire. When Roosevelt decided after the Yalta Conference to go to the Middle East and interview personally the various Oriental potentates, Churchill was "greatly disturbed." [14] The Middle East had long been a British preserve, with a few crumbs left over for the French. Roosevelt's conferences with the tarbooshed King of Egypt, the colorful ruler of Saudi Arabia, and the Ethiopian Emperor, Haile Selassie, could and should have reminded readers of history of similar meetings between the elected representatives of Rome and such old-fashioned Oriental potentates as Massinissa, King of Numidia, or the Ptolemies of Egypt, or any of the numerous Asiatic monarchs who were already if unofficially clients and protégés of the all-powerful Roman Republic. Those were interviews between the pre-Caesarian officials of the globe's most powerful nation and the autocratic relics of a colorful past that was slowly dying out of the modern world.

Each one of the major international conferences—Casablanca, Washington, Quebec, Moscow, Cairo, Teheran—was dominated by Franklin Roosevelt or Secretary of State Cordell Hull. Roosevelt was the initial sponsor of the "unconditional surrender" doctrine that backfired so dramatically after the war. It was Cato's implacable *"Ceterum censeo delendum esse Carthaginem"* all over again,[15] the "total wars" and total destruction that saw the razing of Carthage and Corinth, saturation bombing, the Morgenthau Plan, and other extreme measures of the kind, up to and including the atomic bomb. But it was the President's own policy, not that of Congress or even of his British allies. Of course, he sensed the mood of an emotional and aroused public opinion in a state of exasperation, prepared to countenance any extreme measure against cruel foes. Roosevelt was powerful to the extent that he could interpret public feelings and the storm of protest raised by his handling of the Darlan issue in French North Africa was a reminder that some of these sharp feelings could not be brushed aside for the sake of wise expediency. Yet, as Judge Rosenman stated, in all these conferences, "it was he who made the final decisions; and it was his leadership which dominated the major decisions which involved international diplomacy or politics." [16] And the fact that early in 1943, the current of war began to flow in a direction that was favorable to the United Nations could only reinforce the authority of the President, for whom Churchill's heroic and lonely battle in 1940 and 1941 seemed to have become merely a holding operation.

Just as in Roosevelt's exceptional power and authority there was a premonition of the Caesarism to come, there was in his conceptions of world organization after the war a faint outline of the global "Roman" order to come. As he saw it, the United Nations Organization would replace the former precarious balance of power whose breakdown had finally shattered the modern "Hellenistic" order. His idealistic views prompted him time and again to advocate the voluntary dissolution of all colonial empires, with some form of international trusteeship to take over in case of need. Robert E. Sherwood states in his study on Hopkins that Roosevelt "believed in a system of strategic bases—he gave as examples Dakar, the tip of Tunisia and Formosa—which would be under United Nations control." He then goes on to state that Roosevelt also believed "that France and other occupied countries in Europe should not have to bear the economic and physical burden of rearmament after the war—that the burden of ensuing postwar security should be borne by the nations that were of necessity already armed for combat purposes." [17] These, of course, were the English-speaking world and Russia.

Time and again, throughout the war, Roosevelt discussed the organization of the world of the future and always came back to the obvious solution for difficult problems: a United Nations trusteeship. For instance, strong in his belief that Serbs and Croats could never live together in one composite state like Yugoslavia, he advocated placing Croatia under such international trusteeship.

All this was very well. But if the United Nations Organization was to police the world, who would police the United Nations? Then and there, a new problem was born. As usual, those who establish enduring institutions have only a dim perception of the true historical implications of their own doings. Roosevelt, in his idealistic mood, thought that he was laying the basis of world peace through voluntary cooperation of the victorious powers. He was, in fact, laying the basis of a very different world, of a new "Roman" order revolving around a strong American leadership. What was said of him in connection with the Supreme Court packing scheme could be repeated now in connection with the establishment of the United Nations: he "may not know where he is going, but he is on his way."

Long before the war was over, international agencies began to multiply. November, 1943, saw the establishment of the United Nations Relief and Rehabilitation Administration, of which the United States furnished three quarters of the funds. In July, 1944, at Bretton Woods, the International Monetary Fund and the International Bank of Reconstruction and Development were set up. In 1945, the United Nations Conference was held in San Francisco. To those Americans who felt suspicious of all international commitments, Roosevelt addressed this ultimatum: "There can be no middle ground here. We shall have to take the responsibility for world collaboration, or we shall have to bear the responsibility for another world conflict." [18]

The opposition that had been raised when Roosevelt was nominated for a third term had largely died down when the fourth term came along in 1944. He had by now become a giant straddling America and the world. No one could have replaced him without risking a serious dislocation of the entire war effort, and the only serious objection that could be made against a fourth term was the President's poor health. Before his untimely death, however, Roosevelt was to play again the leading role on the stage of world history.

The Yalta Conference was the supreme triumph of the Soviet "Parthians," a victory of Oriental cunning and diplomatic skill over the uncomprehending stodginess of the "Roman" West. Although a great deal of the subsequent criticism has been leveled at Roosevelt and at the amateurishness with which he handled world problems of infinite complexity, the conference was essentially dominated by the psychological incompatibility between East and West. Idealism was almost completely lacking in the sordid bargaining of the West with the Asian shrewdness of Joseph Stalin. It was a would-be realism that dominated the proceedings, a naïve realism based on misinformation and psychological errors of great magnitude. The British— Churchill especially—were fighting a rear-guard action in defense of an outmoded—"mid-Victorian," said Roosevelt—imperialism. [19] Stalin and Roosevelt agreed that they had entered an age of great superpowers who should take charge of policing the world. In justification of the steady stream of concessions made to Soviet Russia, the argument was consistently put forward that Stalin could make a separate peace with Nazi Germany—ignoring the fact that under the most autocratic dictatorship, the exacerbated passions of a Russian population that had fought an utterly ruthless invader on its own territory could never tolerate such a thing. Paralyzed by illusory fears, Roosevelt and his advisers found themselves at the mercy of the Orient's most skillful negotiator.

But behind the profound mistakes made by the West lay the unquestionable reality of Russia's colossal land army and of the inability of the West to limit its floodlike progress in Europe except by matching its military power on the spot. Far more than the bombings or the landings in Normandy, it was the Russian military machine that had destroyed Hitler's Wehrmacht and the most skillful negotiators in the world could not have altered this fact. But there was another reality that was not sufficiently taken into account by the pragmatic Anglo-Saxons. Behind the armed might of Soviet Russia lay another active force in the realm of ideas and passions, the religion-like force of Marxist philosophy extending to many lands from France to China, shading off into many different hues on its periphery but always linked by ruthless discipline to the Kremlin. And behind Marxist philosophy lay a deep distrust of Western Civilization as such. In this the rustic patriotism of the Russians joined the widening revolt of Asia's crippled civilizations against the West.

Of all this, the naïve Western negotiators at Yalta had little conception. They were facing an East that was rejecting Western Civilization as the Central Asians, Indians, Persians, and Mesopotamians had rejected Classical Civilization two thousand years before. Marxism was a far more complex movement than the Western leaders thought, often a mask for more profound feelings of hatred for Western culture and values. Lack of true understanding of the past, lack of profound knowledge of history paralyzed Western statesmen. Anglo-Saxon pragmatism was all very well in the Western world, but it had no appeal beyond its borders—and these borders were receding while the area influenced by European Culture was shrinking. In this conflict, which vastly transcended mere politics, which symbolized the clash of antagonistic civilizations, and which included in its compass philosophy, religion, science, art, sociology, economics, and differing views of man's destiny, the pragmatists were hopelessly disarmed. Lack of a sound theoretical basis, lack of an all-inclusive philosophy, became telling and paved the way for endless trouble.

The Americans displayed their atomistic outlook in refusing to consider the problem as a joint military-political-social-economic-cultural puzzle that had to be solved synthetically. They always considered each aspect of the problem separately. The Marxists had been trained by their dialectical philosophy of history to look at separate problems only as parts of an integrated whole. The Americans took up only one problem at a time—in 1944 and 1945 the military defeat of Germany and Japan—without being willing to understand that each military move would have far-reaching repercussions in every other field after the hostilities had ended.

It was not so much Communist sympathizers and conspirators who scuttled America's foreign policy as a defective mental approach that finds its distant roots in the outlook of the Age of Enlightenment's rationalism. The American defense leaders and chiefs of staff wanted no military offensive in Central Europe and the Balkans because, however judicious politically, it was not sound military strategy in the war against Germany. They wanted Russian participation in the war against Japan regardless of the political disasters that might subsequently occur in the Far East.

Whenever an over-all philosophic approach is lacking, the only alternative is to concentrate absolute power within the hands of one man. This, the West did, as Rome had been compelled to do, for the very same reasons. Unfortunately, Franklin Roosevelt's stature as a world statesman could no longer rise to this greatest of all challenges. He could not, for instance, look upon the Polish problem as that of Poland herself. To him, the only problem was its effect on the vote of American citizens of Polish descent. Roosevelt had full power; only he could have looked at the global problem as an indissoluble whole. But he was a man of his time, a mental prisoner of the system under which he operated and which he could not dominate.

All the lessons of history showed that the transfer of the English-speaking world's center of gravity from London to Washington, the virtual dissolution of the British Empire, and the dislocation entailed by this inevitable redistribution of power within the Western world —the historical equivalent of Rome's civil wars from the time of Marius onwards—implied the hectic metamorphosis of a loose aristocratic empire into a more compact, centralized and democratic world-empire under Caesarian leadership. Though nominally a monarchy, Britain was in fact an aristocratic republic, whereas, though nominally a republic, the United States was gradually becoming a Caesarian monarchy under Franklin Roosevelt. Britain and America represent, respectively, the modern equivalents of different phases of Rome's social evolution.

The far-reaching implications of this metamorphosis remained largely unnoticed. Obsessed by their anticolonialism, the Americans made it easier for the Russians to play on the divisions within the Western bloc and divert American attention from more fundamental issues. The redistribution of power within the Anglo-Saxon world made it easier for the modern "Parthians" to make deep inroads in Europe and Asia, and roll back the frontiers of Western Civilization.

An American historian, criticizing Franklin Roosevelt's personal conferences, his by-passing of representatives of his own administration, his committing the United States beyond possibilities of recall by Congress, stated that "the concentration of power of the enemy was thereby matched, but the game was played according to the enemy's rules." [20] This situation which also weighed heavily on the Roman statesmen of the first century B.C. is the contagious element that often tends to make adversaries or chance partners increasingly alike. The impulse to imitate the opponent and duplicate his method comes from the fact that enemies have to fight it out on a common ground and with similar weapons. Not only did the American leaders have to match the Nazi concentration of power but, thrown in temporary intimacy with the Russians during the war, they had to listen to Russian sermons on the unchallengeable power of dictatorial machines and take advice as to how to lead the American people. At the Yalta Conference, Andrei Vishinsky, after having claimed that small nations should never be allowed to pass judgment on the behavior of big powers, went on to state categorically that "the American people should learn to obey their leaders." [21]

Such remarks, repeated generation after generation, can never fail to alter the psychological climate and induce the democratic leaders to assume gradually the trappings of Caesarism. Sooner or later, the political coloring of the East begins to come off on the West. The transition from Sulla to Caesar and from Caesar to the absolutism of Vespasian was partly the result of the growing orientalization of Rome and the decline in prestige of elective institutions. In the modern instance, it is clear that "democrat" Roosevelt was not half as much repelled by Stalin's views on strong executive power and absolute supremacy of the great superpowers as "conservative" Churchill was.

The America that emerged from the war was very different from the one that had entered it. The nation moved from uncompromising isolationism to world-wide commitments requiring a large military establishment. Presidential power had experienced renewed growth, a growth now bolstered by full control over nuclear power. "In truth, the office of the President had been altered beyond recognition as

Mr. Roosevelt exercised the powers of a dictator," claimed an American historian a few years later.[22] But it was not so much Roosevelt's own doing as that of profound and uncontrollable historical forces. The President was no more responsible for the unquestionable decline in self-reliance and autonomy of the average individual, or for the growth of a huge bureaucracy and the Welfare State, than any one man was responsible for the gradual transformation of Rome between the Gracchi and Caesar. Opponents and partisans of Franklin Roosevelt could have been reconciled if they had been willing to see the profound changes in the light of historical necessity rather than as the whimsicalities of one or several individual men.

The great power of postwar America was due in part to the vast increase in industrial productivity brought about by the war effort, partly to the fact that America was the only great nation untouched by the military devastations that had ravaged France, Britain, Germany, Italy, Central and Eastern Europe, Russia, China, and Japan. The cost in American lives was a fraction of what it had been in Germany or Russia. This tremendous power added to the total collapse of Europe's "Hellenistic" order, the rise of a gigantic Eurasian Marxist empire, and the full-scale revolt of the Orient creates the contemporary setting for the New Roman Age upon which we are entering in the second half of our century.

PART IV | *The Rise of America*

CHAPTER XIX

European Culture and American Civilization

THE great collapse of European values that started with World War I accelerated during and after World War II. A world in full rebellion no longer looked up to Europe for creative inspiration as in the past—no more than it feared the military might before which all the people of the globe had trembled for so long. Europe's physical power was smashed. Could it be also that Europe had ceased to be the fountainhead of cultural creation? And, if so, was modern Culture itself coming to an end?

The Victorian era, with its smug Hellenistic tinge, its discordant mixture of Philistinism and cultural shabbiness, had been a premonitory phenomenon, suggesting the dusk of Europe's cultural pre-eminence. It was a period of transition from a declining Culture to a rising Civilization whose hallmark was going to be unification and organization, feeding on the cultural output of past centuries, without much creative originality of its own. And few could see that this new era that was to begin in the twentieth century would inevitably mean the rise of a New Roman Age—the age of American Civilization.

The social order of Civilization is the end result of the striving toward democratic equality, the long-standing effort to standardize and raise ever higher the general living conditions of the population, rather than to emphasize the cultured refinement of the few at the summit of the social pyramid. That was the profound trend of America's social evolution, long before the full impact of the Industrial Revolution was felt, a new social outlook which focuses on the prototype only to the extent that it can be standardized for the benefit of the majority. Nietzsche, who saw Civilization coming with terror, warned us: ". . . among the Greeks, it was the 'individual' that counted," he explained; "The Greeks are interesting and extremely important because they reared such a vast number of great individuals." [1] But his fulmination against the rising "herd" men was pathetically ineffective. The trend was obvious: Greece had been compelled to bow to Rome, as Europe would be to America. Nietzsche's exasperated attempt to destroy Western Culture's traditional morality was the last outburst of intense individualism based on an *aesthetic* outlook before it goes down before the *ethical* standpoint of civilized society. He thundered that "the object of mankind should lie in its highest individuals," but with the onset of Civilization, *society* inevitably predominates over the *individual*. In Nietzsche, we have the last, most conscious and passionate exponent of anti-Civilization to rise in a declining Europe.

The social basis of a civilized order rests on the final rise to supremacy not of an oligarchy or proletariat but an immensely broad, town-dwelling middle class. Society is no longer a hierarchical pyramid but a vast middle-class plateau. Civilization is a predominantly urban phenomenon, and the gradual decline of rural America emphasizes this trend toward town-dwelling. In 1954, the farm population of America had declined to less than twenty-two million, hardly more than 13 per cent of the total population, down from thirty million or more than the 23 per cent in 1940. The decline is continuous and by no means terminated. The time may soon come when the farm population will represent less than 5 per cent of the total population.

Civilization implies also the rise to supremacy of economic thinking and the decline of truly creative Culture, whose conflicting ideas and theories, stimulating when formulated, end up causing the breakdown of a Culture's political and social structure because they are taken too seriously. All the way from the post-Renaissance Wars of Religion to Robespierre and Hitler, there were tragic attempts to materialize theoretical schemes, to impose abstract philosophies of life on one's neighbors by all means, fair or foul, and fight to the bitter end without thought of compromise. It takes many generations for men to grow tired of philosophies and abstractions but this creeping fatigue eventually overcomes intellectual curiosity and doctrinal proselytism. And with exhaustion, comes a desire for the harmony of compromise, for a constructive peace devoted to economic welfare rather than cultural pursuits that always spill out into the political world, become monstrously distorted, and end in bloody disaster. The age of Nazism's monstrous Wagnerian drama comes to a close in a cataclysmic Twilight of the Gods. From now on, culture will no longer be taken in dead earnest but rather as a marginal activity that will not be allowed to interfere with Civilization's serious pursuit—the establishment of security and economic well-being for as many human beings as possible. It will be a secondary culture of Ciceros and Senecas growing in the shade of the greatness of the original Culture.

This will be the world as shaped by American Civilization, and in this world many will echo the striking remark of Rome's most famous engineer, Sextus Julius Frontinus, who headed Rome's water department and was justly proud of his massive aqueducts: "Who will venture to compare with these mighty conduits the idle pyramids, or the famous but useless works of the Greeks?" [2] Undisguised contempt for culture and remarkable economic efficiency were the legacies of Rome, the marks of a Classical Civilization that the Greeks had been unable to establish—an unrivaled record of order, peace, prosperity, organization, and efficient construction of roads, bridges, aqueducts, circuses, public baths, and good sewers. The Roman Age was one of maximum security, of free trade throughout the civilized world, of a transportation system that was unmatched with its sixteen broad highways converging in Rome to the Golden Milestone and its fifty thousand miles of good roads crisscrossing the civilized world. One could travel more than fifty miles a day on these roads—an average speed not reached on American roads until well into the nineteenth century. The Mediterranean was circled with good harbors and lighthouses, covered with multitudes of ships plying between three continents on regular lines of sailing. Grain elevators and warehouses dotted the landscape. It was the triumph of a world-wide free-trading commercial organization that could handle commercial transactions stretching from Portugal to the Caucasus, from Scotland to the Indian Ocean.

This miracle of civilized order was made possible by men who, at first sight, did not seem to be blessed by great gifts. The worst features of the Romans—heaviness, poor imagination, little sensitivity, indifference to form, instinctive distrust of individuality and originality —were, however, well compensated for. It was their other qualities

—a taste for action rather than thought, practicality, a concrete rather than abstract outlook on men and things, precision, taste for team-work, discipline, tenacity, genius for efficient organization and sound government, strong patriotism and indestructible belief in the superi-ority of the Roman way of life, a powerful faculty of absorption and assimilation—that made the Romanization of the Classical world possible. More than anything else, it was what Pliny the Elder de-scribed as *"omnium utilitatum et virtuum rapacissimi,"* the remark-able ability to borrow and adapt anything invented by others that could possibly be used in a practical way.[3]

How do the Romans of the modern world compare with their Classical predecessors? The duplication fits remarkably well. Amer-icanism is to the modern world the equivalent of what Tertullian called *"Romanitas"* was to the Classical: the sum total of all the psychological traits, customs, habits of thought that their respective Civilization Men take for granted. Americans are Civilization Men, not Culture Men. All their characteristics point to organization, pro-ductive efficiency, and earthly success. In a chaotic world where sensi-tive men are baffled and often despair, they are not easily baffled and never despair. They can be nonplused, checked by what seems to them irrational reactions of other nations—but only temporarily. Their basic vitality is too great. The shape of things to come depends on many different factors. But one is of transcendent importance: the mind and soul of modern America, as shaped by several centuries of historical growth.

The broader their contacts with the outer world, and the greater the threats to their national security, the more the Americans have tended to become conscious of their Americanism, without always being able to define clearly what America stands for in the world. Americanism is a strange mixture of enduring Puritanism, the ideol-ogy of the eighteenth-century Enlightenment, and the Machine Age. As opposed to Europe with its cultural and aesthetic outlook, Ameri-canism is essentially ethical and moralistic. This was bitingly pointed out by H. L. Mencken: "The American, save in moments of con-scious and swiftly lamented deviltry, casts up all ponderable values, including the value even of beauty, in terms of right and wrong."[4] Moralism, with its implied good faith and reliability, is the founda-tion of all prosperous business life, and business is America's primary occupation. A gradual fusion of the spirit of the Puritan, the pioneer, and the business leader has given American society its typical leader. /Culture thinks in terms of quality, Civilization in terms of quantity, and no people in the world today think so much in purely quantitative, statistical terms as the Americans./The background of America, after all, is *space* and the Americans are sensitive above all to bigness, size, the lateral extension of immensity rather than depth. The background of Europe is *time,* history, and what strikes the European, conservative or revolutionary, in praise or condemnation, is the depth and antiquity of an idea or institution. American imagination is struck not so much by the profundity or intensity of ideas and emotions as by their horizontal expansion among millions of like-minded people.

This, of course, has helped the swift growth of America. The inrush of millions of immigrants from all parts of Europe gave rise to a deliberate policy of Americanization with its emphasis on education. The educational system as a school of citizenship acquired in America a political and social influence that it never had in Europe. The absorption and reshaping of such a vast influx of aliens was only possible through the Americanization of their children, made possible by the profound belief of all Americans in the irresistible influence of environment. The parents made the negative act of will in rejecting Europe and its values. But it remained for their more pliable children to acquire the positive quality of Americanism which their parents could hardly hope to acquire in their lifetime; and the success of the system is proved by the completeness with which children raised in the American environment respond to the treatment.

What American Civilization stands for is symbolized by John Dewey's philosophy—belief in the overpowering influence of environment, a thorough study of practical psychology and its application to mass education. This philosophy is democratic institutionalism pushed to an extreme, based on the premise that there are no differences in essential *Being* among men but only of practical *ability*. Now, Being implies a harmonious synthesis of spirit and matter. It is essentially the "word made flesh," and the primary goal of man, as an individual rather than as a member of society, is to reach a higher state of Being through strenuous self-improvement—not social "adjustment." It is the opposition of the Greek *aretê,* all-round excellence, the full development of the cultured individual in every respect, the dislike of specialization, contempt for mere efficiency—and the Roman *virtus,* which is largely a moral and social quality. Culture means the generalization of this higher state of *aretê* among the elite. It means a new world outlook embodied in concrete matter, whether it be men or works of art. As opposed to this, Civilization is the product of pure intellect, the triumph of conscious intelligence applied to social organization.

Culture is a pulsating organism, endowed with flexibility, in a state of constant growth. Civilization is rigid crystallization, the unavoidable horizontal step on history's stairway, the repose of a society spiritually exhausted by its cultural growth, seeking to digest and distribute mechanically the output of its parent Culture. It is the Roman and American as opposed to the Greek and European ideal. Culture lays the emphasis on the original and unique, Civilization on the common and general. Culture emphasizes that which differentiates men and by way of challenging tensions, produces those historical, epoch-making sparks in literature, art, science, philosophy, and religion through the creation of new styles, new means of expression, new symbols. Civilization emphasizes that which unites men. It is therefore a necessary, unavoidable phase of consolidation, a stage on the road to progress—so long as it is not considered as an end in itself but as a state of transition to a higher Culture.

Dewey's is the practical, earth-bound philosophy of Civilization, that which made it possible for Rome to "Romanize" the world by leveling it. American philosophic thought is almost exclusively educationalist (pragmatic, instrumentalist) or legalistic. The Civilization that springs directly from it is a civilization of instrumentality—in musical terms, the social ideal of the virtuoso as opposed to the creative composer. It implies the practical exploitation of past cultural achievements rather than original creation. This American Civilization, like the Roman, is based on an ethical system that defines what one's moral attitude toward the universe should be rather than on a speculative philosophy that attempts to understand the metaphysical structure of the universe. Its outlook is essentially "behaviorist." It has to involve psychology if it is to be successful, and it has to discard needless abstractions if it is to organize and rule. It may be shallow by European standards but it is eminently workable. Its animating spirit is a blend of Protestant morality and a pragmatism that discards all absolute values. American Civilization is successful because of the remarkable American gift for psychological understanding. Through their practical and intuitive knowledge of men, Americans instinctively counteract their exaggerated appreciation of man's ability as opposed to his Being by sensing the whole human personality, its essence as well as its appearance. When they choose political or business leaders, Americans do so on the basis of their general human qualities rather than their technical proficiency. And an American Civilization that believes more than any other in the "expert," also more than any other has a healthy distrust of all experts.

Americans are not intellectual logicians but highly intuitive men who think in headlines and pictures, very much like the Chinese with their ideograms. This quality gives them a remarkable flair for reality, which is at the root of their political and economic life and largely accounts for their success as men of action. They have a genius for condensing and digesting what the Europeans have been trained to develop, and they reach the heart of a problem with far greater speed than Europeans, who plod along intellectually and often become lost in their own abstractions.

America's destiny is conditioned by the fact that she is an old and not a young nation, as far as *essential* age goes. America represents, in world history, the old age of Europe. Uncle Sam, an elderly gentleman, symbolizes the United States. The Pilgrim Fathers, stern Puritans, Founding Fathers, the grandfatherly character of America's nineteenth-century intellectuals, the moralizing tone of American idealism, the lined parchment-like faces of Fords and Rockefellers, nothing in America's living symbols suggests real youth. The triumph of machinery, the love of gadgets, the mechanization of the mind for the sake of comfort, always denote the oldster's outlook. America's apparent youthfulness has nothing in common with the organic youth of Europe's dynamic Culture in its Gothic and Renaissance phases, with the insatiable curiosity and innate cruelty which is typical of youth. The soul of America is essentially old and mature, as Rome's was, and therefore more qualified to organize the world than the perpetually troublesome Greeks and Europeans who switched abruptly from youth to senility without even being mature.

Yet, in another sense, America is young with the youth of physical dynamism and vigor, a mature, optimistic youth that contrasts with Europe's tired, wizened old age about to enter its second childhood. But this youth applies largely to the economic sphere, where successful development was purchased at the price of virtual petrifaction in most other domains. James Bryce had already remarked generations ago that "the people have the hopefulness of youth. But their institutions are old, though many have been remodelled or new faced; their religion is old, their views of morality and conduct are old." [5] This essential oldness is rooted in an eighteenth-century atmosphere whose optimism still survives in America and wears the mask of youth, but has disappeared in Europe as outdated. It is both a great blessing and a limitation, a psychological disposition that could bloom easily in the vacuum of the last century when America was largely isolated, but is not so easy to preserve in our own turbulent century.

This maturity is the source of America's basic conservatism—once again, in all matters save economic development—which is often masked by a taste for superficial change and a restlessness that has little in common with revolutionary transformation. Here also, Bryce remarked that Americans "have what chemists call low specific heat; they grow warm suddenly and cool as suddenly," [6] and insisting on their basic conservatism in spite of their volatile temperament, he added that "they are like a tree whose pendulum shoots quiver and rustle with the lightest breeze, while its roots enfold the rock with a grasp which storms cannot loosen." [7] It is this fundamental conservatism that gives Americans in the modern world a position almost identical with that of the Romans, a conservatism bolstered by the complete ascendancy of the conservative-minded sex—women. A Civilization can be secured only on conservative foundations, even though its economic development may have revolutionary repercussions in the alien societies that are exposed to it.

Very much like the Romans, the Americans are remarkably unindividualized. Group consciousness among them is paramount, with its attendant worship of quantity, masses, collective impulses, with generalized stereotypes such as the "man in the street" or the "common man." This implies not an advanced but on the contrary an early stage of development, since individualized stages in history evolve out of this primitive phase with the growth of Culture. The dawn of Civilization, therefore, represents a partial return to the unindividualized stage in which group consciousness and social concerns predominate, but on a far higher technical level. Psychologically, it is the primitive tribal collectivism blown up to mammoth dimensions. And this in turn explains the apparent similarities between Americans and Russians in our century, similarities that the alarmed Europeans find often disquieting and always baffling. This psychological collectivism is the historic destination of American evolution, the ultimate goal; to the Russians, it is the starting point, the early stage from which, in centuries to come, we can expect to see the growth and development of a new individualism.

The Pilgrim and Founding Fathers were far more individualized than present-day Americans, who live in a world of compulsory gregariousness and mass suggestion, whose ideal is *normalcy* and whose essential characteristic is *like-mindedness*. Contemporary Americans display a profound hostility toward human differentiation and deny the very existence of differences in human values. It was only on such a basis that democratic equality was made possible. Imbued with a statistical mentality, the Americans were gradually driven to view quantity as a symbol of quality because they lost the ability to differentiate between them.

The constant emphasis on economic well-being and standard of living has led many foreigners to refer to America's "materialism." But it is a fundamental misconception. Americans have, unconsciously and mostly out of sheer idealism, reduced man to an animal level, although an animal in command of fabulous technical powers. The heart of *Behaviorism* lies in this raising and educating human beings as conditioned, domesticated animals. They hardly allow any influence at all to free will and recognize man only as a creature of *habit,* a second nature that can be shaped almost entirely from the outside by the right type of education and environment. Metaphysical or spiritual realities beyond the animal level are simply ignored or given only lip service. Society is the all-inclusive absolute, a substitute for the Almighty. There is nothing beyond but a Platonic realm of abstractions having no vital connections with the world of everyday living.

The fact that many native American institutions—Christian Science, for instance—proclaim the exact opposite means only that they are contrast-phenomena, psychological compensations for the prevailing American outlook on life. Man responds as predictably to a given stimulus as an animal and that is enough. Fundamentalists can vituperate against this prevailing outlook, but they cannot alter it.

The emphasis on man's animal nature can lead only to a virtual destruction of his individual freedom, since it automatically emphasizes the typical inertia of animal nature at the expense of man's greatest human asset: free will, the result of personal striving and conscious suffering. Education, up to a point, has always meant the training of man's animal nature but the conscious emphasis on animalism has never before been as deliberate. Yet, with all its drawbacks and its inevitable impoverishment of human nature, this exaggerated insistence on man's animalism is at the root of America's extraordinary success in technological matters—one that the more refined, differentiated Europeans can never hope to match, one that also gives American youth the typical self-assurance that never fails to astound Europeans.

The result is that, since nothing is done to enhance and develop the exceptional creative talent for its own sake, American man is static in an individual sense although American society as a whole is dynamic. Americans hardly ever make basic discoveries but can endlessly adapt, improve and mass produce European discoveries. They *research* endlessly but rarely *contemplate*. Fundamental scientific discoveries are the result of *disinterested* contemplation. A psychological attitude which tends to concentrate on immediate usefulness is not conducive to the birth of profound thoughts and basic discoveries, since their practical applications are not immediately apparent. Culture provides the necessary atmosphere for disinterested contemplation, Civilization for utilitarian research. One favors thought, the other experiment. From Newton to Einstein, from Pasteur to Fleming, Europe has produced, at very little financial expense, the great thoughts which have rolled back the frontiers of man's scientific knowledge. At an expense of almost four billion dollars a year, American research exploits Europe's basic discoveries but cannot really progress beyond it in a fundamental way. And, not only the utilitarian atmosphere, but also the democratic idea that research's team-work enables the "common man" to substitute for the creative genius, stands in the way of fundamental scientific progress.[8]

The social repercussions of these psychological dispositions are far reaching. Quantitative standards, along with social equality, have given to the dollar sign a symbolic value it has nowhere else. It has nothing to do with the alleged *worship* of money but with its symbolic implications. An artist, professor, or government official in Europe can be and usually is badly remunerated. Yet, the European belief in *qualitative* differences gives them a prestige and consideration that are ample compensation. This has never been the case in America, where mediocre financial returns indicate almost invariably social inferiority. In an equalitarian society, financial income is the only index that is geared exclusively to quantitative standards, and its exclusive domination has had devastating effects on American society. If a title is conferred on a British physician, an academic degree on a German scholar, or a decoration on a French artist, the *prestige* value of money is destroyed. It implies the recognition that along with democratic equality there is a hierarchy of talent that rises above it.

The result is that Americans consistently mistake causes for effects. The democratic habit of considering the verdict of a numerical majority as evidently the best has practically eliminated the notion that the majority can be wrong after all, that an autonomous spirit can have different claims. In their wisdom, the Founding Fathers made provision against such tyranny of the multitude because they still lived in an aristocratic age when the feeling for differences in *Being* was vivid. Today, however, the psychological pressure of conformity is overwhelming and contributes to the degradation of activities that are not strictly businesslike. As a consequence, the constitutional safeguards of the Founding Fathers are being by-passed by the increasing psychological standardization of the American people. The fear of originality and nonconformity has become a far more powerful deterrent than any legal or political oppression, creating a psychological climate in which individual freedom is not destroyed from the outside but effectively and voluntarily crippled from the inside. The resulting type of society, to a foreigner, looks very much like that of an ant heap.

Here again, the Roman-American convergence is remarkable. The Roman *libertas* was as limited when compared with Greece's anarchic *eleutheria* as the American *freedom* when compared with the French *liberté*. Roman and American freedom from arbitrary rule is always lawful and orderly, a freedom fettered by psychological conformity and the subordination of the individual to the welfare of society.

This is no sudden mutation in America but the result of long-term development. More than a hundred years ago, Alexis de Tocqueville had already remarked: "I know no country in which there is so little independence of mind and real freedom of discussion as in America." [9] And he added: "In that immense crowd which throngs the avenues to power in the United States, I found very few men who displayed that manly candor and masculine independence of opinion which frequently distinguished the Americans in former times. . . . It seems at first sight as if all the minds of the Americans were formed upon one model, so accurately do they follow the same route." [10] A psychological disposition that reaches as far back as the Jacksonian era is not going to be reversed easily.

Furthermore, it received added impetus later on with the necessity of absorbing millions of immigrants—the "melting pot" policy with its compulsory uniformization and Americanization. In turn this contributed to create a nation of gregarious extroverts who were purged of all the inherited instincts of the Old World. This resulted in a steady leveling down of all Americans to a common denominator and this growing psychological standardization is made evident by the increasing convergence of all Americans toward one single type, however many the superficial variations. American democracy does not give free play to the development of exceptional talent—as had been fondly hoped by eighteenth-century democrats—but on the contrary to the peaceful destruction of all nonconformist elements. Americans are highly differentiated in their abilities and specializations but they are more uniform as beings, more *true to type* than any other people in the world.

Where, then, does freedom reside in America? Mostly in the fact that the individual American is physically more independent of other human beings than anywhere else in the world. To the extent that he dominates machinery and is not enslaved by it, his technical mastery enables him to be free from the material want that crushes so many other people throughout the world. He can live on a far higher level without depending on human labor. He has become in the modern world the equivalent of the self-respecting Roman citizen whose slaves have been transmuted into mechanical gadgets. And this, not merely as an ideal but as a fact which becomes more definite every day.

American freedom derives additional strength from its emancipation from the shackles of history, from the memory of past loves and hatreds, cramping traditions, a weakening knowledge of past failures —all things that clutter the minds of Europeans and above which they can no longer rise by themselves. Europe in the twentieth century knows its past but no longer possesses enough vitality to dominate it and use it constructively. Europe sighs and groans with the pain of thousands of grievous self-inflicted wounds that can no longer heal because the European body is organically old. America is free from such pain and wounds, free to face a new world optimistically and shape it. With all its limitations the psychological disposition of Americans is a happy one. Through voluntary limitation of its possibilities and interest, through a partial immolation of individualism, American society today comes closer to the utopia men have been dreaming of for thousands of years than any other in the world.

Americans are socialists, *psychological* socialists. This attitude, of which most of them are not aware, results from a combination of three different elements: the herd instinct of the unindividualistic youth, the enduring morality that emphasizes man's social relationships at the expense of his creative individuality, and the predominance of the socially conscious sex: women. The roots lie in the moralism of the Pilgrim Fathers and in the cooperative instincts of the pioneers, the teamwork instinct. Doctrinaire socialism of the European type has no possibility of development in America because it already exists as a psychological reality. The problem European socialists want to solve by external compulsion is already solved in America without compulsion. The gregariousness of Americans, their love of leagues, societies, councils, associations, committees, lodges, fraternities, chambers of commerce, clubs, and other groups is truly fabulous. There are more than two hundred thousand such permanent organizations in the United States. Every year, some seventeen thousand conventions are held at an expense of more than a billion dollars. All these civic activities give to local communities a vitality almost unknown elsewhere, a normal compensation for the uprooted and nomadic mobility of the American people in general. American communities and groups are as cohesive as beehives. The American's pride in his home town is as celebrated as the ease with which he emigrates from it forever.

The psychological socialization of America can lead only to one result: growing conservatism in all areas where it operates, again with the exception of technological development. To repeat once more, Americans are, for all their apparent dynamism and restlessness, essentially conservative. This is unavoidable since initiative belongs to the individual, not to the group, as has been made clear by the increasing power of the one-man Executive and its unavoidable ascendancy over large legislative assemblies. The average American is, psychologically, the most disciplined man in the Western world today—more fundamentally disciplined than the German, who can always seek refuge in the absolute freedom of subjective introspection. The extroverted American has no such refuge. He is open to suggestion and willing to be *bossed* as no other. Mass advertising is based on an unparalleled willingness to be guided, directed, almost hypnotized. The American craves leadership, and the immense power wielded in America by small groups of men—in business as in politics —is due to this utter willingness to follow a leader. Sooner or later, in a crisis, the exceptional man endowed with creative power, imagination, boldness, and initiative, arises and polarizes the immense amount of hero worship that is a permanent part of the American soul.

American socialism is not consciously willed; it is instinctively felt and is, therefore, that much more successful. The lack of cultural activities and interests among American men explains the ease with which a common level of prosperity has been achieved, thanks to an almost inhuman standardization of tastes and living habits. This mental collectivism gives to American society an amazing strength in that it simply ignores all the potential disrupting forces that tear other societies apart in our century. There is no doubt that it helps them to be better adjusted in a world dominated by economic forces. Americans take these forces for what they are, acknowledge their business interests and the profit motive openly, transact their business ethically but strictly—and end up by being free of the increasing frustration and morbid inhibitions of Europeans who profess to despise such "materialistic" preoccupations. Contemplating America, many Europeans become rank hypocrites because they would like to but cannot repress their envy and their greed for material satisfaction. Americans openly acknowledge their almost single-minded pursuit of a higher standard of living and believe that it is perfectly legitimate. Europeans feel that they would like to lead a more satisfactory material life but often shamefully refuse to acknowledge this almost secret desire. The result in America is generosity and good feeling, not greed and selfishness, a fluid society in which wealth circulates with far greater speed than in Europe's crystallized and stratified societies.

The lack of jealousy and resentment is probably the most striking feature of American psychology. It is not equalitarian in a mean, destructive sense but in a constructive way. It is positive and optimistic, not pessimistically negative as in Europe. A strange process of identification allows ill-favored Americans to live vicariously a life of success through their fellow Americans who have succeeded, a psychological disposition made possible only through the complete predominance of the social instinct over the individual. And those who are successful in America are less selfish than other people in the world because their altruism is based on this pervading socialism. The rich are basically disinterested because the pursuit and the attainment of wealth, not its possession, is all that matters.

This lack of social envy and jealousy, remarkable in Britain as it is in America, was one of the main features that distinguished Rome from the rest of the Classical world. Anglo-Saxons, like the Romans, have a deep, instinctive respect for wealth. This, in turn, as in the case of Rome, made them the natural allies of conservatives all over the world—a situation frankly admitted and accepted by the British but resented by the democratic Americans, who would always like to be looked upon as liberals. They have no sympathy for outdated feudalism or unjustified privilege but their natural allies are always the conservative elements and they can no more rid themselves of this "compromising" alliance than the Romans could. In the Classical world, all the way from Hannibal to Mithridates' last defiant clarion call for social revolution, the alignment was always Rome and conservative upper classes of all other lands against Eastern nationalism and the international proletariat.

America's is a dynamic conservatism. The spirit of competition is allowed to develop freely within the narrow limits of American business life in a strictly sportive sense that precludes ill will. This spirit of competition, so characteristic of America and American business —as opposed to the "cartel" spirit of Europe—belongs to the plane of psychological socialism, not to that of the unique individual who, being essentially different from all others, competes with no one. European societies—when they were healthy, which is now rarely the case—saw in the original individual a living cell participating in an organic whole, different from all other cells and competing with none. But American society, pervaded with the spirit of Protestantism and John Locke, is not an organic entity so much as a gigantic machinery of checks and balances in which the spirit of competition between equal, similar, and interchangeable parts is essential.

Thus, the full blossoming of the American individual does not spring from his originality and uniqueness but from his participation in as many different groups as possible—in each one of which he is more conscious of his belonging to the group than of being an individual in his own right. He becomes a point of intersection for as many social activities and interconnections as he can possibly manage. He is, like the Roman, a citizen and a member of a "tribe" or group rather than an autonomous individual. His personality depends essentially on the number and complexity of his various "social" beings.

In turn, this is intimately connected with the American worship of *work,* the disposition to consider that all men, whatever their wealth, should work at something tangible and visible—nothing like self-improvement, meditation, or unpractical cultural pursuits, for instance. There are no shades between the hard-working man and the useless playboy because the very notion that leisure is essential to culture is rarely acknowledged in America. The Puritan roots are still visible. "Those that are prodigal with their time despise their own souls," said the Puritan divine.[11] From Puritan days the worship of productive activity for its own sake is clear. Alexis de Tocqueville had already noticed it in the quieter days before industrialization: "Nothing is more necessary to the culture of the higher sciences or of the more elevated departments of science than meditation; and nothing is less suited to meditation than the structure of democratic society.... In the midst of this universal tumult, this incessant conflict of jarring interests, this continual striving of men after fortune, where is that calm to be found which is necessary for the deeper combinations of the intellect? How can the mind dwell upon any single point when everything whirls around it, and man himself is swept and beaten onwards by the heady current that rolls all things in its course?" [12]

This is why culture in America has become largely the monopoly of women and why feminine *preservation* of culture predominates to such an extent over masculine *creation.* This is why also the worship of work is responsible for the pathetic problem of retirement in an aging society, for the psychological frustrations of old people who cannot stand their idleness and "uselessness," and yet who cannot lead a cultured life because they have never been taught to make culture an integral part of their life. Europe has no such problem.

American idealism, the optimistic idealism of the Age of Enlightenment rather than the stoic and somber idealism of the Pilgrim Fathers, is focused on youthfulness, probably as a compensation for a certain feeling of fundamental oldness. In this sense, it is remarkably impractical. The characteristic of youthfulness, in the human individual, is that it is not yet psychologically integrated. The separate parts of its soul act independently and often in opposition to one another; growth implies the integration of component parts for their mutual benefit and the overcoming of youth's impractical idealism. Extreme idealism is ineffective because its ideals are neither organically related to the whole personality nor geared to concrete reality. American idealism, therefore, is extreme and sees no shades. From this idealization of youth springs conformity, the thirst for popularity, mental passivity. The danger of such idealization of youth as a permanent state rather than as a dynamic preparation for manhood is that it can petrify into a permanent infantilism.

A great deal of this springs from the American attitude toward family life. The school has largely become a substitute for the family. The absorption of a huge influx of immigrants, which could only be carried out by the public schools, has increased the divorce between the generations. In continental Europe, the school is only the fountainhead of intellectual knowledge; the most important part of the education of children is still carried on by the tight-knit family which the husband rules as lord and master. But in England the aristocratic boarding school long ago partly usurped the function of the family and became a training ground for the British Empire's social elite, a sort of Spartan system that developed "character" rather than imparted intellectual knowledge. This British scholastic system was taken over by America, and in keeping with her historic destiny, was drastically democratized.

The American teacher became the guide to the psychological land of Americanism—even for the backward parents the fountainhead of modern, scientific wisdom. Most teachers were women and many came from New England. It was through their agency that Puritanism (its moralistic outlook rather than its religious undertone) came to conquer the whole continent. America found the secret of responsible citizenship, of cohesive and stable democratic society—precisely where Rome had found it—in sound, practical educationalism. In the first century B.C. Rome's educational institutions became the most powerful instruments of democratic leveling in the Classical world. Schools were opened all over Italy, in the smallest country towns, run by educated freedmen, catering to all social classes and admitting no social distinctions. Sons of farmers, senators, freedmen, and businessmen mingled as they do in American public schools.

The requirements of immigration in America had a lasting effect on the American temper. Children are as easily socialized as members of primitive clans and tribes. As early as the kindergarten, adaptation to school is the child's ideal and the American youngster carries it into his adolescent and mature life. Nothing has made as telling a contribution to American conformity and socialism as this pre-eminence of school life that teaches the youngster to cultivate above all the arts of imitation, sociability, and cooperation, that gives him as primary goal the attainment of popularity. He is taught to repress his original personality and develop his social being to the extreme limit. The pressure of social conformity cuts everybody down to common size and even competition, so fierce in past generations, is toned down by the equalitarian trend. It tends now to be rejected to the periphery of life where it concentrates on marginal activities. Everyone must be or become "normal."

All this links up with the best-known characteristic of American life: the hen-pecked nature of American men. In the early days of Puritanism and the southern Cavalier, America was a land of exceedingly dominant men whose social "form" was a stern, almost Biblical patriarchy. No alteration has been as great as that which metamorphosed those self-reliant, iron-willed men into the contemporary American male who is meekly subservient to mother and wife. As fathers and husbands American men are not revered or looked up to. They never appear to embody the superhuman strength and wisdom that children have to look up to if their natural taste for hero worship is to be gratified. Of the two poles between which upbringing always swings, the principle of loving intimacy of the mother and the principle of respectful distance embodied in the father, only one rules, and the childish desire for love that Americans display in their contacts throughout the world is a direct consequence of the absolute predominance of the feminine principle. American men remain basically children and the only grownups are the women—mainly because they are always born adults.

Intimacy, familiarity, lack of reverence have become the dominant themes of American life. Nothing leads more implacably to Caesarism than these traits. The democratic idea that any man is as good as his neighbor automatically destroys the vital tension, the desire to emulate and "reach up to." Even when practiced with as much engaging friendliness as in America, its main result is to nip in the bud any form of self-improvement. The iron-willed Puritan was accustomed to raise his eyes to God, look at Him with reverence and, in his striving, become more spiritualized. His modern descendants have lowered their sights and look horizontally at the "common man." The steady process of humanizing and vulgarizing has destroyed a great deal of vital and creative tension.

At the same time, the American nation as a whole craves love to a degree that baffles foreigners and upsets American foreign relations to a considerable extent. It is a craving not to love but to be loved because America is an outstanding success in the world. What is of primary interest to an average American is not the fact that he may or may not love Englishmen, Frenchmen, or Chinese but the fact that they love or do not love him.

This is a subtle metamorphosis of the Puritan creed, according to which worldly success is a concrete symbol of God's love, and of the corollary belief that lack of success is due to one's sinful nature. Of course, as times changed and as religion lost its former influence, this psychological trait became secularized. Success became a goal in itself, shedding its symbolic meaning, and love became in turn the symbol of success. By this token, dislike or hate implies a frightening failure. If America is not loved abroad, it implies that she is not as successful as she thought—and far back in the subconscious, the old religious fears of spiritual rejection and damnation shape up dimly. The gnawing feeling that America is not worthy of love and that Americans are not lovable provokes understandable reactions— usually a horrified recoiling from ungrateful allies, followed by exasperated isolationism.

The gregariousness and fear of loneliness of the contemporary Americans are also due to this overwhelming feeling. Other human beings are the measuring rod by which one's lovableness can be gauged. American conformity springs from the same source, from a thirst for popularity that can be obtained only if one is not enough of an original individual to defy vicarious identification. Like-mindedness is thus directly linked with this thirst for approval.

Let us now knit together all those traits. Having replaced the relationship of respect and consideration by that of a synthetic love and familiar friendship, American equalitarianism encourages a smiling optimism and humor—without which one is deemed insufferably arrogant. American democracy, having proclaimed that all men are born equal and that they differ not in their *essence* but in their practical *ability,* left women out of the picture because the difference between the sexes is the foremost example of difference in essence. With the progress of democratic equality, the inevitable inclusion of women could only lead to their rise to unquestioned pre-eminence. The American woman simply "feels" superior because she is brought up to believe implicitly that she is superior. From this growing feminine ascendancy arose many of the great changes in twentieth-century America: the steady bartering away of precarious freedom for security, the basic conservatism, the idolization of the child, the instinct for the preservation of property, the distrust of individual originality, the increasing fear of personal risk, and the ideal of social respectability. More than ever, the strictly utilitarian, matter-of-fact atmosphere of America is allied to the predominance of women—women always embodying these traits against man's more creative and artistic temperament. In turn, this leads directly to women's monopoly of relations with "human beings," leaving the American men full disposition of the world of inanimate "things." Business deals largely with the relations between man and nature, raw materials, machines. Even the consuming public is a raw material, a common, standardized field open to the hypnotic suggestion of publicity and from which a precious mineral—cash—can be extracted.

The growing ascendancy of women always heralds the dawn of Civilization, emphasizing preservation and security. There was no greater revolution in Rome than the metamorphosis of women's social position at the close of the Hellenistic Age. They became emancipated in the second century B.C., not merely in an economic sense but in every way. They interfered in every department of life, "invaded the realm of politics, attended political conferences," [13] went into business, and took as much liberty as men. Divorces became outrageously frequent. The former despotic authority of the *pater familias* was shaken to its foundations and eventually swept away altogether. "The meek and henpecked Roman husband was already a stock comedy figure in the great days of the Second Punic War." [14] It was left to that old reactionary, Cato the Censor, to exclaim bitterly: "All other men rule over women; but we Romans, who rule all men, are ruled by our women." [15]

Just the same, the days are gone in America when man's authority was upheld by common law and by the Biblical patriarchy of early Puritanism, the days when Blackstone's venerated legal authority could claim: "The husband and wife are one, and that one is the husband." [16] And even though the trend toward complete equality between the sexes was and is world-wide, women in Classical Greece and in modern Europe remained and have remained far more subdued than in Rome and America.

Man's exclusive concern with the taming of nature in America increased this process of feminine emancipation. From the very start, women alone patronized a culture that became a means of social distinction, not an imperative pursuit in itself. As early as the 1850's they had acquired an almost complete monopoly over the determination of the style of living, social relations, churches, charity, art and literature, and largely the press, steadily increasing their over-all ownership of America until the present day when it exceeds 70 per cent of all American assets. American public opinion has become largely feminine and its profound impact on the political evolution of the United States can never be overestimated. The disintegration of republican institutions geared to a more patriarchal age and the steady march toward Caesarism are largely their doing; an increasingly feminine public opinion will look increasingly for a virile Caesar.

What the American individual may have lost in personal development has been gained by American society. The gradual establishment of Civilization throughout the world will be the undertaking of Americans operating as a social body, not as individuals. Because their general standards are so much higher than those of any other country, they have set new high marks in social development that all other nations are tempted to emulate. Increase in wealth and comfort, popular education and popularization of culture, swift urbanization and industrialization—all of these imply the gradual diffusion of a standard of living hitherto restricted to upper classes. This goal can be reached only at a cost: the sacrifice of a great deal of individualism—but then the socially-conscious Americans made this sacrifice early in their history and without regrets. The outstanding success of America is due far more to this sacrifice of individualism than to geographical or economic circumstances.

The first half of our century has already witnessed a growing impact of American habits and tastes on Europe and the rest of the world. Europe was not too conscious of it, at first. When the Viennese waltz still ruled supreme, the first penetration of Negro jazz was hardly perceptible. But it grew steadily along with the influence of Hollywood's sleek motion pictures, American newspapers and magazines, soft drinks, dentistry, slot machines, and standard techniques, which all bore directly on the comfort of living. The requirements of civilized, if uncultured, living streamed out of America, choking the remains of cultural production in Europe, displacing European influence in the Orient. The glossy mass productions geared to the satisfaction of an immense middle class with a rising standard of living have made the artisan-like, small-scale production of more individualistic countries seem drab in comparison. American products have steadily devalued the European prototypes, submerged the peaks of European culture by mass-producing excellent reproductions, copies, duplications, recordings. Although bitterly resented at times, the appeal of a sterilizing civilization seems irresistible.

Roman influence displaced the Greek in the same fashion, overlaying Greek culture with the countless gadgets of Roman civilization. The Greeks of Gaul and Spain were the first to accept Roman rule and Roman customs and in the first century B.C. the Romanization of the Classical world became as momentous a phenomenon as the Americanization of our modern world. Interest in culture waned steadily throughout the century and the philistine Romans laughed at eccentrics like Herod of Judea or King Juba of Mauretania who still encouraged Hellenic culture, or rather what was left of it. Herod's Jewish subjects, outraged by his pro-Greek sentiments, revolted and Ferrero claims that "few examples can show more clearly the extent to which the Roman conquest had roused throughout the East an opposition to literary and philosophic culture, or the universality and vigour of this reaction." [17] Roman tastes and habits and products submerged the entire civilized world—cheap bread and circuses, gladiatorial contests that were repulsive to the more refined Greeks, the colossal public baths, rudimentary central heating, vast commercial warehouses, road and canal building techniques, harbors and lighthouses, all those characteristics of a civilized life whose mas-

sive ruins still dot the landscapes from England to Arabia and from
Morocco to Armenia. The ideas, originally, were Greek, but the
amplification, standardization, and mass production were Roman.

The irresistible Americanization, like the Romanization that preceded it, arouses bitter resentment, sometimes envy, often admiration.
The ambivalent nature of this reaction is striking in contemporary
Europe. European critics forget, however, that America is the Old
World's offspring and that there is not one facet of American life,
good or bad, that was not originally conceived by European brains.
What makes this Americanization irresistible is that it presents all
the features of a Civilization that is the child of Europe's great Culture, the natural conclusion of a thousand years of European history
and the inevitable standard of the future. There is not a single criticism that can be leveled at America today that could not be leveled
ten times over at most European nations—cheapness, lack of culture
and refinement, vulgarity. Whether one likes it or not, mass civilization is today a world-wide fact. The choice is no longer between
European Culture and American Civilization because European Culture is moribund. The choice lies between the high marks set by
America or the increasingly shabby standards set by contemporary
Europe.

CHAPTER XX

Dawn of the New Roman Age

WHAT is a "Roman Age" in world history? Essentially, an age of increasing unity, not merely a local or even continental unity, but the unity of the entire civilized world. What was a haunting dream for centuries becomes a concrete reality. The ebb and flow of world history show us the recurring cycles of unity, dissolution, and re-emergence of new forms of unity, from the early spiritual unity of Olympic Greece and Gothic Europe to their subsequent fragmentation and collapse and overpowering thirst for the old forsaken unity.

In Classical days the civilized world centered around the Mediterranean and this was the chaotic world that had to be organized and united. In modern times, the civilized world is centered around the Atlantic, but it extends also to the far corners of the globe, to Australia, Africa, and the maritime fringe of the Orient, as Rome's Mediterranean world extended to such distant lands as Britain, Armenia, and Arabia. This is the multinational world that is emerging from the twilight of Europe's pre-eminence into the bright dawn of the coming unity and cooperation under American auspices. It can never be merely the limited union of the Greek or European worlds, the perennial dream that must remain an illusion without any concrete realization, but their integration into a much larger union forged by those superpowers whose entire political history can be summed up in two words: growth and union, the mottos of Rome and America. Defeated by their own brilliant intellectualism, modern Europeans can never translate their theoretical schemes into concrete actuality, any more than the Greeks could. Rent by passions and bitter memories, their spiritual unity shattered by their declining vitality, they are left stranded by the receding tide of Culture. It is only the super-states, concrete-minded and practical, the harbingers of Civilization, who can come forward and work out peace and unity on a scale to dwarf the former homelands of Culture.

The Second World War was the inevitable consequence of the First World War. The latter had left an unbalanced and unhealthy world in which effective military power, economic development, social stability, national pride, and imperial pretensions were fragmented and totally unrelated to one another. There was little correspondence between potential and actual power. None of the European nations were really world-wide powers although their national pride claimed that distinction. Their economic structures were too weak to support their huge military establishments. The victorious democracies—Britain and France—were fundamentally weaker than Germany, their defeated foe; this weakness eventually led to their fateful sur-renders of Munich and Godesberg. Their colonial ventures in the Middle East were hopelessly outdated at a time of waning colonialism. Italy's imperial pretensions were farcical. Japan's might was largely artificial and highly vulnerable, although the ruthless spirit animating it was a symbol of the anti-Western revolt of Asia. Russia was in a chaotic state of transition from an agricultural society to a highly industrialized one. The Orient was slowly awakening, but China had fallen to pieces and the far-flung British Empire was beginning its slow disintegration. Britain, Germany, and Japan were economically vulnerable because they were not self-sufficient, their industries vitally dependent on overseas raw materials and markets. Their small geographical scale in relation to emerging continental powers paralyzed them. France was far more exhausted by the war than had seemed apparent in the first flush of victory.

In the ensuing chaos of conflicting greeds, ambitions, delusions, and fears there were all the seeds of an unavoidable conflict. International conferences and councils of all kinds, including the League of Nations, were powerless because there was no world-wide leadership.

The modern world was in the same insupportable condition as the Classical world in the second century B.C. Rome did not want to put an end to the similar chaos of nations in transition from nominal independence to incorporation in a larger political unity. There were constant wars between Carthage and Numidia, Egypt and Cyrene fighting over the possession of Cyprus, petty Greek states in a turmoil of civil and national wars. Solicited by one side or the other, Rome increased the chaos through her well-meaning but clumsy interference. As Mommsen ironically remarked, "It was the epoch of commissions." [1] Roman commissioners went to and fro from one country to another, wrote reports, appointed committees and councils, and achieved nothing. Roman supremacy, like the American in our century, gave neither peace nor security.

What was needed, and eventually came about after the Roman Senate realized the imperative need and faced up to its responsibilities, was the forcible integration of all these conflicting, anachronistic states into a larger political unit under strict Roman supervision and leadership. Roman domination at first was heavy and harsh, but it was a crude world that could respond only to crude treatment. Our twentieth century is far more sophisticated and the reorganization of our own world has to be carried out with far greater discretion.

The social and economic structure of Rome made her expansion into a world state inevitable. Rome was a slave state, with an intricate organization relying on a steady importation of enslaved manpower and food supplies from all over the world. America is the most highly industrialized nation in the world, where slaves have been transmuted into mechanical gadgets. But American economics are just as tightly and vitally woven into the global economic fabric; the gradual extension of this weaving and of the fabric itself make an effective organization of the world imperative.

It could be argued that America is economically far more self-sufficient than Roman Italy, with her dependence on vast importations of cereals from Egypt. But the difference is only apparent. America's raw materials are not as plentiful as they used to be; it was estimated in 1955 that the United States absorbs 10 per cent more raw materials than she produces, whereas at the turn of the century she produced 15 per cent more than she needed. Today the United States consumes half of the world's unrenewable resources and it is estimated that by 1980 it will be consuming 83 per cent at the present rate of growth. The development of nuclear power will not substantially alter the picture since it will merely substitute one raw material for another. Very soon, the bulk of America's iron ore will have to come from Labrador and Venezuela. It might be that America's dependence on Arabian oil and Malayan tin will become vital in the future. Many of her nonferrous metals now have to be imported.

Furthermore, Britain, whose welfare is as essential to America as Sicily's was to Roman Italy, has to import massive quantities of raw materials and foodstuffs and find vast markets for her exports in order to live at all. The welfare of Germany and Japan, economically as vulnerable as Britain, is almost as essential to America's safety. Ultimately, the problem is the same: Rome and America, having contributed substantially to create world economy, are inexorably compelled to police the world economically—and sooner or later politically as well. World War II was the dramatic illustration of this need for a new "Roman Age." [2]

Though World War II may have been the inevitable consequence of World War I, it is not at all the inevitable seed of a third global conflict. The situation is radically different today, the reason being that the second war swept away almost all the discrepancies that had distorted the post-World War I situation. At one stroke, Britain, France, Germany, Italy, and Japan lost their status as world powers. Two world powers remain, America and Russia. The powers of the periphery of Eurasia were crushed between these two giants, regardless of their attitude as friend or foe.

What is today striking is that the world is balanced in military might as it is geopolitically, and world tension operates between two antagonistic blocs that are fairly well matched. One rules the oceans, its center of gravity in the American continental island; the other rules the heart of the Eurasian land mass. This partition of the globe results in a certain equilibrium for the simple reason that neither of the global powers can effectively conquer and subdue the other, any more than a shark can destroy a tiger if the tiger stays on dry land. The two great powers are fairly well matched in nuclear weapons and airpower so that neither has a decisive advantage over the other.

If the logic of geography does not seem sufficiently convincing, we can always appeal to the prophetic vision of past analysts. When the Iron Curtain fell in 1946, the fundamental opposition between East and West finally assumed the aspect that had been in the making for generations. The prophet who gives us this clue is Alexis de Tocqueville, who wrote more than a century ago: "There are at present two great nations in the world, which started from different points but seem to tend towards the same end. I allude to the Russians and the Americans." And he added: "Their starting point is different and their courses are not the same; yet each of them seems marked out by the will of Heaven to sway the destinies of half the globe." [3] Tocqueville would have been unable to forecast the complex state of the world as it was in 1926, yet he was able to prophesy what it would be in 1946, twenty years later. Nothing more is needed to make us understand that there is a fundamental difference between the aftermath of the two World Wars. Today, we see a globe split between a Communist "Eurasiatic" empire stretching from Germany to Indochina, gathering under its Pharaonic yoke some nine hundred million subjects and an outside "Oceanic" world revolving with more or less reluctance around America.

If we glance back two thousand years at the Classical world, we can see an amazing duplication of this phenomenon: "The true character of the Parthian-Arsacids and of the Iran over which they ruled for nearly four centuries is gradually emerging as the result of research into their history, religion, art and civilization. At first, it was no more than a conquest by a small and insignificant outlying province of the Seleucid Empire, but gradually it eliminated the traces of dying Hellenism. The Arsacid [Parthian] advance towards the West had its counterpart in that of Rome towards the East. Eventually the two people . . . came face to face on opposite banks of the Euphrates" [4] and each swayed the destinies of half of the known world of their times.

World War II accelerated the most important event of our times: the gradual falling away of the Orient, with its determined rejection of European values and economic domination, the secondary manifestations being the inclusion of China in the Marxist empire, the collapse of European colonial empires, and the geopolitical shrinking of Europe to its western maritime fringe. All this happened more or less simultaneously with the gradual rise of America to a position of pre-eminence within the Western world. In all respects, this evolution is similar in scope and significance to the rise of the Parthian power in the Orient two thousand years ago, its rejection of Greek culture at the time when Rome was driven to assume leadership of the Classical world. With the addition of Tigranes' Greater Armenia, Mithridates Eupator's Asiatic empire, the Maccabean Jews and other western Semites, this rebellion of the Orient was in all respects similar to that of Russia and her Asian allies or sympathizers in the twentieth century.

Such a conflict takes place on all levels simultaneously: military, political, social, economic, and cultural. When Mithridates went to war against Rome in 88 B.C., the Asians sided with the ruthless King of Pontus, and so did the Greek proletariat. Roman capitalists, businessmen, and tax-farmers had become hated throughout Greece and the East; speculating on the widespread anti-Roman feeling, Mithridates Eupator ordered the general slaughter of all Roman Italians in Asia. Playing up to his role as leader of a revolution, he put forth a socialistic program, promised freedom to all slaves, a 50 per cent remission of debt to all those who killed their creditors. This rising of the Orient and of the Greek proletariat coincided to a large extent with Rome's own grave social upheavals in Italy, as the Russian and Asiatic revolutions in the twentieth century coincided with bitter social conflicts in Europe and America.

Greece and the Orient saw, under Mithridates' leadership, the gory massacre of one hundred thousand Romans and Italians in one single day. In Appian's own words: "The Ephesians tore away the fugitives who had taken refuge in the Temple of Artemis and were clasping the images of the goddess, and slew them. The Pergamenes shot with arrows the Romans who had sought sanctuary in the Temple of Aesculapius. The people of Adramyttium followed into the sea those who sought to escape by swimming, and killed them and drowned their children. The inhabitants of Caunus (in Caria) pursued the Italians who had taken refuge about the statue of Vesta, killed the children before their mothers' eyes, then the mothers, then the men. . . . By which it was made plain that it was as much hatred of the Romans as fear of Mithridates that impelled these atrocities." [5] Mithridates next ordered the confiscation of the fortunes of wealthy Levantines and Greeks, and even the wealth of the Jewish bankers of the islands of Cos, and their subsequent distribution to the populace. The revolutionary appeal of the East reached Athens and Greece. The proletariat joined the bitterly anti-Roman intellectuals, philosophers, and university professors, even in friendly Athens, and revolted against the tyranny of mere wealth that Roman influence had indirectly promoted.[6]

Mithridates even attempted to create an international revolutionary organization on the pattern of the modern Third International, allying himself with the revolutionary proletariat on the Italian continent, incorporating in his armies large numbers of disgruntled Italians who had been ruined by Roman capitalists, making common cause with the anti-Roman Samnites and Lucanians.

In such ages of transition, when every human value is put in question, wars and revolutions blend the military, political, social economic and cultural elements together. Behind the slogans and rallying cries, lies the basic conflict between alien civilizations. When it was not Mithridates Eupator or Tigranes of Armenia, it was the Parthians who arose as champions of an East that refused to be Romanized and debased to the level of a nondescript proletariat without identity or personality. They would rather be first-rate Asians than third-rate Romans. They fought not merely an economic or political domination but a cultural domination that they rejected with even greater horror because it threatened their innermost being. They fought an alien domination that did not appeal to them, brushing aside the decadent Greeks and fighting directly their successors and heirs, the Romans. They had overthrown Greek Culture and now attempted to avoid the imposition of the Roman Civilization that fulfilled it. And many embittered Greeks were willing to help the Orientals out of anti-Roman spite, just as many Europeans help communism today out of anti-American spite.

In our more sophisticated age, things are often less obvious, concealed behind pseudoscientific or "progressive" formulas, armed with all the technical trappings of industrialization. Today, the Orient masquerades in Western clothes. Tigranes, the anti-Roman ruler of Armenia, appeared in public in the sumptuous apparel befitting the successor of Xerxes and Darius as if to symbolize his rejection of Classical culture. His feelings and historical role were made plain when his purple caftan and high turban brushed aside centuries of Greek influence. But we can almost as easily see the Byzantine-Mongolian profiles of Tzars Ivan the Terrible and John the Dread behind Lenin and Stalin, just as we can see the intellectual arrogance and contempt for foreign devils of the imperial mandarins among the ruling Chinese Communists, many of whom are the actual lineal offsprings of old mandarin families.

There are permanent antagonisms that go far deeper than the superficial conflicts on which our attention is too often fixed. It is because these antagonisms were not studied after the challenge of World War I that the next decades were so full of surprises. Perhaps the most outstanding surprise of all was the complete metamorphosis of America under the leadership of Franklin Roosevelt, from the scuttling of the London Conference of 1933, in response to the overwhelming isolationism of the country, to the acceptance of global leadership ten years later, with its crushing responsibility involved in reorganizing the postwar world.

The postwar drama started when the incongruous alliance between the Anglo-Saxons and the Russians collapsed. Realistically, the British had foreseen the coming estrangement. Adept at the game of "balance of power," they had foreseen that the Russians would grab all the spoils if left free to do so. They knew how to bargain with the Soviets and were willing to do so, exchanging countries and spheres of influence with an Oriental cunning equal to Joseph Stalin's, as if trading in a bazaar with centuries of such experience behind them. Rumania, Bulgaria, and central Europe to Russia; Greece, Italy, and the major slice of Germany and Austria to the West. The British instinctively knew how to match effective power and demands, knew more or less how far they could go, and knew that postwar politics would be largely shaped by the war's military campaigns.

America refused to enter into any such bargains. The war was fought for ideals and, according to democratic ideals, all liberated nations should have been free to choose their own form of government. How this program was to be enforced, in view of the geographical and military preponderance of the Soviet empire, was never examined. This sincere idealism could not and did not survive the cynicism displayed at Yalta. The subsequent disillusionment was as shattering as it had been after World War I. But there could be no return to isolationism, no rejection of world-wide responsibilities. America had been stepping out of a century of nature-taming in comparative isolation, into the wider world of nations and empires with conflicting standards, values, cultures. Europe's "Hellenistic" order had collapsed and no longer served as a buffer between America and the rest of the world.

For a time, the United States attempted to ignore this stark reality. Having given in at Yalta, then attempted to stand up at Potsdam, realistic statesmen had to face a widening chasm. During the year and a half following the end of the war, several councils of foreign ministers saw the Russians increasingly adamant and the puzzled West increasingly weak. American public opinion had forced a swift demobilization of America's armed forces, which destroyed her bargaining power, possession of the atom bomb being ineffective, since it would obviously be used only in a contest of global proportions. British public opinion whittled down Britain's armed forces just as speedily.

But there was no peace, and when the dust of war began to settle, a dramatic reality confronted America. She stood alone in a hostile world, without her former protective belt of strong, like-minded nations, without self-reliant allies. Europe had broken down and Nationalist China was collapsing. The first sign of this catastrophic weakening came in February, 1947, when Britain informed Washington that she was compelled to pull out of the Near East, leaving Turkey and Greece to their own devices. The British Empire was fast disintegrating, battered by wartime exertions, economic weakness, and the passionate wave of Asian nationalism. Caught in the vise of a financial and economic collapse of catastrophic magnitude, Britain's imperial lion gave up the ghost in 1947. The withdrawal from Cairo to temporary quarters in the Suez Canal area, abandonment of the Near East, independence of Pakistan, India, Ceylon, and Burma—all these were landmarks in a disintegration that nothing could prevent.

The void thus created had to be filled, and the New Rome was compelled to step in. This time, however, the fundamental weakness of European powers was not hidden, as it was in the 1920's. It was now plain—glaring. America had no more sturdy allies, nothing but exhausted satellites. In 1947, the former European masters of the world were close to starvation and social collapse. Towering over this bankruptcy, Soviet power seemed ready and willing to grab the fragments and snuff out the pitiful remains of a once-great Culture.

Hesitation was impossible and America rose to the emergency with the lightning speed of intuition. Without profound study or long-range plan, the United States stepped into the Near East and at the initial cost of four hundred million dollars, picked up the Greek and Turkish burden the exhausted British had dropped. This was the start of the Truman Doctrine, of global commitments that impelled America to erect a new "Roman" line of defense against the growing threat of Marxist Eurasia.

Even bolstered in this way, the Near East was only a fragment of the immense imperial frontiers of Western Civilization, a few sandbags that could never dam up the Communist flood. The prize item was Western Europe with its large human and industrial resources, and it was to reconstruct the Old World that the Marshall Plan was devised in the summer of 1947 as the natural corollary of the Truman Doctrine. The aim was to make Europe healthy and self-reliant, able to stand on its own feet and act as a buffer for America. The long-range result resembled far more the integration of Western Europe into a new imperial system whose ghostly contours were hardly perceptible as yet. But that American power, energy, and technical ability would be the center of this new system, there could no longer be any doubt.

Bolstering foreign states to make them self-reliant and capable of acting as bulwarks against common enemies had long been the essence of Roman policy. When Rome destroyed Antiochus' empire in the great war that made the rise to power of the Parthians inevitable, she was reluctant as always to acquire overseas possessions. She merely broke up the empire and distributed slices to Rhodes, Cappadocia, and Armenia. The Romans bolstered independent states like Pergamum as they had bolstered Numidia in Africa, expecting them to act as buffer states. And, once again, Roman fleets and armies evacuated the East, only to be compelled to return a few years later for new wars against aggressors like Perseus of Macedonia. There was no end to involvements, each one of them committing Rome to further involvements, solidifying her influence over individual states into virtual protectorates, a prelude to their metamorphosis into provinces of a world-wide empire. Macedonia was broken up into four republics, Illyria into three. The battle of Pydna, which destroyed Macedonian power for all times was Rome's last attempt to respect her cardinal principle: no overseas possessions. But it was the decisive event that, under the appearance of nominal independence for the overseas nations, established Rome's *de facto* imperium over the entire civilized world. The Roman Senate was, from then on, recognized as the supreme court of justice for kings, princes, and republics in the entire Classical world. And when Rome's Senate bowed to the coming Caesars, all independent states and nations bowed simultaneously to world government under Roman leadership.

America saved Europe from total collapse between 1945 and 1950 at the cost of twenty-seven billion dollars. Another ten billion was spent between 1950 and 1955, mostly on the build-up of Europe's military establishment. A collapse would have entailed the prompt scrapping of the postwar democratic structures in Western Europe, the rise of some form of local dictatorship or integration in the expanding Communist empire, entailing a deadly threat to America herself. There was no choice and the United States set out to rebuild the shattered Old World, proving once more that idealism and enlightened self-interest could be successfully combined. What had been done since 1945 haphazardly, as stopgap measures that were quite unable to stanch Europe's mortal bleeding, was integrated in 1947 in a long-range plan to reorganize the civilized life of more than two hundred million bankrupt human beings. Masters of the world only a generation before, they were now mere pawns—pawns like the unhappy Greeks who were caught between the Romans and the Asians in full revolt. The European working classes led substandard lives, the middle classes had seen their savings wiped out by inflations. The former were tempted to reject all the values of a civilization that seemed to condemn them to everlasting misery; the latter were bitter, demoralized, ready to bow to strong-minded dictators who would promise to restore their former privileges. Unable to rescue themselves from the moral peril into which they had been thrown by their own folly, the Europeans grudgingly came to accept the help and advice of America.

The Marshall Plan started in 1948, sending a vast American bureaucracy to Europe to screen requests for funds, supervise their spending, give advice, issue virtual commands, reconstruct defective agencies, and influence directly or indirectly the local and national policies of most European nations. It was the triumph of economic necessity over outdated and parochial politics. It aimed at the rebuilding of Europe's industries, the scrapping of obsolescent plants, the reshaping of economic structures and currents, swift technical improvements, training of technicians—in other words an attempt to help Europe bridge the fantastic gap in economic productivity that had opened at the turn of the century when productivity and standard of living were roughly equivalent in Europe and America. This gap could be easily measured in terms of the seven or eight horsepower of energy at the disposal of the American worker, as compared with the two or three for his European counterpart—or the three hundred billion dollars' worth of national production of one hundred fifty million Americans compared with half that amount produced by almost twice as many Europeans. Narrowing this gap involved not only the complete overhauling of defective economic sectors but the internal standardization of production and the unification of the European market.

The economic integration of Europe gradually became the primary goal of Marshall Planners, enforced by the American-inspired Organization of European Economic Cooperation and the European Payments Union. Refusing to deal with each one of the eighteen nations separately, America forced upon them a grudging cooperation, a pooling of needs and requirements that lightened the load thrust on American planners. The United States did not want to assume the crushing leadership of a fragmented Europe but to assist the birth of a new European leadership with which it could deal on a basis of equality. By 1949, the complete unification of Europe had become the long-range goal of the Marshall Plan, and of America's policy toward Europe in general. In this, it failed. No European leadership developed, nor could any ever develop—any more than it could have developed in Classical Greece.

The Marshall Plan had one major defect: it was only a partial substitute for the drastic lowering of American tariffs that many European and especially Britsh economists advocated—"Trade, not aid" was their motto. But America would not hear of this. Europe would be rebuilt as a separate, autonomous economic unit, under American supervision, according to long-range plans. The lowering of trade barriers between Europe and America might start a free-for-all and entail dislocation of the delicate economic fabric of the entire world.

In spite of grumbling and recriminations, the success of the Marshall Plan as it stood was spectacular. But the economic integration remained as much a dream as it had been in the past; the financial structure of Europe with its petrified jungle of holding companies, trusts, and cartels remained unshakable. European leaders wanted none of the free-enterprise competition that had made America great. The American dream of counteracting the appeal of Communism by raising the European working class to middle class status was obviously failing because it was mostly the well-to-do who benefited from the economic recovery. By 1950 the Marshall Planners were aware of this social problem and were prepared to attack boldly through a determined display of American authority—when the whole project came brutally to an end with the outbreak of war in Korea.

The threat that had seemed merely political and social in Europe now assumed a more deadly aspect in the Far East. Economic rehabilitation in Europe gave way to rearmament. As usual in America, there were no shades, no gradual transition. The switch was brutal, from a peace economy to a semi-war economy and with greater or lesser reluctance, the rest of the Western world had to follow suit. In 1950, not a cent of the Marshall Plan was spent on military items. Two years later, 80 per cent of the American aid was made up of weapons and the rest went indirectly into bolstering the military defense of the Old World. The change was brutal but unavoidable and in 1952, the remnants of the Marshall Plan were fused with the Military Defense Aid Program.

This development gave concrete expression to two related movements: the political and military unification of Europe and the consolidation of the Atlantic Community. The first was and will remain an outstanding failure; the second is a temporary success with implicit promise of greater success in the future. The vague impulse toward a political union of Europe's disparate nations took shape in 1949 when twelve governments set up the ineffective Council of Europe in Strasbourg, an arena for unemployed politicians. But from empty political talks obviously leading nowhere, the best minds in Europe turned once again to the only force that could create a common European outlook: economics. So it was that the Schuman Plan, the only concrete realization of European unity, concentrated exclusively on an economic integration of Europe's industrial heart: the geographical triangle comprising the German Ruhr, Holland, Belgium, France's north and east. The economic union was to merge the coal and steel industries of six antagonistic nations under the supervision of a High Authority, sovereign and independent in its own right. This was conceived of as the nucleus of an economic integration that would soon draw into its orbit every economic sector of Western Europe. The High Authority of the European Coal and

Steel Community began to function creakily, in spite of the obstacles raised by adverse nationalist feelings, and was kept alive by American loans (one hundred million dollars in 1955) advanced by Washington's Export-Import Bank.

But when global politics forced the Western nations to switch from economics to rearmament, everything went wrong. Initiated in 1950 by the alarmed French who refused to sanction the rebirth of a separate German army, the European Defense Community took four long years to die, a sordid period of renewed intra-European suspicions and squabbles, of murky memories of past misdeeds that poisoned the atmosphere and almost wrecked the modest Schuman Plan itself. Prodding, needling, enticing, or commanding in turn, America attempted to raise Europeans above their cruel history, to dispel their memories, and show them the bright light of union for the sake of common defense. American planners at SHAPE (Supreme Headquarters, Allied Powers, Europe) took apart the Pleven Plan and put it together again so that the German combat units should have real military value. American diplomats framed the supra-national authority—assembly, council of ministers, budget—which would have full sovereignty over this European army. Finally, America put full pressure on the various European nations—hustled the French, pressed the Germans, jostled Belgians and Dutch. But it was no use. The dream of military integration through the EDC (European Defense Community) went the way of political integration and many fears were awakened that the modest beginning of economic integration would follow them.

European unity, alone, is a dream without any possibility of ever becoming a reality. The first insurmountable obstacle is Britain's determined refusal to join, economically, politically, or militarily. The reason is obvious: Britain belongs half to Europe, half to the New World. The Channel may be only a moat but, psychologically, it is as wide as an ocean. Britain is half "Greece" and half "Rome" and her determination to remain halfway between America and Europe is unshakable. And without Britain, European unity is meaningless. "Europe" then becomes merely the maritime fringe of Western Europe, an agglomeration of disparate nations split by bitter memories, jealousies, hatreds. Spain and Portugal hardly belong to Europe at all; their semi-African character is unmistakable. Switzerland and Sweden are staunchly neutral. And any hope of European integration rests on the impossible solution of a Franco-German integration, with Germany herself fundamentally uncertain, torn between East and West.

If unity is to come, it will have to be from extra-European sources and take place within a much larger framework. It will have to be based on the only unity that has any concrete reality: the Atlantic Community, the geographical unit of Western Civilization.

It was the good fortune of the West that it did not wait for European unity to devise a larger alliance more consistent with the profound trend of history. This new framework became the North Atlantic Treaty Organization, an alliance of fourteen Atlantic nations amounting to almost four hundred million people under American leadership, representing the closest approach to a realistic "Roman" order attempted in modern times—and consequently the most tangible sign of America's acceptance of the full leadership of Western Civilization. The movement is still rudimentary but it is a step in the right direction, the alliance of men united by centuries of common culture and common ideals, forced together in a defensive alliance against the rising forces of alien ideologies and neobarbarism. They are set apart from the rest of the world by their underlying unity. The histories of Europe and America are understandable when studied together, meaningless if taken separately. They cannot be separated because they would not be today what they are if the other sections had not existed. The whole complex Europe-America is an integrated universe in which the various stars and planets are made of the same stuff and revolve around a mobile center of gravity that has shifted across the Atlantic in our century, from the Old to the New World. But this joint history sets them apart from all other civilizations. It does not require direct references to Russia or Asia or Africa to be comprehensible. It is a self-contained unit of its own, a living organism, whereas Europe alone is not.

The birth of NATO (the North Atlantic Treaty Organization) is now lost in the fog of uncertainty that gripped the statesmen of America and Britain when the wartime alliance with Russia collapsed in 1947. The idea germinated slowly because it involved a radical departure from America's traditional policy of aloofness. But, with the Marshall Plan, isolationism was already virtually dead and NATO looked very much like the natural extension to military defense of the plan's economic cooperation. Britain had started by organizing the small and ineffective Brussels Pact. It was only a gesture, an invitation to America to step in, broaden it and take the lead. This was done when the Atlantic Pact was signed in April, 1949, by twelve nations as a new type of alliance, one that was no longer based on a community of political or economic interests, but an epoch-making union of like-minded nations for the defense of a *way of life*—the defense of a Civilization. With it, the long-standing fragmentation of the West that had started with the Renaissance and the Reformation was at last reversing itself: the West was moving back, once again, to growing integration and eventual unity.

The military limb of the Atlantic Community is SHAPE and while the moribund European union was dragging along wearily through hopeless discussion and arguments, NATO was able in a few years to put up a respectable number of Western legions to stand guard along the frontiers of Civilization—almost a hundred divisions in various stages of readiness in 1955. The military vacuum that had left those frontiers virtually defenseless after the war came to an end. From Norway to Greece, the modern *limes* are in place and effectively garrisoned. American, British, and European troops stand guard, under American supervision, equipped and bolstered by millions of tons of American supplies.

NATO appears to be a mere coalition but it is not, because it cannot be. It has a unified command that can steam-roller any reluctant European nation. Only America, and Britain to a limited extent, can provide the necessary leadership, the bulk of the supplies and equipment, the advanced technology, the experienced commanders in the higher echelons. Control is overwhelmingly in the hands of the English-speaking partners. The unified command itself was not adopted right away. Democratic sentiments and national prejudices had favored the system of Regional Planning Groups, loose committees which could not provide effective leadership. It was the 1950 disasters in Korea that swiftly altered the thinking of the Americans and led to the creation of SHAPE with General Eisenhower as Supreme Allied Commander.

Two years later, as a result of the Lisbon Conference, the military organization received its political counterpart: the Permanent Council of the Atlantic Treaty. With this, at last, the West came to recognize that definite goals, years of peril, precise timetables, and dates of Soviet aggression were unrealistic—that, in fact, this was no temporary coalition but a permanent union similar to a super-state. The world was permanently split, although not necessarily by a cold war. And many in the West came to understand that Civilization was not to be a bright era of world peace and international understanding but a precious treasure located in a definite geographical era, to be tirelessly looked after and jealously guarded. The function of NATO is to be the political guardian of Western Civilization, to be the nucleus of a supranational government whose sovereignty might become, in time, supreme over that of the participating nations. In NATO, the authority and power of America stand supreme, even against a unanimous coalition of all the other members.

NATO is a refinement of Roman imperium, adapted to a more sophisticated age when power is not brutally naked but judiciously disguised; and it is only a beginning, destined to grow through many vicissitudes and temporary setbacks. It should not be overlooked that even Rome was cautious in her involuntary imperialism and that Roman authority was secure only when it was fully accepted by the smaller nations. Such imperialism is fully accepted only to the extent that it is the only protection against frightful catastrophes, to the extent that it becomes the common property of both the imperial and imperialized nations for the sake of common defense, to the extent that they both constitute a true commonwealth defending a common way of life.

The present weakness of the Atlantic Community is immediately visible if compared to the compact, monolithic structure of the Communist East. It is still a percariously embryonic structure, even if slowly on the way to becoming a united commonwealth. It lacks flexibility because every individual member has to be consulted, even if this is only a formality. It cannot match the swiftness of decision of the Red power and its conflicting public opinions still have too much weight, can paralyze a farsighted policy-making, indeed could temporarily break up the alliance. In fact, NATO today is at the stage reached by America at the time of the Articles of Confederation. It needs a new constitution and a strong executive. It has, in fact, to become a living organism with a soul, not an alliance of frantic powers and sluggish nations constantly at odds because the real leader, America, does not dare bulldoze the other partners. Time and stress will be needed to make this fact plain.

The decade following World War II saw the establishment and consolidation of an American imperium over a large part of the globe. It is gradually being crystallized into a permanent, world-wide structure. In 1955, America maintained almost 1,400,000 combat troops in about 950 foreign installations throughout the world. Although NATO is the core of this new "Roman" empire and absorbs half a million American soldiers, sailors, and airmen, it is not the whole of it, by any means. America has another frontier to defend and a backyard to keep quiet. The backyard is weak and divided Latin America, the former object of the one-sided Monroe Doctrine and now the nominal partner in the Pan-American organization. The relative preponderance of America is much greater today than in the days of Monroe and Latin Americans are still wary of *Yanqui imperialismo*. But here again, progress in sophistication and international psychology has led to a rewording of America's supervisory protectorate. Ostensibly, the Pan-American defense system as set up in 1947 is a cooperative arrangement between equal partners. In fact, its real purpose is to make certain that no part of the Western Hemisphere can be used as a base of attack against the United States.

The other frontier that must be defended is the remote Far East. From America's first involvement across the Pacific (the opening of Japan in the 1850's) to the 1950's, a tremendous extension of American power has taken place. Nor was it entirely unforeseen or unpremeditated. Commodore Perry, who had led his squadron into Yeddo Bay and compelled Japan to open her gates to American influence, had proclaimed: "It is self-evident that the course of coming events will ere long make it necessary for the United States to extend its jurisdiction beyond the limits of the western continent, and I assume the responsibility of urging the expediency of establishing a foothold in this quarter of the globe as a measure of positive necessity to the establishment of our maritime rights in the east." [7]

A century later, the results of this imperial extension are plain. The defeat of Japan has given to America a number of semiprotectorates strung all along the coast of Asia, economically dependent on the United States, garrisoned by American troops, guided by American advisers. From Korea to Japan, to the American fortress of Okinawa, Formosa, the Philippines, and South Vietnam, America has been unwittingly driven to create a new frontier to replace the crumbling system of European bases and colonies. In 1955, for instance, the United States had four hundred warships in the Far East with 350,000 navy men, 300,000 army troops and thirty squadrons of jet fighters and bombers—without mentioning the nuclear power of Strategic Air Command's long-range bombers. Twenty South Korean divisions were maintained with American technical and financial help amounting to six hundred million dollars, four hundred thousand Nationalist Chinese on Formosa at a cost of 300 million, a hundred thousand Vietnamese at an additional cost of several hundred million.

But in Asia, the problem is far more complex than in Europe. Except for the Philippines, all the countries are staunchly Asian in culture and cannot fit into a *Western* commonwealth. Their standards of living are much lower than Europe's, their way of life entirely different. American efforts are largely paralyzed politically because the United States stands, inevitably, as the successor of European colonialism, as the Romans inherited the Greek legacy in the East.

It is the whole of these world-wide commitments that form the canvas of the future of Roman Age. Even NATO looks small within the much wider network of American protection that includes tremendous air bases in North Africa, Spain, the Azores, Greenland, Iceland, and Alaska, a growing network of strictly American defenses that stand outside NATO and overhang it like a gigantic umbrella. The Strategic Air Command controls this global network along with the five-thousand-ship American navy, which is equal to all the other navies of the world combined, whose technical superiority over the others increases steadily. Behind it all, stands America's immense nuclear power, the result of a colossal investment of more than twelve billion dollars of public funds during and immediately after World War II, of a fusion of European brains and ideas (Alfred Einstein, Niels Bohr, Enrico Fermi, Leo Szilard) and America's gigantic resources bolstered by her genius for organization and concrete application. This nuclear power stands outside and above NATO, whose members knew and agreed in December, 1954, that its disposal would be entirely at the discretion of the President of the United States. There could be no democratic vote in the NATO Council but only acceptance of the President's decision.

The psychological consequences of this new situation are far-reaching. With the collapse of their colonial empires, the European nations are gradually losing whatever global vision they had in the past. They dwindle in size, mentally as well as physically, becoming parochial and therefore, that much more subordinate. Meantime, America is gradually compelled to develop a world-wide vision and policy that no European nation can possibly match. The European countries shrink to the size of provincial fragments of a global puzzle that America alone can put together.

But this is not all. The most ominous development, which has come about largely unnoticed, is the peculiar way American influence has made itself felt in Europe since the Marshall Plan. Help and control on such a staggering scale could no longer be content to use the normal diplomatic channels through which "sovereign" nations communicate with each other. Those narrow channels were soon flooded and direct contact was established between the controlling American departments and their European counterparts. This is the ominous development that shows us the pattern of things to come. The American bureaucracy will be directly *geared* onto its European counterparts, steadily increasing its influence and control with each military and economic crisis. European statesmen and politicians will continue debating within the framework of their increasingly impotent parliamentary systems, taking themselves as seriously as in the past; they will not notice that a growing portion of the bureaucracies that are nominally their servants (and in France, for instance, were actually running the country) will have changed masters. European political structures will not be brutally abolished; they will simply atrophy and die. By then, a gigantic American-European bureaucracy, centered in Washington, will have become an established fact.

Thus, it is obvious that Europe is not only losing its foreign and colonial positions; it is gradually becoming "protected" by America, the prelude to a future "integration" within a unified "Western Empire."

Along with the development of American bases all over the world, came the spreading of American economic and technological assistance. Point Four, and other related organisms have extended their work and influence to the far corners of the world. In mid-century, for instance, America maintained twenty-five hundred American officials and four ambassadors in Paris alone. Each official is an expert in some economic, social, or political problem. Trade, banking, atomic energy, engineering, labor unions, social security, radio, press, films, minerals, oil, aviation, artillery—everything conceivable was surveyed, chartered, analyzed, gauged, and handled with an eye on its world-wide implications. All over the world, the American expert, adviser, army officer, proconsul, diplomat, and businessman has become the Roman of our times, living apart from the native of the land, insulated behind mountains of pasteurized and sterilized supplies and equipment. In the same way, the Romans settled down all over the Classical world as the tax-farmers, army contractors, slave dealers, merchants, managers, and employees of Roman trading corporations, army officers, engineers, bankers, and landowners. They were organized in self-governing, autonomous colonies, the *conventus Civium Romanorum,* the self-appointed advisory councils of Roman ambassadors, governors, and proconsuls, separated from the bulk of the subject populations by their higher standard of living, their political and social prerogatives. The American businessmen abroad today are simply reincarnations of the Roman *negotiatores* (who operated on their own account, with their own capital) and *publicani* (who handled governmental business under contract).

Modern Americans suffer to an extent from the same sort of distrust, envy, dislike that most men in the Classical world extended to the Romans. The rather swift metamorphosis of the former friendliness and good will for Americans all over the world into the present global distrust is understandable. In Europe, it is an inevitable byproduct of the hectic transition from one historical phase to another, the mutation of Europe's former superiority into an inferiority complex. In the Orient, it simply transfers to the Americans the deep-rooted anti-Western feelings hitherto reserved for the dominant Europeans, as the Romans inherited the anti-Greek feelings of the Orient. This heartbreaking alteration of feeling was predictable, even though it clashes violently with the American thirst for love and friendship. The era of irresponsible popularity is closed and the sooner Americans come to accept the position held by the British in the last century, the better. The trend is irreversible, the responsibility cannot be shirked.

Instead of looking upon America as she is—the New Rome—the puzzled and embittered Europeans prefer to see in her a new Carthage—soulless, exclusively dedicated to the pursuit of material wealth, vaguely hypocritical, the land of sharp and ruthless Yankee businessmen. They fail to see that America today, and alone in the world, has the necessary ingredients of a stable *civilized* order: moral ideals and ethical purpose. Few Europeans saw in the Marshall Plan the great act of statesmanship and generosity that it was; they prefer to look exclusively at the other side of the coin: the preservation of American tariffs, the warding off of an economic depression in the United States itself, and the undoubted increase in American power and influence over the internal affairs of European nations.

Responsibility for this estrangement lies largely with America's atomistic outlook, extreme pragmatism, distrust of intellectual theories, and therefore, the inarticulate character of her idealism. Idealism is always contagious, but it has to be transferable. It must be thought out clearly and lived out concretely. American idealism, unfortunately, is extremely difficult to explain to other nations because Americans have never been able fully to understand themselves, because, so far, they have not understood the significance of their past in relation to world history.

Caesars are preceded by men of vision who instinctively understand the requirements of a new age. A world ruled or influenced by the Roman Senate remained in chaos because Rome did not want to assume responsibilities, and because Rome's executive power was weak. It took Lucullus' campaigns against Mithridates' revolutionary power to bring the truth home to Roman statesmen. And it was Lucullus who was the first to understand that to put an end to the chaos, Rome had to assume burdens and responsibilities, who also saw that Rome's foreign policy was paralyzed by irrational fears of her inflated enemies, exaggerated reliance on the nonexistent strength of allies, slackness and lack of continuity, misinformation about the real strength alike of friend and foe. Rome had always preferred diplomacy to war, had refused to lay down long-term policies, and had always preferred to solve problems in a pragmatic and piecemeal way that took only the present and not the future into account.

Lucullus had to prove to Rome that the Near East had the shadow but not the substance of power, that a strong policy would always be respected and lead to lasting peace if it was farsighted and generous. Pompey and Caesar were, in this respect, nothing more than his disciples. In a sense, Lucullus was to Rome what Douglas MacArthur was to America—the imperious but capable conqueror who shows the path to a new type of generous imperialism, more conscious of its duties and responsibilities than its prerogatives. "MacArthur warned against exerting American influence 'in an imperialistic manner, or for the sole purpose of commercial advantage'; our influence and our strength, he insisted, must be expressed 'in terms of essential liberalism' if we are to retain the friendship of the Asian peoples." This is no more and no less than the true Caesarian policy in the Classical world, from Lucullus to Julius Caesar himself. "Unlike the merely brisk and efficient commanders of the Lucius Clay type, MacArthur felt that he was performing not one more army assignment but an exalted historical mission. He communicated his sense of high historical significance to the Japanese, swept them up in the great drama and mystery of reconstruction, and gave them a feeling of spiritual purpose in a moment of unsurpassed national disaster." [8]

Lucullus and MacArthur were both political conservatives who were able to rise above the limitations of their own traditions and put a brake on unchecked capitalism. Lucullus' severe repression of Roman capitalists, tax-farmers, bankers, and usurers was the counterpart of MacArthur's distinctly "New Deal" reconstruction of postwar Japan. MacArthur himself claimed that it was "extraordinarily successful. I don't think that since the Gracchi effort at land reform in the days of the Roman Empire there has been anything quite as successful of that nature." [9]

And yet, both Lucullus and MacArthur were unable to become true Caesarian figures, in spite of their ambitions, because they lacked the popularity with their troops and the democratic masses at home that goes with Caesarian genius. Both were disliked by their men because of their inflexibility and both forfeited to others brilliant political careers. Lucullus' recall in 67 B.C. in semi-disgrace and MacArthur's in 1951 were comparable events. Lucullus was on the verge of dealing a death blow to Mithridates' revolutionary power when the Senate deprived him of his command and jeopardized Rome's position in the East for generations afterward. President Truman's recall of MacArthur implied America's tacit acceptance of a new and powerful Red empire in the Far East, as well as her reluctance to reclaim her European heritage in China by forcible means, just as Rome forsook her Hellenistic heritage beyond the Euphrates.

Today, the question therefore arises: is the Western world compelled to stand guard along its global frontier forever, or is there some way whereby the world can be unified and made safe for the Western way of life? For centuries after the Parthians had rubbed off the Hellenization of the Orient, the Romans nursed the dream of a reconquest in order to retrieve Alexander's legacy. The destruction of Parthian power remained the long-term goal of Rome's foreign policy, the ideal toward which Roman and Classical public opinion looked with insistence. The dream never came true.

The new Roman Age, with its defensive frontiers girdling the globe, is the *reality* of our times. The United Nations is the precarious materialization of the idealistic *dream* woven during World War II—a more sophisticated dream than the rather brutal and simple dream of the Classical world—an attempt to reconquer the Communist East peacefully and ideologically.

CHAPTER XXI

United States and United Nations

LONG before the collapse of Europe's "Hellenistic" order, a dream had taken hold of Western thinkers and statesmen, the dream of a world organization dedicated to the unification of mankind. Like all such dreams, it had deep roots in human psychology. All great empires, as distinct from monarchies or republics, have had universalist pretensions. The dream of Roman unity was sufficiently haunting to leave us a number of legacies after its collapse—the Holy "Roman" Empire in Germany, the Byzantine and its Russian successors in the east, whose Kaisers, Basileus, and Tzars were crude replicas of Rome's Caesars. The Muslims had viewed their Caliph as the universal leader of all true believers, actual and potential—that is, the whole of mankind. The Chinese conceived of only one empire "Under Heaven" for civilized mankind. And as the human race began its fabulous multiplication on the surface of our planet two hundred years ago, the dream of organizing it peacefully became more insistent and general. But it was only after the turn of our century that the dream gradually became a reality.

The first step was the foundation of the International Court of Justice at The Hague. The establishment of an international law of universal validity is the first requisite for an enduring world order. Rome took this step when she recognized an international law (*jus gentium*) above her own Twelve Tables as amended by Sulla, as well as above all other national legislations applicable to local communities. It grew to become a legal code for all civilized men;

under it, as the famous jurist Ulpian stated, "all men are equal," a legal code that protected all individual men against the encroachments of any state—whether their own or Rome's universal state, with equal rights and freedom of speech for all.[1]

After law, politics. It was the first World War, with the subsequent break-up of so many "universalist" empires, the disappearance of Kaisers, Tzars, Caliphs, and the release of so many captive nations, that sparked the first political attempt. Faced with this Balkanization of the world and the virtual anarchy of international relations, some attempt had to be made to reconstruct the political structure of a world seared with uncontrolled nationalism. Something had to be done to rescue the world from the void into which the collapse of the antagonistic empires had precipitated it. None of the emancipated nations could really stand on their own feet and few were even competent enough for self-government. At a time when political atomization had reached the limits of its absurd possibilities, there was a growing thirst for peace, unity, and international understanding.

The League of Nations was the clumsy offspring of this first attempt, ill-fated but instructive in its very failure. It was a double attempt, to organize the world on a global scale, and on a lower level, to unify Europe (still the center of the world in those days). It was this second, restricted view that was taken by an isolationist America when Woodrow Wilson's proposals were rejected by Congress. Left stranded, a creaky mechanism without leadership and without a soul, closely dependent on Europe's precarious stability, the League collapsed with the breakdown of Europe's "Hellenistic" order.

It was during the Second World War that America realistically faced the fact that the problem rested on a simple alternative: either one organized world or no world at all. The Declaration of the United Nations was signed by twenty-six countries in Washington on the first day of 1942—and the name itself, designed to wipe out the unhappy memory of the deceased League's failure, was symbolic. It seemed to ease the transition from United States to United Nations, and under American supervision, implied a promise to apply to the ordering of the world of the future the rich experience learned during the constitutional evolution of the United States. The charter of the UN included a great deal of America's own constitutional past and the initiative itself was largely American. It is highly significant that the Declaration was signed in Washington, that the first Assembly gathered in San Francisco, and that the permanent seat of the United Nations should be in New York—always on American soil and under American auspices. And, to date, the only military success of the UN, highly relative though it may seem, was entirely due to America's dynamic leadership in Korea. But even then, it was made possible by a blunder of the Russians, who could have vetoed UN participation in the Korean War if they had not temporarily withdrawn from the Security Council.

In the fall of 1956, Britain and France made a last, desperate attempt to retrieve their dominant position in the Middle East. Their military operations in the Suez Canal zone came to a halt when the UN, spurred by the United States, ruled overwhelmingly against them. They were compelled to evacuate Egypt. But it was not so much the will of the UN as the effective pressure of America that doomed the effort of the two leading European imperial powers. Britain's position in the Middle East, hinge of the British Empire, was destroyed. Europe's control over Middle Eastern sources of vital raw materials and international waterways, collapsed. America's prestige in the Middle East and the Orient rose as Britain's and France's declined. And thus, year after year, decade after decade, American power gradually substitutes for that of Europe. This great historical evolution takes place quite legally within the framework provided by the UN. But when it comes to dealing with areas out of American control, the Communist bloc for instance, the UN proves to be tragically impotent.

What paralyzes the UN is the obvious division of the world into two major blocs and a number of splinter groups. Technically, this profound division is expressed by the veto power, a built-in potential for self-destruction that is a pernicious legacy of the deceased League of Nations. No impersonal organization with such suicidal features can bridge the historical clash between antagonistic civilizations, one of which simply does not believe in liberal democracy at all, while the UN itself is an attempt to establish an international democratic procedure on a global scale. Here, it should be recalled that the democratic world, as it emerged in the last century, had two fundamentally opposed types of political structure: the *parliamentary* and the *presidential*. The basic weakness of both the League of Nations and the UN is that they are awkward duplications of the parliamentary system, but without all the elements that go into making its traditional strength in Britain. No vast assembly with its multitude of overlapping councils and committees can ever hope to organize the world and give it the strong leadership that it so badly needs, the real structure which a human race in the process of unification craves: world administration on a superfederal scale.

Leadership of this kind can grow only in a *presidential* structure because it, alone, can cope with the massive democratization of the world. It was the practical genius of America that enabled her to devise such a plastic structure that, through change and adaptation, real executive leadership could arise with perfect legality.

What holds true for America holds true for the world. What a world organization needs is a sound structure with a philosophy behind it. It has to serve a purpose other than being a mere platform for antagonistic powers. It has to be, in fact, more than a powerless gathering of ambassadors appointed by their national governments. It must not only preserve world peace but protect all individuals against the encroachments of their own local governments. The *individuals,* rather than the various *states* and *nations,* will one day be recognized as having inalienable rights. Local states will have to abandon their sovereignty, parochial politics will have to bow to world-wide economic welfare.

The prestige of America lies in that she represents the practical anticipation of a world order in which the sacred rights of the individual and efficient economic development are paramount. This is the bedrock of American Civilization. Before it, outdated political problems are bound to wither away, however painful and hectic the period of transition in which we are living today. Before going out forever, the flame leaps up once more, and the political explosions of our century are nothing more than the climactic blaze that precedes the extinction of virulent nationalism. It is on this basis alone that a world order can come into being, on the respect, first and last, for the "private" rather than the "national" life of the individual human being.

America's prefiguration of a world order of the future explains why it is that, regardless of the mistakes and failures of the UN as a political forum, international organizations of a strictly technical, nonpolitical nature have been steadily growing and expanding. The UN not only took over, lock, stock and barrel, the entire technical organization of the League of Nations but multiplied it a hundredfold. It is this growth that enables farsighted thinkers to foresee the inevitable rise of some form of global administration in the distant future. As the Industrial Revolution enters a new phase of increased acceleration and inaugurates the age of nuclear power, the globe has figuratively shrunk to a far smaller dimension than the Roman Empire. Technically, it is a far more compact unit. The imperative need for worldwide organisms is reflected in the birth, on a very modest scale so far, of an international bureaucracy that extends its tentacular influence to the remotest places, sends its representatives all over the world, probes into every problem, devises solutions and assists in carrying them out. There is not one patch on this globe that will not sooner or later come under the scrutiny of a multitude of such specialized agencies. All backward areas slowly become the province of bureaucratic experts who supply guidance and financial assistance to develop the unused potential.

Roman power was able to unify the Mediterranean world politically only because the world had, beforehand, become an economic unit, because industry and trade had developed to an amazing extent, and the economically interdependent nations had instinctively broken down tariff barriers and outdated political obstacles. When Julius Caesar unified the Classical world's currencies and standardized weights and measures, he was only carrying out a universal wish for the common benefit of all civilized men.

One of the most important United Nations agencies, and the most overlooked in its immense potentialities, is the Trusteeship Council. Its importance springs from the growing discrepancy that is coming to light under our very eyes: the destruction of great empires, the emancipation of multitudes of nations and yet, their obvious inability to rule themselves. The trusteeship idea stands at the climax of the historic evolution that began with the destruction of great imperial structures. Since the destruction of former empires is not so much due to the wisdom and strength of the emancipated nations as to the relative weakening of their former overlords, it is evident that they will eventually stand in need of guidance on a grand scale. Yet, a return to the old colonial system is obviously quite impossible. If anything, the breakdown of all existing colonial regimes should be accelerated and the subject nations emancipated as early as possible: the emerging notion of international solidarity will substitute for the waning colonialism of former days.

The pattern of the future becomes clear if one recalls the early transition from the feudal order to the modern forms of society. Feudalism was characterized by the personal allegiance of individual vassals to individual suzerains within a pyramid of interconnecting loyalties. When feudalism broke down, the former pyramid of autonomous authorities with its interlocking allegiances collapsed and the former feudal lords were compelled to give up their private realms; they now banded together and became an aristocracy, ruling "collectively" the whole state. In this sense, a colonial empire is a feudal system in which vassals are individual nations, colonized and colonizing. But now, instead of being the colonial dependency of one suzerain nation, former colonies or liberated nations will gradually be brought under international control through their very membership in international organisms. Instead of being under the exclusive domination of France, Britain, Spain, Portugal, Belgium, or Holland, they will fall *de facto* under the authority of a more impersonal and abstract entity: the UN: This evolution will put an end to the national feudalism of the colonial era and substitute, as it did socially in Renaissance Europe, a more up-to-date international "aristocratic" structure in which those nations endowed with superior technical knowledge, political wisdom, and social stability are bound to become world-wide aristocrats leading those who have not yet reached the same level.

The small native oligarchies that have replaced the departed colonial rulers are often likely to be far more oppressive and inefficient than their predecessors. The intrusion of an international power dedicated to substituting economic welfare for the shallow satisfaction of nationalistic vanity, can only be beneficial to the average man. As an expert employed by an international agency, a Dutchman can go back to Indonesia, or a Frenchman to Syria, and engage in technical work without implying old-fashioned colonial domination. This gradual metamorphosis will be very similar to that which began to take place in the Mediterranean world in the second century B.C.: the collapse of Greek and Hellenistic colonial empires, but also the effective loss of independence of the numerous allies, protectorates, and client states of Rome, and their progressive transformation into provinces of a world-wide commonwealth, run by Rome for the benefit of all civilized men.

Nationalism as such is just as bankrupt all over the world as colonialism. What goes under the name of nationalism is merely a destructive resurgence of old civilizations that had fallen under alien domination. It is often a desperate and doomed effort to recapture a way of life made obsolete by modern industrial standards.

Today, the UN is an entirely soulless organization. It has brains, nerves, blood vessels, and limbs—assemblies, committees, agencies, experts. But it is not a living entity. It has no heart, no will, no initiative. Its permanent organism is an embryo of a world federal structure but its assemblies are simply platforms for political propaganda. The Communist world stands largely outside it, although it can paralyze its machinery from the inside, and does not share the idealism that gave birth to it.

However, behind this apparent weakness, there are two important facts that are bound to loom large in the future. The first is the existence of an indispensable and expanding international bureaucracy. The permanent nonpolitical agencies bring into close contact the fully developed strength of the leading Western nations and the patent weakness of the rest of the world. These agencies represent the accepted channels through which the power and influence of America flow down into the rest of the undeveloped world, the extent of this influence being conditioned by the nature and degree of weakness displayed at the other end of the line. When American technicians travel abroad, it is mostly to teach or advise. When European or Asian technicians come to America, it is mostly to learn. There is no likelihood that this pattern will change in the foreseeable future. The technological gap that opened between America and the rest of the world fifty years ago widens steadily, since the momentum of America's technical and economic progress increases ceaselessly—because it represents the collective effort of a highly skilled, dynamic, disciplined, and single-minded community of almost two hundred million human beings dedicated to the promotion of economic well-being. The haphazard progress of unassisted nations compares with this gigantic collective effort as the handicraft of individual artisans compares with mass productions' mechanized assembly lines.

What America represents, therefore, is not merely a massive and dynamic power, but also a pattern into which small but progressive nations—Canada, northern Europe, Australasia—will fit in quite naturally. American influence is not resented in Scandinavia or Holland, where the way of life tends to approximate America's in its almost single-minded devotion to economic development. It is far more resented in Latin countries where such single-mindedness seems repulsive. It can be intensely disliked, even hated in Asian countries where old cultures and traditions are totally opposed to the new way of life. But everywhere, none the less, it is making impressive inroads.

Therefore, the United Nations can be effective to the extent that the United States breathes life into the organization, shaping it according to American ideals. Only America, which conceived the structure of the UN, can give the international organism the necessary leadership. Producing more than half the world's output of goods, possessing the highest standard of living, and leading the rest of the world for reasons made plain during the course of her history, America will be driven to assume an increasingly great ascendancy over the world organization. The proof that her leadership is not yet being fully exerted lies in the existence of America's numerous alliances and commitments *outside* the UN, of the duplication of technical agencies, some of which are merely the limbs of the federal government, others being UN agencies largely financed and staffed by Americans. The former represent the instinctive response of America to unforeseen problems, emergencies, and threats. They belong to the concrete world of plain facts and represent stopgap measures with political and military undertones. The latter, the international agencies in which American influence is predominant although not as absolute as in the former, represent the ideal toward which the world was tending before the Communist world broke away. The two will have to merge before any real progress toward a world order can come about.

In any case, this world organization will represent the second layer of the new "Roman" commonwealth of the future, one never dreamed of but therefore all the more probable. The Atlantic community of Western nations will remain the hard core of this new "Roman" order; but a more complex and sophisticated world demands a wider and looser structure through which Western Civilization can effectively rule scores of proud non-Western nations that would never submit to open domination. While the individual nations of Europe will tend to become, in the course of time, provinces of this global commonwealth, non-European nations will be handled more gingerly. Flattering new names will have to be devised to soothe their ruffled feelings. This world organization will effectively regulate international relations, bring under close control all those areas that are obviously unfit for self-government, and yet satisfy them—as Rome satisfied the provincials by giving the masses a sound administration and their elites full possibilities of development through the channels and within the framework of their new world order. It will be a new form of empire in tune with a far more sophisticated epoch than any known to history. The contemporary human race craves the same peace and unity under strong leadership that the Classical world craved at the dawn of the Roman Age.

One should not think of the Roman Empire as ruled exclusively for the benefit of Rome. That was true of its very beginning, of the age of conquest and transition before Julius Caesar, when Rome shifted uncertainly from one extreme to the other, from irresponsible isolationism to ruthless imperialism. But it was no longer true when Rome came of age. Roman imperialism became generous. When in 12 B. C. an earthquake devastated Asia Minor, for instance, Roman public opinion was so aroused with pity that charitable assistance was immediately extended to the victims and all their taxes remitted for decades. Humanitarianism had made such progress that the old days of plundering imperialism were completely forgotten.

In the same way, the America of today can never revert to the America of the nineteenth century, with her ruthless expansionism and irresponsible capitalism. America is becoming as responsible and humane as Rome once was and her world organization will, in the long run, benefit the people of the world just as much as Rome did. By the time of Trajan, the Roman Empire had become a commonwealth, a world-wide *res-publica* run for the benefit of all civilized beings, often by non-Romans. The legions were recruited from a dozen different nationalities, the administration was just as much Gallic or Greek as it was Roman. Senators and emperors came from all parts of the empire: Trajan was a Spaniard, Severus an African, Diocletian and Constantine were Illyrians. Almost none of the great figures of Latin literature—Cicero, Virgil, Horace, Juvenal, Tacitus, Livy—were of Roman origin.

Free trade and free immigration everywhere had spread Roman

ideals and methods or organization. Roman emigration had settled Roman communities in every country around the Mediterranean by the first century B.C. These autonomous Latin communities enjoyed a great deal of local self-government and their existence entailed the gradual disappearance of the distinction between Roman Italy, ruled by civil law, and the provinces, ruled by martial law under proconsular supervision. From the days of Caesar onward the whole world was gradually welded into a civilized community of equal citizens sharing the same feelings of veneration for the *pax Romana* that had put an end to anguish and bloody chaos.

What Rome offered then, America offers today: not merely a concrete, massive power, but a living pattern, a common denominator that might repel Culture Men but which is the only one around which all human beings can be reconciled in the dawning age of Civilization.

Besides being the embryo of a superfederal structure dealing largely with technical matters, the UN today has another function that is strictly political: it is a platform on which the various contenders can air their disagreements. In this sense, it is an entirely new phenomenon in history. We know that civilization today has its "Roman Wall" stretching all around Eurasia, guarded by millions of soldiers. But those *limes* also extend beyond the military and geographical areas and slice the UN itself into antagonistic fragments. Its role, thus, is to attempt to transcend war as the ultimate argument of politics and transfer its alternative to the debating platform. Rome's frontiers were never transcended and finally broke down. The modern world's frontiers can be transcended if the civilized community understands clearly the nature of the challenge, which the Classical world never did. In turn, this implies that the Western world has to avoid Rome's errors: the freezing of the geographical frontiers, the static outlook, the reliance on military garrisons, the anti-intellectual pragmatism and lack of over-all philosophy. The struggle takes place in the minds of men before it does on any battlefield and it is won or lost in their minds—as it was when a large part of the Roman legions became converted to the Mithraic religion from hostile Persia. When so many high-minded Romans bowed to the "Invincible Sun" of the East, they tacitly admitted that Classical Civilization was dead because it had nothing more to offer. When its Civilization died, the Roman Empire became an empty shell, at the mercy of barbarian hordes. It is always a struggle of ideas that precedes physical battles, a struggle which Classical Civilization lost but which ours can win.

The UN's platform is a precious substitute for war. Its world-wide appeal is so potent that the Communist nations dare not leave it although they are largely outvoted. It is not a limited platform such as the League of Nations offered but a global arena in which the struggle for ideological mastery of the world can be won by the West. World War III is no more inevitable than America's Civil War. It can be patiently argued away if the awareness of reality and the spirit of compromise that served America's development so well are extended to international relations.

Today we are living in the shadow of the possible nuclear destruction of the entire human race. To many it might seem that this is an entirely new development, since man has never before possessed such deadly knowledge and power over the inner forces of nature. However, from a psychological viewpoint, the situation is hardly new. In the generations that preceded and followed the lifetime of Christ, a large part of the civilized world was swept by an apocalyptic fear of the imminent end of the world, of the conflagration prophesied by John the Baptist. A cosmic terror was born that had never been experienced in the buoyant, vigorous world of Classical Culture. It was a feeling of world-anxiety that was no less real than ours even though modern nuclear power was unknown. Men lived in anguish and terror, often sublimated into spiritual visions. This wave swept the East and shook the West. Virgil himself seems to have had a presentiment of the coming of Christ in his remarkable Fourth Eclogue, *Upon the Golden Age,* which he wrote in the darkest hour of the Classical world when the legions of Anthony and Octavian destroyed their opponents at Philippi, during the appalling massacres and revolutionary wars when the world was threatened with utter chaos. The poignant sadness of a Classical world about to enter its Civilization era gripped even the melancholy Horace.

It was with them as it is with us today. We know the same growing fear of the end of the world and pathetic yearning for the unity of mankind, two opposed and yet complementary feelings, indissolubly welded to a vision of a new world to come. However, one immense difference between then and now has to be emphasized. Then it was a psychological fear. Today it is a stark reality in the concrete world of facts. Until our times, man was lord of creation in his imagination only, not in reality. He was merely a super-animal among others. History is nothing but the tale of man's long struggle to overcome his animal nature—and history will come to an end only when this goal is achieved. Man will then understand that he is not merely going through a change of historical phase but that, in the coming centuries, he will be stepping out of history altogether into a new "geological" age. Man is gradually becoming the "leading fossil" of this new geological age—man alone, distinct from all other mammals. He is becoming, for the first time, a planetary phenomenon.

It is against this cosmic background that the problem of world unity has to be seen.

<table>
<tr><td>CHAPTER
XXII</td><td>*The*

Coming Caesars</td></tr>
</table>

↙THE legitimacy of all institutions rests on one factor: *time*. Those that endure over a long period of time are legitimate. Those that happen to seem logical at the immediate moment are not necessarily legitimate. This is the cardinal difference between Caesarism and tyrannies or dictatorships. Legitimacy involves a slow build-up over a period of generations, not a sudden seizure of power. Aristotle had already observed, from Greek experience, that tyrannies are short-lived. Not so Caesarism, which is a slow, organic growth within a society tending toward democratic equality.↙

↙Western society today, and especially American society, presents the spectacle of an immense multitude of equal and similar men and women who think alike, work alike, and enjoy the same standardized pleasures.↙The more uniform the level, the less the inequality and greater the compact emotional power of the multitude of like-minded men. But this power has to be concentrated and personalized by one man who acts as its articulate spokesman. Who can this man be, today, except the incumbent of the most powerful office in the most powerful state in the world—the President of the United States?

The United States Congress has repeatedly expressed its fear, especially since the New Deal and World War II, that the Constitution and the separation of powers is being steadily undermined—and so it is. Under present conditions, democratic equality ends inevitably in Caesarism. No system of checks and balances can hold out against this profound evolution, a psychological alteration that by-passes specific institutions. The thirst for equality and distrust of any form of hierarchy have even weakened Congress itself through its seniority rule. Dislike for aristocratic distinctions eventually ends by eliminating that most indispensable of all elites—the aristocracy of talent. This is the elite that in Britain, substituting for the former aristocracy of birth and wealth, makes the parliamentary system workable. Since most of the work of the U. S. Congress is done in committees, there is little occasion for great debates on the floor of either House or Senate comparable with the dramatic debates of European parliaments. The need of Americans to personalize and dramatize all issues can be satisfied only by concentrating attention on the President—thereby giving him increasing power. Because he can now communicate over the head of Congress with the nation, he can always dominate legislative proceedings. He can dramatize, Congress cannot—or if it does, as in the case of Senator Joseph McCarthy, it is largely because of presidential failure or unwillingness to use the immense potentialities vested in the White House.

Long ago, James Bryce discounted the usual fears of Americans and Europeans who thought that some ambitious President might attempt to seize absolute power through a brutal *coup d'etat*. But he added this warning: "If there be any danger, it would seem to lie in another direction. The larger a community becomes, the less does it seem to respect an assembly, the more it is attracted by an individual man." [1] The reason for this is plain: the larger the masses, the more they display *feminine* traits by emphasizing emotional reactions rather than rational judgment. They instinctively tend to look for masculine leadership as a compensation—the leadership they can find in a strong man but never in an assembly, which is after all only a reproduction in miniature of their own faults and weaknesses. Instinct always prevails in the end. The great predominance of women in contemporary America can only bolster this trend.

Alongside this internal evolution, another trend asserts itself unmistakably: the development of imperial expansion, military might, and foreign commitments continues to increase the power of the American Executive. This trend was still concealed a century ago when Alexis de Tocqueville wrote: "The President of the United States, it is true, is the Commander in Chief of the army, but the army is composed of only six thousand men; he commands the fleet, but the fleet reckons but few sail; he conducts the foreign relations of the Union, but the United States is a nation without neighbors. Separated from the rest of the world by the ocean, and too weak as yet to aim at the dominion of the seas, it has no enemies and its interests rarely come into contact with those of any other nations on the globe." [2] Now, compare this picture with the present: armies of millions of men, the most powerful fleets in the world, commitments all over the globe, and vast nuclear power.

The President's role as Commander in Chief has now become preponderant in an age of world-wide wars and tensions. His role as director of American foreign policy has grown correspondingly. He can take many steps that are beyond recall or repair. He can start a war according to his own judgment. Singlehanded, he can influence decisively the political situation in scores of foreign nations. President Truman sent American troops into the Korean fray without waiting for Congressional approval, in spite of Senator Taft's vehement protests. But there can be no collective initiative, no collective action, and no collective responsibility.

President Truman's formula "the buck stops here" sums up the immense responsibility of the one man who heads the American government. His cabinet is entirely his own tool because he alone decides on policy and is not bound to consult its members as a prime minister in a parliamentary regime. New emergencies after World War II led to the creation of the National Security Council in 1947, a body independent of both the cabinet and Congress. And to what extent can Congress control the actual working of the Atomic Energy Commission? The President's already considerable veto power has been reinforced by the new possibility of applying it to single items of the appropriation bills. The veto becomes more sensitive and discriminating. From being largely negative, the President's legislative power becomes increasingly positive, fulfilling Henry Clay's dire prophecy.* His power has been increasingly emphasized in the annual legislative program submitted in the "State of the Union" message, and if he controls his party, through his overriding influence in pushing it through.

In truth, no mental effort is required to understand that the President of the United States is the most powerful single human being in the world today. Future crises will inevitably transform him into a fullfledged Caesar, if we do not beware. Today he wears ten hats—as Head of State, Chief Executive, Minister of Foreign Affairs, Chief Legislator, Head of Party, Tribune of the People, Ultimate Arbitrator of Social Justice, Guardian of Economic Prosperity, and World Leader

* See p. 149.

of Western Civilization. Slowly and unobtrusively, these hats are becoming crowns and this pyramid of hats is slowly metamorphosing itself into a tiara, the tiara of one man's world imperium.[3]

Wars are the main harbingers of Caesarism. The Punic and Macedonian wars proved to Rome that great undertakings in an increasingly equalitarian society can be the responsibility of one man only, never of a democratic assembly. In grave emergencies, leadership can never be collective, and we are now living in an age of permanent emergency. Presidential power in America has grown as American power and expansion have grown, one developing within the other. This fact has not remained unnoticed in America since the passing of Franklin Roosevelt and a great deal of the postwar developments in American politics can be written down as Congressional reaction against the power of the White House.

Although by no means a weak President, Harry Truman did not have the authority of his predecessor and Congress raised its head once more. And when the Republicans came back to power in 1952, a deliberate effort was made by President Eisenhower to restore to Congress that dignity and prestige which had been so damaged during the New Deal and World War II. A similar reaction took place in Rome when Sulla attempted to undo some of the worst features of Marius' New Deal and eliminate all possibility of another such concentration of supreme power in the hands of one man.

After World War II, the American Congress voted a Constitutional amendment forbidding future Presidents more than two terms of office. But the precedent has been set and in America historical precedents have an overwhelming influence. Such belated moves can no more halt the trend toward Caesarism than those of Sulla limiting all offices to a one-year tenure, specifying that no one could ever be, as Marius had been, both Commander in Chief and supreme magistrate, and handing back military authority to the Roman Senate.

Sulla, the victorious foe of Mithridates, was a determined conservative. He came back from his campaigns in the Hellenistic East after having destroyed the power of the redoubtable "Hitler" of the Classical world. Although endowed with absolute power, he had regularly consulted the Assembly and the Senate before carrying out any reform. He did not have to be murdered or thrown out of office by force. He resigned of his own free will in 79 B.C. hoping that his reforms would endure, and that Rome would never again have to bow to a one-man rule. This conservative reaction was doomed, not because of any shady ambition lurking in the breasts of would-be dictators but because it was far too late to sidetrack an historical evolution. A volatile and emotional public opinion looked increasingly for the one-man Executive, for the inspiring leadership of one responsible human being. Sulla's reforms, like those of our modern republicans, were noble-minded but unworkable in the long run because of the profound social and political evolution. They merely skimmed the surface by legislating instead of working in depth to correct the psychological and social trends. Sulla struck down Rome's most powerful office, the Tribunate, but it bounced back to power after his death. Then as now, the problem was not so much constitutional as psychological. It is a human problem and only human will can preserve liberty. More honest and more perceptive than many of our contemporaries, Cicero, without the benefit of our historical perspective, pointed it out clearly: "It is due to our own moral failure and not to any accident of chance that, while retaining the name, we have lost the reality of a republic." [4]

New emergencies and the ceaseless trend toward democratic equality brushed aside Rome's conservative reaction. There was no more ruling class and there was urgent need for a strong, farsighted ruler. We today, who stand roughly in a "Sullan" period, can now see this clearly. The gradual convergence of historical trends joins ever closer together the unconscious longing for Caesarism and the external emergencies that bring it about. We stand on the threshold of a mysterious future and try to discern its broad outline. But let us once more look at the past, the remote past that was once the present, long before our Western history was born. Before facing the future, let us once again project the full meaning of Rome's most dramatic epoch: the coming of the imperial Caesars.

Time and again, before and after Sulla, the Romans tried not to interfere in the East for fear of being dragged into the infinite spaces of the Orient and lost among the multitude of hostile Asians—just as no sane Westerner today would contemplate with equanimity the prospect of invading the vastness of Russia, China, and Central Asia. The Romans even retreated for a time, refusing to accept Egypt, bequeathed to Rome by her ruler in 81 B.C. The Romans were patient and long suffering, sluggish and often unable to make up their collective mind. Circumstances made it up for them, and war started again, because this time the Romans had decided to accept a new legacy willed to them by the King of Bithynia.

The irresponsible agitation of political parties in Rome and the disasters in the Orient finally smashed what was left of Rome's republican institutions. The decadent Senate was totally unable to cope with the situation and Rome drifted again into a new one-man rule, that of Pompeius. In 67 B.C. the popular Assembly, panic-stricken, transferred the administration of the state from the Senate to Pompeius. The elaborate safeguards of Sulla were swiftly brushed aside. It was then that desperate, high-minded Romans began to see the hated specter of monarchy take shape on the horizon.

Public opinion was by and large still in favor of the old constitution of the republic, but without being willing to make the necessary sacrifices to uphold it. Everywhere, it was a sentimental attachment to constitutional forms rather than to the substance of freedom. All that could now be done was support one strong man against another and, eventually, throw Pompeius against Julius Caesar, who had become the leader of the democratic *Populares* party, standing on a platform of "people and democratic progress." The struggle was on between two strong men, not between an unavoidable Caesarism and a doomed republic. The conservative *Optimates,* who believed that they could control strong men like Pompeius and restore the republican institutions, were only fooling themselves. As usual, it was only when the democrats rose to power in 67 B.C. that real imperialism started again and that Roman power was restored throughout the Mediterranean basin. But democracy is an expansive state of mind, not a system whereby an extensive empire can be ruled. The Romans had to choose a leader.

Democracy endures only so long as it expands, and the seeds of Caesarism lay in its very expansion. Crassus, the millionaire, joined the democratic party and showed it the road to a further rise in the people's standard of living through the annexation of Egypt and the appropriation of her corn harvest. The moral scruples of the conservative Senate were brushed aside when Crassus appealed over its head to Rome's imperialistic masses. When Caesar moved on to the conquest of Gaul, he was the acknowledged leader of Rome's democratic party. He did not embark on a deliberately imperialistic conquest but on a war conducted in self-defense against the incursions of Germanic hordes—thus proving to Rome, in Guglielmo Ferrero's words "that only the democrats could defend her against the northern barbarians." [5] He helped the Gauls against their hereditary enemy but ended up by conquering and absorbing them.

Julius Caesar was a bold democrat whose "notion was to found at Rome a democracy similar to the democracies of Greece, which dispensed with a Senate and governed their empires single-handed through the deliberative assembly of the people." [6] The conservatives, traditionally isolationist, did not want the conquest of Gaul but they were unable to stem the imperialistic tide. This, however, was a new form of imperialism, generous and world-wide. Julius Caesar was, in fact, a great internationalist who attempted to carry out the dream of many generations: the unification of the world, the foundation of an Italo-Hellenic empire in which all worthy men would be citizens with equal rights. He made every effort to internationalize the Classical world, destroy the remnants of vicious nationalisms and narrow-minded chauvinism. He used the powerful but scattered Jewish communities as "effective leaven of cosmopolitanism and of national decomposition." [7]

The fact that Julius Caesar was elected Tribune for life in 48 B.C. did not subtract anything from his sincerity when he claimed that he came "not to destroy liberty but to fulfill it." [8] He most likely believed it. But the plain truth was that his power was far greater than that of the old kings because now there was no civic-minded upper class to check it, no complex network of traditions and social inequalities to cramp his style. There was nothing but a vast multitude of anonymous, conformist men thirsting for peace and security.

Faced with creeping Caesarism, there are some who are blind and imitate freedom-loving Cato, who committed suicide at Utica. There may be others, however—reflective men like Cicero—who understand the new requirements of new historical times. Cicero was no blind admirer of Caesar's, but he knew that the old order had passed away, that the old republic was dead in all but name. Leadership was required and would spring up whether the old traditionalists liked it or not. Cicero, the typical representative of the new middle class, looked for a powerful executive, not a tyrant, an enlightened ruler who would look upon himself as an Aristotelian leader: *esse parem ceteris, principem dignitate*—to be the first citizen in a republic of citizens with equal rights. Neither Caesar nor Cicero could force the masses to be responsible citizens rather than slavish subjects. That was entirely beyond their power. Cicero wanted a strong president, not an absolute monarch of the Asiatic type, and it was Octavian, his vindictive foe, who was eventually to embody this type of leadership under the name of Augustus.

In Cicero, also, we have the first man of a new age, the man who stands on the threshold of Civilization and world empire even as he looks back on an epoch of frightful wars and revolutions. He saw the greatest curse of his time in the increasing division of labor and the extreme specialization that had deprived leading men of the encyclopedic outlook which belongs to the well-balanced, comprehensively cultured man. The talents of lawyers, orators, military commanders, businessmen, farmers, statesmen had in the past been fused within the vigorous personalities of the ruling class; they were now dispersed among multitudes of men who could not rise above their narrow specialization. Of course, the situation rings true to us now, because this is exactly what we are suffering from today, in America perhaps more than elsewhere. Overspecialization and the atomization of intellectual knowledge account for the inconsistencies of Western statesmanship and leaves us wide open to some form of absolute autocracy that will seek to reunite the disconnected fragments.

The real founder of Rome's Caesarism was Octavian, not Caesar. When Brutus and his die-hard conservative associates murdered Julius Caesar, they failed to understand the full meaning of historical requirements. The past was dead and done for. There was no hope of resuscitating a republic that had actually died generations before, of inspiring the amorphous citizens of Rome with a desire for true political freedom when they had long ago bartered it away for equality and security. Murdering Caesar solved nothing and chaos was the result, leading directly to the bloody Proscriptions of the Triumvirate and the gory massacre of upper classes and capitalists. Exterminated by the Proscriptions in Rome, the last remaining forces of the republicans were hopelessly crushed at Philippi. Their futile attempt to stem the tide of history only made it certain that the Caesarism of the future would degenerate into an Oriental despotism in spite of the efforts of the coming Caesars themselves. Brutus destroyed with his own hands the pitiful remains of what he wanted to save, instead of associating it in a constructive manner with the unavoidable Caesarism— and therefore curbing it. Compromise is the essence of enduring institutions and discarding compromise only makes it certain that the institutions one is out to save will eventually perish altogether.

Once more, it should be emphasized that enduring Caesarism, just like enduring imperialism, is an involuntary development, not the result of any one man's ambition. It is of prime importance to recall Suetonius' words: *"De reddenda republica bis cogitavit: primo post oppressum statim Antonium"*—Octavian wanted to abandon power after Actium and restore the republic.[9] If he became Augustus, invested with the full "imperial" dignity inherited from his adoptive father, it was because public opinion wanted it so, not because of his own personal ambition. Caesars no more seize and hold supreme power against the wishes of public opinion than enduring empires build themselves up on oppressed and unwilling populations. Both are called into being by voids begging to be filled. Octavian was prudent, cold, and cautious, saturated with wealth and glory. Physically weak, plagued by poor health, he dreamed of retiring like Sulla rather than attempting to reshape the world like Caesar.

Having reluctantly accepted the responsibility of rebuilding a shattered world, Octavian had to make a fundamental choice. Should he continue to develop the cosmopolitan bureaucratic state on the Hellenistic pattern that Sextus Pompeius and Julius Caesar had started, or should he revert to the constitutional traditions of Rome and enhance the elective system? Deciding in favor of the latter, he moved to bolster the authority of the Senate. In vain. The Senators refused to assume any responsibility.

Long before the advent of Augustus, an insidious belief had taken hold of the Roman world. This was the belief in the "indispensable man," a feeling that becomes so potent at that stage of history that it finally results in canceling the short tenure of office and tends to prolong supreme power almost indefinitely in the hands of the same man. Continuity in office becomes essential. What is more, a world power no longer belongs exclusively to the citizens who promoted it. A world power belongs to the world that it dominates and its government is as much responsible to the noncitizens as to its electors. The power and prestige of its Executive in other lands requires that he adapt himself to satisfy many vastly different psychological tempers.

One of the chief reasons that forced Augustus to give up his idea of resigning in 28 B.C. was that he had become, in fact, King of Egypt, a land of proud people devoted to the monarchical principle who could never be ruled by the proconsul of an alien republic. President of the Roman republic for life, Augustus could remain an Oriental monarch in the eyes of the Egyptians—but only so long as he remained the supreme magistrate of the Roman state. He became a Janus-like ruler, the republican side turned toward Italy, the monarchical toward the East. And since Egypt's food supplies were of paramount importance to Rome, there was nothing to do but humor both Egyptians and Romans, and alter the Roman constitution. Is it any different in our contemporary world? When the Emperor of Japan had to divest himself of his divinity in 1946 it became obvious that General MacArthur retrieved the fallen dignity without too much reluctance.[10]

But, to return to Rome, there was no complete break with the former constitution, although Octavian was both consul and proconsul, two offices that were deemed incompatible in the old days. What it amounted to, in fact, was that Octavian "agreed to accept an appointment for ten years as sole President of the Latin republic, with supreme military command and wide but constitutional powers, rather resembling those of the federal President in America than of an Asiatic monarch." [11] He became *princeps,* the first citizen of the republic, as visualized by his unfortunate enemy Cicero, and finally brought to maturity all the potentialities of the Tribuneship. In the words of a British historian, "the Principate was not a dictatorship or a kingship or a more potent consulship, but a magnified Tribuneship. It definitely linked the Princeps with the popular traditions of the Gracchi and of Julius, and set him before the world as pre-eminently the guardian of the plain man's interests." [12] And the *res gestae,* Augustus' "Memoirs," proves that he understood it as such and placed the highest of all values in this office.

Psychologically, it is easy to understand why the republican ideal had survived all those wars and upheavals. "The Roman republic, far from falling beneath the yoke of foreign monarchs, had destroyed every monarchy founded by Alexander. Thus it was inconceivable that a system of government which had enjoyed such vast successes should be abolished at any moment by the act of one man or of a small party." [13] It also explains why the Caesars themselves attempted time and again to bolster those failing institutions that had raised Rome above all other nations, and also why they could not find the men to do so. It was not the republican institutions as such but a high-minded ruling class that had raised Rome above all other nations, and this class no longer existed.

For forty-one years after the restoration in 27 B.C., Augustus attempted to reform the Roman state along the lines laid down by Cicero in his *de officiis*. His policy was conservative whereas that of Julius Caesar had been frankly revolutionary. Caesar was a bold, imaginative, aristocratic revolutionary, endowed with immense charm and generosity. Augustus, the grandson of a usurer of the city of Velitrae, was the prudent, pragmatic, calculating representative of the now dominant middle class that had gradually become reconciled to Caesarism for fear of republican chaos—and eventually became Caesarism's mainstay. The middle class populations of the entire Classical world refused to look far into the future, were determined to move slowly and cautiously, and to make the preservation of world peace their paramount task. As their representative, Augustus tried strenuously to inculcate a respect for the constitution and revive the "rule of law" that the exaggerated adulation of the Roman masses and the Oriental populations for his person made difficult. He was forced by the popular will to become the absolute monarch he did not want to be. It was the long-term change in psychological climate, not the formal breaches of the constitution, that destroyed the republic.[14]

Time and again, Augustus absented himself from Rome so as to accustom the Senate and Assembly to think and act for themselves instead of always coming to him for advice and command. But it was useless. The Senate remained lethargic. There were not even enough candidates for the public offices: the twenty Quaestorships in 25 B.C. could not be filled. Formerly, in a more aristocratic Rome, magistrates were content with the prestige of an unpaid office and the satisfaction of fulfilling a duty. But the long predominance of Big Business and the mercantile worship of money, linked with the rising taste for democratic equality, had destroyed the old prestige of social distinctions. Augustus was now forced to pay them salaries, transform elective offices into administrative appointments, transform elected magistrates into government officials, and lay the foundations of a bureaucratic state which gradually superseded the elective one of the old days. From Julius Caesar's foundation of an imperial secretariat under Oppius and Balbus to the full-fledged establishment of a salaried civil service under Claudius, the growth of the imperial bureaucracy was uninterrupted, dwarfing and eventually eliminating Senate and Assembly altogether.

On the other hand, all of Augustus' initiatives were approved without opposition. He attempted to revive the Senate by a massive infusion of new members, but to no avail. When in 27 B.C. physical illness made him wish to resign and retire to private life, consternation and panic swept Rome. Begged to remain in power, Augustus took the opportunity to revise the constitution, relieving himself of the burdens imposed by the Caesarian tradition of cumulative offices, retaining merely the proconsular dignity and the Tribuneship. He attempted to induce the Senate to resume its former responsibilities in the conduct of foreign affairs. But the Senate referred everything back to him, thus abandoning forever its former prerogatives by transferring full authority, of its own free will, into the hands of one man. And when, almost simultaneously, famine made its appearance in Rome, the people rioted in the streets, threatened to burn down the Senate, and proclaimed Augustus dictator. Not yet convinced, Augustus attempted in 18 B.C. to divide the executive office by splitting it up between two Princeps nominated for a five-year term.

Augustus was wise enough to know that it was the decadence of the ruling class and the trend toward democratic equality that had led directly to Caesarism. He knew that liberty thrives only on a certain amount of inequality and nonconformity. But there was no more ruling class, only an *owning* class of new rich, the spineless *novi homines* who could substitute socially, but never politically, for the fallen aristocracy. Augustus could not stem the tide of history, although he was not the last one to try. Austere, stern, and unbending, Tiberius tried to instill self-reliance into the Senate, refused to allow it to take an oath to support all his decisions and, in exasperation at the contemptible fawning of which he was the object, exclaimed in despair: "O men, ready for slavery!" [15]

Growing public indifference to politics was already deplored in Caesar's days, lamented by Augustus, and bitterly resented by Tiberius. But it was too late. With Caesarism and Civilization, the great struggles between political parties are no longer concerned with principles, programs, and ideologies but with *men*. Marius, Sulla, Cato, Brutus still fought for principles. But now, everything became personalized. Under Augustus, parties still existed, but there were no more *Optimates* or *Populares,* no more conservatives nor democrats.

Men campaigned for or against Tiberius or Drusus or Caius Caesar. No one believed any more in the efficacy of ideas, political panaceas, doctrines, or systems, just as the Greeks had given up building great philosophic systems generations before. Abstractions, ideas, and philosophies were rejected to the periphery of their lives and of the empire, to the East where Jews, Gnostics, Christians, and Mithraists attempted to conquer the world of souls and minds while the Caesars ruled their material existence.

Caesars were not crowned monarchs, since monarchy had become as meaningless a symbol then as it has largely become today. They remained powerful lifetime Presidents of what was still technically the Roman Republic. From Augustus to Trajan they observed the old constitutional forms and stately traditions of the republic. Trajan himself, upon his inauguration, "swore before the consul's tribunal that he would observe the law." As Gibbon pointed out, the emperors remained mere citizens: "In all the offices of life they affected to confound themselves with their subjects and maintained with them an equal intercourse of visits and entertainments. Their habit, their palace, their table was suited only to the rank of an opulent senator. . . . Augustus or Trajan would have blushed at employing the meanest of the Romans in those menial offices, which in the household and bedchamber of a limited monarch, are so eagerly solicited by the proudest nobles of Britain." [16]

The rise of Caesarism in America is considerably eased by a number of American features. In the first place, democratic equality, with its concomitant conformism and psychological socialization, is more fully developed in the United States than it has ever been anywhere, at any time. There are no social barriers, such as existed in Rome's remnants of aristocratic tradition, because Britain's ruling class played that part on behalf of America. Whatever tensions there were within the Roman state are partly transmuted in our modern world into international tensions between Britain and America.

The next most important feature is that Caesarism can come to America constitutionally, without having to alter or break down any existing institution. The White House is already the seat of the most powerful tribunician authority ever known to history. All it needs is amplification and extension. Caesarism in America does not have to challenge the Constitution as in Rome or engage in civil warfare and cross any fateful Rubicon. It can slip in quite naturally, discreetly, through constitutional channels. ✓

The psychological climate is almost ripe. What irked the Romans of the stamp of Brutus was not so much Julius Caesar's effective power as the ostentation with which he displayed it. Republican institutions can long be dead and still survive as a sacred ideal in the minds of men. Most Romans were ready to admit the reality of Caesarism but not the symbol of a hated monarchy. It is not too different today. Ideology, the realities of geography, and insularity have made of the Americans tamers of nature rather than subduers of men. Americans have always tended to be repelled by open display of authority over men as much as they enjoy power over "things." So far, they have been nonmilitaristic out of circumstances rather than conviction. Individually, they are far from disliking violence. Their nonmilitaristic disposition does not spring from dislike of effective power—hero worship and bossism are marked American features— nor from dislike for military discipline, since they are more disciplined, group-minded, and eager for leadership than most Europeans. It comes simply from their instinct for equality, which makes them dislike the inevitable hierarchy of military organization. They frown on any form of hierarchy whatsoever. They have no feeling of awe or reverence for other human beings and would, if circumstances warranted it, behave as did the Romans who hurled insults and mocked the victorious generals during their "triumph" in order to deflate their swelling vanity and thus compensate for the supreme honors decreed to them. Americans have no appreciation for the majestic symbolism that moves Englishmen when they face their powerless Crown. They enjoy calling their President Tom, Dick, or Harry, even though he is probably the most powerful human being in the world.

✓ Americans will accept immense, almost autocratic power over them so long as they do not have to see in it a transcendant authority, and they will always attempt to "humanize" such authority with the help of humor or incongruity. What they will always seek to cut down is not effective power but its awe-inspiring character. Through the gap thus opened between appearance and reality, the coming Caesars will march in if left free to do so. We shall legislate against them and rave against them. But there they will be, towering over us, far above such petty attacks, symbols of a mortal disease within our Western Civilization. And, like a Shakespearean Brutus, all that will be left to us will be to cry in despair:

> *"O Julius Caesar, thou art mighty yet!*
> *Thy spirit walks abroad, and turns our swords*
> *in our own proper entrails."*

Appendix

HAVING examined the great drama of Western history, it might be appropriate to look back at the broad panorama of world history and consider some of the basic ideas that make it intelligible. But before doing so, it should be pointed out that *The Coming Caesars,* although a complete work in itself, is also part of a larger whole, a comprehensive philosophy of history in several volumes, which will include in its compass a study of all the other societies, past and present. What follows, therefore, is both an elaboration of the theme of *The Coming Caesars* and a prelude to the following works.

In contrasting the Classical and Western societies, we contrast the two most similar evolutions known to history. Before we glance at the other civilizations, it is essential to keep in mind the reasons for such similarity.

When a Civilization perishes and disintegrates, the Culture that preceded it and was "preserved" by it does not disappear completely. Many of its most important elements are absorbed by the barbarian successors of the deceased Civilization and go into building up a new Culture—which, therefore, and in spite of all the cyclical repetitions, stands on a higher level than its predecessors. In particular, this is what happened in the case of the West. Western Europe was the heir to Greek Culture and Roman Civilization and, having absorbed a great deal of this Classical legacy, made it an organic part of its Culture. It was inevitable, under the circumstances, that there would be great similarities between the evolution of these two societies.

Furthermore, they have other features in common. Besides the fact that they both spring from related human stock and live partly on the same soil and under the same climate, they have an important geopolitical similarity. Both are centered around wide expanses of water, the Mediterranean and the Atlantic. This geopolitical disposition is unique in history and makes for considerable differences from all the other major civilizations. The Egyptian, Babylonian, Chinese, Indian, Islamic, Aztec, and Inca civilizations all developed on continental grounds, in contiguous areas where inland waterways (rivers and canals) played the part that seas and oceans play in the history of Classical and Western societies.

A final distinguishing feature is the fact that both the Classical and the Western worlds were and are in contact with eastern neighbors, Iranians and Russians, organically younger than themselves, whose existence had and has a marked influence on their historical evolution. Except for the Islamic, all other Cultures have developed freely, in comparative isolation. It was only when they had reached the stage of petrified Civilizations that these other Cultures came into contact with alien societies, and by then their historical role was played out.

All these close similarities between the Classical and Western situations give a certain sharpness to their cyclical evolutions, whereas those of other societies appear rather blurred in comparison. It is therefore all the more remarkable and significant that, in spite of their differences, the societies of the world should have all displayed so many parallel traits; and it is such universal parallels that allow us to make bold generalizations that might not seem justified by the study of only two societies.

Before presenting a rough sketch of the other cycles, let us take a closer look at the basic concepts that make up the canvas of our interpretation of history.

We have explained in the Introduction, and exemplified throughout this work, the basic distinction between Culture and Civilization. Every so often, we have also contrasted, but without going into philosophical detail, the two concepts of Space and Time. This pair of opposite concepts is of fundamental importance because all other human concepts can be grouped and organized around them. It is in their instinctive attitude toward them that all the great Cultures of the world have developed their own particular world-picture, and it is in a more profound conception of their sharp opposition that our own Western Culture has distinguished itself. In this conception lies the very justification of this present interpretation of history.

Kant has posited that Space and Time are two fundamental categories of the human mind, basic intuitive forms around which man builds his world-picture. Now, Space is the true dimension of what is general and "reversible"; it is the domain of Causality, discursive Reason, and pure intellectualism. Time, on the contrary, is the dimension of the "irreversible," the domain of Fate and Will. Any sound attempt at understanding the profound essence of history has to take into account the fundamental nature of the process of Time and discard at once the notion that history can be dealt with along the lines of physical sciences and mathematical laws—all of which deal with space, the domain of the inorganic and the lifeless. Time is life itself, the domain of the organic; its interpretation can be based only on symbolic analogy, not mathematical law.[1]

All the great creations of the higher Cultures came about spontaneously, as if propelled outward from the hearts and minds of creative men by some inner Will that discursive Reason cannot explain. That is why the philosophic student of history, who wishes to discover some ultimate cause, eventually comes face to face with the same insoluble mystery that confronts the scientist who peers into interstellar space. It is the same mystery, and yet, it is another aspect of it. The scientist who delves into space does so in order to reach a greater understanding of nature, of that which stands *outside* of man. The philosopher who delves into the mystery of time and history does so in order to reach a greater understanding of man himself. Man is essentially what his *past* has made him and he studies his past in order to gain self-knowledge; in fact, in order to "psychoanalyze" himself, not as an individual, but as a species. And every psychologist knows that he looks for *symbols* in the inner world of man's consciousness, whereas the scientist looks for *facts* in the outer world of nature. Historical reality is not physical but *symbolic* and all interpretations of history that pretend to be scientifically factual fall to the ground. At best, a philosophy of history can be deeply religious, at worst it can be merely ethical. Outside this alternative, there is no valid interpretation of history whatsoever.

Of course, this does not mean that we are at liberty to tamper with the past in order to suit ourselves. Our symbolic interpretation has to be firmly grounded on factual evidence; and to the extent that the organization of this factual evidence can be scientific, it has to be along biological and psychological lines, not along the lines of mathematical physics. Only then can we look upon history as a gigantic symbolism—the greatest of all because it contains all the others, religious, poetic, and artistic. And we can do no better, before gathering our material, than take the attitude of the world's great Cultures toward history itself as the starting point of our inquiry.

All the great Cultures plunge their roots deep into some form of religious outlook; and it is in their religious attitude toward history that they differ at the outset from one another.

The most extreme form of complete rejection of history and of the process of *historical time* (as distinct from *cosmic time*) is that of Indian Culture. Nothing but the immutable and changeless Absolute had any metaphysical reality for the Hindu devotee. Where man comes from and where he goes on this planet was of no concern to him. As a result, India did not produce a single historian before the advent of Islam. In striking contrast, Chinese Culture was essentially historically minded, to the extent of largely substituting a rudimentary philosophy of history for its former religion. The early substitution of *ancestor worship* for the former local cults and *nature worship* were symbolic of this new outlook. The Chinese were not concerned about *Eternity* but with the process of *Time,* looking ever backward to discover in the past a guide into the future, concerned about the *Tao,* the road of man's pilgrimage on earth rather than with final causes and absolutes. There can be no greater contrast than between India's timeless Brahman and China's time-bound, ethical Tao.

If we move toward the West, we encounter in the Classical world a lack of interest in history almost as great as it was in India. Greece had few historians and those were merely chroniclers. Such a thing as a history of Greece was inconceivable to them—not to mention a universal history such as that of the Bible. They could deal only with a limited succession of essentially parochial events, with a well-defined beginning and end, limited in time to one or two generations.[2] The Greeks were never interested in man's remote *past* or distant *future* and persisted in living in a timeless *present.*

As a matter of fact, this is why Classical Civilization eventually collapsed. The great religious and philosophic contest between the Classical world and the prophetic religions from the Middle East was not over polytheism versus monotheism. Polytheism had already broken down by the time Socrates, Plato, and Aristotle expounded their fundamentally monotheistic philosophies. The contest took place on other grounds.

The Zoroastrians, Jews, Mithraists, and Manichaeans, groping in pre-Cultural darkness, were beginning to evolve a new and superior outlook, one which the Greeks, for all their intellectual brilliance and profundity of thought, were unable to comprehend: the Messianic notion that the process of Time had metaphysical significance, that history had a meaning, the apocalyptic notion of Revelation, of the Prophet who sees God not merely in Eternity but also in Time, not merely in *nature's* universe but in the very process of man's *history.* All prophetic creeds saw in the historical development of mankind the most profound revelation of Divine Wisdom; and it was in Christianity that this revolutionary outlook eventually assumed its full dimensions, in the idea of Christ as the hinge between Time and Eternity. Christ became the concrete manifestation of Eternity in History, of the Timeless in Time. In the words of the Bible, "When the fullness of time was come, God sent forth his Son."[3]

Thus, the new faiths of the East added a new dimension to Classical man's world-picture. Their devotees felt dimly, and could not explain intellectually as yet, that their outlook was as far superior to the Classical as the vision of a man with two eyes is superior to that of a one-eyed man. Unless the fast-petrifying Classical world took steps to understand this new outlook, incorporate it within its own culture, and thereby display a renewed ability to grow organically, it was doomed. And doomed it was, because it closed its eyes to the challenge. All the great creations of Classical Culture were no shield against this onslaught of awakening barbarians. The Classical soul withered away under the Roman Caesars and when the Teutonic hordes struck, it was nothing but an empty shell—save in the East where the new Byzantine world was entirely taken over by the new faiths.

Early Christians, Jews, and Muslims looked upon history as being essentially *linear* and not *cyclical:* history was going somewhere and in a straight line. It was this conception of history that European Culture inherited at its birth, a thousand years after Christ, and to which it clung with desperate energy until our own times. Its eschatological viewpoint on mankind's final goal altered and became secularized like everything else. In the eighteenth century the thinkers of the Age of Enlightenment sought for a purely rationalist interpretation of history but preserved the universalist, apocalyptic, and linear characteristics of the early prophetic concepts. The historical purpose of man's development throughout the ages was his progress toward Reason, and the Age of Enlightenment itself was the new apocalypse.

Yet, without being conscious of it, the Western conception of history was widely different from that of the Eastern Christians, Jews, and Muslims. Although it clung to the linear conception of development and endowed it with a directional movement aimed at a fulfillment, the Eastern —by now mostly Islamic—conception was essentially *discontinuous:* time was not an objective dimension of human understanding, flowing regularly and continuously, but an essentially subjective, discontinuous dimension, its flow erratic and unpredictable because it depended essentially on the capricious revelations of the Almighty and His Prophets. Time had its greatest density in the past in the days of Muhammad (for the Muslims), and would acquire the same density again in the future when the expected Mahdis, Khalifas, and Imams would reveal themselves as Allah's messengers. In between, the flow of time was of no account and history was not a continuous record of the important events but a discontinuous narrative, jumping erratically from one prophet and one revelation to another.

The Western conception was entirely different. Time was an *objective* dimension standing outside of man, its flow *continuous* and, after the Renaissance, its evolution *progressive*. History was no longer a haphazard collection of remarkable events taking place at the discretion of the

Almighty with meaningless intervals between; it became a homogeneous and abstract dimension of human understanding, flowing continuously and chronologically (the invention of the wheel-clock in the eleventh century was the first indication of this new conception of Time). The greatest symbol, perhaps, of this new outlook on history was the birth in Western Europe of the *dynastic* idea, so alien to all other societies, especially the Islamic. From France's Capetian dynasty onward, kings were no longer known by some concrete qualification (such as, for instance, Charles the Bald, Louis the Pious, and other rulers of Merovingian and Carlovingian times) but were numbered in good chronological order— symbol of a new conception of *chronological* Time. Kings became historical landmarks rather than specific individuals.

Of course, this new outlook on history was only one aspect of the total world outlook of a new Culture. From the very beginning of Western Culture, Western man has been moved by some extraordinarily dynamic impulse to add to his understanding of reality. This is no place to analyze this process of Western Culture's development to its conclusion in modern science. What should be emphasized, however, is that in order to be able to build this towering scientific structure on which we stand today and which we take for granted, Western man had to develop an extraordinary ability to divorce *objective* from *subjective* reality, man from his natural environment, and study this environment with cold detachment. More than any other, Western man has stood outside of nature, determined to overpower his environment by analyzing it with complete objectivity. Even in his arts, he has manifested a will to conquer and dominate nature that has no equivalent in other cultures—in his stained-glass windows that incorporated into his dynamic Gothic architecture the boundless space of nature (in all previous architectural styles, windows were merely "holes" in the walls), in his three-dimensional painting that injected, for the first time in history, true geometrical laws of perspective, in his French-style gardening that imposed his mathematical concepts on nature.

Western man's instinctive outlook on Time and Space, history and nature, was all of one piece in his Culture's springtime. But something happened after the Renaissance that shattered this harmony. Some time after the start of the Reformation, history fell into disfavor as philosophic material. From Descartes onward, rationalistic thinkers turned away from history to nature, from Time to Space. Discarding the *symbolic* outlook of the Gothic era, they expelled history from their philosophic speculations and began organizing the *facts* that the physical sciences were discovering. Overwhelmed by the truly explosive character of scientific progress, they began to seek, once more, the Timeless—but it was a new "scientific" Timeless in the world of Space where discursive logic and reason rule supreme, where everything is reversible and can be endlessly repeated. Newton's mechanical universe became the pattern upon which the rationalistic Age of Enlightenment sought to model human institutions. And with the Industrial Revolution's rapid development of the Western world, there seemed to be less reason than ever to understand man's historical past.

It was precisely this *ahistorical* outlook that the Puritans took with them to the New World, and it was both the remoteness of the United States from the scenes of history-making in Europe and Asia and the *spatial* vastness of America that confirmed the Americans in their neglect of history. Of course they are fast giving up this indifference, now that history itself has caught up with America.

But, and this was a great irony, Western science and the Industrial Revolution, its legitimate offspring, could not remain satisfied to overpower external nature. Science began searching in Time also, digging out and collecting historical data with a realistic objectivity unmatched before the nineteenth century. And as time went on, man's collective past began to emerge as an independent universe of its own, begging to be interpreted and understood on the same terms as nature's own physical universe. As our factual knowledge of history grew, it became obvious that the linear outlook Western Culture had inherited from its predecessors was no longer acceptable. It became obvious that man's progress over the ages had not been a continuous advance along a straight line, and it was rather a complex evolution marked by advances and retreats, that the torch of progress was transmitted continuously from one human society to another, and that each of these societies had a life of its own, going through all the biological phases of birth, growth, decay, and death.

Here again, we cannot go into the complex history of the cyclical conceptions of history, starting with Giambattista Vico. We should merely keep in mind that, at last, the truly Western conception of history was coming into its own, slowly freeing itself from the narrow outlook of past ages. It began to apply to its interpretation of the past the truly objective treatment that hitherto had been reserved to its scientific investigation of nature, looking upon its own Western society as only one among many other similar societies. The cyclical interpretations were by no means the final answer; they were simply overdue reactions against a linear outlook that was proving more obsolete every day. This obsolescence was due to two widely different, but converging, elements. One was the factual data unearthed by archeology and the related sciences, which pointed toward alarming similarities between the evolution of all human societies. The other was the contemporary evolution of Western society itself, the collapse of the rationalistic dream of the Age of Enlightenment, the obvious decline in cultural vitality, and the political and social crises, wars, and revolutions that have finally brought our Western world to the threshold that so many other societies have crossed in past ages.

The final answer to the riddle of history, the true answer, is a synthesis of the linear and cyclical interpretations. In contrasting Classical and Western Cultures, we have made it plain that Western Culture stood on a much higher level, although its organic evolution paralleled the Classical. The true answer, therefore, is that historical progress moves along the lines of a *spiral*. At one time or another, we may emphasize the cyclical or the linear aspect of evolution, but we should never assume that one or the other interpretation is the only valid one. And when we emphasize the traditional linear interpretation, we should always concentrate, not on material progress and technological advances, which are only by-products, but on the spirit underlying the vast changes that gave birth to them, centuries ago. For him who really wants to understand the inner structure of Western history, the prophetic dreams of Roger Bacon are far more important than the Industrial Revolution, which was only the concrete materialization of such dreams.

We are now in a position to give a rough sketch of the evolution of the other great Cultures not mentioned in the body of this work. In keeping with our emphasis on political and social history, we shall leave aside all the stunning parallels between their scientific, literary, and artistic evolutions.

When, how, and why are the higher Cultures born? Although there seems to be a fundamental mystery as to the genesis of every Culture, one fact seems clear. A new Culture is born of the cross-fertilization of two life-units in some pre-medieval Dark Age. A new Culture is the spontaneous creation of a new people, new men who are always the offspring of two complementary groups: a refined and decadent people who have lost their creative vigor, and invading barbarians who have the dynamic aggressiveness and primitive vitality that their victims lack. Thus, the Chou invasions in China, the barbarian invasions of Egypt after King Menes, the Aryan invasion of India, the Dorian in Greece and Germanic in Western Europe, all resulted in an almost complete fusion between invaders and invaded, and all gave birth to a new type of man as carrier of a new Culture. Other invasions did not result in the birth of a new Culture (for instance, the countless invasions suffered by China in the past two thousand years) because the Civilization itself was strong enough to absorb the invaders and mold them; because it preserved a certain cultural vitality and, with it, a certain capacity for organic growth; and also because there was no contiguous Culture able to undermine the cultural foundations of the Civilization. And so, whereas the Classical world collapsed under a double-barreled assault (the destruction of its cultural foundations by the rising Culture of the Middle East, and the physical invasions of Germanic hordes) the contemporaneous Chinese world, whose Chinese Caesar Shih Huang-ti brought about its Civilization two centuries earlier than the Classical world, lived on more or less intact until the twentieth century.

All societies went through the same phases, in the same sequence, beginning with a feudal phase that contrasted strongly with the previous social organization. Whether it was primitive masses of men organized along clannish lines or similar masses of decadent remains from a collapsing Civilization (Pharaonic Egypt, for instance) did not matter. The birth of feudalism in the China of the Chou era, in Vedic India, in the days of Egypt's Old Kingdom, always symbolized the beginning of a Culture and the beginning of the emancipation of the *individual* from the massive, anonymous conformity of pre-Cultural times. Egypt's hereditary *nomarchs,* Vedic India's independent *rajas* or China's Chou *princes* were all similar to Greece's Homeric lords or Europe's feudal barons. This feudal period is always intensely religious but its religions are always in a state of dynamic growth, not hieratic petrification as in a mature Civilization. Feudal eras are too dynamic, "medieval" men have too much vitality to suffer from doubt and skepticism. Religious feeling is profound and religious truths are self-evident. Man is still close to the soil, and all social relations take place along vassal-suzerain lines.

But with growth and development come the *city* and the rise of middle classes who challenge the fast-decaying feudal structure. Feudal territories begin to lose their autonomy, begin to merge with one another and form distinct states. This consolidation and social evolution took place in China during the Spring and Autumn era, in India at the close of the Vedic era, in Egypt from the fifth dynasty onward. And with this gradual destruction of the "medieval" structures, starts the destruction of the old "catholic" religions at the hands of reformers. They strike all at once against traditional beliefs and the entire social structure that went with them. Buddha raised the "protestant" banner in India by denying the divine character of the Vedas and simultaneously struck a powerful blow at the entire caste system. The Egyptians did likewise when the Heliopolitan clergy harked back to the original sun-god Râ and, after having attempted to destroy the goddess Isis as the European reformers rejected Mary, eventually defeated the last "catholic" reaction of King Shepseskaf. And we have the most successful "Reformation" of all: Islam, the "protestant" movement of early Christianity and of the late offshoots of Zoroastrianism, which all but wiped out Eastern "catholicism," which destroyed the Semitic and Iranian feudal structures that had arisen since the beginning of the Christian era, which was first and foremost the creed of the new middle classes of the Middle East—bankers, traders, merchants, and traveling salesmen. Muhammad the Prophet, who was a Middle Eastern Calvin and Cromwell combined, rejected monasticism, clergies, and a large part of the art that had been part and parcel of the Culture of the Middle East. Islam had its puritans, its iconoclasts, its social levelers.

And with reformation, philosophical inquiries begin to detach themselves from religion. Rationalism takes over, to be followed by skepticism, agnosticism, cynicism, and eventually outright rejection of all the foundations of religion and the Culture that went with it. India had its materialists such as Lokayata, rationalists such as the Tarkikas, sophists such as the Paribbajakas, cynics such as Kautilya. China had her fantastic profusion of philosophic schools and doctrines in the three centuries following Confucius—Mo Ti the religious utilitarian, Tzu Ssu the Confucianist, Mencius the moralist, Shang Yang the totalitarian, and crowds of epicureans, cynics, materialists, agnostics, skeptics. Islam, too, had its great philosophic and intellectual flowering during its first four centuries—great names such as al-Kindi, al-Farabi, al-Ghazali, and many others who deserve to rank among the great thinkers of all times—and soon enough, even Islamic thinking began to slide into the rationalism of the Mu'tazila, who insisted boldly that discursive logic should be applied to theology, who had fittingly started as religious puritans and who ended by helping themselves liberally to Greek philosophy in their effort to "purify" Islam. They too ended up, often enough, in agnosticism, atheism, and pessimistic skepticism, which reached its peak with the great Persian thinkers and poets.

While Culture slowly draws closer to the end of its historical development and while its philosophic outlook collapses into conflicting and discordant doctrines, political and social upheavals of great magnitude begin to sweep its world. All Cultures have thus ended in a chaos of "world wars" and revolutions—the famous period of the Warring States in China when the "great powers" Wei, Han, Chao, Ch'u, and others fought each other with mass slaughters; in India, where the powerful states of Kosala, Avanti, Vidha, and Licchavi recklessly destroyed each other in the three centuries following Buddha; the so-called Hyksos period in Pharaonic Egypt; the wars that eventually destroyed the Mayan world and the Culture that had bloomed in the brilliant cities of Copan, Naranjo, Tikal, and Piedras Negras and collapsed when the "Hellenistic" powers such as Uxmal, Mayapan, and Chacmultun failed to put an end to their "world wars" through leagues of nations (the Mayapan League, for instance). And the same applies to the collapse of Sumerian Culture after the great wars that ravaged Ur, Uruk, Nippur, Eridu, and Lagash. The same applies to the wars and revolutions that put an end to Islam's *"ancien régime,"* the Omayyads of Damascus, and saw the rise of such socialistic and communistic movements as the Khurramiyya and Muhayyida, and the revolutionary Muhammira, the "Reds" of Babik al-Khurrani.

These great epochs of history are dramatic watersheds, the final world-conflagrations that put an end to great Cultures torn apart by their inner contradictions and call forth the establishment of Civilizations. Growing revulsion against the cataclysmic disorders which corrode their respective societies, growing distrust of all philosophies and ideologies, a gradual return to religion and revival of religious faith, and a flight from dangerous liberty into the strong hands of capable Caesars—these are the hallmarks of this era of transition. And nothing is as significant as the voluntary surrender of that measure of freedom without which no true Culture would ever have developed. Democratic equality has done away with hereditary aristocracies everywhere, and in all cases, gigantic bureaucracies recruited "democratically" take their place—the most convenient tools in the hands of the Caesars: the Chinese mandarins who replaced the dying aristocracy, the Egyptian bureaucracy created by Pharaoh Amenemphat I in replacement of the aristocratic *nomarchs* of former times, and so on. The growth of Caesarism is always closely related to the destruction of the aristocracies. In Tocqueville's words, "Of all societies in the world, those which will always have most difficulty in escaping absolute government will be precisely those societies in which aristocracy is no more, and can no more be." [4]

In all cases, there is, on the geographical margin of the Culture's homeland, one Civilization-people seemingly predestined to take in hand the destinies of the entire civilized world—because it has established the necessary political and social pattern beforehand. Thus, the "Roman" state of Ch'in that eventually swallowed up the whole of China, the people of Maghada who did likewise in India, the practical Akkadians who were interested only in economic development and conquered the Sumerian world, the Central Asian Turks who organized the Islamic world the Arabs were no longer able to dominate. Just the same, it was no longer the Mayan world that could set up the pre-Columbian Civilization; while Chichen-Itza, Uxmal, and Mayapan slowly reverted to the jungle from which human striving and imagination had conjured them, the "Roman" Aztecs from faraway Tenochtitlan defeated the "Macedonian" Toltecs and established their rule over the civilized world of Central America, while the ultimate war between Itzas and Xius wrecked forever what was left of Mayan power. And so it was, also, with the "Romans" of the Andes, the Incas, who, as efficient imperialists, had few peers in history and who swallowed up the entire world of Andean Culture—the coastal city-states of Pachacamac, Chimu, and Nazca, the Aymara-speaking people of the highland around Lake Titicaca, and others. Like the people of Ch'in who had found the secret of organic growth by assimilating Tibetans, Huns, and other semibarbarians, or the Aztecs who displayed the same unconscious genius in unifying the area of Anahuac as Rome had unified Italy, Civilization-people usually displayed a remarkable ability to incorporate other people into their more democratic, fluid, "open" societies.

In all cases, these Civilization-people had a more democratic social structure than their cousins in the old Culture areas. They were all strong, practical, self-disciplined men who were far less individualized than their Culture-cousins, individually uncreative but collectively powerful, men who borrowed from the parent Culture all the ethical, legalistic notions on which to build enduring Civilizations. Whenever they did not base their political philosophy on sound morality, they had to give way to more ethically minded men as soon as their work of unification by sword and fire was accomplished. Such was the case of Ch'in, for instance, whose dynasty lasted only one generation and was replaced by the Hans, their cynical Legalist philosophy withering away soon after, leading to a rebirth of ethical Confucianism. In India, original Buddhism, practical and unphilosophic, was nothing more than the ethical side of Brahmanism without the metaphysical and aesthetic aspect of Hindu religion which Buddha rejected.

These Civilization-people all emphasized the Rule of Law with a rigor unknown in former Culture days, and took a legalistic view of all human relations. The very same Legalists who unified China were the first in the Chinese world to develop law systematically in the state of Ch'in. If the name Hammurabi, Babylonian Civilization's Caesar, has become so familiar, it is largely on account of his remarkable code of laws. And when the Islamic faith ceased to develop and grow, and the Islamic Civilization entered its winter, the most important residue that held it together was the paramountcy of Koranic law.

It was the profound appeal of democracy's social equality—relative though it was, and still is with us today—within these Civilization-states that drove them on to what was usually an involuntary and unconscious imperialism. Their democracy was successful because it was always based on psychological conformity and had accepted the autocratic rule of an all-powerful Executive, a development the more individualistic Culture-people rejected. When the great world crisis started, when wars and revolutions devastated the Culture areas, the great bulk of the Culture-people themselves began to long for peace and security at any price, for the constructive stability displayed by the Civilization-states. It was the appeal thus involuntarily created that compelled the Civilization-people to take over the leadership of their respective worlds, that compelled them to extend their more democratic social structures to the rest of civilized mankind, and which tightly linked democracy and imperialism. And so the democratic Legalists of China, the Buddhist destroyers of caste distinction in India, the equalitarian Turks in Islam, the Hyksos in Egypt, the "democratic" Aztecs of Mexico, and the "communistic" Incas of Peru—all of them came forth as imperialistic champions of an orderly and far more equalitarian social organization. The price paid was simply the loss of that measure of real liberty without which the individual cannot create and without which there would never have been any great Culture.

And when all those transformations were over, the civilized worlds surrendered to world Caesars. The silence of death replaced the stimulating and destructive conflicts of former times. In forsaking their former freedom, they also forsook all further organic growth and real progress, leaving it to other people, younger and more dynamic, to build a new Culture on the ruins of former Civilizations.

By now, the meaning is clear. Like a giant wheel of destiny, this cyclical rhythm of historical evolution has operated in the past with unfailing regularity. Factual evidence suggests that this rhythm is essentially biological, that great human societies develop like spiritual organisms in their own right and are likely to die when their souls depart. Once established, Civilizations can last almost indefinitely—China, for instance. But they are empty shells, soulless and inadaptable.

In itself, this cyclical rhythm has no profound metaphysical significance. It is a fate that binds us, like individual birth and death, and from which we can free ourselves only by an effort of collective will. Long ago, Hegel (the most penetrating of the "linear" philosophers of history) remarked: "The changes that take place in Nature ... exhibit only a perpetually self-repeating cycle; ... only in those changes that take place in the region of Spirit does anything new arise."[5] The true significance of history lies in linear development, not in cyclical repetition. History does go somewhere and does have a meaning; but it is up to us to go somewhere and give it meaning by overcoming the cyclical conditioning of our future.

We know where we stand today. Do we have to go through the same phases as all other societies before us? And while they had the blessing of going through those phases blindfolded, through lack of historical perspective, as animals go through life unaware of eventual death, do we have to go through the same phases with our eyes wide open?

The obvious answer is that we do not. We are still free agents and it is our very understanding of the past that frees us, if we want to be free. But this freedom to alter this biological rhythm of history depends essentially on one condition: that we have the courage to consider the great extent to which our future is already conditioned. It will avail us nothing to deny that such a cyclical rhythm exists—indeed, it is the best way of making sure that we will be its victims.

The will to overcome this rhythm implies that we have to work "in depth" in order to shape our future. We shall put no obstacles in the path of the coming Caesars simply by legislating against them; we would be attempting only to cure the symptoms, not the profound disease. The problem is far more complex. It is nothing less than the discovery of the ways and means of reviving our moribund Culture while retaining all the good and necessary features of Civilization. In other words, handing back to the creative *individual* the functions and dignity which *society* has usurped. The Caesars of the future, if they eventually materialize, will only be a terrible symbol of something more terrible still: the death of our Western soul—and the body would not be long in following it to the grave of history. And as has already been pointed out in the Introduction, this might imply the destruction of the entire human race as well. Advanced technology and fast superficial changes do not speed up or significantly alter the historical process; they merely make more certain that the next world conflagration will put an end to history altogether. Once again, what was an episodic drama in the past might be final tragedy tomorrow. It is up to us, who know better, to prevent this tragedy.

Notes and References

INTRODUCTION

1. The distinction between Culture and Civilization, popularized by Friedrich Nietzsche, Thomas Mann and Oswald Spengler, was pointed out for the first time by John Stuart Mill. Attempting to define the word "civilization" in his *Logic,* Mill stated: "A volume devoted to explaining what civilization is and is not, does not raise so vivid a conception of it as the single expression that Civilization is a different thing from Cultivation." (*Logic,* book iv, chap. 4.) But, significantly enough, it is mostly Russian thinkers of the nineteenth century who elaborated upon it—such Slavophils as Alexander Herzen and K. Leontiev who emphasized this distinction in an effort to define the true historical relationship between Russia and Europe (see Berdyaev, *The Beginning and the End,* p. 223).

CHAPTER I

1. Apollo was the shimmering sun-god of poetry and plastic arts, the presiding deity of Greece's "Middle Ages," the symbol of harmony and beauty. The Apollinian outlook was essentially harmonious whereas the Dionysiac was tense and extreme—essentially a reaction against the Apollinian "medievalism." Dionysius invaded Olympus around the seventh century B.C.; he was the god of music as an antiplastic symbol and ended as the son of the Almighty perishing to save mankind. His mythical career was a somber drama; his worshipers mourned his suffering and death with savage pain and celebrated his resurrection with ecstatic orgies. He was a symbol of mounting antagonism toward the disintegrating Olympic faith and was borrowed from Thrace as the European Renaissance borrowed its forms from Classical Rome and the Reformation from the Semitic East.

357

2. Orpheus, who was also borrowed from Thrace, was probably a re-forming priest of Dionysus. In any case, Orphism was directly related to the Dionysiac movement and was a further step in the development of Greek "protestantism." Its moral code was far superior to the Dionysiac and it introduced a great many beliefs which later passed into Christianity: original sin, judgment after death, resurrection of all men into an afterlife of reward and punishment. It took the revo-lutionary step, in Classical Greece, of looking upon the body as evil and the soul divine. Its puritanical asceticism rebelled against the loose morals of the "catholic" Olympians and set up a stern code of ethics. It probably influenced the Pythagoreans, handed its puritanism to Plato, and was probably the main source and inspiration of Stoi-cism.

3. Wish, *Society and Thought in Early America,* p. 4.

4. Pater, *Plato and Platonism,* p. 141.

5. Russell, *History of Western Philosophy,* p. 141.

CHAPTER II

1. Ghirshman, *Iran,* p. 195.

2. Wish, *Society and Thought in Early America,* p. 34.

3. Tawney, *Religion and the Rise of Capitalism,* p. 177.

4. Buchan, *Augustus,* p. 206.

5. The similarity of the Roman and Puritan characters has been noted by many students of Classical times. Concerning the theater, for instance, one of them remarks: "The Roman never overcame his ob-jection to acting, and a drama which is not written for acting does not flourish. Like the Puritan he thought it wrong to surrender one's own personality and to assume another's: it offended against a sense of 'gravity.' The more successfully it was done, the more it led to emo-tional and, therefore, moral instability" (Barrow, *The Romans,* p. 119). It is well known that for generations, well into the eighteenth century in fact, no public theater was tolerated in New England (see Commager, *The Growth of the American Republic,* i, p. 108).

6. "*Gravitas* means a 'sense of the importance of the matter at hand,' a sense of responsibility and earnestness . . . it is the opposite of *levitas,* a quality that Romans despised, which means trifling when you should be serious, flippancy, instability. *Gravitas* is often joined with *constantia,* firmness of purpose, or with *firmitas,* tenacity; it may even be seasoned with *comitas,* which means the relief given to over-seriousness by ease of manner, good humour, and humour. *Dis-ciplina* is the training which produces steadiness of character; *indus-*

tria is hard work; *virtus* is manliness and energy; *clementia* the willingness to forego one's rights; *frugalitas*, simple tastes. . . . They are moral qualities; they may even be dull and unexciting. There is nothing among them to suggest that intellectual power, or imaginativeness, or sense of beauty, or versatility, or charm . . . appealed to them as a high ideal. The qualities which served the Roman in his early struggles with Nature and with neighbours remained for him the virtues above all others. . . . Perhaps they can be summed up under *severitas*, which means being stern with oneself" (Barrow, *The Romans*, p. 22-23).

7. Mommsen, *The History of Rome*, p. 19.
8. Ibid., p. 16.
9. Ibid., p. 11.

CHAPTER III

1. Tawney, *Religion and the Rise of Capitalism*, p. 207.
2. Russell, *History of Western Philosophy*, p. 636.

CHAPTER IV

1. Rossiter, *Seedtime of the Republic*, p. 405.
2. Agar, *The Price of Union*, p. 12.
3. Rossiter, *Seedtime of the Republic*, p. 431.
4. Ibid., p. 430.
5. Ibid., p. 435.
6. Ibid., p. 436.
7. Ibid., p. 336.
8. Agar, *The Price of Union*, p. 22.
9. Jensen, *The Articles of Confederation*, p. 34.

CHAPTER V

1. Agar, *The Price of Union*, p. 31.
2. Bryce, *The American Commonwealth*, i, p. 21 footnote.
3. Agar, *The Price of Union*, p. 40.
4. Bryce, *The American Commonwealth*, i, p. 34 footnote.
5. Barrow, *The Romans*, p. 43.
6. Mommsen, *The History of Rome*, p. 56.
7. Jensen, *The Articles of Confederation*, p. 3.
8. Agar, *The Price of Union*, p. 46 footnote.
9. Ibid., p. 118.

10. Bryce, *The American Commonwealth*, i, p. 39.
11. Agar, *The Price of Union*, p. 42.
12. Ibid., p. 77.

CHAPTER VI

1. Polybius, ix, p. 2.
2. Chaeronea was the fateful battle in which Philip of Macedon defeated the Athenians, and Valmy the first victory of the army of the French Revolution over the anti-revolutionary European coalition.
3. Ghirshman, *Iran*, p. 240. A perfect example of intellectual confusion brought about by lack of precise terminology is the following sentence of a highly reputable scholar: "...Babylonian civilization was a city civilization like the Greek and not a country one like the Iranian" (Tarn, *The Greeks in Bactria & India*, p. 56). Now, the etymology of the word *civilization* implies the building of "cities"; by definition, there can be no such thing as a "country" civilization.
4. Ghirshman, *Iran*, p. 154.

CHAPTER VII

1. Agar, *The Price of Union*, p. 95.
2. Commager, *The Growth of the American Republic*, ii, p. 361.
3. Agar, *The Price of Union*, p. 116.
4. Ibid., p. 71 footnote.
5. Bryce, *The American Commonwealth*, i, p. 94.
6. Adams, *History of the United States*, i, p. 378.
7. Agar, *The Price of Union*, p. 131.
8. A great historian of the Classical world has summed up in a few lines the development of Rome's involuntary imperialism: "Rome's policy ... was dictated at the outset, not by any desire to increase her empire by adding to it territories in the East, but by a feeling of uneasiness aroused by the policy of Philip and Antiochus, just at the time when she had emerged victorious but exhausted from the Punic wars. Hannibal had invaded Italy; why should not Philip (a former ally of Hannibal) and Antiochus attack Rome and invade Italy in their turn? There was nothing impossible in the surmise. Alexander—such was the firm belief of the leading historians of the time—had been determined to add the West to his world empire, and since his day Pyrrhus had shown that there were men in Greece willing and able to make the attempt and to unite against Rome all

who disliked her supremacy in Italian affairs. Rome was suspicious of the Hellenistic East, with its glorious military traditions and its reputation of being the home of all the great inventions in the field of strategy, tactics and war machinery. Rome felt herself in this respect a pupil of Greece and was afraid of her teacher. This fear was never quelled in the Roman mind" (Rostovtzeff, *The Social and Economic History of the Hellenistic World*, i, pp. 52, 53).

9. Tardieu, *Devant l'Obstacle*, p. 9.
10. Adams, *History of the United States*, ii, p. 130.
11. Agar, *The Price of Union*, p. 74.

CHAPTER VIII

1. Ferrero, *Ancient Rome and Modern America*, p. 39.
2. Rossiter, *Seedtime of the Republic*, p. 34.
3. Ibid., p. 15.
4. Tocqueville, *Democracy in America*, i, p. 277.
5. Rossiter, *Seedtime of the Republic*, p. 34.
6. Tocqueville, *Democracy in America*, ii, p. 355.
7. Ibid., ii, p. 335.
8. Agar, *The Price of Union*, p. 99.
9. In spite of fundamental differences in their inner workings, British and American legal systems have always aimed successfully at one thing: protection of the individual against the arbitrary power of the state. The same difference that separated Roman and Greek legislation separates the Anglo-Saxon and the continental European. Even the Romans, who did not enjoy the favorable insular protection of the English-speaking people, built their towering legal edifice on this sound basis. "A more remarkable testimony to the Roman faith in law and due legal process as the remedy for disputes was the creation in 242 B.C. of the office of second Praetor to deal with cases in which foreign residents and visitors to Rome were involved. His title was *Praetor peregrinus*. With the establishment of this new judge, the Romans laid the foundations of a new view of justice. Instead of regarding law as applicable only to Roman citizens, they extended it to protect private persons as such. By recognizing the need to allow for the rights as well as the different customs of foreign peoples the Romans paid tribute to that Rule of Law, the elaboration of which is their greatest, because their most enduring, contribution to human civilization" (Cowell, *Cicero and the Roman Republic*, p. 136).
10. Agar, *The Price of Union*, p. 195.
11. Ibid., p. 263.

CHAPTER IX

1. Gibbon, *The Decline and Fall of the Roman Empire*, i, p. 29.
2. Cowell, *Cicero and the Roman Republic*, p. 253.
3. Agar, *The Price of Union*, p. 315.
4. Ibid., p. 308.
5. Ibid., p. 319.
6. Trollope, *North America*, p. 7.
7. Commager, *The Growth of the American Republic*, i, p. 714.

CHAPTER X

1. "The 'First Families of Virginia,' a rural aristocracy of native origin, reproduced the high sense of honor and public spirit of the English aristocracy, as well as the amenities of English country life. They frequently combined planting with the practice of law, but left to their inferiors, commerce to the agents of British mercantile firms, and navigation to the Yankees. Prepared by private tutors or at schools kept by Scotch clergymen for Princeton or William and Mary, trained to administration by managing their large estates, and to politics by representing their counties in the Virginia Assembly, the planters stepped naturally and gracefully into the leadership of the nation. It was no accident that Jefferson of Virginia drafted the Declaration of Independence, that Washington of Virginia led the army and became the first President, that Madison of Virginia fathered the Federal Constitution, that Marshall of Virginia became the greatest American jurist, and that he and Taylor of Virginia led the two opposing schools of American political thought" (Commager, *The Growth of the American Republic*, i, p. 316).
2. Tocqueville, *Democracy in America*, i, pp. 316, 17.
3. Ibid., i, 355.
4. Commager, *The Growth of the American Republic*, i, p. 450.
5. Agar, *The Price of Union*, p. 204.
6. Binkley, *American Political Parties*, p. 99.

CHAPTER XI

1. The Hortensian Law declared that henceforth all decrees of the plebs in their *Comitia Tributa* or Assembly (from which patricians were excluded) had equal force with the decrees of the Senate.
2. Buchan, *Augustus*, p. 108.
3. Agar, *The Price of Union*, p. 233.

4. Ibid., p. 275.
5. Ford, *The Rise and Growth of American Politics*, p. 182.
6. Tocqueville, *Democracy in America*, i, p. 413.
7. According to Mommsen, "Everything with these political clubs was bought and sold; the vote of the electors above all, but also the votes of the senator and the judge; the fists, too, which produced the street riot, and the ring-leader who directed it. The associations of the upper and of the lower classes were distinguished only in the matter of tariff. The hetaeria decided the elections; the hetaeria decreed the impeachment; the hetaeria conducted the defense; it secured the distinguished advocate; and it contracted, in case of need, respecting an acquittal with one of the speculators who prosecuted on a great scale the lucrative traffic in judges' votes" (Mommsen, *The History of Rome*, p. 327).

CHAPTER XII

1. Agar, *The Price of Union*, p. 46 footnote.
2. Ibid., p. 297.
3. Tyler could not be a radical Jacksonian Democrat and yet refused to lead the Big Business Whigs. In fact, he vetoed every important law sponsored by the Whigs (see Agar, *The Price of Union*, p. 301).
4. Ibid., p. 397.
5. Commager, *The Growth of the American Republic*, i, p. 634.
6. Santayana, *Character and Opinion in the United States*, p. 1.
7. Commager, *The Growth of the American Republic*, i, p. 376.
8. Lincoln's message to the special session of Congress, July 4th, 1861.
9. Bryce, *The American Commonwealth*, i, p. 94.
10. Agar, *The Price of Union*, p. 434.
11. Ibid., p. 425.
12. Ibid., p. 436.

CHAPTER XIII

1. Agar, *The Price of Union*, p. 446.
2. Ibid., p. 452.
3. Binkley, *President and Congress*, p. 159.
4. Agar, *The Price of Union*, p. 552.
5. Bryce, *The American Commonwealth*, i, p. 121.
6. Bentham, *Introduction to the Principles of Morals and Legislation*, Chap. I, Sec. 4.
7. Ferrero, *Ancient Rome and Modern America*, p. 25.

CHAPTER XIV

1. Commager, *The Growth of the American Republic*, ii, p. 112.
2. Agar, *The Price of Union*, p. 609.
3. Ibid., p. 595.
4. Ibid., p. 601.
5. Ibid., p. 650.
6. Ibid., p. 638.
7. Roosevelt, *Autobiography*, p. 437.
8. Commager, *The Growth of the American Republic*, ii, p. 320.
9. Adams, *Letters*, ii, p. 461.
10. Agar, *The Price of Union*, p. 623.
11. Ibid., p. 650.
12. Wish, *Society and Thought in Modern America*, p. 390.
13. Ibid., p. 393.
14. Ibid., p. 391.
15. Tocqueville, *Democracy in America*, i, p. 429.
16. Wish, *Society and Thought in Modern America*, p. 395.
17. Bryce, *The American Commonwealth*, ii, p. 908.
18. Agar, *The Price of Union*, p. 660.

CHAPTER XV

1. As a symbol of the exasperated patriotism that ends by destroying all because it is basically cynical and not ethical, this sketch of Clemenceau's feelings by John Maynard Keynes is apt: "He [Clemenceau] felt about France what Pericles felt of Athens—unique value in her, nothing else mattered. . . . He had one illusion—France; and one disillusion—mankind, including Frenchmen" (Keynes, *The Economic Consequences of the Peace*, p. 32).
2. Grey, *Twenty-Five Years*, ii, p. 20.
3. Fustel de Coulanges, *La Cité Antique*, p. 453.
4. Mommsen, *The History of Rome*, p. 187.
5. Ibid., p. 221.
6. Ghirshman, *Iran*, p. 241.
7. Ibid., p. 205. Also, Davies, *Dead Sea Scrolls*, p. 76.
8. Davies, *Dead Sea Scrolls*, p. 90.
9. Ghirshman, *Iran*, p. 252.

CHAPTER XVI

1. Agar, *The Price of Union*, p. 671.
2. Galbraith, *The Great Crash*, p. 19.

3. Ibid., p. 33.
4. The collapse of the prestige of European Big Business had taken place more than a decade earlier. World War I and its revolutionary aftermath did to European capitalism what the Great Crash did to its American counterpart. John Maynard Keynes gave a startling description of its condition, writing in 1920: "We are thus faced in Europe with the spectacle of an extraordinary weakness on the part of the great capitalist class, which has emerged from the industrial triumphs of the nineteenth century, and seemed a very few years ago our all-powerful master. The terror and personal timidity of the individuals of this class is now so great, their confidence in their place in society and in their necessity to the social organism so diminished, that they are the easy victims of intimidation. This was not so in England twenty-five years ago, any more than it is now in the United States. Then the capitalists believed in themselves, in their value to society, in the propriety of their continued existence in the full enjoyment of their riches and the unlimited exercise of their power. Now they tremble before every insult. . . . They allow themselves to be ruined and altogether undone by their own instruments, governments of their own making, and a press of which they are the proprietors. Perhaps it is historically true that no order of society ever perishes save by its own hand" (Keynes, *The Economic Consequences of the Peace*, pp. 237, 238).
5. Galbraith, *The Great Crash*, p. 143.

CHAPTER XVII

1. Sherwood, *Roosevelt and Hopkins*, p. 40.
2. Robinson, *The Roosevelt Leadership*, p. 55.
3. Ibid., p. 56.
4. Sherwood, *Roosevelt and Hopkins*, p. 41.
5. James Bryce was referring to the following incident: "The Aetolians chose for an inroad the time when the official year (of the Achaian general) was drawing to its close, as a time when the Achaian counsels were sure to be weak. Aratos, the general-elect, was not yet in office; Timoxenos, the outgoing general, shrank from energetic action so late in his year, and at last yielded up his office to Aratos before the legal time" (Bryce, *The American Commonwealth*, i, p. 71).
6. Robinson, *The Roosevelt Leadership*, p. 108.
7. Mommsen, *The History of Rome*, p. 386.
8. Robinson, *The Roosevelt Leadership*, p. 150.

9. Ibid., p. 193.
10. "... the storm of popular indignation at Rome fell upon individuals, not on the rotten system of senatorial government" (Mommsen, *The History of Rome*, p. 253).
11. Ibid., p. 265.
12. Ibid., p. 408.
13. Robinson, *The Roosevelt Leadership*, p. 204.

CHAPTER XVIII

1. Kennan, *American Diplomacy*, p. 64.
2. The antihistorical attitude of Americans, succinctly expressed by Henry Ford when he claimed that "History is bunk," was even more strikingly displayed by the fact that, as late as 1880, there were only eleven professors of history in American colleges (Muller, *The Uses of the Past*, p. 34).
3. Sherwood, *Roosevelt and Hopkins*, p. 67.
4. Robinson, *The Roosevelt Leadership*, p. 243.
5. Ibid., p. 245.
6. Ibid., p. 253.
7. Sherwood, *Roosevelt and Hopkins*, pp. 196, 197.
8. Ibid., p. 274.
9. Robinson, *The Roosevelt Leadership*, p. 265.
10. Ibid., p. 269.
11. Ibid., p. 281.
12. Sherwood, *Roosevelt and Hopkins*, p. 631.
13. Ibid., p. 509.
14. Ibid., p. 871.
15. "Besides, I think that Carthage must be destroyed," the terrible sentence with which Cato ended every one of his speeches in the Senate.
16. Robinson, *The Roosevelt Leadership*, p. 304.
17. Sherwood, *Roosevelt and Hopkins*, p. 708.
18. Robinson, *The Roosevelt Leadership*, p. 317.
19. This anticolonialism of America had its precise counterpart in the Classical world when Roman power, already supreme in the Mediterranean, encouraged all the anti-Hellenic nationalism of the East. Writes Rostovtzeff: "The Romans helped forward all the processes that were ruining the political stability of the Hellenistic world; separatist tendencies within the monarchies, dynastic troubles, civil wars, wars between the several States, they always encouraged, or at least hardly ever put a stop to. She contributed to their economic

ruin. By doing this, she undermined Greek civilization throughout the Hellenistic area, and made the advance of orientalization easier and more rapid. . . . Left alone, the Hellenistic States certainly would have existed longer than they did, and would have offered a stronger and more effective resistance to the growth of Parthia and Armenia and to the rapid rise of the oriental tide." This is a striking parallel with our times, this gradual disintegration of European power in the East and the relative indifference of the United States—until the day comes when America has to pick up the Western burden dropped by Europe. And Rostovtzeff adds: "Thereafter she [Rome] did her best during two centuries to secure peace for the East and re-hellenize it. This is her enduring merit. But why begin by crushing Hellenism alike in the East and in the West and then try to save what little was left of it?" (Rostovtzeff, *The Social and Economic History of the Hellenistic World*, i, pp. 71-73).

20. Robinson, *The Roosevelt Leadership*, p. 363.
21. Sherwood, *Roosevelt and Hopkins*, p. 852.
22. Robinson, *The Roosevelt Leadership*, p. 374.

CHAPTER XIX

1. Nietzsche, *Thus Spake Zarathustra*, p. X.
2. Frontinus, *Stratagems and Aqueducts*, i, p. 16.
3. Homo, *La Civilization Romaine*, p. 37, quotes Pliny the Ancient.
4. Editors of *Fortune* Magazine, *U.S.A., The Permanent Revolution*, pp. 68, 69.
5. Bryce, *The American Commonwealth*, ii, p. 853.
6. Ibid., ii, p. 294.
7. Ibid., ii, p. 296.
8. *Fortune* Magazine, *The Strange State of American Research*, April 1955.
9. Tocqueville, *Democracy in America*, i, p. 263.
10. Ibid., i, p. 264.
11. Tawney, *Religion and the Rise of Capitalism*, p. 241.
12. Tocqueville, *Democracy in America*, i, p. 42.
13. Mommsen, *The History of Rome*, p. 503.
14. Cowell, *Cicero and the Roman Republic*, p. 219.
15. Plutarch, *Lives*, chap. "Cato the Elder." In a memorable speech, Cato elaborated with great bitterness on this theme: "If we had, each of us, upheld the rights and authority of the husband in our own households, we should not today have this trouble with our women. As things are now, our liberty of action, which has been annulled by female despotism at home, is crushed and trampled on

here in the Forum. . . . If you now permit them to remove these restraints . . . and to put themselves on an equality with their husbands, do you imagine that you will be able to bear them? From the moment that they become your equals they will be your masters" (Livy, *History of Rome*, I, xxxiv).

16. Wish, *Society and Thought in Early America*, p. 416.
17. Ferrero, *Greatness and Decline of Rome*, v, p. 338.

CHAPTER XX

1. Mommsen, *The History of Rome*, p. 205.
2. What the advent of the Roman Age meant economically for the entire Classical world has been admirably summed up by one of the leading authorities on such matters: "I allude to the closer political, social, and economic connexion of the two parts of the civilized world of that time: the Western, centered around Italy and Rome, and the Eastern, more or less reunited under the pressure of the Roman protectorate. For the Eastern region the increasingly intimate interpenetration of the two worlds meant not only a new market for its goods, a market continuously increasing in size and purchasing capacity, and perhaps a new field for emigration (mostly through slavery), but also an influx of new capital and new energies from the West. These made their way into the East with the steady flow of enterprising and well-to-do new settlers, the 'Roman' *negotiatores*. What the *negotiatores* brought with them was not only a brisk business spirit but also capital ready for investment" (Rostovtzeff, *The Social and Economic History of the Hellenistic World*, ii, p. 1030).
3. Tocqueville, *Democracy in America*, i, p. 434.
4. Ghirshman, *Iran*, p. 287.
5. Appian, *Roman History*, xii, 4.
6. Ferrero, *Greatness and Decline of Rome*, i, p. 83.
7. Commager, *The Growth of the American Republic*, ii, p. 315.
8. Schlesinger, *The General and the President*, p. 77.
9. Ibid., p. 79, footnote.

CHAPTER XXI

1. Muller, *The Uses of the Past*, p. 202.

CHAPTER XXII

1. Bryce, *The American Commonwealth*, i, p. 68.
2. Tocqueville, *Democracy in America*, i, p. 126.

3. A perusal of the latest works published on this topic in 1956 gives us a variety of opinion. Some authors claim that the President's immense power is justified because it is the will of the people that he should have it (Rossiter, *The American Presidency*). Others are definitely uneasy (Corwin, *The Presidency Today*). But then, as Justice Jackson said when President Truman seized the steel industry after World War II: "I have no illusion that any decision by this court can keep power in the hands of Congress if it is not wise and timely in meeting its problems. . . . If not good law, there was worldly wisdom in the maxim attributed to Napoleon that 'the tools belong to the man who can use them.' We may say that power to legislate for emergencies belongs in the hands of Congress, but only Congress itself can prevent power from slipping through its fingers" (Hyman, *The American President*, p. 308). On this score, the record of history speaks for itself.

4. Barrow, *The Romans*, p. 43.

5. Ferrero, *Greatness and Decline of Rome*, i, p. 323.

6. Ibid., i, p. 322.

7. Mommsen, *The History of Rome*, p. 513.

8. Ibid., p. 488.

9. Ferrero, *Greatness and Decline of Rome*, iv, p. 121, footnote.

10. "As the years went by, he almost seemed to take on the divinity renounced on January 1, 1946, by Hirohito. 'We look on MacArthur' said one Japanese . . . 'as the second Jesus Christ.'" After MacArthur had solemnly addressed a joint meeting of Congress after his recall in 1951, "some people were so deeply affected by the speech that they thought it must have been celestial in origin. This was an unexpected development," adds the historian. "In the Philippines and Japan, where the pantheons are capacious and stand always in readiness for new annexes, MacArthur had long been regarded by some people as a figure of supernatural proportions; it was not, however, to be supposed that Americans . . . would associate the General with deity" (Schlesinger and Rovere, *The General and the President*, p. 82).

11. Ferrero, *Greatness and Decline of Rome*, iv, p. 134.

12. Buchan, *Augustus*, p. 108.

13. Ferrero, *Greatness and Decline of Rome*, iv, p. 137.

14. Pliny made it clear that, constitutionally, the Caesarian *princeps* was still the "first servant of the state" and that the law was still supreme: *"Non est 'princeps supra leges' sed 'leges supra principem'"* (Buchan, *Augustus*, p. 283). But a modern historian has pointed out that under interpretative legislation of the Roman (and we might add, American)

type, such nominal supremacy of law is no barrier against a perfectly legal assumption of absolute power by one man: "The Romans had lived for centuries mainly under the rule of interpreted or judge-made law, and now the Roman world, enlarged and unified, looked for guidance not to the "comitia,' which were in decay or to the Senate, whose contact with the provinces was ever becoming less, but to the one interpreter who was known to every judge and every litigant, and whose utterances could be heard at the furthest ends of the earth. It was the force of circumstances, not any constitutional theory, which made the Princeps the highest of all legislative, because the greatest of all interpreting, authorities" (Greenidge, *Roman Public Life*, p. 381, quoted by Buchan, *Augustus*, p. 290).

15. Suetonius reports that he claimed that "in a free country, there should be freedom of speech and thought" (Suetonius, *Works*, p. 27).
16. Gibbon, *The Decline and Fall of the Roman Empire*, i, p. 60.

APPENDIX

1. In Hegelian terminology, "History in general is ... the development of Spirit in *Time*, as Nature is the development of the Idea in *Space*" (Hegel, *The Philosophy of History*, p. 72).
2. See Collingwood, *The Idea of History*, pp. 27, 28.
3. Galatians, 4:4.
4. Tocqueville, *L'Ancien Régime*, Pref. XVI, quoted by Buchan, *Augustus*, p. 283.
5. Hegel, *The Philosophy of History*, p. 54.

Bibliography

The subject matter of this volume is so large that a truly comprehensive bibliography would be unwieldy. Therefore, I have included only those works that I have quoted directly, or those that might be of interest to readers anxious to go deeper into some of the topics discussed in this book. Most of the following works have extensive bibliographies of their own, making it even less necessary to extend my own list.

ADAMS, H.—*History of the United States,* 9 vols., New York, 1889-91
ADAMS, H.—*Letters,* 2 vols., Boston, 1930
AGAR, H.—*The Price of Union,* Boston, 1950
ALLEN, F. L.—*The Big Change,* New York, 1952
APPIAN—*Roman History,* 4 vols., Loeb Classical Library
BARROW, R. H.—*The Romans,* Harmondsworth, Middlesex, 1955
BARZUN, T.—*Teacher in America,* New York, 1945
BEARD, C. A.—*The American Leviathan,* New York, 1930
BENTHAM, J.—*Introduction to the Principles of Morals and Legislation*
BERDYAEV, N.—*The Beginning and the End,* London, 1952
BERDYAEV, N.—*The Russian Idea,* London, 1947
BERENSON, B.—*Aesthetics and History,* London, 1948
BERLE, A. A. Jr. & MEANS, G. C.—*The Modern Corporation and Private Property,* New York, 1932
BINKLEY, W.—*American Political Parties,* New York, 1943
BINKLEY, W.—*President and Congress,* New York, 1947
BROGAN, D. W.—*Politics in America,* New York, 1954
BRYCE, J.—*The American Commonwealth,* 2 vols., New York, 1912
BUCHAN, J.—*Augustus,* Leipzig, 1938
CARNEGIE, A.—*Autobiography,* New York, 1920
CHESTERTON, G. K.—*What I Saw in America,* New York, 1922
CICERO—*De Re Publica,* Loeb Library
CLEVELAND, G.—*Presidential Problems,* New York, 1904
COLLINGWOOD, R. G.—*The Idea of History,* Oxford, 1946

COMMAGER, H. S. & MORISON, S. E.—*The Growth of the American Republic,* 2 vols., New York, 1953

CORWIN, E. S.—*John Marshall and the Constitution,* New Haven, 1919

CORWIN, E. S.—*The President, Office and Powers,* New York, 1940

CORWIN, E.S. & KOENIG, L. W.—*The Presidency Today,* New York, 1956

COULANGE, F. de—*La Cité Antique,* Paris, 1876

COWELL, F. R.—*Cicero and the Roman Republic,* London, 1948

CURTI, M.—*Bryan and World Peace,* Northampton, Mass., 1931

DAVIES, A. P.—*Dead Sea Scrolls,* New York, 1956

DAVIS, E.—*But We Were Born Free,* New York, 1952

DE VOTO, B.—*The Year of Decision,* Boston, 1943

DIODORUS SICULUS—*Library of History,* Loeb Library

FERRERO, G.—*Greatness and Decline of Rome,* 5 vols., New York, 1910

FERRERO, G.—*Ancient Rome and Modern America,* New York, 1914

FISCHER, E.—*The Passing of the European Age,* Harvard, 1948

FLYNN, E. J.—*You're the Boss,* New York, 1947

FORD, H. J.—*The Rise and Growth of American Politics,* New York, 1898

FORTUNE, EDITORS OF—*U.S.A., The Permanent Revolution,* New York, 1951

FRANK, T.—*An Economic History of Rome,* London, 1927

FRONTINUS—*Stratagems and Aqueducts,* Loeb Library

GALBRAITH,—*The Great Crash,* New York, 1955

GHIRSHMAN, R.—*Iran,* Harmondsworth, Middlesex, 1954

GIBBON, E.—*The Decline and Fall of the Roman Empire,* 3 vols., Modern Library.

GOMPERS, S.—*Seventy Years of Life and Labor,* 2 vols., New York, 1925

GORER, G.—*The Americans,* London, 1948

GRANT, U.—*Personal Memoirs,* 2 vols., New York, 1885-86

GREELY, H.—*Recollections of a Busy Life,* New York, 1868

GREY, E.—*Twenty Five Years,* 2 vols., New York, 1925

HASKELL, H. J.—*The New Deal in Old Rome,* New York, 1939

HEGEL, G. W. F.—*The Philosophy of History,* New York, 1944

HOFSTADTER, R.—*Social Darwinism in American Thought, 1860-1915,* London, 1944

HOFSTADTER, R.—*The American Political Tradition, and the Men who Made it,* New York, 1948

HOMO, L.—*La Civilization Romaine,* Paris, 1930

HYMAN, S.—*The American President,* New York, 1954

JENSEN, M.—*The Articles of Confederation,* Madison, Wisconsin, 1940

JOUVENEL, B.—*Power,* London, 1948

KENNAN, G.—*American Diplomacy,* New York, 1951

KEYNES, J. M.—*The Economic Consequences of the Peace*, New York, 1920

KITTO, H. D. F.—*The Greeks*, Harmondsworth, Middlesex, 1954

KEYSERLING, H.—*America Set Free*, London, 1930

KEYSERLING, H.—*Europe*, New York, 1928

KOHN, H.—*The Idea of Nationalism*, New York, 1944

LIPPMANN, W.—*The Public Philosophy*, Boston, 1955

LIVY, T.—*History of Rome*, 6 vols., Everyman Library

MADARIAGA, S. de—*Englishmen, Frenchmen, Spaniards*, Oxford, 1928

MAHAN, A. T.—*Sea Power in Its Relations to the War of 1812*, 2 vols., Boston, 1905

MEYER, E.—*Caesars Monarchie und das Principat des Pompejus*, Stuttgart, 1918.

MOMMSEN, T.—*The History of Rome*, New York, 1889

MULLER, H. J.—*The Uses of the Past*, New York, 1954

MYRDAL, G.—*An International Economy*, New York, 1956

NEVINS, A.—*The American States during and after the Revolution*, New York, 1924

NEVINS, A.—*The Emergence of Modern America*, New York, 1928

NEVINS, A.—*Frémont, Pathmaker of the West*, New York, 1939

NIETZSCHE, F.—*Thus Spake Zarathustra*, Modern Library, New York

ORTEGA Y GASSET, J.—*Toward A Philosophy of History*, New York, 1941

ORTEGA Y GASSET, J.—*The Revolt of the Masses*, New York, 1950

PARES, SIR B.—*A History of Russia*, New York, 1953

PARKMAN, F.—*The Oregon Trail*, Boston, 1886

PATER, W.—*Plato and Platonism*, London, 1910

PLUTARCH—*Lives*, 3 vols., Everyman Library

POLYBIUS—*Histories*, 6 vols., Loeb Library

ROBINSON, E. E.—*The Roosevelt Leadership*, New York, 1955

ROOSEVELT, T.—*Autobiography*, New York, 1913

ROSSITER, C.—*Constitutional Dictatorship*, Princeton, 1948

ROSSITER, C.—*Seedtime of the Republic*, New York, 1953

ROSSITER, C.—*The American Presidency*, New York, 1956

ROSTOVTZEFF, M.—*Social and Economic History of the Roman Empire*, 2 vols., Oxford, 1926

ROSTOVTZEFF, M.—*History of the Ancient World*, Oxford, 1928

ROSTOVTZEFF, M.—*The Social and Economic History of the Hellenistic World*, 3 vols., Oxford, 1941

RUSSELL, B.—*History of Western Philosophy*, London, 1946

SANTAYANA, G.—*Character and Opinion in the United States*, New York, 1946

SCHLESINGER, A. M. JR.—*The Rise of the City*, New York, 1933

SCHLESINGER, A. M. JR.—*The Age of Jackson,* New York, 1945

SCHLESINGER, A. M. JR. & ROVERE, R.—*The General and the President,* London, 1952

SHERWOOD, R.—*Roosevelt and Hopkins,* New York, 1948

SOROKIN, P.—*Social Philosophies in an Age of Crisis,* London, 1952

SPENGLER, O.—*The Decline of the West,* 2 vols., New York, 1926-28

STRAUSZ-HUPÉ, R.—*The Zone of Indifference,* New York, 1952

SUETONIUS—*Works,* Loeb Library

TARDIEU, A.—*Devant L'Obstacle,* Paris, 1927

TARN, W. W.—*The Greeks in Bactria and India,* Cambridge, 1938

TAWNEY, R. H.—*Religion and the Rise of Capitalism,* New York, 1947

TOCQUEVILLE, A. de—*Democracy in America,* 2 vols., New York, 1945

TROLLOPE, A.—*North America,* New York, 1951

WILSON, W.—*Constitutional Government in the United States,* New York, 1908

WISH, H.—*Society and Thought in Early America,* New York, 1950

WISH, H.—*Society and Thought in Modern America,* New York, 1952

Index

Aberdeen, Lord, 133
Achaemenian Empire, 98
Achaen League, 91
Adams, Henry, 110, 112, 193, 219
Adams, John, 64, 66, 73, 102, 107, 120, 140, 162, 175
Adams, John Quincy, 144, 145
Adams, Samuel, 65
Administrative agencies, 234-35, 237, 252
Aequi, 124
Aeschines, 91
Aeschylus, 54
Aetolian League, 206
Agencies, *see* Administrative agencies; International agencies
Agrigentum, 34
Ahenobarbus, Domitius, 186
Air bases, 310
Akbar, 33
Alabama, 139
Alaska, 194
Alexander the Great, 87, 92, 100, 150, 193, 210
Alexander the Molossian, 102, 134
Alexandria, 87, 89, 90, 125
Amendments, Constitutional, 116, 190, 199, 331
American civilization, 269-91, 319
American Federation of Labor, 176
Americanism, 272-73
Americanization, 128, 291
American Railway Union, 190
American Resettlement Administration, 242
American Revolution, 60, 63, 64-69, 119, 126
Anaximander, 20
Ancient Rome and *Modern America*, 117

Anglican Church, *see* Church of England
Anthony, Mark, 326
Antioch, 87, 89, 125
Antiochus III, 209
Antipater, 90
Antiphon, 90
Aquinas, Thomas, 29
Archimedes, 88
Aristarchus, 89
Aristophanes, 90, 213
Aristotle, 29, 30, 31, 88, 90, 328
Army Corps of Engineers, 250
Artaxerxes, 92
Arthur, Chester, 178
Articles of Confederation, 70, 72, 106
Athens, 78, 89, 96, 122, 123, 126, 206, 208
Atlantic Charter, 254
Atlantic Community, 304, 306-09, 323
Atlantic Pact (1949), 307
Atomic Energy Commission, 330
Augustus, 147, 336-37, 340
Australia, 258

Babylon, 33, 87
Bach, John Sebastian, 59
Bacon, Francis, 35
Bacon's rebellion, 44, 45
Baltimore, Lord, 43
Balzac, Honoré, 212
"Bank holiday," 234
Bank of America, 155-57
Bank of England, 155, 157
Beard, Charles A., 254
Beethoven, Ludwig von, 205
Behaviorism, 277
Bellini, Charles, 103

375